THE ORIENTAL INSTITUTE OF THE UNIVERSITY OF CHICAGO

STUDIES IN ANCIENT ORIENTAL CIVILIZATION · NO. 31

PREHISTORIC INVESTIGATIONS IN IRAQI KURDISTAN

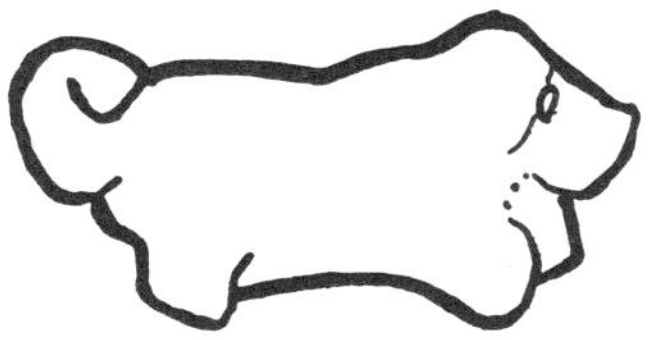

BY ROBERT J. BRAIDWOOD

AND

BRUCE HOWE

WITH CONTRIBUTIONS BY HANS HELBAEK · FREDERICK R. MATSON · CHARLES A. REED · HERBERT E. WRIGHT, JR.

THE ORIENTAL INSTITUTE OF THE UNIVERSITY OF CHICAGO

STUDIES IN ANCIENT ORIENTAL CIVILIZATION · NO. 31

THE UNIVERSITY OF CHICAGO PRESS · CHICAGO · ILLINOIS

International Standard Book Number: 0-226-62404-8
Library of Congress Catalog Card Number: 60-8969

THE UNIVERSITY OF CHICAGO PRESS, CHICAGO 60637
THE UNIVERSITY OF CHICAGO PRESS, LTD., LONDON

TABLE OF CONTENTS

LIST OF ILLUSTRATIONS

PLATES

Text Figures

LIST OF WORKS CITED

Adametz, Leopold, and Niezabitowski, E. de Lubicz. 1914. Über die in Zloczow in Ostgalazien gefundenen Pferde- und Ziegenknochenüberreste (Equus sp., Capra prisca, n. sp.). L'Académie des sciences, Cracovie. Classe des sciences mathématiques et naturelles. Ser. B: Sciences naturelles. Bulletin, 1914, pp. 761-75.

Adams, Robert M. 1960. Early civilizations, subsistence, and environment. In City invincible: A symposium on urbanization and cultural development in the ancient Near East. Oriental Institute special publication. Chicago.

Albright, William F. 1954. A survey of the archeological chronology of Palestine from Neolithic to Middle Bronze. Robert W. Ehrich (ed.), Relative chronologies in Old World archeology, pp. 28-33. Chicago.

Alimen, Henriette. 1957. The prehistory of Africa. London.

Allouse, Bashir E. 1953. The avifauna of Iraq. Iraq Natural History Museum. Publication III.

Altmann, Margaret. 1957. Grunt, my wild boar. Animal kingdom LX 9-10.

Amschler, J. Wolfgang. 1939. Tierreste der Ausgrabungen von dem "grossen Königshügel" Shah Tepé, in Nord Iran. Expedition to the North-Western Provinces of China (The Sino-Swedish Expedition). Publication IX 35-129.

Arambourg, Camille. 1929. Les mammifères quaternaires de l'Algérie. La Société de histoire naturelle afrique du nord. Bulletin XX 63-84.

Arkell, J. A. 1949. Early Khartoum. London.

_______. 1953. Shaheinab: An account of the excavation of a Neolithic occupation site carried out for the Sudan Antiquities Service in 1949-50. London.

_______. 1956. Man's beginnings in Africa. New biology XX 112-22.

Arnold, J. R., and Libby, W. F. 1951. Radiocarbon dates (September 1, 1950). Science CXIII 111-20.

Asil, Naji al-. 1949. Barda Balka. Sumer V 205-6.

Ayrton, Edward R., and Loat, W. L. S. 1911. Pre-dynastic cemetery of El Mahasna. Egypt Exploration Fund. Memoir XXXI. London.

Barker, Harold. 1958. Radiocarbon dating: Its scope and limitations. Antiquity XXXII 253-63.

Barnett, Lincoln. 1956. The epic of man. IV. Man shapes his environment. Life magazine, April 16, 1956, pp. 74-98.

Barth, Fredrik. 1953. Principles of social organization in southern Kurdistan. Universitets etnografiske Museum. Bulletin VII. Oslo.

Bate, Dorothea M. A. 1930a. Animal remains from the Dark Cave, Hazar Merd. American School of Prehistoric Research. Bulletin VI 38-39.

_______. 1930b. Animal remains from the Zarzi cave. American School of Prehistoric Research. Bulletin VI 23.

_______. 1942. The fossil mammals of Shukbah. Prehistoric Society. Proceedings (n.s.) VIII 15-20.

_______. 1951. The mammals from Singa and Abu Hugar. British Museum of Natural History. Fossil mammals of Africa II 1-28.

Blanc, Alberto C. 1938. Le glaciaire considéré aux points de vue paléobiologique et géomorphologique. L'Anthropologie XLVIII 260.

_______. 1957. On the Pleistocene sequence of Rome—paleoecologic and archeologic correlations. Quaternaria IV 95-109.

Bobek, Hans G. 1940. Die gegenwartige und eiszeitliche Vergletscherung im zentralkurdischen Hochgebirge (Osttaurus, Ostanatolien). Zeitschrift für Gletscherkunde XXVII 50-87.

_______. 1954. Klima und Landschaft Irans in vor- und frühgeschichtlicher Zeit. Geographische Jahresbericht aus Österreich XXV 1-42.

Bodenheimer, Friedrich S. 1958. The present taxonomic status of the terrestrial mammals of Palestine. Research Council of Israel. Bulletin No. 7B:165-86.

Boesch, Hans H. 1939. El-Iraq. Economic geography XV 235-61.

Bordes, François. 1955. Le Paléolithique inferieur et moyen de Jabrud (Syrie) et le question du pre-Aurignacien. L'Anthropologie LIX 486-507.

Bordes, François, and Müller-Beck, H. 1956. Zur Chronologie der Lössedimente in Nordfrankreich und Süddeutschland. Germania XXXIV 199-208.

Bradley, P. L. 1958. An assemblage of arthropod remains from a Roman occupation site at Saint Albans. Nature CLXXXI 435-36.

Braidwood, Linda. 1946. Artifactual materials of the terminal food-gathering stage of North Africa and the Near East. In Human origins: An introductory course in anthropology. Selected readings II. 2d ed. Chicago.

_______. 1951. The Jarmo flint and obsidian industry. Sumer VII 105-6.

_______. 1952. Early food producers: Excavations in Iraqi Kurdistan. Archaeology V 157-64.

_______. 1953. Digging beyond the Tigris. New York.

Braidwood, Robert J. 1946a. A synoptic description of the earliest village-culture materials from the Aegean to the Indus. In Human origins: An introductory course in anthropology. Selected readings II. 2d ed. Chicago.

_______. 1946b. Terminology in prehistory. In Human origins: An introductory course in anthropology. Selected readings II. 2d ed. Chicago.

_______. 1951a. Discovering the world's earliest village community. Illustrated London news, Dec. 15, 1951, pp. 992-95.

_______. 1951b. A preliminary note on prehistoric excavations in Iraqi Kurdistan. Sumer VII 99-104.

_______. 1951c. From cave to village in prehistoric Iraq. American Schools of Oriental Research. Bulletin No. 124:12-18.

_______. 1952a. The Near East and the foundations for civilization. Eugene, Oregon.

_______. 1952b. From cave to village. Scientific American CLXXXVII 62-66.

_______. 1956a. Reflections on the origin of the village-farming community. Saul S. Weinberg (ed.), The Aegean and the Near East: Studies presented to Hetty Goldman, pp. 22-32. Locust Valley, New York.

_______. 1956b. The world's first farming villages. Illustrated London News, April 28, 1956, pp. 410-11.

_______. 1957. Jericho and its setting in Near Eastern history. Antiquity XXXI 73-81.

_______. 1958a. Near Eastern prehistory. Science CXXVII 1419-30.

_______. 1958b. Über die Anwendung der Radiokarbon-Chronologie für das Verständnis der ersten Dorfkultur-Gemeinschaften in Südwestasien. Österreichischen Akademie der Wissenschaften, phil.-hist. Klasse. Anzeiger, Jahrgang 1958, No. 19:249-59.

_______. 1959. Note to the editor. Kush VII 236-37.

_______. 1960. Prelude to civilization. In City invincible: A symposium on urbanization and cultural development in the ancient Near East. Oriental Institute special publication. Chicago.

Braidwood, Robert J., and Braidwood, Linda. 1950. Jarmo: A village of early farmers in Iraq. Antiquity XXIV 189-95.

_______. 1953. The earliest village communities of southwestern Asia. Journal of world history I 278-310.

_______. 1960. Excavations in the Plain of Antioch. I. The earlier assemblages. Oriental Institute publications LXI. Chicago.

Braidwood, Robert J., and Reed, Charles A. 1957. The achievement and early consequences of food-production: A consideration of the archeological and natural-historical evidence. Cold Spring Harbor symposia on quantitative biology XXII 19-31.

Braidwood, Robert J., et al. 1952. Matarrah: A southern variant of the Hassunan assemblage, excavated in 1948. Journal of Near Eastern studies XI 1-75.

_______. 1953. Symposium: Did man once live by beer alone? American anthropologist LV 515-26.

_______. 1954. The Iraq-Jarmo Project . . . 1954-1955. Sumer X 120-38.

Brandtner, Fritz. 1956. Lösstratigraphie und paläolithische Kulturabfolge in Niederösterreich und den angrenzenden Gebieten. Eiszeitalter und Gegenwart VII 127-75.

Broecker, W. S., Turekian, K. K., and Heezen, B. C. 1958. The relation of deep sea sedimentation rates to variations in climate. American journal of science CCLVI 503-17.

Brooks, Charles E. P. 1926. The evolution of climate. 2d ed. London.

_______. 1949. Climate through the ages. Revised ed. London.

Brunnacker, Karl. 1958. Zur Parallelisierung des Jungspleistozäns in den Periglazialgebieten Bayerns und seiner östlichen Nachbarländer. Geologischen Handesanstalten der Bundesrepublik Deutschland. Geologisches Jahrbuch LXXVI 129-50.

Brunton, Guy. 1927. Qau and Badari I. British School of Archaeology in Egypt and Egyptian Research Account. Publication XLIV. London.

_______. 1929. The beginnings of Egyptian civilization. Antiquity III 456-67.

_______. 1937. Mostagedda and the Tasian culture. British Museum Expedition to Middle Egypt, first and second years, 1928, 1929. London.

_______. 1948. Matmar. British Museum Expedition to Middle Egypt, 1929-1931. London.

Brunton, Guy, and Caton-Thompson, Gertrude. 1928. The Badarian civilization and predynastic remains near Badari. British School of Archaeology in Egypt and Egyptian Research Account. Publication XLVI. London.

Büdel, Julius. 1951. Die Klimazonen des Eiszeitalters. Eiszeitalter und Gegenwart I 16-26.

_______. 1953. Die "periglaziale"-morphologische Wirkungen des Eiszeitalters auf der ganzen Erde. Erdkunde VII 249-60.

Butzer, Karl W. 1957a. Mediterranean pluvials and the general circulation of the Pleistocene. Geografiska annaler XXXIX 48-53.

_______. 1957b. The recent climatic fluctuation in lower latitudes and the general circulation of the Pleistocene. Geografiska annaler XXXIX 105-13.

_______. 1957c. Late glacial and postglacial climatic variation in the Near East. Erdkunde XI 21-35.

_______. 1958. Quaternary stratigraphy and climate in the Near East. Bonner geographische Abhandlungen XXIV.

Capart, Jean. Primitive art in Egypt. London.

Carruthers, Douglas. 1949. Beyond the Caspian: A naturalist in central Asia. Edinburgh.

Caton-Thompson, Gertrude. 1952. Kharga Oasis in prehistory. London.

Caton-Thompson, Gertrude, and Gardner, E. W. 1934. The desert Fayum. 2 vols. London.

Chang, Tso Kan, and Landauer, Walter. 1950. Observations on the skeleton of African dwarf goats. Journal of morphology LXXXVI 367-79.

Childe, V. Gordon. 1928. The most ancient East. London.

_______. 1934. New light on the most ancient East. London.

_______. 1935. Changing methods and aims in prehistory. Prehistoric Society. Proceedings (n.s.) I 1-15.

_______. 1941. Man makes himself. London.

_______. 1942. What happened in history. Harmondsworth.

_______. 1950. Cave men's buildings. Antiquity XXIV 4-11.

_______. 1952. New light on the most ancient East. 4th ed. London.

Clark, J. Desmond. 1959. The prehistory of southern Africa. Harmondsworth.

Clark, J. G. D. 1954. Excavations at Star Carr. Cambridge, England.

Coon, Carleton S. 1951. Cave explorations in Iran in 1949. Philadelphia.

_______. 1952. Excavations in Hotu cave, Iran, 1951: A preliminary report. American Philosophical Society. Proceedings XCVI 231-49.

_______. 1954. The story of man. New York.

_______. 1957. The seven caves. New York.

Crowfoot, Grace M. 1954. Textiles, basketry, and mats. In Charles Singer, E. J. Holmyard, and A. R. Hall (eds.), A history of technology I. Oxford.

Dahr, E. 1937. Studien über Hunde aus primitiven Steinzeitkulturen in Nordeuropa. Lunds University. Arsskrift, n.s. 5, sect. 2, XXXII, No. 4. [Not seen; cited from Sauer, 1952.]

Davies, D. Hywell. 1957. Observations on land use in Iraq. Economic geography XXXI 122-34.

De Candolle, Alphonse. 1883. Origine des plantes cultivées. Paris.

Degerbøhl, Magnus. 1927. Über prähistorische, dänische Hunde. Dansk naturhistorisk Forening. Videnskabelige Meddelelser LXXXIV 17-71.

De Morgan, Jacques. 1924. Le monde oriental avant l'histoire: L'Asie antérieure et l'Égypte. L'Anthropologie XXXIV 17-56.

_______. 1926. La prêhistoire orientale II. Paris.

De Mortillet, Gabriel. 1885. Le préhistorique antiquité de l'homme. Paris.

De Terra, Hellmut, and Paterson, T. T. 1939. Studies on the Ice Age in India and associated human cultures. Carnegie Institution of Washington. Publication No. 493.

De Vaumas, Etienne. 1955. Études irakiennes. La Société de géographie d'Égypte. Bulletin XXVIII 125-94.

De Vries, Hugo. 1958. Radiocarbon dates for upper Eem and Würm interstadial samples. Eiszeitalter und Gegenwart IX 10-17.

De Vries, Hugo, and Barendsen, G. W. 1954. Measurements of age by the Carbon-14 technique. Nature CLXXIV 1138-41.

Dobson, Ronald M., and Stachell, J. E. 1956. Eophila oculata at Verulamium: A Roman earthworm population? Nature CLXXVII 796-97.

Dubertret, Louis. 1946. Géologie du site de Beyrouth avec carte géologique au 1:20,000. Délégation générale de France au Levant, section géologique. Beirut.

Dubertret, Louis, and Weulersse, J. 1940. Manuel de géographie: Syrie, Liban et Proche Orient. Première partie. La péninsule arabique. Beirut.

Duerst, J. Ulrich. 1908. Animal remains from the excavations at Anau. Carnegie Institution of Washington. Publication No. 73:339-442.

Dunand, Maurice. 1956. Rapport préliminaire sur les fouilles de Byblos en 1954 and . . . 1955. Musée de Beyrouth. Bulletin XIII 73-78 and 79-86.

Dyson, Robert H., Jr. 1953. Archeology and the domestication of animals in the Old World. American anthropologist LV 661-73.

Ellerman, J. R., and Morrison-Scott, T. C. S. 1951. Checklist of palaearctic and Indian mammals, 1758-1946. London.

Emiliani, Cesare. 1955. Pleistocene temperatures. Journal of geology LXIII 538-78.

Erman, Adolf, and Grapow, Hermann. 1925. Wörterbuch der aegyptischen Sprache I. Leipzig.

Evans, J. V. 1956. Blood groups in ruminants and human migration. British Association for the Advancement of Science. The advancement of science XIII 198-200.

Ewart, J. Cossar. 1913. Domestic sheep and their wild ancestors. I. Sheep of the mouflon and urial types. Highland and Agricultural Society of Scotland. Transactions, ser. 5, XXV 160-97.

Ewing, J. Franklin. 1947. Preliminary note on the excavations at the Palaeolithic site of Ksar 'Akil, Republic of Lebanon. Antiquity XXI 186-96.

Fairservis, Walter A., Jr. 1955. Wool through the ages. New York.

Falkenstein, Adam. 1936. Archaische Texte aus Uruk. Ausgrabungen der deutschen Forschungsgemeinschaft in Uruk-Warka II 1-76.

Field, Henry. 1956. Ancient and modern man in southwestern Asia. Coral Gables, Florida.

Fink, Julius. 1956. Zur Korrelation der Terrassen und Lösse in Österreich. Eiszeitalter und Gegenwart VII 49-77.

Firbas, F. 1939. Vegetationsentwicklung und Klimawandel in der mitteleuropäischen Spät- und Nacheiszeit. Naturwissenschaften XXVII 81-89, 104-8.

Fisher, William B. 1952. The Middle East. 2d ed. London.

Fisk, H. N., and McFarlan, E. 1955. Late Quaternary deltaic deposits of the Mississippi River. Geological Society of America. Special paper No. 62:279-302.

Fleisch, Henri. 1956. Dépôts préhistoriques de la côte libanaise et leur place dans la chronologie basée sur le Quaternaire marin. Quaternaria III 101-32.

Flohn, Hermann. 1953. Studien über die atmosphärische Zirkulation in der letzten Eiszeit. Erdkunde VII 266-75.

Frankfort, Henri. 1939. Cylinder seals: A documentary essay on the art and religion of the ancient Near East. London.

_______. 1951. The birth of civilization in the Near East. Bloomington, Indiana.

Fraser, F. C., and King, J. E. 1954. Faunal remains. Clark, 1954, pp. 70-95.

Freising, H. 1957. Neue Altsteinzeitfunde aus Nordwürttemberg und ihr erdgeschichtliches Alter. Fundberichte aus Schwaben XIV 7-27.

Frenzel, B. von, and Troll, C. 1952. Die Vegetationszonen des nördlichen Eurasiens während der letzten Eiszeit. Eiszeitalter und Gegenwart II 154-67.

Funkenstein, Daniel H. 1955. The physiology of fear and anger. Scientific American CXCII 74-80.

Gaillard, Claude. 1934. Contribution a l'étude de la faune préhistorique de l'Égypte. Muséum d'histoire naturelle de Lyon. Archives XIV 1-125.

Garrod, Dorothy A. E. 1928. Notes on some Mousterian finds in Spain and Irak. Prehistoric Society of East Anglia. Proceedings (for 1927) V 268-72.

_______. 1930. The Palaeolithic of southern Kurdistan: Excavations in the caves of Zarzi and Hazar Merd. American School of Prehistoric Research. Bulletin No. 6:8-43.

_______. 1932. A new Mesolithic industry: The Natufian of Palestine. Royal Anthropological Institute of Great Britain and Ireland. Journal LXII 257-69.

_______. 1938. The Upper Palaeolithic in the light of recent discovery. Prehistoric Society. Proceedings (n.s.) IV 1-26.

_______. 1951. A transitional industry from the base of the Upper Paleolithic in Palestine and Syria. Royal Anthropological Institute of Great Britain and Ireland. Journal LXXXI 121-30.

_______. 1953. The relations between South-West Asia and Europe in the Late Palaeolithic Age. Journal of world history I 13-38.

_______. 1956. Acheuleo-Jabroudien et "pre-Aurignacien" de la grotte du Taboun (Mont Carmel). Quaternaria III 39-60.

_______. 1957. Notes sur le Paléolithique Supérieur du Moyen Orient. La Société préhistorique française. Bulletin LIV 439ff.

_______. 1958. The natufian culture: The life and economy of a Mesolithic people in the Near East. British Academy. Proceedings XLIII 211-27.

Garrod, Dorothy A. E., and Bate, D. M. A. 1937. The Stone Age of Mount Carmel I. Oxford.

Ghirshman, Roman. 1954. Iran from the earliest times to the Islamic conquest. Harmondsworth.

Gobert, E.-G. 1950. Le gisement paléolithique de Sidi Zin. Karthago I 1-64.

Greiss, Elhamy A. M. 1955. Anatomical identification of plant remains and other materials from (1) El-Omari excavations at Helwan from the Neolithic period; (2) the excavations at Helwan from the First Dynasty. L'Institut d'Égypte. Bulletin XXXVI 227-35.

Gross, Hugo von. 1954. Das Alleröd-Interstadial als Leithorizont der letzten Vereisung in Europe und Amerika. Eiszeitalter und Gegenwart IV/V 189-208.

_______. 1958. Die bisherigen Ergebnisse von C-14 Messungen und paläolithischen Untersuchungen für die Gliederung und Chronologie des Jungpleistozäns in Mittel-Europa und den Nachbargebiete. Eiszeitalter und Gegenwart IX 155-87.

Guyan, Walter U. 1954. Das jungsteinzeitliche Moordorf von Thayngen-Weier: Das Pfahlbauten-Problem. Schaffhausen.

Hahn, Eduard. 1896. Die Haustiere und ihre Beziehungen zur Wirtschaft des Menschen. Leipzig.

Hamerton, J. L. 1958. Problems in mammalian cytotaxonomy. Linnaean Society, London. Proceedings CLXIX 112-25.

Hamilton, Archibald M. 1958. Road through Kurdistan. 2d ed. London.

Harding, G. Lankester. 1958. Recent discoveries in Jordan. Palestine exploration quarterly, 1958, pp. 7-18.

Harlan, Jack R. 1951. New World crop plants in Asia Minor. Scientific monthly LXXII 87-89.

Harper, Francis. 1945. Extinct and vanishing mammals of the Old World. American Committee for International Wild Life Protection. Special publication No. 12. New York.

Hatt, Robert T. 1959. The mammals of Iraq. University of Michigan. Museum of Zoölogy. Miscellaneous publications CVI.

Heer, Oswald. 1865. Die Pflanzen der Pfahlbauten. In Mitteilungen der antiquarischen Gesellschaft in Zürich.

Helbaek, Hans. 1953a. Archaeology and agricultural botany. University of London. Institute of Archaeology. Annual report IX 44-59.

_______. 1953b. Early crops in southern England. Prehistoric Society. Proceedings (n.s.) XVIII 194-233.

_______. 1953c. Queen Ichetis's wheat. Det kongelige danske videnskabernes Selskab. Biologiske Meddelelser XXI, No. 8

_______. 1954. Store Valby—Kornavl i Danmarks første neolitiske Fase. Aarbøger for nordisk Oldkyndighed og Historie, 1954, pp. 198-204. Copenhagen.

_______. 1955a. La recherche paletnobotanique. Sibrium II 225-32. Varese, Italy.

_______. 1955b. Ancient Egyptian wheats. Prehistoric Society. Proceedings (n.s.) XXI 93-95.

_______. 1958a. Grauballemandens sidste Måltid. Kuml: Årbog for Jysk arkaeologisk Selskab, 1958, pp. 83-116. Århus, Denmark.

_______. 1958b. Plant economy in ancient Lachish. Olga Tufnell, Lachish IV 309-17. London.

_______. 1959. Notes on the evolution and history of Linum. In Kuml. Århus.

Herzfeld, Ernst E. 1930. Die vorgeschichtlichen Töpfereien von Samarra. Forschungen zur islamischen Kunst II, Vol. V. Berlin.

Hildebrand, Milton. 1955. Skeletal differences between deer, sheep, and goats. California fish and game XLI 327-46.

Hilzheimer, Max. 1932. Dogs. Antiquity VI 411-19.

_______. 1936. Sheep. Antiquity X 195-206.

_______. 1941. Animal remains from Tell Asmar. Studies in ancient oriental civilization No. 20. Chicago.

Howell, F. Clark. 1952. Pleistocene glacial ecology and the evolution of "classic neanderthal" man. Southwestern journal of anthropology VIII 377-410.

_______. 1959. Upper Pleistocene stratigraphy and early man in the Levant. American Philosophical Society. Proceedings CIII 1-65.

Huzayyin, Suliman Ahmad. 1941. The place of Egypt in prehistory: A correlated study of climates and cultures in the Old World. L'Institut d'Égypte. Mémoires XLIII.

ILN. 1956. An Egyptian queen's watch-dog of 5000 years ago, and domestic dogs of the Near East, 6000-650 B.C. Illustrated London news, June 23, 1956, p. 782.

_______. 1958. Ancestry of the domestic dog: A family tree showing lines of descent. Illustrated London news, Oct. 11, 1958, pp. 614-15.

Ingholt, Harald. 1957. The Danish Dokan Expedition. Sumer XIII 214-15.

Isserlin, B. 1955. Ancient forests in Palestine: Some archaeological indications. Palestine exploration quarterly, 1955, pp. 87-88.

Iversen, J. 1941. Land occupation in Denmark's Stone Age. Danmarks geologiske Undersøgelse II 34.

Jacobsen, Thorkild, and Adams, R. M. 1958. Salt and silt in ancient Mesopotamian agriculture. Science CXXVIII 1251-57.

Jackson, J. Wilfred. 1937. The osteology: Report on the animal remains. Egyptian Exploration Society. Memoir XLII 254-58.

Josien, Thérèse. 1955. La faune chalcolithique des gisements palestiniens de Bir es-Safadi et Bir Abou Matar. Israel exploration journal V 246-56.

Junker, Hermann. 1929-30, 1932-34, 1940. Vorläufiger Bericht [Nos. 1-5, 7] über die Grabung . . . auf der neolithischen Siedlung von Merimde Benisalâme (Westdelta). Kaiserlich Akademie der Wissenshaften, philos.-hist. Klasse, Wien. Anzeiger, 1929, pp. 156-249; 1930, pp. 21-83; 1932, pp. 36-99; 1933, pp. 54-97; 1934, pp. 118-32; 1940, pp. 3-25.

Kantor, Helene J. 1953. Prehistoric Egyptian pottery in the Art Museum. Princeton University. Record of the Art Museum No. 12:67-82.

_______. 1954. The chronology of Egypt and its correlation with that of other parts of the Near East in the periods before the Late Bronze Age. Robert W. Ehrich (ed.), Relative chronologies in Old World archeology, pp. 1-27. Chicago.

Kellersohn, Heinrich. 1953. Die Landwirtschaft im Irak. Erdkunde VII 276-88.

Kenyon, Kathleen. 1957. Digging up Jericho. New York.

_______. 1959. Earliest Jericho. Antiquity XXXIII 5-9.

Klatt, B. 1927. Entstehung der Haustiere. Handbuch der Verebungswissenschaft, Berlin.

Klebelsberg zu Thumburg, Raimund von. 1949. Handbuch der Gletscherkunde und Glazialgeologie. II. Historisch-regional Teil. Vienna.

Koby, F. 1954. Y a-t-il eu, à Lascaux, "un Bos longifrons?" La Société préhistorique française. Bulletin LI 434-41.

Kökten, İ. Kılıc. 1952. Anadolu'da prehistorik yereşme yerlerinin dagılışı üzerine bir araştırma. Ankara Universitesi. Dil ve tarih-coğrafya fakültesi dergisi X 167-207.

_______. 1955. Ein allgemeiner Überblick über die prähistorischen Forschungen in Karaïn-Höhle bei Antalya. Türk Tarih Kurumu. Belleten XIX 284-93.

Krishraswami, V. D. 1953. Progress in prehistory. Ancient India IX 53-79.

Lauer, J.-P., Laurent-Täckholm, Vivi, and Aaberg, Ewart. 1951. Les plantes découvertes dans les souterrains de l'enceinte du Roi Zozer à Saqqarah (IIIe Dynastie). L'Institut d'Égypte. Bulletin XXXII 121-57.

Lawrence, Barbara. 1956. Cave fauna. Harvard University. Peabody Museum of Archaeology and Ethnology. Papers XLVIII 80-81.

Leach, Edmund R. 1940. Social and economic organization of the Rowanduz Kurds. London School of Economics. Monographs in social anthropology III.

Lees, G. M., and Falcon, N. L. 1952. The geographical history of the Mesopotamian plains. Geographical journal CXVIII 24-39.

Life. 1955. Amiable boar. Life magazine, June 13, 1955, pp. 87-90.

Lines, Joan L. 1953. The al 'Ubaid period in Mesopotamia and its Persian affinities. Unpublished Ph.D. dissertation, University of Cambridge.

Lloyd, Seton. 1947. Twin rivers. 2d ed. Oxford.

_______. 1948. The oldest city of Sumeria. Illustrated London news, Sept. 11, 1948, pp. 303-5.

Lloyd, Seton, and Safar, Fuad. 1945. Tell Hassuna. Journal of Near Eastern studies IV 255-89.

Lorenz, Konrad Z. 1955. Man meets dog. Boston.

Lucas, Alfred. 1948. Ancient Egyptian materials & industries. 3d ed. London.

Lutz, Henry F. 1923. Textiles and costumes among the peoples of the ancient Near East. Leipzig.

Lydekker, Richard. 1893. Horns and hoofs, or chapters on hoofed animals. London.

_______. 1913. Catalogue of the ungulate mammals in the British Museum (Natural History) I. London.

Mallowan, M. E. L. 1933. The prehistoric sondage of Nineveh, 1931-32. Annals of archaeology and anthropology XX 127-86.

_______. 1946. Excavations in the Baliḫ Valley, 1938. Iraq VIII 111-49.

_______. 1947. Excavations at Brak and Chagar Bazar. Iraq IX 1-266.

_______. 1956. Twenty-five years of Mesopotamian discovery. Plymouth, England.

Mallowan, M. E. L., and Rose, J. Cruikshank. 1935. Excavations at Tall Arpachiyah 1933. Iraq II 1-178.

Massoulard, Émile. 1949. Préhistoire et protohistoire d'Égypte. Paris.

Matson, Frederick R. 1955. Ceramic archaeology. American Ceramic Society. Bulletin XXXIV 33-44.

_______. 1956. Techniques of the Early Bronze potters at Tarsus. Hetty Goldman, Excavations at Gözlü Kule, Tarsus II 352-61. Princeton.

Matthey, Robert. 1954. Chromosomes et systématique des Canidés. Mammalia: Morphologie, biologie, systématique des mammifères XVIII 225-30.

McBurney, C. B. M., and Hey, R. W. 1955. Prehistory and Pleistocene geology in Cyrenaican Libya. Cambridge.

McCown, Donald E. 1954. The relative stratigraphy and chronology of Iran. Robert W. Ehrich (ed.), Relative chronologies in Old World archeology, pp. 56-68. Chicago.

McFadden, E. S., and Sears, E. R. 1946. The origin of Triticum spelta and its free-threshing hexaploid relatives. Journal of heredity XXXVII 81-89, 107-16.

Meinertzhagen, Richard. 1954. Birds of Arabia. Edinburgh.

Mellaart, James. 1958. Excavations at Hacilar. Anatolian studies VIII 127-56.

Menghin, Oswald. 1932a. The excavations of the Egyptian University at Ma'adi. Ancient Egypt XVII 108-9.

_______. 1932b. Die Grabung der Universität Kairo bei Maadi. Deutsches Institut für ägyptische Altertumskunde, Cairo. Mitteilungen II 143-47.

_______. 1932c. Die Grabung der Universität Kairo bei Maadi. 2. Grabungsjahr. Deutsches Institut für ägyptische Altertumskunde, Cairo. Mitteilungen III 150-54.

_______. 1934. Die Grabung der Universität Kairo bei Maadi. 3. Grabungsjahr. Deutsches Institut für ägyptische Altertumskunde, Cairo. Mitteilungen V 111-18.

Menghin, Oswald, and Amer, Mustafa. 1932. The excavations of the Egyptian University in the Neolithic site at Maadi. First preliminary report (season 1930-31). Egyptian University. Faculty of Arts. Publication XIX 1-65. Cairo.

_______. 1936. The excavations of the Egyptian University in the Neolithic site at Maadi. Second preliminary report (season 1932). Cairo.

Moore, H. T., and Boswell, Charles. 1956. Field observations on the birds of Iraq. II. Pteroclidae-Timaliidae. Iraq Natural History Museum. Publication X.

Mortensen, Hans. 1957. Temperaturgradient und Eiszeitklima am Beispiel der pleistozänen Schneegrenzdepression in den Rand- und Subtropen. Zeitschrift für Geomorphologie I 44-56.

Moustafa, Y. Shawki. 1955. Canis familiaris aegyptica from predynastic Maadi, Egypt. L'Institut d'Égypte. Bulletin XXXVI 105-9.

Movius, Hallam L., Jr. 1944. Early man and Pleistocene stratigraphy in southern and eastern Asia. Harvard University. Peabody Museum of American Archaeology and Ethnology. Papers XXX 3.

Mumford, Lewis. 1956. A study of history. Diogenes XIII 11-28.

Murie, Adolph. 1944. The wolves of Mount McKinley. U. S. National Parks Fauna series V.

Murdock, George Peter. 1957. Culture areas of Africa. Still unpublished paper read at the 1957 meetings of the American Anthropological Association, Chicago.

Murray, George W. 1951. The Egyptian climate: An historical outline. Geographical journal CXVII 422-34.

Myres, John L. 1911. The dawn of history. London.

Neumann, Heinrich. 1953. Die physisch-geographischen Grundlagen der künstlichen Bewässerung des Iran und Irak. Museum für Länderkunde zu Leipzig. Wissenschaftliche Veröffentlichungen XII 4-46.

Neuville, René. 1951. Le Paléolithique et le Mésolithique de désert de Judée. Archives de l'Institut de paléontologie humaine. Mémoire XXIV.

Neuweiller, E. 1905. Die praehistorischen Pflanzenresten Mitteleuropas. In Botanische Exkursionen und Pflanzengeographische Studien in der Schweiz. Zürich.

Newberry, P. E. 1928. The pig and the cult-animal of Set. Journal of Egyptian archaeology XIV 211-25.

Nybom, Nils. 1954. Mutation types in barley. Acta agriculturae Scandinavica IV 430-56.

Okladnikov, A. P. 1956. Peshtera Dzhebel. Southern Turkmenistan Archeological Complex Expedition. Publications VII 11-219. Ashkhabad. [In Russian.]

Olson, Edwin A., and Broecker, W. S. 1959. American Journal of science CCLVII 1-28.

Passemard, M. E. 1926. Les terrasses alluviales de l'Euphrate et les industries qu'elles contiennent. Académie des sciences, Paris. Compte-rendus CLXXXIII 365-68.

Peake, H. J. E., and Fleure, H. J. 1927. Peasants and potters. Oxford.

Pearcy, G. Etzel. 1959. The Middle East: An indefinable region. United States Department of State. Bulletin XL 407-16.

Peet, T. Eric. 1914. The cemeteries of Abydos. II. 1911-1912. Egypt Exploration Fund.

Memoir XXXIV. London.

Perkins, Ann Louise. 1949. The comparative archeology of ancient Mesopotamia. Studies in ancient oriental civilization No. 25. Chicago.

Perrot, Jean. 1952. Le Néolithique d'Abou-Gosh. Syria XXIX 119-45.

_______. 1957. Le Mésolithique de Palestine et les récentes découvertes à Eynan (Ain Mallaha). Antiquity and survival II 91-110.

Peters, J. L. 1940. Check-list of the birds of the world IV. Cambridge, Massachusetts.

Peterson, Roger, Mountfort, Guy, and Hollom, P. A. D. 1954. A field guide to the birds of Britain and Europe. London.

Petrie, W. M. Flinders, and Quibell, J. E. 1896. Naqada and Ballas, 1895. London.

Pfannenstiel, Max. 1952. Das Quartär der Levante. I. Die Küste Palästina-Syriens. Akademie der Wissenschaften, Mainz. Mathematisch-naturwissenschaftlichen Klasse. Abhandlungen VII 375-475.

Picard, Leo. 1937. Inferences on the problem of the Pleistocene climate of Palestine and Syria drawn from the flora, fauna, and stratigraphy. Prehistoric Society. Proceedings (n.s.) III 58-70.

_______. 1943. Structure and evolution of Palestine, with comparative notes on neighboring countries. Hebrew University. Geology Department. Bulletin IV 1-134.

Pilgrem, Guy E. 1947. The evolution of the buffaloes, oxen, sheep, and goats. Linnaean Society, London. Journal of zoölogy XLI 272-86.

Pomel, A. 1898. Les ovidés. Algeria. Service de la carte géologique. Paléontologie monographies XIII. [Not seen; cited from Arambourg, 1929, and Bate, 1953.]

Poser, Hans. 1948. Boden- und Klimaverhaltnisse in Mittel- und Westeuropa während der Würmeiszeit. Erdkunde II 53-68.

Prošek, Fr. von, and Ložek, V. 1957. Stratigraphische Übersicht des tschechoslowakischen Quartärs. Eiszeitalter and Gegenwart VIII 37-90.

Quibell, J. E. 1900. Hierakonpolis I. Egyptian Research Account. Memoir IV. London.

Ralph, Elizabeth K. 1955. University of Pennsylvania radio-carbon dates I. Science CXXI 149-51.

Randall-MacIver, David, and Mace, A. C. 1902. El Amrah and Abydos 1899-1902. Egypt Exploration Fund. Memoir XXIII. London.

Redfield, Robert. 1953. The primitive world and its transformations. Ithaca, New York.

Reed, Charles A. 1957. Comment on "early goats." Antiquity XXXI 38-39.

_______. 1959. Animal domestication in the prehistoric Near East. Science CXXX 1629-39.

Reed, Charles A., and Marx, Hymen. 1959. A herpetological collection from northeastern Iraq. Kansas Academy of Science. Transactions LXII 91-122.

Reilly, E. B. 1940. Test excavations at Tilkitepe (1937). Türk tarih, arkeologya ve etnografya dergisi IV 156-65.

Reynolds, Sidney H. 1939. A monograph of the British Pleistocene mammalia. London.

Rhotert, Hans. 1938. Transjordanien: Vorgeschichtliche Forschungen. Stuttgart.

Romer, Alfred S. 1938. Mammalian remains from some Paleolithic stations in Algeria. Beloit College. Logan Museum. Bulletin V 173-84.

Rosselli, Collette. 1957. Beauty and the beast. This Week magazine, July 14, 1957, pp. 8-10.

Rütimeyer, Ludwig. 1862. The fauna of middle Europe during the Stone Age. Smithsonian Institution. Annual Report, 1861, pp. 361-67.

Rust, Alfred. 1950. Die Höhlenfunde von Jabrud (Syrien). Neumünster.

Ryder, Michael L. 1958. Follicle arrangement in skin from wild sheep, primitive domestic sheep and in parchment. Nature CLXXXII 781-83.

Sauer, Carl O. 1952. Agricultural origins and dispersals. New York.

Schwarz, Ernst. 1935. On ibex and wild goat. Annals and magazine of natural history (London), ser. 10, XVI 433-37.

Scott, John P. 1954. The effects of selection and domestication upon the behavior of the dog. National Cancer Institute. Journal XV 739-58.

Şenyürek, Muzaffar, and Bostancı, Enver. 1956. The excavation of a cave near the village of Mağracik in the Vilâyet of the Hatay. Anatolia I 81-83.

Shalem, N. 1950. Attributed climatic changes in the Levant. Sixteenth International Congress of Geographers, Lisbon, 1949, II 593-649.

_______. 1953. La stabilité du climat en Palestine. Research Council of Israel. Special Publication II 153-75.

Shepard, Anna O. 1956. Ceramics for the archaeologist. Carnegie Institution of Washington. Publication No. 609.

Shepard, F. P., and Suess, H. E. 1956. Rate of postglacial rise of sea level. Science CXXIII 1082-83.

Soergel, Wolfgang. 1919. Lösse, Eiszeiten, und paläolithische Kulturen. Jena.

Solecki, Ralph S. 1955. Shanidar cave, a Paleolithic site in northern Iraq. Smithsonian Institution. Annual Report, 1954, pp. 389-425.

_______. 1957. The 1956 season at Shanidar. Sumer XIII 165-71.

Solecki, Ralph S. and Rubin, Meyer. 1958. Dating of Zawi Chemi, an early village site at Shanidar, northern Iraq. Science CXXVII 1446.

Stekelis, Moishe. 1951. A new Neolithic industry: The Yarmukian of Palestine. Israel exploration journal I 1-20.

Stekelis, Moishe, and Haas, G. 1952. The Abu Usba cave (Mount Carmel). Israel exploration journal II 15-47.

Steward, T. Dale. 1958. First views of restored Shanidar I. Sumer XIV 90-96.

Strahler, Arthur. 1951. Physical geography. New York.

Sushkin, Peter P. 1925. The wild sheep of the Old World and their distribution. Journal of mammalogy VI 145-57.

Tauber, H. 1958. Difficulties in the application of C-14 results in archaeology. Archaeologia Austriaca XXIV 59-69.

Taylor, Walter W. 1957. The identification of non-artifactual archaeological materials. National Research Council. Publication No. 565:1-64.

Tobler, Arthur J. 1950. Excavations at Tepe Gawra II. Philadelphia.

Toynbee, Arnold J. 1935. A study of history. 6 vols. 2d ed. London.

Tsalkin, V. I. 1951. European and Asian mountain sheep. Moscow Society of Naturalists. Zoölogical Section. Materials for the recognition of the fauna and flora of the USSR (n.s.) XXVII 1-343. [In Russian.]

Van Buren, E. Douglas. 1939. The fauna of ancient Mesopotamia as represented in art. Analecta orientalia XVIII 1-113.

Van der Heide, S. 1957. Correlations of marine horizons in the Middle and Upper Pleistocene of the Netherlands. Geologie en Mijnbouw, 19th year, pp. 272-76.

Vaufrey, Raymond. 1939a. Paléolithique et Mésolithique palestiniens. Revue scientifique de la France et de l'étranger VI-VII 390-406.

_______. 1939b. Faune de Sialk. Roman Ghirshman, Fouilles de Sialk près de Kashan, 1933, 1934, 1937 II 195-97. Paris.

_______. 1951. Étude paléontologique. I. Mammifères. Archives de l'Institut paléontologie humaine. Mémoire XXIV 198-217.

Vavilov, Nikolai I. 1926. Studies on the origin of cultivated plants. In Bulletin of applied botany and plant breeding. Leningrad.

Vesey-Fitzgerald, Brian. 1957. The domestic dog: An introduction to its history. London.

Vignard, Edmond. 1920. Station Aurignacienne à Nag Hamadi (Haute Égypte). L'Institut français d'archéologie orientale. Bulletin XVIII 1-20.

von Fritsch, K. 1893. Zumoffen's Hölenfunde im Libanon. Naturforschende Gesellschaft zu Halle. Abhandlungen XIX 41-81.

von Fürer-Haimendorf, Christoph. 1955. Culture history and cultural development. Yearbook of anthropology I 149-68.

von Wissmann, Hermann. 1957. Ursprungsherde und Ausbreitungswege von Pflanzen- und Tierzucht. Erdkunde XI 81-94.

von Wissmann, Hermann, et al. 1956. On the role of nature and man in changing the face of the dry belt in Asia. W. L. Thomas (ed.), Man's role in changing the face of the earth, pp. 278-303. Chicago.

Voute, Caesar. 1957. A prehistoric find near Razzaza (Karbala Liwa). Sumer XIII 1-14.

Waechter, J. d'A. 1952. The excavation of Jabrud and its relation to the prehistory of Palestine and Syria. University of London. Institute of Archaeology. Annual report VIII 10-28.

Waechter, J. d'A., and Seton-Williams, V. M. 1938. The excavations at Wadi Dhobai, 1937-1938, and the Dhobaian industry. Palestine Oriental Society. Journal XVIII 172-85.

Washburn, S. L., and Howell, F. Clark. 1960. Human evolution and culture. In Sol Tax (ed.), Evolution after Darwin. II. The evolution of man. Chicago.

Wasylikowa, K. 1956. Cultivated plants from a Hallstatt fort in Kamieniec (Poland). Acta

Societas botanicorum Poloniae XXV 479-512. Warsaw.

Weidenbach, F. 1953. Zeitliche Einordnung der jungpleistozänen Ablagerungen Mitteleuropas. In Actes du IV Congrès international du Quaternaire.

Wetzel, René, and Haller, J. 1945. Quaternaire de la region de Tripoli. La Mission géologique de la délégation générale de France au Levant. Notes et mémoires IV 1-48.

Wheeler, Sir Mortimer. Archaeology from the earth. Oxford.

White, Theodore E. 1952-55. Observations on the butchering technique of some aboriginal peoples I-IX. American antiquities XVII 337-38, XIX 160-64, 254-64, XXI 170-78.

Willett, H. C. 1950. The general circulation at the last (Würm) glacial maximum. Geografiska annaler XXXII 179-87.

Willey, Gordon R., and Phillips, Philip. 1958. Method and theory in American archaeology. Chicago.

Wirth, E. 1958. Morphologische und bodenkundliche Beobachtungen in der syrisch-irakischen Wüste. Erdkunde XII 26-41.

Witherby, Harry F., et al. 1938. The handbook of British birds. II. Warblers to owls. London.

Woldstedt, Paul. 1954. Saaleeiszeit, Warthestadium, und Weichseleiszeit in Norddeutschland. Eiszeitalter und Gegenwart IV/V 34-48.

_______. 1955. Die Gliederung des Pleistozäns in Norddeutschland und angrenzenden Gebieten. Geologiska föreningen i Stockholm. Förhandlingar LXXVII 525-45.

_______. 1956. Über die Gliederung der Würm-Eiszeit und die Stellung der Lösse in ihr. Eiszeitalter und Gegenwart VII 78-86.

_______. 1958. Eine neue Kurve der Würm-Eiszeit. Eiszeitalter und Gegenwart IX 151-54.

Wright, Herbert E., Jr. 1951. Geologic setting of Ksâr ʾAkil, a paleolithic site in Lebanon —preliminary report. Journal of Near Eastern studies X 115-19.

_______. 1952. Geologic setting of four prehistoric sites in northeastern Iraq. American schools of oriental research. Bulletin No. 128:11-24.

_______. 1955. Geologic aspects of the archeology of Iraq. Sumer XI 83-91.

_______. 1958. An extinct wadi system in the Syrian desert. Research Council of Israel. Bulletin No. 7G:53-59.

Wright, Herbert E., Jr., and Howe, Bruce. 1951. Preliminary report on soundings at Barda Balka. Sumer VII 107-18.

Zeuner, Frederick E. 1945. The Pleistocene period. London.

_______. 1953a. The three Mousterian shorelines. Actes du IV Congrès international du Quaternaire, pp. 547-53.

_______. 1953b. The colour of the wild cattle of Lascaux. Man LIII 68-69.

_______. 1954a. Riss or Würm? Eiszeitalter und Gegenwart IV/V 98-105.

_______. 1954b. Domestication of animals. In Charles Singer, E. J. Holmyard, and A. R. Hall, A history of technology. Oxford.

_______. 1955. The goats of early Jericho. Palestine exploration quarterly, 1955, pp. 70-86.

_______. 1956. The domestication of animals. Scienta L 1-6 (pagination of reprint).

_______. 1957. Stone Age exploration in Jordan, I. Palestine exploration quarterly, 1957, pp. 17-54.

_______. 1958a. Dating the past. 4th ed. London.

_______. 1958b. Dog and cat in the Neolithic of Jericho. Palestine exploration quarterly, 1958, pp. 52-55.

Zohary, Michael. 1950. The flora of Iraq and its phytogeographical subdivisions. Directorate General of Agriculture, Baghdad. Bulletin No. 31.

I

THE GENERAL PROBLEM

This is the story of the first three field campaigns of an archeological expedition—the Iraq-Jarmo Project—in the Kurdish hill country of Iraq. Usually archeologists working in the Near East concern themselves with some particular site, such as Ur of the Chaldees or Roman Antioch, or with a particular thing, such as the tomb of Tutankhamon or the palace of the Assyrian king Sargon at Khorsabad. The expedition described here is different in that it is working toward the solution of a general problem: How are we to understand those great changes in mankind's way of life which attended the first appearance of the settled village-farming community?

The appearance of the village-farming community marked a transition, in cultural history, of great import for what was to follow. Before it were some half a million years of savagery during which small wandering bands of people—living sometimes in caves and sometimes in the open—led an essentially "natural" catch-as-catch-can existence. After the transition, urban civilization followed within a short five thousand years.

Here are some of the possible factors of the transition for which just enough evidence in the archeological record is at hand to warrant further investigation. On the upswing to the transition we note (1) a growing ability (and perhaps some motivation) for intensifying and localizing the exploitation of a given piece of terrain by food-collectors and (2) their increasing tendency to dwell in the open. As traces of the achievement of the transition become apparent, the archeological record makes it reasonably clear that (3) the domestication of plants and (4) the domestication of animals had taken place. What were the interrelationships of these factors (and possible other factors) in the establishment of the first village-farming communities?

Understanding of the transition as a problem of general culture-historical importance is thrown into relief if we ask whether urban civilization is conceivable at the level of a food-collecting economy. Civilization in the full sense of the word—the city, the formal political state, writing, great art and architecture, and the highly specialized crafts such as metallurgy—is already familiar to us in the Near East from the writings of the conventional ancient historians. Civilization began, first of all, in southern Mesopotamia about 3500 B.C. The foundations upon which Mesopotamian civilization arose were laid in an adjacent locale, we believe, by some of the first farmers. By about 7000 B.C., they had apparently established themselves in little villages on the hilly flanks of the Fertile Crescent in southwestern Asia.

How the great change from cave to village, from food-collecting to food-production, came about will be understood, we believe, only by patient attention to the debris contained in little village mounds or other inconspicuous encampments and in the upper layers of caves in the hill-flank country above the Fertile Crescent. The original names of caves and villages have long since disappeared; the names by which we now call them are the Arabic, Kurdish, Persian, or Turkish denominations of the local inhabitants today. The original dwellers had no writing; it takes every tool in the prehistoric archeologist's bag, plus all the help he can get from his natural-scientist colleagues, to make their debris give up its history. Full understanding of how the great transition was made from the level of food-collecting cave-dwellers to that of the settled village-farming community is a faraway goal. We may not ever reach it completely, although our tools for understanding grow increasingly sharp. What follows here is not a complete story but rather only a beginning. The goal of understanding that we seek will not come within the lifetime of this expedition's staff. All we can hope to tell here, in the most tentative way and before the completion of our laboratory research, is how we began work on the problem during our first three seasons in the field and the rough conclusions that we can draw from our field observations.

The general theoretical framing of the problem is not new. Without a long excursion into the history of ideas, we can, nevertheless, note Myres' (1911, p. 124)—to us rather quaint but perceptive—geographical localization of the problem area, which localization was emphasized by Peake and Fleure (1927, p. 140), who also laid some stress on the importance of agricultural settlements as a new way of life. The great British prehistorian V. Gordon Childe wrote much on the theoretical importance of the transition, characterizing it as one of the great revolutions in human history, although he (Childe, 1935) credited Elliot Smith with the idea. But the general notion certainly antedates Smith. Late in the last century, for example, De Mortillet (1885, p. 576) wrote: "La domestication, dans l'histoire de la civilisation, est un fait immense, un découverte des plus importantes. . . ."

Until the end of World War II, however, the problem could still be framed only in its theoretical sense. Field archeology had done little to recover the necessary details of evidence, so that the compilers of ancient history and prehistory, like Childe, could rarely point up their theorizing with fact. Several distinguished excavators had concerned themselves with the more remote ranges of the prehistory of the Pleistocene (or "Ice Age") in the caves of western Asia. But the bulk of archeological excavation in the area had rather been concerned with the developed phases of conventional ancient history, attention being given primarily to particular sites or things, as we remarked above. Such sites as Babylon, Nineveh, Byblos, Megiddo, and Jericho were all excavated, but the intellectual frame of reference of their excavators was biblical or conventional ancient history. Occasionally narrow slit trenches or deep pits were driven down into the lowest levels of some of the great sites, and these operations yielded snatches of prehistoric material. Nevertheless, there were definite economic restrictions on prehistoric excavations of this type, especially in instances where continuous millenniums of living had followed upon the very spot where a prehistoric village was first established. To dig the prehistoric depths of one of the great mounds, it was first necessary to remove the thousands of tons of overburden containing the later levels (see Pl. 1A). Thus the "prehistoric pits" exposed very restricted areas, and their yields were restricted as well. It did not occur to the earlier archeologists to search for inconspicuous little sites (e.g. Pl. 1B) which had not been occupied during the milleniums following their prehistoric establishment. Therefore, our comprehension of prehistoric village life was a thing of shreds and patches at best.

Understanding of the great transition to the cultural level of the village-farming community, tied as we logically reason it must have been to a new way of food-getting, also demands detailed knowledge of the ancient environment in which the transition took place. Botanical, climatological, geological, and zoölogical attention did come to be focused on the Near East in general before the end of the 19th century, and on the problem of the origins of agriculture and animal domestication in particular. But with very little firsthand excavated archeological evidence bearing on the time of the transition itself, the interests of the natural scientists were restricted mainly to a speculative level. Archeology then provided little to substantiate the generalizations of Brooks (1926) on climate, De Candolle (1883) on cultivated plants, and Hahn (1896) on domesticated animals. Egypt may be an exception, but in late prehistoric times it apparently lagged behind western Asia culturally. Vavilov's (1926) very interesting reconstruction of the original centers of plant distribution was based on theorizing from present-day areas of greatest diversity and not from archeologically derived evidence. But as Harlan (1951) has shown, in noting the great genetic diversity developed by many New World plants which reached Turkey after the discovery of America, centers of great diversity need not be the original centers of plant domestication. The whole problem of understanding how and, more exactly, where the great transition took place, in its cultural historical <u>and</u> its natural historical aspects, demands the examination of primary firsthand evidence. Such evidence can only come from the ground—from the upper levels of caves and from the debris of the little villages in which once lived the men who brought about the great transition. The way to reclaim the evidence is by archeological excavation specifically pointed toward the problem.

At the end of World War II, a chart (Braidwood, 1946a; cf. 1956a) made for inclusion in one of a series of essays prepared for a new course in "Human Origins" in the University of Chicago's Department of Anthropology demonstrated that there was clearly a gap in our knowledge of the transition from the final levels of the cave-dwelling food-collectors to those of well established food-producing villages in the Near East. The sequence seemed to jump from a late aspect of the cave stage immediately into the level of flourishing village-farming communities. We would have a comparable situation if the history of the city of Chicago were to be based on a catalogue of what Joliet and Marquette saw among the Indians at Che-kag-ong in 1673 and on nothing else but the mail-order catalogues of the 1950's. Claims of evidence of a transition in Palestine had been examined (Linda Braidwood, 1946) and found to be unconvincing. At the same time, we realized that only within the range of still-undiscovered archeological materials would understanding of the great transition be found.

Our thinking was strongly influenced by the writings of Childe (e.g. 1934) and by discussion with our colleagues in both the Department of Anthropology and the Oriental Institute. Moreover, it seemed increasingly clear that there was rather a high degree of facile assumption and some inconsistency in the generalizations about the transition which were being made by most cultural and natural historians. Some of these assumptions came from purely chance finds of prehistoric or protohistoric materials in areas which now appear to have been peripheral, and some stemmed from archeologically baseless speculations of the earlier natural historians. On the other hand, we had no reason to suspect from the evidence available that traces of the transition should be sought outside western Asia. There were clearly traces of human occupation in western Asia well back in the Pleistocene, for example in the cave of Zarzi (Pl. 10A). In caves in southern Lebanon and Palestine the sequence of stone-age archeology seemed fairly complete, ending in the apparent cultural richness of the levels called "Natufian." True, we could not see signs of a direct transition from the level of culture suggested by the Natufian catalogue to that of the then available basal layers of Jericho or other such minute early village exposures. Nevertheless, all indications suggested that such traces of early village-farming communities as had been found in western Asia were the earliest available anywhere in the world. We were quite prepared to see independent beginnings in food-production, based on other plants and sometimes animals, in other parts of the world (Braidwood, 1952a), but we reasoned that these were later experiments than the Near Eastern instance.

There were also just enough present-day field observations by naturalists and historical clues—from either written documents or artistic representations—to point to the "hilly flanks of the Fertile Crescent" (see Fig. 2) as a natural "nuclear" area. It was reasonable to suspect that the transition took place there. Within the hilly-flanks zone occur in nature (or, in the case of some of the larger animals, occurred until recently) a remarkable constellation of the very plants and animals which became the basis for the food-producing pattern of the Western cultural tradition. Nowhere else in the world were the wild wheats and barley, the wild sheep, goats, pigs, cattle, and horses to be found together in a single natural environment. Such is still the case (save for the extinct wild cattle and horses) in the range of elevations and rainfall concentrations which the hilly-flanks zone represents. The coincidence of the distribution of such early village sites as were known within the hilly-flanks zone itself was striking when mapped (Braidwood, 1952a).

Real understanding was far from precise, however. The early village sites available for plotting on the distribution map were few in number and certainly somewhat later than would be pertinent to the transition itself. The map might not be very significant, since it did not directly give the physical evidence for the natural history of the area for the time of greatest concern. Were the climate pattern and general ecological situation of the hilly-flanks zone in the millenniums around ten thousand years ago roughly similar to or radically different from those of more recent historical and modern times? Is it fair to project the present-day observations of the naturalists back some ten thousand years? Clearly, much more work was necessary.

Nevertheless, it did seem to us that the general theory was approximately correct. Childe and some other (but not all) generalizers assumed that the first great transition to the cultural level of the village-farming community took place in western Asia sometime after ten thousand years ago. But the theory needed much more pointing up with field evidence. We believed that the scene could be localized in the hilly-flanks zone, but to prove this, we would have to reconstruct an extinct environment. For this reconstruction we would need not only archeological excavation oriented directly toward the problem but also on-the-spot assistance of natural scientists. At the same time, we were very conscious of the fact that plants and animals do not domesticate themselves, nor does an environment domesticate them. The domesticator is man, and our chief problem in understanding the great transition would be one of assessing the levels of culture of just before, during, and immediately after the time during which the transition took place.

As our thinking and writing developed, furthermore, we abandoned such Grecized terms as "mesolithic" and "neolithic"; we did for a while follow Childe in emphasizing the "food-producing revolution" as the matter of our real concern, but for the last several years we have been labeling our problem the "appearance of the effective village-farming community." This label, we believe, is a fuller and more precise term for the broad societal changes which the transition brought about. The permanent, architecturally manifested village community, based on an economy of farming and small crafts, was the expression of an entirely new way of life for mankind. Our research goal is both cultural and natural historical reconstruction, and this reconstruction must have clearly defined concepts and terms for the shifting stages and elements of cultural history. But, as cultural historians, we hope that our most useful contributions will be to the understanding of how revolutionary changes in technology and economics—themselves closely linked to natural environment—affect and change or are themselves conditioned by the whole cultures of man. If we are to achieve proper reconstruction, any archeologically derived knowledge of the transition from the cultural level of the cave to that of the village-farming community must be viewed in a disciplined way that is not bound by traditionally imposed conceptions. The inevitable accumulation of new data will increasingly impose the use of conceptual schemes which fit the realities of the case.[1]

---

[1]Adequate basic terminology for the classification of the long range and great variety of prehistoric archeological materials is not easy to devise. This is hardly the place to develop our ideas (see Braidwood, 1946b), but we feel that the currently used neo-Grecisms do not lead to easy communication of ideas. In brief, even though the factor of place (provenience) is of necessity expressed separately, the neo-Grecisms are often used indiscriminately for any one or all of the other three factors which need to be taken into account: (1) time (chronology), (2) technological-typological description (e.g. the presence of chipped or of polished stone tools, of metal tools, of the techniques used in their manufacture, etc.), (3) culture-historical interpretation (e.g. restrained but legitimate generalizations on levels or stages of socio-cultural achievement). We are convinced that these factors cannot simply be lumped under a single word, such as "neolithic," if understanding is to ensue. Cultural evolution was multilinear and not always evenly paced in each line. Both homotaxis and the principle of the sloping horizon as regards diffusions are demonstrable in the archeological record. Certain cultural lines did not contain each of the levels of an ideally complete ascending classificatory scheme. Our alternatives to the neo-Grecisms are as follows:

(1) For "chronology," to make such informed guesses, in terms of years, as the available fabric of radiocarbon determinations and our own judgment of the comparative or real stratigraphic sequence allows.

(2) To use the type-site nomenclature for assemblages of artifactual materials, giving for each assemblage a basic "technological-typological description" of its contents (see chap. v).

(3) To supply our "culture-historical interprepation" of the prehistoric archeolog-

Few scientists work in a vacuum, and, happily, there has been since World War II some archeological activity in the Near East which has dealt in part with the reclamation of evidence approaching the problem of our concern. Unhappily, on the other hand, there are too few archeologists who have the good fortune to be placed in a great research university with the means (or money-getting potential vis-à-vis the learned foundations) and the personnel for continuing intellectual commitment to a single research problem. The antiquities yielded by excavation of very early village sites and caves are seldom of a character which fascinates conventional museums or private donors. In this sense, the work of the Iraq-Jarmo Project has been uniquely blessed by the character of the University which activated it. Our colleagues outside this University have been less fortunate; very few of them would have been able both to concentrate on and to persist in excavations oriented toward the problem of the transition to the village-farming community, even had it been their primary interest.

The first conscious and knowledgeable selection of a small and easily excavatable village site in southwestern Asia, because of surface indications of its prehistoric content, can probably be credited to Mallowan (Mallowan and Rose, 1935) for his work at Tell Arpachiyah, just east of Mosul, in 1933, although such a judgment is somewhat difficult to make. Well before Mallowan's time, tests had been made in southern Mesopotamia and Susiana of prehistoric mounds with attractive painted pottery, but there was no clear comprehension of the overall culture-historical problem. Likewise, in deep pits on historic mounds, prehistoric levels had sometimes been excavated. It is quite clear, however, that Lloyd and Safar's (1945) excavation at Tell Hassunah, south of Mosul, was the result of deliberate and informed choice, based on surface indications that it contained the earliest of the then available village material of the northern Iraqi sequence. This represents the first attempt to disclose in some detail a horizon then considered to represent the earliest village material.

Meanwhile, working upward through Pleistocene prehistoric time, archeologists in Palestine were approaching evidence for the transition from the opposite direction. The brilliant successes of Professor Dorothy Garrod in caves on Mt. Carmel, supplemented by further cave excavations in the Judean hills by M. René Neuville, by Dr. Alfred Rust at Yabrud (Syria), and by the Jesuits at Ksar Akil (Lebanon), stimulated some thought concerning the characteristics of the transition which must have followed the latest paleolithic layers of these caves, but there was little action designed to elucidate them. The most interesting of these latest layers of certain of these caves included an assemblage or catalogue of Natufian artifacts, which was sometimes classified as "mesolithic" and sometimes as "neolithic."[2] The Natufian tool kit does suggest that its makers were probably in a phase of incipient cultivation. We will reconsider this suggestion and some of the following matters in our conclusions. There seems to have been little direct survey to locate open-air aspects of the Natufian and its assumed descendants, although the work of Stekelis and Haas (1952) at the Abu Usba cave and that of Perrot (1952) at the Abu Ghosh open site, both in Palestine, appear to have resulted from the selection of sites solely for their prehistoric content. More recently an undoubted open-air Natufian site has been excavated by Perrot (1957) at Ain Mallaha, in northern Israel. In northeastern Iraq, Solecki (1957) discovered, at Zawi Chemi Shanidar near Ruwanduz, an open site of the same essential character as Karim Shahir (see pp. 52-54).

In the main, however, the postwar excavators of southwestern Asia have continued

---

ical materials of our concern (see chap. xii), using a device of levels of subsistence-settlement types.

After some soul-searching, we have, however, decided to retain the single neo-Grecism "paleolithic"; we believe we have restricted it to the factor of "technological-typological description."

[2] In her latest study of the Natufian, Garrod (1958, p. 226) clearly recognizes the terminological difficulties.

to concern themselves—if they have sought prehistoric materials at all—with deep trenches of restricted size in the great sites of historic times. Highly provocative attempts under such circumstances have been made by Miss Kenyon (1957) at Jericho and by Dunand (1956) at Byblos. In Iraqi Kurdistan, a Danish expedition under Harald Ingholt has recently announced tapping levels of the Jarmo phase (see p. 49) at Tell Shimshara (Ingholt, 1957). But when our field work began, there was no material from any of the postwar excavations that was directly pertinent to the great transition.

Several direct attacks on the Pleistocene prehistory of the caves have been made since the war. The excavations of the Jesuits at Ksar Akil, north of Beirut, were completed (Ewing, 1947), but the site did not yield materials as late as the beginning of the transition. Solecki's (1955 and 1957) topmost consistent level in the cave of Shanidar, in Iraqi Kurdistan, paralleled in the main the materials of the Zarzi and Palegawra caves (see pp. 57-60); his purpose appeared at the beginning to favor the exposure of earlier Pleistocene levels. Coon's (1957) soundings in Iran and later in Syria were also pointed primarily toward the Pleistocene, but certain upper layers of two of his caves, Belt and Hotu, lying in the lush and specialized ecological niche of the south Caspian coastal plain, yielded materials which may be indirectly pertinent to the great transition. We believe that the Belt and Hotu materials represent cultures which (while they may be quite central in their own terms) may prove to be largely peripheral to those of the nuclear area of the hilly-flanks country. They show, we believe, the persistence of the food-collecting level in such a periphery after the appearance of the village-farming community in the nuclear area (Braidwood, 1958a).

It is not our intent here to analyse the results of our colleagues' postwar excavations. Were we to make such an analysis, the work in the basal levels of Tell al-Sultan (Jericho) would hold much of our attention. In these excavations, Miss Kenyon (1957) has exposed successive stages of a well developed architectural complex. Thick masonry fortification walls, which included a tower with interior staircase and a surrounding rock-cut ditch, inclosed a town-size cluster of mud-brick houses in an area of approximately 8 - 10 acres. But the two earliest phases of the site, as so far published, did not yield pottery, and several radiocarbon determinations, which range from about 6800 to 5800 B.C., have been announced for them. There is also news that a Natufian-like variant, with a radiocarbon determination of approximately 7770 B.C., lies under these earliest phases. Miss Kenyon and her collaborators have accepted these radiocarbon determinations at face value and have made somewhat extravagant interpretations for "civilization" at "Urban pre-pottery Neolithic Jericho." The advisability of this terminology and of these interpretations has been questioned on the basis of present evidence (Braidwood, 1957 and 1958a).

These doubts do not detract from the importance of the site of Tell al-Sultan. Although we at first suspected its importance was that of a relatively early provincial town in a somewhat specialized ecological niche, the recent news of Natufian-like strata and of a certain continuum in the typological sequence upward into the overlying nonceramic town deposits is also of considerable importance. This news tends to support a picture of a perhaps predominantly indigenous evolution for the subsistence and settlement pattern about Jericho during the transition period in this particular quarter. Regardless of dating problems, these archeological efforts in the Jordan valley and those in Iraqi Kurdistan will prove to be interdependent and related. Regardless also of the question of specific ecological niches, both efforts lie within the general area that we feel may be crucial to the great transition. Both investigations have already yielded characteristic cultural remains and sequences which, though dissimilar from one another, strengthen a working concept that would see perhaps a multiplicity of localized readaptations taking place within several subregions, each drawing on its own local indigenous forerunning traditions. This concept tends frankly to emphasize the role of an isolated locality wherein certain traditions had already been imposed and to minimize the role of cross-cultural or even immigrating influences. The two roles may have been equally powerful, but lack of evidence seriously restricts our assessment of the second role. The total possible amount of evidence is so far from canvassed that one cannot yet presume to see the relative combinations of the two roles (isolated cultural evolution versus regional cultural interchange) in the final outcome. A great variety of possibilities must be allowed for. For the present, however, two tentative lines are being pursued by means of fragmentary and dissimilar evidence in only two limited spots of a potentially very large field. Our report tries to give an overall presentation of the facts and the imponderables as they appear in the sampling from Iraqi Kurdistan.

It gives us satisfaction to note the general increase in intellectual interest in the transition to the established village-farming community and in the realization of its importance as a major landmark in human history. This increase is no doubt in fair part due to the popularity of the late V. Gordon Childe's writings, especially Man Makes Himself and What Happened in History, which have tended to flourish in the intellectual milieu which also made Toynbee's A Study of History a best seller. Toynbee, in fact, utilizes Childe's development of Brooks' theory of the postglacial northward shift of the rain winds with resulting desiccation in northeastern Afrasia as his "challenge" in explaining the "genesis of Egyptaic civilization." This theory (see pp. 72-73, 122-23) attempts to explain the appearance of agriculture and animal domestication on the basis of the assumption of an enforced withdrawal of plants, animals, and men to oases and river valleys with the disappearance of a glacially-induced southern storm track. Lewis Mumford (1956) takes Toynbee to task for not stressing enough the positive aspects of the transition.

There is danger that Childe has overstressed the realm of technology in his treatment of the character of the transition and of the way of life of the early village-farming community. His great familiarity with such primary archeological evidence as existed when he wrote and his tendency toward a materialistic philosophy of history rather forced his interpretations into the realm of changes in what Redfield (1953) referred to as the technical order, to the exclusion of attention to changes in the moral order. Childe could quite justifiably have answered that the archeologists had provided him only with evidence of things (mainly tools, weapons, objects of daily use)—and few enough of these—and that he was on much sounder ground in interpreting the meaning of an ax to an extinct culture than he was in interpreting the meaning of a design which the people used in painting their pottery. Here lies, in fact, one of the great enigmas of prehistoric archeology. How are we to arrive at justifiable interpretations of the moral order by which people of an extinct culture lived? What is the utmost degree in which it is possible to make such interpretations from the material traces of an extinct culture?

We believe the prospects for success in interpreting the moral order are remote but by no means hopeless. To oversimplify, we believe the first step should be the disentanglement of the very complicated knot comprising the two strands, the technical and moral orders. In disengaging the strand of the technical order, so that that of the moral order will lie bare for observation, we shall need the help of the natural scientists. Working with them, the archeologist can place the present imponderable factors of the ancient environment and a culture's utilization of its natural resources in their proper perspective. The disengagement can go forward only with much more imaginative archeology than we have had up to now. We shall often need the natural scientists in the field with us for mutual stimulation. We shall have to think, in our clarification of the technical order, in terms of extinct crafts as entities. To do this, we must focus on all the artifacts possibly belonging to each craft and on the position of these artifacts in the site, thus going beyond the more convenient and initially necessary excavator's classification based merely on such formal aspects as shape and raw material. One of the more challenging and thought-provoking categories now assembled from Jarmo consists of several thousand animal and human figurines and associated pieces displayed in great variety and undoubtedly bearing on both the technical and the moral order. In our approach to the moral order we need much larger exposures in our excavations so that architectural arrangements for family life and the communal aspects and activities of village life may be more adequately studied. In this realm, too, we shall increasingly need to turn to the ethnologists and social anthropologists. Studies of contemporary peoples with approximately comparable cultural levels and natural environments may be informative. Such studies must be made soon, for such peoples are fast becoming "modern." We envision not the familiar old-fashioned archeology of digging royal tombs for fine-arts museums but an "idea archeology" aimed at broad culture-historical problems, in which antiquities as such are meaningless save as tools for understanding the ways of mankind.

II

SCENE OF THE FIELD WORK

The geographical locale of the great culture-historical sequence leading to full civilization in western Asia may be likened to an enormous amphitheater with its stage toward the south. On the west, the tiers rise to the Judean, ante-Lebanon, and Lebanon mountains which border the Mediterranean Sea. To the north and east, they rise to the high ranges of Anatolia and Persia. The amphitheater serves as a basin for the Euphrates-Tigris drainage system. These rivers cut down from the high tiers on the north and run in roughly parallel courses through the vast orchestra pit of the Syrian desert to flow onto extreme left stage in classic southern Mesopotamia at the head of the Persian Gulf. On extreme right stage lies Palestine with Egypt beyond it to the southwest. In center stage are the desert wastes of Arabia. This analogy becomes comprehensible when one refers to a map (e.g. Figs. 1-2), for the mountain flanks of the amphitheater do run like tiers. The mountains, especially the Anatolian flanks and the Zagros on the north, northeast, and east, build up in a series of ridges which are concentric about the orchestra pit. North of Lebanon, on the Syrian coast east of Cyprus, the rim of the tiers is low, and this low portion is known as the "Syrian saddle." Through the saddle, from the east Mediterranean over Cyprus, come the rain-bearing winter winds. Their moisture is precipitated along virtually all of the mountain rim of the amphitheater to the north and northeast of the saddle, as far as the Persian Gulf (Fisher, 1952, Map II).

In moving north and northeast from the center of the orchestra pit to the mountain rim of the amphitheater, we find it useful to delineate five zones or types of landscape, climate, and vegetation. The lowest zone is the band of alluvium adjacent to the rivers Euphrates and Tigris as they cut southward. Below the latitude of Baghdad the alluvium spreads out to encompass all of classic southern Mesopotamia and stretches irregularly beyond its bounding rivers. The second zone is the desert-steppe, trenched by the Tigris and the Euphrates in their middle courses. The portion of the desert-steppe lying between the two rivers is upper Mesopotamia or the Jazirah (Arabic for "Mesopotamia," i.e., the land between water, the island), and there is further desert-steppe beyond the bounding rivers. Both the alluvial and desert-steppe zones are of low elevation and have little relief; they receive little rainfall. The rivers meander through these zones, especially as they reach the alluvial plain, often shifting their beds. Truly effective agriculture is possible on the alluvium only by means of irrigation. The desert-steppe soil is of a poor gypsum, heavy and not suitable for agriculture even with irrigation.

To the north and east, above the desert-steppe and alluvial zones, lies the piedmont zone, with elevations which approximate 750 to 1,250 feet above sea level. The piedmont's average annual rainfall is about 12 to 20 inches, and the relief is of low rolling hills. This is natural grassland, and grain may be grown without irrigation in years of normal rainfall. Tributaries of the Tigris cut down through the piedmont to join the main river. The part of the piedmont about the junction of the Tigris and Greater Zab Rivers was the heartland of ancient Assyria.

The fourth zone comprises foothills and intermontane valleys at elevations of 1,250 to 3,000 feet above sea level. This is the characteristic "hilly flanks of the Fertile Crescent," with yearly rainfall averaging about 20 to 30 inches. Since the rocky structure of the "Crescent" flanks builds up in concentric folds, the main intermontane valleys between these ridges run from northwest to southeast in Iraqi Kurdistan but turn to run from west to east along the Turkish flanks. The streams and rivers which drain these intermontane valleys break through the lower ridges at points of structural weakness. This situation is

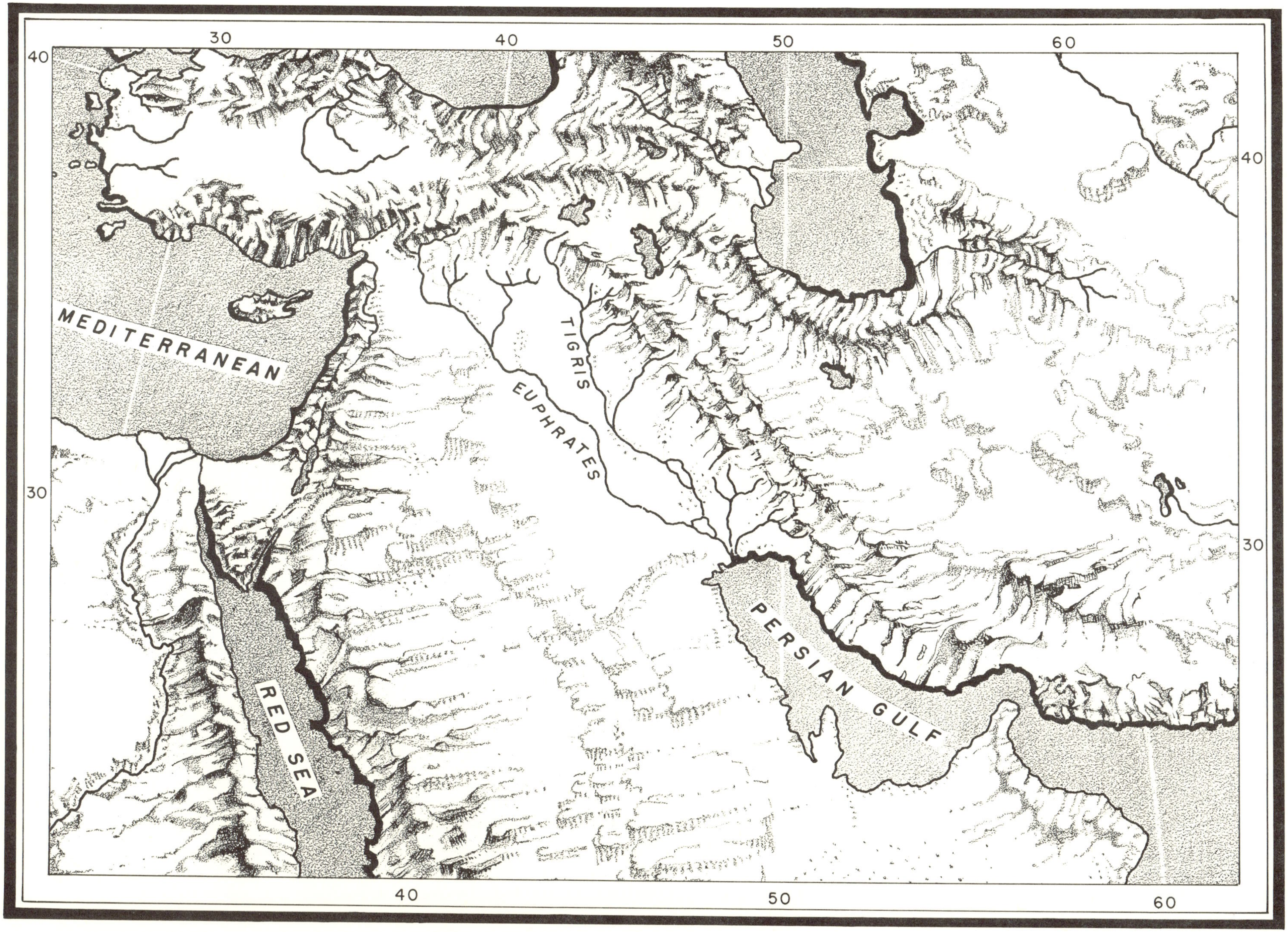

Fig. 1. Physiographic map of southwestern Asia

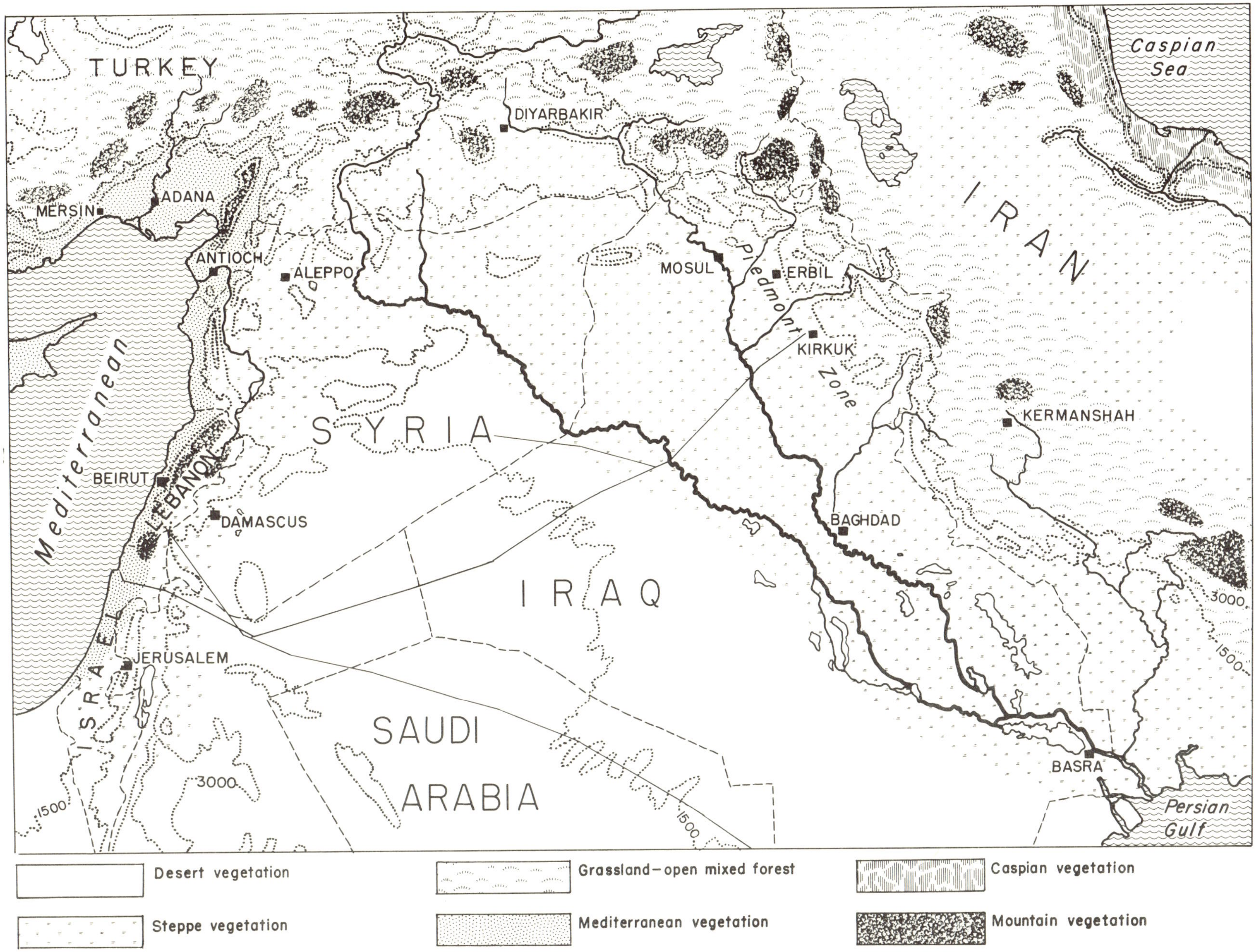

Fig. 2. Map of the "amphitheater," with 1,500- and 3,000-foot contours and indication of the vegetation zones. After Times Atlas I, Pl. 6 (1957). Cf. a rainfall map (e.g. Braidwood, 1952a; Dubertret and Weulersse, 1940; Fisher, 1952).

well expressed in Iraqi Kurdistan, where the major Tigris tributaries (the Greater Zab, the Lesser Zab, and the Diyala) gather many intermontane-valley streams and themselves break through the successive ridges to the piedmont, at the lower edge of which they join the Tigris. The zone of foothills and intermontane valleys contains much open grassland in the valley bottoms and still has scrub oak on many of its intervening ridges. It is good grain, tobacco, and orchard country.

Finally comes the higher grandeur of the Turkish and Kurdish mountains, rising to peaks above the timber line of 11,000 feet in Iraq and even higher in Turkey and Iran. Some of the higher elevations receive more than 40 inches of annual rainfall. At these elevations the two Zabs, the Diyala, and the Tigris itself become mountain streams, gathering in tributary streams as they rush down toward the lower zones. This country is too rugged for normal farming, but some grain and tobacco are now grown on hillsides, grapes are cultivated, and animals are herded. There is still some virgin timber, which includes oak, pine, and juniper.

The characteristics of the five zones—alluvium, desert-steppe, piedmont, foothills and intermontane valleys, high mountains—are in fact most clearly defined in the northern (Turkish) and northeastern (Iraqi Kurdistan) arcs of the amphitheater. The Turkish portion is broad and has all but the two lowermost zones well expressed. The Iraqi Kurdistan area also is an embayment of some size, with fingerings through several lower passes in the high Zagros onward into northern Iran in the Lake Urmiyah region. To the southeast, in Persian Khuzistan, the scarp is somewhat more abrupt, the piedmont is less broad and clearly defined, and the intermontane valleys of the intermediate altitude are less extensive. In the west, the five-zone system seems to break down even more.

In the western portion of the amphitheater, the weather pattern is different from that of the north and northeast. The piedmont is broad, but much of it is screened from the Mediterranean rains by high Lebanon (see Fig. 2). The wind and rain track through the Syrian saddle, as noted above, waters the Turkish and Kurdish arcs of the amphitheater, but does not hook back southward to water the inland flank of the ante-Lebanon. Aleppo, well seated in the Syrian saddle, and Mosul, on the Tigris, have very similar climatic diagrams (yearly patterns of rainfall and temperature). The rain-shadow effect of the Lebanon and ante-Lebanon mountain screen is readily apparent when one notes the differences between Damascus and Erbil. Damascus, in the mountain-screened portion of the Syrian piedmont, although it lies at an elevation of approximately 2,250 feet, receives only 9 inches of rainfall annually; its gardens depend on irrigation from the mountain streams of the ante-Lebanon. Erbil, in the highest portion of the piedmont of Iraqi Kurdistan, lies at an elevation of only 1,350 feet but receives about 17 inches of annual rainfall. The point, of course, is that Erbil is within the wind and rain track, while Damascus is not.

The coastland beyond the western rim of the amphitheater, fronting outward toward the sea, enjoys climate and vegetation which are essentially Mediterranean. Thus anything south of the town of Tripoli and the Syrian saddle—essentially the Lebanese and Palestinian littoral—lies outside the climatic scheme of the amphitheater. In fact, along the Levant coastlands, short stretches of climates and environments in great variety may be found on the face of the mountains or in the intermontane valleys as one moves upward in altitude or back from the sea. This situation is also reflected along the broader coastland and Judean hill flanks of Palestine. There is a small saddle which opens between Mt. Hermon and Mt. Carmel and allows rains to penetrate along the higher western slopes of the trans-Jordan highlands. The eastern slopes of the Judean hills and the Dead Sea basin are left very dry.

Increasingly, our evidence in Iraqi Kurdistan which bears on the beginnings of the transition to the settled village-farming community suggests that the band of foothills and intermontane valleys—the "hilly flanks of the Fertile Crescent"—was a zone of very great importance. What evidence we now have indicates that the piedmont probably felt the effects of the transition slightly later, although there may have been some "spilling-out" from the intermontane valleys onto the piedmont at the embouchures of the larger drainage systems.[1]

---

[1] The site of M'lefaat, on the Khazir River (see p. 27), lies at the opening to the pied-

Only time and much more investigation will tell whether the picture we project is true for all of the hilly-flanks zone. Unfortunately, we know as yet practically nothing of the earlier cultural history of the zone of foothills and intermontane valleys in the Iranian, Syrian, and Turkish portions of the arc. One may assume that early developments there would soon have spilled down onto the piedmont. The zone of the high mountain rim about the whole amphitheater never achieved very great importance, probably because of the rugged nature of its landscape. There is enough archeological and ecological evidence to discount the possibility that the transition could have taken place in the lower desert-steppe or alluvial zone, although Adams (1960) suggests that food-collectors adapted to riverine life may have flourished in lower Mesopotamia.

In chapter i we suggested that the hilly-flanks of the Fertile Crescent form a "nuclear" area—a zone in which a constellation of potentially domesticable plants and animals was ready and waiting in nature. This situation, to the degree that we now have evidence to delineate it, obtained in our zone of foothills and intermontane valleys. There is little doubt in our minds that the nuclear area for the appearance of the village-farming community in the Near and Middle East can—as a reasonable working hypothesis—already be taken to coincide with this zone. An extension of the hypothesis would be that the critical part of the zone lay at elevations of approximately 1,250 to 3,000 feet and, then as now, received about 20 or more inches of annual rainfall. Iraqi Kurdistan is one ideal geographical area which must be more fully investigated so that the working hypothesis and its extension can be tested. Tell al-Sultan, in the Dead Sea valley, is ideally situated for testing the negative validity of the extension of the hypothesis. Obviously, a major feature of the testing of an environment will be to discover the degree to which the present observable situation resembles, or is different from, the situation which obtained some eight or ten thousand years ago. Did the zone then, as it does now, naturally contain potentially domesticable plants and animals? We shall see that the available evidence suggests far greater similarity than difference.

We may pass now to a slightly more detailed description of Iraqi Kurdistan (see Figs. 2-4). As one crosses the desert from Syria to Iraq along the Iraq Petroleum Company's pipe-line road, as the expedition staff did in the early spring of 1955, and continues on eastward from the oil fields at Kirkuk to the frontier of Persia beyond Sulimaniyah, he traverses each of the five zones of our amphitheater. The Syrian desert-steppe country, the upper Jazirah, is sparsely occupied, its only inhabitants being the nomad Bedouin Arabs with their flocks and camels, save where the pipe-line road crosses the Euphrates and Tigris. Along the lowest alluvial terrace (the "mud flats") of the rivers, are garden culture and some date palms. For a few weeks in early spring, after the rains, the desert itself is green, especially along a temporary watercourse like that of the Wadi Tharthar (Pl. 2A), which drains southward from the Jabal Sinjar between the Tigris and the Euphrates.

After ascending out of the Tigris trench and driving for some two hours in a northeasterly direction toward Kirkuk, one finds that the desert-steppe country gradually gives way to the piedmont zone less than 20 miles from the city of Kirkuk itself. The westward edge of the piedmont zone, about coincident with the 12-inch annual rain line, comes rather close to the foothills at Kirkuk. The zone narrows off even more to the southeast but expands into the broader Assyrian plain to the northwest of Kirkuk, where its western border even lies west of the Tigris in the vicinity of Mosul. Kirkuk lies at an elevation of about 1,100 feet and receives about 12 inches of rainfall annually; rainfall agriculture becomes increasingly precarious as the piedmont zone thins out southeast of Kirkuk. Culturally the piedmont is now a transitional zone, with a population composed of Arabs, Kurds, Turkomans, and var-

---

mont. Dr. Stuart Harris, of the Hunting Technical Services, Ltd., collected surface materials from a variety of small mounds near the embouchure of the Tauq Chai, some 50 miles south of Kirkuk. Upon examination of the flints from two of Harris' sites, Linda Braidwood and Howe identified them as of the same essential flint industry as that of the site of Jarmo.

Fig. 3. Map of sites in the Kirkuk-Sulimaniyah region

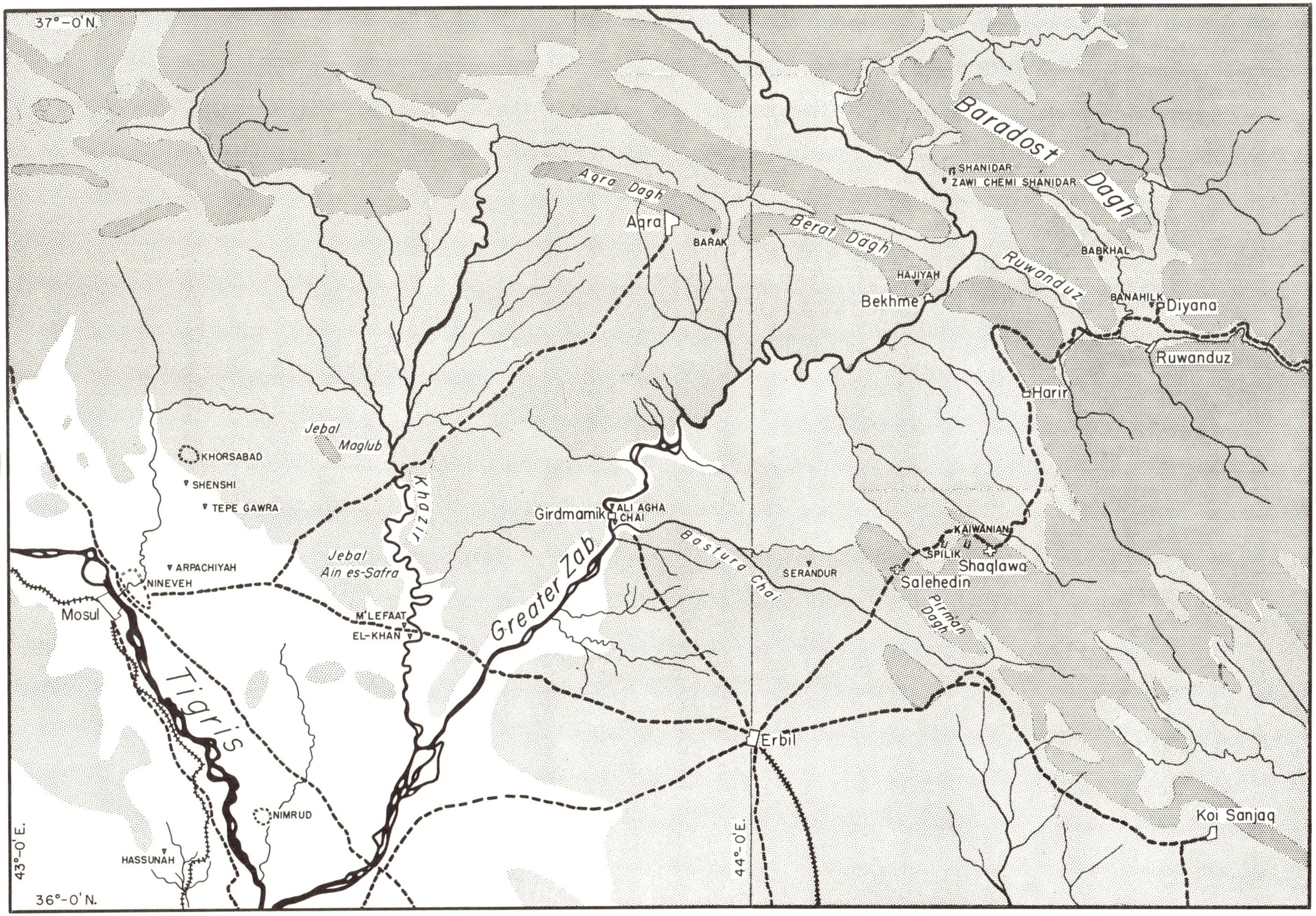

Fig. 4. Map of sites in the Mosul-Ruwanduz region

ious small Christian sects. The Kurds predominate where the piedmont approaches the foothills zone.

The landscape about the city of Erbil, two hours' drive north of Kirkuk, is in fact more representative of the Assyrian-plain piedmont country. With its central core on top of the ancient mound (Pls. 1A, 2B) and with its 1,350-foot elevation and 17 inches of rain, Erbil is a major gateway into Iraqi Kurdistan and a favored Kurdish market. Round about Erbil lie numerous smaller towns and villages of the piedmont zone, with the higher hills and mountains in full view on the northern and eastern horizons.

The piedmont is a rolling to flat grassland plain with fertile alluvial soil, beautifully green from the time of the winter rains into the month of May and turning to bronze in June as harvest time approaches. There are few trees, and the vegetation browns off to a monotonous buff color in summer and autumn. Villages tend to lie near springs or along wadies, few of which flow perennially although they do retain occasional pools of water or yield subsurface water in shallow wells. The village headman, at least, has water carried or channeled to his small garden of onions and tomatoes and for his occasional apricot tree. In late summer and autumn there is little agricultural activity, and the sheep and goats pasture on the stubble of the wheat and barley fields.

The hills build up quickly beyond Kirkuk and a few miles to the east of Erbil. The lowest hills are of gravel, then come low ridges of sandstone, perhaps more gravel, and finally the higher limestone mountain ridges. The axis of the ridges is from northwest to southeast; between the ridges lie the fertile valleys of our study. The more active drainage systems of these valleys cut through the ridges to carry their burden down onto the piedmont and, in the case of the two Zabs and the Diyala, even to the Tigris. This is the foothill and intermontane country. Its population is made up predominantly of Kurds who live in small towns and villages; only Sulimaniyah, three hours' drive east of Kirkuk, approaches the size of a small city with its 25,000 population. The villages are adjacent to springs or streams which, at the elevations and with the rainfall characteristic of this zone, are often perennial. There are oleander bushes and occasional small trees along the watercourses and sometimes a protected tree or grove of trees of considerable height (Pl. 3A). The higher limestone ridges carry scrub oak.

This country is much more colorful than the piedmont. The green of its fields and grasslands lasts longer into the summer and contrasts—often vividly—with the colors of exposed sandstones, shales, and limestones of the ridges which border its valleys. Its spring flowers are magnificent and its crops of wheat, barley, and lentils generally flourishing. Crops are occasionally lost in a year of lean rainfall in the piedmont zone, but such is seldom the case in the zone of foothills and intermontane valleys. Flocks and herds are pastured higher than the valley floors or along the wadi flanks or on fallow land until the harvest is done. Fine tobacco and some rice are grown in the Sulimaniyah province; the government experimental farm at Bakrajo and Shaikh Baba Ali's farm produce excellent fruit, vines, and berries. The villagers use water of smaller streams and springs for garden truck, but the zone is certainly not characterized by irrigation agriculture. As noted above, this zone is approximately 1,250 to 3,000 feet in elevation, and its annual rainfall averages about 20 to 30 inches.

It remains to say that in this zone agriculture is restricted largely to the valleys and to remark again that the major tributary basins allow the lower elevations of the piedmont to finger up into it in the foothills and, vice versa, to provide egress from the foothills to the lowlands. In effect, however, these lower and broader valley extensions of the piedmont receive the same approximate rainfall as the foothills zone in general. Also the Diyana-Ruwanduz, the Rania-Dukan, and the Halabja valley-plains—characteristic intermontane valleys—lie eastward of higher ridges which belong properly to the mountain highland zone. It would take a large and detailed map (cf. Davies, 1957) to plot the zone of foothills and intermontane valleys accurately. Its good arable land is nowhere nearly so great in area as is that of the piedmont, and the zone does tend to be fragmented into separate valley-plains. It is not a region of physically difficult access or communications, although playful tendencies toward brigandage of certain Kurdish tribes in late Ottoman times gave it a reputation for remoteness and danger.

The Kurdish highlands proper, in the ridges of the Zagros Mountains which flank the Iranian border and which lie above 3,000 feet, include some very spectacular country.[2] Here oak and, in the north, pine are common up to the timber line, with interspersed open meadows. Snow remains on the higher peaks until May, and the streams, many of which have the character of mountain torrents, are usually perennial. This is for all intents and purposes pure Kurdish country. The villages are not large, and their architecture contrasts with the mud-walled houses of the piedmont and lower valleys in that flat-roofed stone-walled houses tend to nestle into the hillsides (Pl. 3B). Two of the tribes are still migratory, leaving their summer camps in the high country on either side of the Iraqi-Iranian border with the onset of cold weather and trekking down into the lower valleys or piedmont for the winter season. Our expedition staff had contact with such a movement of the Herki, during the time of our test excavations in the plain of Diyana in early December, 1954.

The high country is not thickly populated. Most of the villagers remain throughout the year. They grow enough field crops to maintain themselves, tend orchards, vineyards, and small gardens, and practice wood-cutting and charcoal-burning. We were told that the men do some hunting in the winter. The highlands, with their majestic scenery, make up a wild country in the physical sense, and it is not surprising that they show slim trace of occupation during prehistoric or early historic times.

Various geographers recently concerned with Iraq (e.g. Boesch, 1939; Davies, 1957; De Vaumas, 1955; Fisher, 1952; Kellersohn, 1953; Neumann, 1953) have not generally distinguished a zone of foothills and intermontane valleys in Iraqi Kurdistan. They tend to divide our foothill zone into a piedmont and a high-mountain classification. We note with interest that Leach (1940)—one of the very few professional ethnologists who has worked in the area—had independently arrived at our zone classification as "having both geographic and ethnographic significance." In terms of exact factors, such as elevation, our zones may be slightly inconsistent. For example, the general average upper limit of elevation in the piedmont is 1,250 feet above sea level, but Erbil—at 1,350 feet—is certainly piedmont in the topographic, climatic, and vegetational senses. Again, Halabja is obviously within an intermontane plain, but it receives almost 40 inches of rainfall annually, although the average of our zone of foothills and intermontane valleys is 20 to 30 inches. Though our subdivision into five zones may be somewhat more impressionistic and less rigidly precise than the geographers', we think it serves best for the story we have to tell.

The activities of the Iraq-Jarmo Project's staff were concentrated in the zone of foothills and intermontane valleys and the upper edges of the piedmont zone because we believe that an important early act in the great drama of the achievement of civilization in the amphitheater of western Asia was played, at least in part, in the tiers of Iraqi Kurdistan. Later, the play moved to a new act, on left stage, in the river alluvium of classic southern Mesopotamia.

---

[2] During recent years, many views of this country have been published in excellent color illustrations in the issues of Iraq Petroleum, the magazine of the Iraq Petroleum Company, Ltd., London.

III

THE DEVELOPMENT OF THE IRAQ-JARMO PROJECT'S FIELD ACTIVITIES

The Oriental Institute's first post-World War II digging in western Asia was done by the Iraq-Jarmo Project, at first called the "Iraq project of the Syrian Expedition." The staff consisted of Robert J. and Linda Braidwood, Charlotte Otten as Department of Anthropology grantee, and Dr. Faraj Basmachi as representative of the Iraqi Directorate General of Antiquities. The Braidwoods were still members of the prewar Syrian Expedition staff, and, in fact, it was first proposed that work be resumed in northern Syria, for the Braidwoods were most familiar with the early village archeology of that area. But in 1947 the newly independent Syrian Government had not yet fully organized its antiquities service and was unready to receive foreign field parties. The Institute's director at that time, Professor Thorkild Jacobsen, proposed that we shift our activities to Iraq. The Iraq Government's Directorate General of Antiquities was fully prepared to accept foreign excavators, and the high quality of both its own scientific interests and its co-operation with foreign excavators was well known. Two of its staff, Sayid Taha Bakir and Sayid Fuad Safar, had received higher degrees in the Oriental Institute, and its then advisor, Mr. Seton Lloyd, had been a member of the 1930-36 Iraq Expedition of the Oriental Institute. In the spring of 1947, we wrote of our intentions and range of interest to our friends in the Iraqi Directorate General of Antiquities, suggesting as a general locale for our activities the higher piedmont and hilly-flanks country northwest of Mosul in the Tigris basin proper.

The Directorate's response was most enthusiastic. It sent us a list of some fifty sites which its own survey inspectors had reported to be in the prehistoric village range and some of which had actually been visited by the senior members of the staff. They advised against the area north of Mosul, in part because it had not yet been surveyed and in part because conditions for living, labor, and security were not so well assured as in the district between Mosul and Kirkuk. They drew particular attention to a small mound called Matarrah (Pl. 7A), located in the piedmont, about twenty minutes' drive south of Kirkuk, and they also invited our attention to a somewhat enigmatic open site called Jarmo (Pls. 4, 8), in the intermontane valley of Chemchemal, an hour and a half's drive east of Kirkuk. Tell Matarrah had yielded surface indication of an assemblage of the same general type as that of basal Tell Hassunah, which Lloyd and Safar (1945) had already excavated and reported on for the Directorate General of Antiquities. The surface of Jarmo had yielded only fragments of flint and obsidian tools and a few bits of ground stone bowls and celts; the Directorate staff thought that the site might be "mesolithic" in content. By any definition of this somewhat slippery word, it sounded as if Jarmo should certainly be within our range of interest.

We decided to ask for a formal concession to excavate Matarrah and for a "sounding" permit at Jarmo. The Iraqi antiquities law allows a foreign field party a concession for only one site at a time, but it also allows tests or soundings in other sites with the permit restricted to one month for each site. Our strategy was to begin at Matarrah, where we could familiarize ourselves with some of the details of the later prehistory of Iraq in a range which had already been tested at Hassunah. We would also be extending knowledge of the Hassunan phase well to the southward of the Mosul area, and we also reasoned—site unseen—that there might possibly be pre-Hassunan materials at Matarrah. Since our first season was to be a short one in any case, we reasoned that we could find out what Jarmo actually did contain in the testing allowed during the month's sounding permit and then lay our plans for the future accordingly.

The excavations of the first field season extended from March into June of 1948. Matarrah (Braidwood et al., 1952) yielded a village of the Hassunan phase but nothing earlier. Jarmo (R.J. and L. Braidwood, 1950), on the other hand, contained materials which certainly appeared to be typologically earlier than those of the Hassunan phase, although the site was that of a settled village and could hardly be called "mesolithic."

Since the expedition's 1948 soundings indicated that Jarmo contained a simpler, more elemental, and apparently earlier catalogue of the materials of a village-farming community than had hitherto been exposed anywhere, the plan for the second field compaign was based primarily on intensive excavation at that site. The second field season began in September of 1950, with a staff consisting of the two Braidwoods, Vivian Broman, Elizabeth West, Robert M. Adams as Department of Anthropology grantee, and Sayid Sabri Shukri as representative of the Directorate General of Antiquities. Early in 1951 the staff was enlarged to include Bruce Howe, of the Peabody Museum of Harvard University, Herbert E. Wright, Jr., of the Department of Geology of the University of Minnesota, and Fredrik Barth, of the Ethnographic Museum of the University of Oslo, with Cornelius Hillen and Gustavus F. Swift, Jr., Oriental Institute graduate students, as part-time volunteers. The enlargement was made possible by participation in the project of the Baghdad School of the American Schools of Oriental Research and by grants to the project from the Axel Wenner-Gren Foundation for Anthropological Research and the American Philosophical Society.

The staff was enlarged so that work on the general problem could be extended to include investigation of the archeology of the final phases of cave occupation in the zone of foothills and intermontane valleys and a search for open-air sites which might have been occupied during the interval between the final cave phases and the Jarmo phase. Wright, as a Pleistocene geologist with one field season's Near Eastern experience with the Jesuits at Ksar Akil in Lebanon, was to make a beginning at the reconstruction of the ancient environment of Iraqi Kurdistan. Barth, who had begun his studies in physical anthropology and paleontology, made the field appraisal of the animal bones from the excavations and gave some attention to the general contemporary ecological situation. In fact, however, Barth's professional interests were already tending to shift to ethnology; he remained in Iraqi Kurdistan after the close of the excavations to study contemporary Kurdish villages (Barth, 1953).

In September of 1950, camp was extablished in a mud-brick house near the Jarmo excavations. The operations comprised a completion of the sounding begun in 1948 and the opening of a somewhat larger area on the crest of the mound. Once work on the site itself was well started, the staff devoted as much time as it could afford to a survey for sites earlier than Jarmo in the Chemchemal intermontane plain. Howe took over this survey upon his arrival, and—sometimes with Wright, sometimes with Sayid Sabri—extended it to valleys adjacent to the Chemchemal valley.

The best type of survey is undoubtedly an intensive one on foot, with every bit of land which is arable and adjacent to a supply of drinking water—either now or conceivably in the past—being examined closely. But an intensive survey for surface indications of sites, especially in hilly country where mounds blend into the contours of the hills, is extremely time-consuming. We thus became increasingly dependent on the reports of our workmen, who were Hamavend Kurds from several different villages. As boys, they had all wandered over the countryside with their flocks of sheep and goats. Flint and steel are still utilized for fire-making, and obvious occurrences of flint thus tend to be noticed by shepherds as potential sources of supply. Once the workmen were familiar with the normal yield from Jarmo, they began to recall other places in the valley where they had seen flint, obsidian, broken bits of pottery, and other traces of antiquity. We would then give them bags and send them to collect from the surface at the places they recalled. In this way we acquired a number of surface collections, which could be washed, sorted, and classified in the base camp. We ourselves then visited the sites which yielded the most promising collections. Several dozen surface sites were located before Howe's arrival, and at least half a dozen of these looked very promising.

The Chemchemal valley runs northwest-southeast and is perhaps 35 miles long and 10 miles in greatest width. The ridge which flanks it to the south and west is mainly of gravel and contains no caves or rock shelters. Minor secondary ridges of rock which are occasionally exposed within the valley are mainly of shale or sandstone and also do not contain caves or shelters. The ridge to the north and east, the Kani Shaitan Hasan-Sagirma Dagh ridge, is of limestone; it does have a few caves, but we had found no promising indications in any of these before Howe's arrival. Howe extended the survey into the Bazian valley, which is the next beyond that of Chemchemal, over the Sagirma Dagh ridge. In fact, Howe extended his survey into the next valley beyond that of Bazian, the upper reaches of the Sulimaniyah plain, on the eastern edge of which is the city of Sulimaniyah. Visits were made to the two caves, Zarzi and Hazar Merd, in that region which were excavated in 1928 by Garrod (1930).

In March of 1951, we had made our selections and received a consession—in the name of the Baghdad School of the American Schools of Oriental Research—to excavate an open site called Karim Shahir (Pls. 1B, 9A) and a sounding permit for a rock shelter called Palegawra (Pl. 10B). The Palegawra cave is in the Baranand Dagh ridge, which flanks the northeastern edge of the Bazian valley. Karim Shahir is about a mile up the wadi which runs by the base of Jarmo in the Chemchemal valley.

Karim Shahir proved, on excavation, to be the site of a single shallow layer of occupation, probably of one or more temporary encampments, and it yielded a catalogue of materials which is certainly earlier than that of Jarmo on typological reckoning. The Palegawra materials are of a late phase of the Zarzian industry, which Garrod described originally as "Upper Aurignacian" (1930, p. 22), later as "Upper Gravettian" (1938, pp. 14, 23, 24), and more recently as "Upper Palaeolithic . . . evolving towards the Mesolithic" (1953, p. 22) and "paléolithique supérieur très évolué" (1957, p. 446). The results of these excavations and those at Jarmo have been briefly described (Braidwood, 1951a-c and 1952a-b; R. J. and L. Braidwood, 1953; Linda Braidwood 1951-53). One further test during the 1950/51 season was a brief examination made at Barda Balka for the Directorate General of Antiquities by Wright and Howe (1951). This testing of the occurrence of paleolithic stone tools—including Acheulean type hand axes, pebble tools, and flake tools—in gravels near the town of Chemchemal itself, gave Wright a cultural check point within late Pleistocene times in his geological sequence and fixed the stratigraphic position of the early tools. Wright (1952) made his own brief report on his geological survey of the general area.

The plan of our 1954/55 field campaign was based on the assumption that Jarmo had been adequately tested in depth in the 1948 and 1950/51 seasons. We reckoned that three month's work in the spring would give us an adequate test of the allover village plan, if only of the uppermost levels (but see p. 23). While spring is ideal for digging, autumn is the best time for surface survey; drier stream beds facilitate cross-country movement and, since the vegetation browns off during the summer, the collection of surface materials is much easier. Anticipating that Jarmo would be adequately tested for the purposes of culture-historical generalization by the end of the 1954/55 season, though it would take perhaps twenty-five seasons and much expense to exhaust the site completely, we proposed spending the autumn of 1954 in a survey of the upper piedmont and the zone of foothills and intermontane valleys in the basin of the Greater Zab River (Fig. 4, Pls. 5A and 7B). This would take us into new country 100 or more miles to the northwest of the Chemchemal valley, and we anticipated that within the cultural phases of our concern we might be able to recognize interesting regional variations.

We also proposed to extend the natural-sciences aspect of the investigation which had been so fruitfully begun by Wright and Barth. A substantial grant was made in favor of the project to the Department of Anthropology of the University of Chicago by the National Science Foundation; further grants were made to the Oriental Institute by the Wenner-Gren Foundation for Anthropological Research, the American Philosophical Society, and generous friends of the Institute itself. Wright received both Guggenheim and Wenner-Gren postdoctoral fellowships, and the Baghdad School of the American Schools of Oriental Research appointed Howe as its annual Baghdad professor with a stipend for his field work. The staff consisted of the Braidwoods (Mrs. Braidwood and their son joining the field party in the spring of 1955), Vivian Broman, Hans Helbaek of the Danish National Museum as botanist, Howe, Frederick R. Matson of the Pennsylvania State University as technical specialist, Mrs. Matson as volunteer, Charles A. Reed of the University of Illinois as zoölogist, Mr. and Mrs. Mayo Schreiber as Oriental Institute volunteers, Mrs. Patty Jo Watson (nee Andersen) as Department of Anthropology grantee, and Wright, with Mrs. Wright and three Wright sons as volunteers. Sayid Hussain Azzam and Sayid Sabri Shukri represented the Directorate General of Antiquities, with Sayid Muhammad Ali and Sayid Subhai Anwar serving for shorter periods. Reed was assisted by Sayid Yusuf Mansur of the Natural History Museum of Baghdad in the autumn.

The staff established itself in late September of 1954 at the summer hotel in the village of Salahedin on the Pirman Dagh ridge, overlooking the upper piedmont near the city of Erbil and the basin of the Greater Zab. Not having a core of familiar workmen to call on for advice about sites bearing surface material, we were on our own. We moved along such primary and secondary roads and such tracks as we could follow with fourwheel-drive vehicles. We also examined, on foot, major parts of the Khazir, Bastura, Harir-Barazan, and Diyana-Balikian valleys tributary to the Greater Zab and of the Berat Dagh northwest of Bekhme and, by collapsible boat, a stretch of the Greater Zab itself. Our route maps show total distances of about 400 miles covered; we must have walked twice that far in zigzagging back and forth, but the area is very large and cannot yet be said to have been intensively surveyed. Reed and Wright also made extended trips into the higher mountain country, toward both the Iranian and Turkish borders in far northeastern Iraq.

By the middle of November, 1954, we were able to select three localities with promising open sites and four localities with cave or rock-shelter sites for a series of soundings. There were two open sites near Girdemamik (Pl. 7B), a village on the Greater Zab in the piedmont north of Erbil. One of these, Gird Chai, yielded material at least as early as that of Karim Shahir, but its catalogue was not clear because of the presence of intrusive pits made in much later times. The second Girdemamik site, Gird Ali Agha, revealed a little village which must have flourished during a time roughly parallel to that of the upper levels of Jarmo. The next open site we sounded was Gird Banahilk (Pl. 6A), near the village of Diyana in the intermontane plain extending northwest of Ruwanduz. It yielded traces of a village whose catalogue included painted pottery of the Halafian style. In the piedmont about Mosul, the Halafian painted style of pottery generally follows the pottery of the Hassunan phase, and it was interesting to see the catalogue of a village so close to the higher mountain zone and with Halafian style pottery. The third locality with open sites was at the point where the Khazir tributary passes from the foothills to the piedmont, midway between Erbil and Mosul. Here, Tell al-Khan and Tell M'lefaat lie on either side of of the road, on the Mosul end of the Khazir River bridge (Pl. 6B). Al-Khan yielded material more or less analogous to that of Hassunah III, but nothing earlier. M'lefaat, on the other hand, showed a catalogue which on typological grounds suggests a cultural level rather close to that of Karim Shahir. For our purposes it was the most interesting of the open sites sounded.

The rock shelter Kaiwanian, northwest of Shaqlawah town, proved on testing to have been badly disturbed. The same proved true of the large cave of Hajiyah (Pl. 11B), in the ridge between the villages of Bekhme and Bia northwest of the Bekhme gorge of the Zab, and, to some extent, in the cave of Barak (Pl. 11A), east of Aqra. It was at least clear, however, that Hajiyah and Barak had been occupied by people who used a series of flint tools similar to those of the Zarzi and Palegawra occurrences. The third locality with rock shelters was immediately above the village of Havdian, northwest of the larger village of Diyana (and of Gird Banahilk) in the Ruwanduz country. The most fruitful of these rock shelters was Babkhal, which yielded paleolithic material of Mousterian type like that first reported in Iraq at Hazar Merd by Garrod (1930). Above this material at Babkhal was a somewhat disturbed layer containing Zarzi-Palegawra types of flint tools. During the spring of 1955, a test was made in the cave called Spilik, adjacent to the main road between Salahedin and Shaqlawah; this also yielded a Mousterian flint industry. The results of the survey and soundings during the autumn of 1954 are briefly described by Braidwood et al., 1954.

In January of 1955, the staff left Iraq temporarily for an archeological tour of sites in the general range of our interest which are situated in the countries of the Mediterranean littoral—Jordan, Lebanon, Syria, and southern Turkey. There were two major points to this tour. First, we hoped to collect surface materials from or near the major excavated sites of the late cave and earliest village ranges and, further, to secure radioactive-carbon samples from old trench faces of the original excavations in as many of the sites as possible (Pl. 5B). The Braidwoods, Broman, and Swift had covered some of the proposed route in June of 1951, and we believed that much could be learned and collected. The second point was to afford the natural scientists on the staff opportunity to observe the range of present-day environmental situations in which the archeological material now available occurs. Thus—except for the territory now included in the state of Israel—we would be observing parts of the northwestern and western arcs of the hilly flanks of the Crescent and the Syro-Palestinian regions beyond.

We left Mosul on January 4, 1955, and arrived in Aleppo, Syria, on January 9th, crossing the piedmont just south of the Turkish border. This route allowed us to inspect the sites of Grai Resh, Tell Brak, Tell Chagar Bazar, Tell al-Halaf, and Tell Fakhariyah and to examine unexcavated sites in the Jabal Sinjar plain and the upper Syrian Jazirah. From Aleppo, we made a quick trip down to Beirut, Lebanon, to take up our winter base in a summer pension at Shemlan, a half hour's drive above Beirut. We stayed at the winter base in Shemlan from January 11th to February 27th, during which time we visited most of the known sites in Jordan, Lebanon, and the inland piedmont of Syria. The major excavated sites visited included the caves of the Wadi Kharaitun and the mound at Jericho in Jordan, the Yabrud caves and Khirbat al-Ombashi in Syria, and the coastal caves of Abu Halka, Nahr Ibrahim, Ksar Akil, and Adlun and the site of Byblos in Lebanon as well as the major prehistoric localities associated with geological features along the coast. On leaving Shemlan, we visited Tabbat al-Hammam and Ras Shamra on the Syrian coast, the Amuq sites, Tarsus, and Mersin in Cilician Turkey, and Baghuz on the Euphrates in Syria. The Matsons visited Egypt and secured further radioactive-carbon samples, while Howe and the Wrights went to the Anatolian plateau to inspect the obsidian beds near Aksaray. We reached Kirkuk and Jarmo on March 8th, to end the winter tour.

With our camp re-established at Jarmo, excavations were resumed on March 19th, as the final phase of the 1954/55 field season began. There was still some activity in addition to the excavations proper. Matson and Schreiber made trips to both the northern and the southern excavated Iraqi sites of the earlier ranges, mainly for the collection of surface pottery and to secure radioactive-carbon samples. Reed and Helbaek made a further tour into the high country beyond Ruwanduz for zoölogical and botanical purposes. Wright made journeys onto the Iranian plateau beyond Kermanshah and out into the Iraqi portion of the Syrian desert beyond Rutbah as well as further trips into the high country in northeastern Iraq. In June he traveled north into Turkey to the high Hakari country on the northern side of the Turko-Iraqi frontier, before finally traversing the Anatolian plateau to the west on the way home. For preliminary generalizations on the geological aspects of archeology in Iraq see Wright, 1955.

The system of a grid of small squares (Pl. 8) by which we had hoped to test the village plan of the upper levels of Jarmo taught us much of the overall stratification of the site. However, it raised more problems than it solved, and the decision may be reached that Jarmo needs another season of excavation before it can be considered completed. Howe was able to complete the American Schools' excavation at Palegawra, which he had first tested in 1951. The 1954/55 field season closed on June 3d; so far, only a brief description of the season's results at Jarmo has been published (Braidwood, 1956b).

IV

DESCRIPTION OF THE SITES

The archeological sites excavated or tested by the Iraq-Jarmo Project in the 1947/48, 1950/51, and 1954/55 field seasons are listed below, also the more important sites which were located but not tested. The list runs generally from latest to earliest. The order of presentation (cf. Braidwood et al., 1954) depends on our assessment of the typological development, that is, on the increasing simplicity of the catalogues of material from the different sites as one moves backward in time.

Gird Banahilk

This is a low mound somewhat over 5 meters high (Pl. 6A) with a roughly ovoid plan of about 100 x 159 meters. It is less than a mile southwest of the village of Diyana, in the plain north of Ruwanduz: about 36° 40' N., 44° 32' E., elevation above sea level about 2,200 feet. The plain itself is only about 5 x 10 miles in breadth and length; it is rolling and well watered, and the high peaks of the Kurdish mountains surround it. Several streams join in the southwest corner of the plain to become the Ruwanduz River, which enters the spectacular Guli Ali Beg gorge at this point.

Adjacent to the site on the south is an aeroplane landing strip built by the British and their Assyrian Levies in the 1920's and later utilized by the Iraqi army (Hamilton, 1958, p. 90). There are traces of a gun emplacement on the summit of the site, three or four slit-trenches, and a large cut on the northeast slope from which earth had been taken. The catalogue of materials from Banahilk includes painted pottery of the Halafian style. Restricted as our testing necessarily was, it nevertheless gave a more rounded picture of all categories of a Halafian assemblage than is otherwise available in the literature.

Tell al-Khan

This mound (Pl. 6B) is immediately south of the Erbil-Mosul road on the right bank of the Khazir River at the Manguba bridge. Its co-ordinates, elevation, and physical surroundings are essentially the same as those of Tell M'lefaat, which lies just north of the road (see p. 27). Al-Khan is a small mound of about 80 x 100 meters and perhaps 4 meters high, practically surrounded by a British Army World War II tank-trap trench, and with remains of a concrete pill box and an entrenched gun emplacement on its crest. Apparently the Khazir crossing was strongly fortified on both banks in anticipation of a possible Nazi airborne invasion into northern Iraq in 1941. The tank-trap trench facilitated our testing of al-Khan, whose contours may originally have been somewhat different from what they are now. Below a thin surface layer of Islamic (and perhaps some Assyrian) material, there was a rather thick band of sterile silt. Below this, we encountered a thin layer of material of Hassunan type. The generous scatter of broken Hassunan pottery over the surface of the mound must have resulted from the British entrenching operations. Wright tentatively suggests that the sterile silt layer was the result of a wash of silt from the gravel hills to the northwest of the mound in post-Hassunan times. Had the tank-trap trench not been put in, it is very doubtful that any Hassunan sherds would have occurred on the present surface—a side light which has disquieting implications for the order of completeness of any intensive surface survey.

Tell Matarrah

The mound of Matarrah (Braidwood et al., 1952) is some 20 miles south of Kirkuk: 35° 23' N., 44° 22' E., elevation above sea level about 750 feet. It is on the piedmont plain and is not large as mounds of this zone go, being about 200 meters in diameter and about 8 meters high (Pl. 7A). Only the upper half consists of occupational debris; apparently the original village was built on a small natural hill, a curious anomaly in that it rises above the general level of the piedmont plain at this point. About 3 miles east of the mound is the low Kani Domlan-Jabal Tasak ridge, first of the series which builds up to the Kurdish mountains. This ridge is the source of water, and a small wadi—now dry save in the rainy season—flows from it to pass by the foot of the mound and has even eroded away a bit of the mound. Turning away from the ridge on the east, one sees in all other directions the vast stretch of the piedmont plain, here becoming flat, its horizon broken occasionally by mounds which were occupied predominantly in periods later than that of Matarrah. About 10 or 15 miles to the west of Matarrah, these mounds begin to thin out and disappear; as noted above (p. 13), the rainfall belt of the piedmont is not broad south of Kirkuk. The catalogue of archeological materials from Matarrah closely resembles that of the Hassunan type site. We guess, in fact, that Matarrah represents a somewhat impoverished southern variant of the Hassunan phase of culture. If this is true, Matarrah reflects the situation today, for the villages of the piedmont south of Kirkuk are too near the danger line of meager rainfall to be as flourishing as the villages of the Assyrian plain proper to the north.

Gird Ali Agha

This mound lies on a gravel hill on the first major terrace of the left bank of the Greater Zab, nearly a mile north of the village of Girdemamik (Pl. 7B): about 36° 27' N., 43° 48' E., elevation above sea level about 1,000 feet. The site covers an area of about 80 x 100 meters and probably has a depth of debris of over 2 meters. A relatively modern cemetery covers its southern surface. Ali Agha lies in a country of rolling gravel hills and river terraces. From the point of view of absolute elevation, the immediate region is piedmont, but it much more resembles the foothill zone in general topography and rainfall. The right bank of the Zab just opposite Ali Agha is an almost vertical cliff of gravel, well over 100 feet high, which screens from view the mountains of the Aqra ridge to the north. Just south of Girdemamik village, the broad wadi of the Bastura Chai reaches the Zab; in its lower reaches, the wadi now carries water only during the rainy season.

The catalogue of archeological material from the short test at Ali Agha indicates a phase of culture roughly similar to that of the upper levels at Jarmo or the basal levels of Tell Hassunah.

Qalat Jarmo and Possibly Germane Unexcavated Sites

The Chemchemal intermontane plain lies between the Kani Domlan-Jabal Tasak and the Kani Shaitan Hasan-Sagirma Dagh ridges and is about 10 miles wide and 35 miles long, with its axis northwest to southeast. By the main road from Kirkuk, it is about 28 miles to the town of Chemchemal itself, which lies in the northwest center of the valley and approximately on the valley's northwest-southeast watershed. The land surface of the valley consists of broad stretches of silt, occasionally interrupted by minor ridges of exposed bedrock (Pl. 8), but the broad green fields of the silt surface are seriously dissected by deep wadies which drain the higher slopes of either ridge (Wright, 1952). A few of these wadies have perennial streams; most of them have springs or pools which are also perennial sources of water. The site of Jarmo lies above one of these wadies, the Cham-Gawra, some 7 miles east of Chemchemal, within that part of the drainage pattern which flows out of the southeastern end of the valley: about 35° 33' N., 44° 57' E., elevation above sea level about 2,500 feet. Its present size is about 90 x 140 meters, with a depth of deposit of over 7 meters at its highest point. Wright believes a fair portion of the original mound may have been eroded away by the stream of the wadi. The catalogue of archeological materials indicates a very early but full-fledged village-farming community. The site contains about a dozen architectural levels of buildings and their renovations, and coarse pottery vessels appeared only in the upper third of the deposit. These have some points comparable with the pottery of the basal levels of the Hassunan phase.

Two sites encountered on survey in the Chemchemal valley, Kani Sur (less than a mile south of Jarmo) and Khora Namik (ca. 3 miles northeast of Chemchemal), yielded surface material which appears to parallel approximately that from Jarmo. A more impressive site—Kharaba Qara Chiwar—also not yet tested beyond the collection of surface materials, lies on the left bank of the upper Tauq Chai, the main stream of the southeastern drainage of the Chemchemal valley. This is a mound on a gravel hill about a mile and a half below the village of Qara Chiwar and some 28 miles southwest of Jarmo. At this point, the Tauq Chai has turned westward as it breaks through the Jabal Tasa ridge onto the piedmont. Sayid Sabri Shukri had discovered this site during his own earlier surveys and led us to it; we hope to test it during our next field season in Iraq. The surface evidence contains a variety of elements, and it is not clear whether the total assemblage will be found more closely comparable with that of Jarmo or with that of the general horizon of M'lefaat, Karim Shahir, and Gird Chai. Our assessment of the surface yield inclines us somewhat toward the latter.

Fragments of coarse pottery which appeared to be of Hassunan type appeared on the talus wash of two larger mounds northwest of Chemchemal, Tell Sargarden and Tell Ibrahim Aga. These, taken with the Samarran and Hassunan ceramic occurrences noted in the Danish expedition's test pit at Tell Shimshara (Ingholt, 1957), suggest that some aspect of the Hassunan phase was not entirely restricted to the piedmont zone. The stratification at Tell Shimshara assures the sequence, with Jarmo-like materials below the Samarran-Hassunan levels.

Tell M'lefaat

This small mound lies on a gravel hill immediately north of the Erbil-Mosul road, just west of the Manguba bridge over the Khazir River (Pl. 6B) and only a few meters north of the crest of al-Khan (see above): approximately 36° 18' N., 43° 33' E., elevation above sea level about 950 feet. It seems to cover an area of roughly 90 x 120 meters, and its depth is over 1.5 m. (below which level none of our tests on the crest were taken). Gravel hills and the limestone system from Jabal Maglub to Jabal Ain al-Safra build up rather quickly just north of M'lefaat; the Khazir, which is a perennial stream of some size, cuts through the hills to reach the Assyrian plain at this point. In effect, both M'lefaat and al-Khan are exactly on the border of the piedmont with the foothills zone, at a point where the Khazir is easily fordable. To the south and west roll the grasslands of the Assyrian plain—in fact, that portion of the plain identified as Gaugemela (where Alexander defeated Darius). The site has a concrete-faced machine gun emplacement left over from the World War II fortification of the bridge and ford; the tank-trap trench flanks it on the west, and the ruins of a small barracks nestle between the mound and the river bank on the east.

The archeological catalogue of M'lefaat—as the results of our very limited test showed it—indicates a flint-tool kit very little different from the kits of Gird Chai and Karim Shahir and somewhat better-made large ground stone tools than either of those sites yielded. Since one of the test trenches indicated five levels of deposit to a depth of over 1.5 m., M'lefaat may have been a settlement of some degree of permanence. There are even traces of primitive architecture. Hence we initially assessed M'lefaat (Braidwood et al., 1954) as a very elemental type of little village. Final assessment will depend on more extensive exposure by excavation and on insights which may be gained through Solecki's (1957) work at Zawi Chemi Shanidar. The latter site is on the Greater Zab at the foot of the Baradost Dagh and close to the cave of Shanidar, some 15 miles northeast of Aqra. It has yielded a flint industry of the same general complexion as that at M'lefaat, Karim Shahir, and Gird Chai and, like M'lefaat, has some traces of rudimentary architecture.

Karim Shahir and Possibly Germane Unexcavated Sites

The earliest of the open-air sites exposed by our excavations in any considerable area is on top of a high silt bluff at Karim Shahir (Pls. 1B, 9A), roughly a mile east of Jarmo, on the right bank of the Cham-Gawra, which flows below Jarmo (Braidwood, 1951c, pp. 13-15; 1952a, pp. 24, 26, 27). The area with marked surface indication of settlement at Karim Shahir measures about 60 x 70 meters. The relatively thin occupation level, virtually coincident with the present surface on the crest of the rise, has a thin slope-wash cover which reaches 30 cm. in thickness on the down-slope side of the excavations. There was also some displacement along the eroding bluff face, and, as at Jarmo, an unknown proportion may well be lost because of erosion along this bluff face. The co-ordinates are approximately 35° 33' N., 44° 58' E., the elevation above sea level about 2,600 feet. Like Jarmo, Karim Shahir lies in the typical intermontaine valley of Chemchemal, with the Kani Shaitan Hasan-Sagirma Dagh ridge in full view just east of it.

The catalogue of archeological materials of Karim Shahir, preponderantly a flint-blade industry but with some ground stone objects, and the thinness of its deposit suggest that it was not a village-farming community but rather a temporary encampment (or a series of recurrent encampments) of somewhat earlier times.

Two other interesting open-air sites of a range at least as early, Turkaka and Kowri Khan, were located during the surface survey in the Jarmo vicinity in 1950 (see p. 20). The Turkaka occurrence consisted of a surface scatter of certain flint blade tools and microliths, on a hill above the left bank of the Cham-Gawra, about half a mile northeast of Jarmo. The crown of the hill is not quite as extensive in area as that of Jarmo; the area is crescent-shaped about a little wadi which heads in a small spring in a rock overhang. The Kowri Khan occurrence was on a small ridgelike hill which forms a promontory between two branches of the Cham Chalga (the wadi which flows below Chalga village), less than a mile and a half west of Jarmo. A small ruined khan (probably an Ottoman control post, several centuries old at most) lies on a lower hill just south of the ridge. Again the surface scatter consisted of flint blades and bladelets, with no later material. Howe (pp. 156 f.) considers it possible that both these groups of materials may be somewhat older than those of Karim Shahir.

Gird Chai

The occupation site on the gravel hill at Gird Chai, overlooking the Greater Zab from its left bank about half a mile west of Girdemamik village, was tested at the same time as was Gird Ali Agha (see above). Its situation and co-ordinates closely parallel those of Ali Agha. Our testing was brief; while the site yielded a flint-tool industry rather closely resembling that of Karim Shahir, we found it to have been riddled with later grain-storage pits and traces of a medieval Islamic occupation and possibly of some slightly earlier phases. To untangle it completely would have been very time-consuming, and we anticipated that further survey would surely reveal other sites of its range of time which are uncontaminated by later occupation.

Ishkaft Palegawra

This rock shelter (Pl. 10B) in the Baranand Dagh ridge, which flanks the northeast side of the typical intermontane valley of Bazian, is some 14 miles northeast of Jarmo:

approximately 35° 37' N., 45° 9' E., elevation above sea level about 3,250 feet (Braidwood, 1951c, pp. 13, 14; 1952a, pp. 23, 24, 26, 27). The shelter is below the village of Sulimani Girde, within a small stream-bearing side valley of the Baranand ridge; it opens to the southeast and is about 70 meters above the level of the Bazian plain, from which it may be seen at one point on the main Chemchemal-Sulimaniyah road. The Bazian valley is considerably smaller than that of Chemchemal, somewhat better watered, and not so seriously dissected. The remarkably fine view from the mouth of the shelter commands the southeastern portion of the Bazian valley and the ridges which flank it. The shelter opening is 3 meters high. Its chamber has a maximum breadth of about 6 meters and extends back from the opening only some 5 meters, so that all parts of it are well within the reach of daylight. The depth of the deposit proved to be nearly 2 meters. The artifactual yield from the principal undisturbed layer is restricted almost completely to chipped flint tools. The industry indicated by these tools appears to represent an even later development of the Zarzian tradition than those Garrod (1930) described.

Ishkaft Barak

This was the most satisfactory of a group of rock shelters tested immediately east of the village of Jouna, some 3 miles east of the town of Aqra, on the southern flank of the Aqra ridge: about 36° 45' N., 43° 58' E., elevation above sea level about 2,650 feet. The opening of the shelter (Pl. 11A) fronts to the southwest, but from the terrace the broad expanse of the hills on the eastern end of the Aqra plain is in full view. The shelter is on the left flank of a side valley into the ridge; the valley has a stream and springs. The shelter is about 12 meters wide and extends 8 meters into the rock beyond its opening, but the remnant of ancient living debris was concentrated only on the talus. The yield is a small but interesting quantity of a flint-blade industry, typologically Zarzian.

Ishkaft Hajiyah

This rock shelter is one of the group recommended to our attention by the Directorate General of Antiquities. It lies in the wooded country of the Berat Dagh just east of the village of Bia, on the left flank of a narrow valley which opens out at Bekhme village at the exit of the Greater Zab from the Bekhme gorge: approximately 36° 42' N., 44° 13' E., elevation above sea level approximately 2,350 feet. Hajiyah is a shelter of some size, 7-12 meters in breadth and extending 24 meters into the rock. Its opening (Pl. 11B) fronts to the south; while none of the interior is fully dark during daylight hours, it is by far the most truly cavelike of any of our sites. Under present conditions, water is available at a spring on the opposite flank of the valley, nearly half a mile away, and the view from the front gives only on the little valley itself and its opposite flank. Our tests within the shelter yielded no significant archeological deposits, but a trench midway down the talus slope in front of it exposed a flint-tool industry of Zarzian type, but with an admixture of Islamic and pre-Islamic potsherds.

Ishkaft Kaiwanian

A small shelter above the village of Kaiwanian, over 2 miles northwest of Shaqlawah on the main Shaqlawah-Erbil road, was tested for a day and a half but abandoned because of very shallow deposit and unpromising yield. Flint tools of Zarzian type did occur scattered down the talus slope.

Ishkaft Babkhal

This shelter is one of a group in the spur of the Baradost ridge which rises immediately north of the village of Havdian, on the western flank of the Diyana plain. Babkhal fronts to the southwest, in the valley between the spur and the main ridge of the Baradost, and does not overlook the plain: about 36° 42' N., 44° 28' E., elevation above sea level about 2,500 feet. This is the most open of all our shelters, the deposit lying at the foot of a near-by vertical cliff face and extending into the rock only about a meter beyond its overhang; it might best be considered a sheltered open-air site. Water is available immediately around the corner of the base of the spur. Babkhal revealed two archeological levels. The upper level was thin and contained a Zarzian type of blade-tool industry mixed with both earlier and later materials. The lower level yielded a flint flake-tool industry of Mousterian type as known from Hazar Merd (Garrod, 1930) and certain other caves (see below).

At Havdian village we observed a practice which may explain why so little archeological debris is left within some of the larger shelters, as at Barak and Hajiyah. The large Havdian shelter looks down over the village and is in the part of the spur which fronts immediately on the Diyana plain, the smaller Babkhal shelter being around the point of the spur to the west. As we approached Havdian village at the time our tests were to begin, we were surprised to see smoke pouring out of the big Havdian shelter. On arrival at the shelter we were told by the inhabitants that the year's layer of sheep and goat dung on the floor of the inner chamber was being burned off. The whole floor on the inside was aglow with a blue flame. It was not clear whether the purpose was simply to clean the floor or whether some notion of heating the rock for the winter was not involved as well. We were told that, when the fire had burned out, the floor would be scraped and the rough screen wall across most of the shelter front would be repaired so that sheep and goats could be kept there during the coming winter. If such burning and scraping have gone on for millenniums, they would explain why little archeological debris is left in some of the more commodious shelters. A later sounding at the threshold of the big Havdian shelter was entirely unproductive, although microliths had been reported from the talus slope below (Field, 1956, p. 15).

Ishkaft Spilik

This shelter lies in full view across a wadi from the Shaqlawah-Erbil road, some 6 miles northwest of Shaqlawah: about 36° 24' N., 44° 16' E., about 2,800 feet above sea level. This is scrub-oak country; the wadi is now dry in summer and early autumn, but there are springs adjacent. The shelter fronts to the north and is protected by ridges in a bend of the wadi; it has a breadth of about 15 meters and extends into the rock about 8 meters, although two narrow flanking chambers each extend inward for about 8 meters more. Beneath a rather thick layer of animal dung and debris containing only a handful of recent potsherds, we encountered a horizon which yielded flint flake tools of Mousterian type as seen at Hazar Merd (Braidwood, 1956b).

The Mousterian industry of the general type found at Spilik and Babkhal was first encountered in this region at the cave of Hazar Merd (Garrod, 1930); knowledge of it has recently been extended by Solecki (1955 and 1957), in level D of the Shanidar cave, where neandertaloid skeletons also were found.

Telegraph Pole 26/22 and Serandur

A coarse Mousterian industry was indicated in mixed surface collections from gravels at two open-air localities discovered during our survey: at telegraph pole 26/22 just west of Chemchemal and at a hill spur called Serandur, on the right bank of the Bastura a mile west of the Erbil-Shaqlawah road. In 1927, Garrod (1928) found a few roughly comparable coarse Mousterian tools in gravels near Kirkuk. The generalized coarse techno-typological aspect of these three open-air occurrences differs from the more carefully made Mousterian tools of Hazar Merd and the other caves.

Barda Balka and Possibly Germane Unexcavated Sites

Barda Balka was located by Dr. Naji al-Asil and Sayid Fuad Safar during a survey by the Directorate General of Antiquities in 1949 (Asil, 1949). In 1951, Howe and Wright excavated it on behalf of the Directorate (Wright and Howe, 1951). It is an open-air site, with its stone tools contained in certain specific Pleistocene gravels on a hilltop and in part consolidated within the breccia of a peculiar natural columnar remnant (Pl. 9B) of this same gravel system which first drew attention to the locality. The site is immediately south of the main Chemchemal-Sulimaniyah road, 2 miles northeast of Chemchemal, in the rolling country which flanks a major tributary wadi of the Chemchemal branch of the headwaters of the Tauq Chai: about 35° 33' N., 44° 52' E., elevation above sea level about 2,250 feet. The yield from the three-day sounding included core-biface tools of Acheulean type, pebble tools, and utilized flakes. This is certainly the earliest paleolithic material yet excavated in Iraq.

Two other occurrences of the Barda Balka horizon (see also p. 62) were encountered during our survey of the Chemchemal valley. The tools lay on the surface but were weathered out from the same specific gravels. At Cham Bazar, where the main Chemchemal and Jarmo tributaries of the Tauq Chai join, some 3 miles southeast of Chemchemal, hand axes and flake tools occurred. Hand axes also appeared on a slope immediately adjacent to Jarmo.

V

THE ARCHEOLOGICAL ASSEMBLAGES

As in chapter iv, the order of description is from latest to earliest. Here our assessment of the typological sequence will become obvious, since the catalogues grow increasingly simple as we move from the more complex village sites back to the rock shelters.

Gird Banahilk

The soundings[1] were made in four modest test trenches (two other trenches, yielding obviously disturbed material, being abandoned at shallow depth). The total area exposed beyond a superficial depth was about 70 square meters. About half of this total area yielded mixed material with wheel-made pottery and fragments of iron as well as a scatter of Halafian style painted pottery. The architectural traces in this mixed zone consisted of remains of stone-founded houses with rectilinear plans. Since archeological information concerning the developments in the historical periods in this remote part of Iraq is practically nonexistent, we do not know the exact age of the later elements from the mixed zone. It is conceivable that some of the stone foundations pertain to the time of the prehistoric village. In the two tests on the north and northeast slopes of the mound no appreciable amount of mixed material was encountered, and the following description of the Banahilk variant of the prehistoric village assemblage with Halafian painted pottery is based on these two operations. Virgin soil was encountered 4 meters below the surface in the test on the northeast slope.

Architecture was poorly represented in the tests. A fragment of a limestone-founded, apparently <u>tauf</u> (see p. 40), wall of a rectilinear building was encountered. In the test on the north slope, traces of a built hearth or oven of fire-hardened clay appeared. Successive floor levels were easily visible, and the fill contained an appreciable number of cracked limestone boulder fragments which probably had some architectural purpose originally.

The Halaf-style painted ceramic falls within the range of pottery vaguely called "Eastern Halaf." In texture it is more like the Tell Arpachiyah and Tilki Tepe (Şamıramaltı) wares than those of Tell al-Halaf, Tell Chagar Bazar, and Yunus-Carchemish. The paint is of the usual Halafian rather lustrous monochrome type. Banahilk, unlike the upper levels of Arpachiyah, yielded only one sherd showing the use of white paint (and only seven or eight sherds showing deliberate use of both red and black paint). Moreover, there are no more than three vessels with the characteristic "cream-bowl" profile. Otherwise shapes comprise simple round-sided bowls with typical Halafian painted bands and square-sectioned rims which nearly always show closely set painted tick marks, shallower bowls, many pieces of rounded bowls with drawn-in lips, very handsome large high-collared jars (similar to smaller ones from Arpachiyah), many smaller lower-collared jars, and some very squat pots with bulging sides (the "Büchse" of Tell al-Halaf). A few miniature vessels

---

[1] Mrs. Watson had immediate supervision of the soundings, and the following is abstracted from her notes. She visited the Hittite Archeological Museum in Ankara in June, 1955, and with the permission and aid of Dr. Necati Dolunay, director, and Miss Saadet Onat, assistant, examined the unpublished Halafian painted pottery from Tilki Tepe, near Lake Van, in detail. She also had access to the Oriental Institute's and Matson's surface collections from Tell Arpachiyah, Tell al-Halaf, and Tell Chagar Bazar.

of various kinds are also represented.

The design motifs of the Banahilk painted pottery (Pl. 12) contribute little to those already known, especially from Tell al-Halaf and Arpachiyah. The "bucranium" is rare at Banahilk, as at Tilki Tepe (at least among the 150 or so sherds seen from the latter site). The few Banahilk examples show Mallowan's so-called "stylized bucranium" (Mallowan and Rose, 1935). The combination of quatrefoil and Maltese cross is, on the other hand, fairly common, and one representational example of a bird occurs.

There is no Samarran-style or Hassunan-style painted pottery in our Banahilk sample.

The plain ware of Banahilk is interesting, though no comparative statements are made here since so little information on plain wares is published for most other Halafian sites. At Banahilk there are two basic fabrics, though they grade into each other. One is orange-surfaced and chaff-filled; the other is heavier, with brown surfaces, sometimes lightly burnished on the outside, and little or no chaff. The shapes include sloping-shouldered jars and simple bowls in both fabrics, flat-bottomed trays, and lugged jars or pots. The lugs (most of which had been broken off in antiquity and were found loose) are sometimes quite large, projecting 5-6 cm. from the body and being 3-5 cm. thick; they were apparently quite functional.

In our Banahilk sample, the Halafian painted pottery approximates 60% of the total sherd bulk, with the plain ware making up the remainder.

A fair variety of apparently utilitarian objects in clay appeared. These include spindle whorls, sieves (baked-clay disks 4-5 cm. in diameter, pierced with many holes), funnel-shaped objects, and baked-clay disks and rings. Potsherds were utilized for pierced disks (whorls?) and for chipped scrapers, the latter perhaps for flaying but more likely for the working of pottery. Figurines, notably those of the "mother-goddess" type, did not appear in our exposures.

The flint industry at Banahilk is not impressive, consisting generally of casual flakes and flake-blades rather than of well trimmed blades from pyramidal cores. Sickle flints are usually of flake-blades with no retouch except for some occasional blunting. Sheen and occasional traces of bitumen(?) hafting are observable. Otherwise the flint tools recovered include a few scrapers, three or four simple drills, and a few microliths, of which there are five of the transverse or trapezoidal-point category, one lunate, and one small double-pointed object. Obsidian was present in some quantity, mainly as used or plain blades. A few of the used blades are notched.

In the heavier ground stone categories, mortars, pestles, and other milling-stone types were present. There are a number of fragments of well made stone bowls. Fully ground celts with cutting ends of ax type occurred. There were also traces of an industry of relatively well formed ornamental stone objects. This included ground obsidian ornaments, pendants or seals with simple crosshatched engraving, and stone beads. Awls or punches produced from metapodial bones occurred.

Reed's preliminary sorting of the animal bones shows domesticated goat (Capra hircus); forms for which the status (domesticated or wild) is uncertain from our evidence, that is, cattle (Bos sp.), dog or wolf (Canis sp.), pig (Sus scrofa); and wild forms including roe deer (Capreolus capreolus), fox (Vulpes vulpes), goat (Capra aegagrus), leopard (Panthera pardus), beech marten (Martes foina), and an unidentified small cat. Rare equid bones occurred, seemingly all from the surface layers and thus probably not of Halafian context. The shells of a large land snail (Helix salomonica) were common. The study of such plant impressions as occurred has not been completed.

Banahilk seems to have been essentially a one-period site, but with some traces of later occupation at least on the crest of the mound and to the west. Certainly a strong manifestation of pottery in the Halafian painted style occurs in an interesting and well developed assemblage. Despite the restricted size of the sample, the absence of "mother-goddess" figurines is enigmatic, raising again the question (R. J. and L. Braidwood, 1953) as to whether they were really a normal item in the "classic" Halafian assemblage. In the absence of any well described Halafian flint industry, Banahilk's rather uninspired industry recalls that of the Hassunan in the piedmont. This contrasts strikingly with the earlier industries of well made blades at Jarmo and Karim Shahir in the zone of foothills and intermontane valleys, in which Banahilk also lies. The presence of microliths at Banahilk suggests that their assumed absence in other sites with Halafian painted pottery may be due simply to lack of observation. On the basis of its painted pottery, Banahilk would appear to have been occupied at about the same time as Tilki Tepe and the pre-TT 6 levels of Arpachiyah. Relatively small as is the bulk of material recovered from the tests at Banahilk, when fully analyzed it will yield the first full-bodied description of the total archeological assemblage of a site containing Halafian pottery.

Tell al-Khan

The British tank-trap trench was utilized for the test at al-Khan.[2] Somewhat over 5 meters of its crumbling face on the western slope of the mound was trimmed up in steps in such a way that it gave a clean vertical section down to virgin soil, at a depth of about 3 meters. In the surface humus, Islamic (and possibly some Assyrian) pottery occurred in some quantity; below this, to a depth of approximately 2 meters, was a layer of clean and well consolidated silt. A few random bits of Hassunan pottery were found in the silt, but no compacted floors or concentration of material occurred above approximately the 2-meter depth. Several rather ephemeral "floors" were found below this depth, and these yielded Hassunan pottery in quantity. No architectural traces were encountered, however, and the materials recovered consisted almost entirely of potsherds and fragments of stone tools.

In spite of its limitations the potsherd sample from al-Khan (see p. 66) closely approximates the pottery of level III at Tell Hassunah. In the coarse category, husking trays and a few milk jars are represented. Fine ware includes sherds of Hassunan standard incised, standard painted-and-incised, and standard painted types. Samarran painted sherds were restricted to a handful.

The chipped stone industry of the al-Khan sample is a poor one indeed, which also approximates the general Hassunan tradition. The smallness of the sample may account for the lack of proper blade tools and of obsidian tools.

A few bits of ground stone, mainly fragments of pestles and milling stones, occurred. A single short truncated conical bead of polished black stone was found.

Such animal bones as did occur have not yet been studied, and there were no other nonartifactual finds.

The general similarity of the al-Khan yield to that of the type site, Tell Hassunah (actually only 25 miles to the southwest), and the stratigraphic peculiarity of the thick silt layer did not encourage us to enlarge our sounding. If, as suggested by Wright (p. 25), the silt layer is due to a post-Hassunan wash from the hills to the northwest, then the present contours of al-Khan may not indicate the original Hassunan center of the tell at all. More advantageous sites for the elaboration of knowledge of the normal Hassunan assemblage are certainly to be found in the general region.

Tell Matarrah

The Matarrah assemblage can certainly be considered a somewhat impoverished southern variant of the normal Hassunan assemblage. Since a report has already been

---

[2]Miss Broman had immediate field supervision of the sounding, and the following is based on her field notes, save for the section on pottery. Dr. Joseph R. Caldwell (now of the Illinois State Museum and in 1955-57 a graduate student in the Department of Anthropology of the University of Chicago) and Dr. Matson have jointly undertaken the detailed study of the al-Khan pottery, the remarks here depending on Caldwell's preliminary study.

published (Braidwood et al., 1952), its description here is held to a minimum. Some 460 square meters were exposed, about 365 of which were opened in the three principal operations. The greatest thickness of deposit encountered above virgin soil was about 5 meters, which seems to include approximately five or six levels of architectural renovation or change.

The Matarrah houses were relatively well built rectilinear structures with tauf walling (see p. 40). The best preserved example encountered had four rooms and appeared to front southwestward onto a court. Traces of ovoid ovens or parching hearths, which had been at least partially arched over with mud, were found (cf. p. 42). In the base of the deepest of the three major operations a strange arrangement of long ovoid pits with fire-hardened walls was dug into virgin soil.

The coarse pottery closely resembles that of Tell Hassunah, with husking trays, a few proper milk jars, and large jars with shoulders low on the body (erroneously called "milk jars" in our original report). There is finer simple ware, also somewhat more elaborate incised ware, than is known from Tell Hassunah itself. Following the opinion of Lloyd and Safar, the excavators of Tell Hassunah, we tend to see the painted pottery of Matarrah as belonging more in the Samarran than in the standard Hassunan painted tradition. The finer simple ware, elaborate incised decoration, and painted decoration do not occur in the lower levels of Matarrah.

Sling missiles and whorls are the most common baked-clay objects, but a rather amorphous "mother-goddess" figurine and a few fragmentary bits of animal figurines did occur, as well as odd disks and plaques.

Again, in the general Hassunan tradition, the flint industry runs to poorly produced flakes and flake-blades with proper blades being very rare. Sickle elements with sheen and traces of bitumen hafting are most commonly of flake-blades and flakes, although a few are on blade sections. Strangely, the characteristic Hassunan chipped hoe did not occur. Obsidian is present and tends to run to blades (or to random chips), while a few pieces of microlithic scale occur, including a peculiar transverse "side blow blade-flake" of a type known at Jarmo (see p. 45 and Pl. 18B, 4th row).

It is worth noting that the chipped stone industry of Tell Hassunah itself may not be quite so wretched as its Matarrah counterpart. This opinion of one of our younger colleagues, Frank Hole, is based on surface collections from Tell Hassunah, made during visits to the site in 1951 and 1954/55. Hole has in mind not the obviously Syro-Cilician type of "javelin" projectile point (cf. R. J. and L. Braidwood, 1953, p. 304) but some technically well trimmed flint blades and a number of microdrills.

Among the ground stone objects, mortars, pestles, and other types of milling stones are most common. Celts were not common. One ax-type and several adz-type examples were found; they are essentially fully ground but seem to have been made on asymmetrical and casually selected pebbles. The Hassunan chipped hoe did not appear, nor any chipped-and-ground celts. There are a fair number of rather simple stone beads and a roughly rectangular stamp-seal type of object. Stone nails, a sort of circular stud with curved tank (Fig. 5, left), and a loop-bored marble bead which seems to simulate a cowrie-shell bead (Fig. 5, right) are somewhat more significant for comparative purposes (see below).

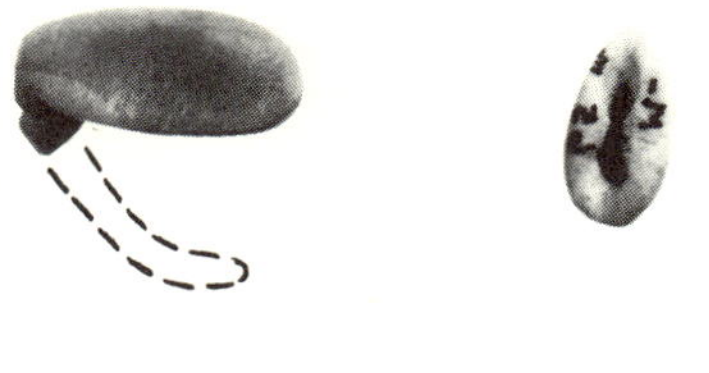

Fig. 5. Stone stud with curved tang and simulated cowrie-shell bead in marble

Bone awls were fairly common, some with the articular surface of the metapodial bone intact. Bone pin and needle fragments also occurred, as well as rib-blades and gouges. There are bone beads, one of which is grooved, and beads made of snapped pieces of dentalium shell were common.

Studies of the nonartifactual materials, including invertebrate and vertebrate fauna, are not yet complete. Helbaek (1953a) has identified two-row barley.

A few rather poorly preserved burials showed no consistent burial practice.

In spite of the general resemblance of the Matarrah assemblage to the "standard" Hassunan assemblage, certain characteristic features of the type site—such as the Hassunan archaic painted ware, the standard painted and painted-and-incised wares, and the minor strain of dark-faced burnished pottery—seem missing. So also are the Hassunan chipped hoe and the bitumen-coated grain bin. If, as Lloyd and Safar suggest, the painted pottery of Matarrah is all to be seen as a more or less successful production of the Samarran painted style, then it is interesting to note that the marble simulated cowrie-shell bead and the bent-tanged stud have so far otherwise been reported only from Samarra itself (R. J. and L. Braidwood, 1953). Nevertheless, the overall complexion of the Matarrah assemblage is Hassunan, and as suggested above (p. 26), Matarrah probably represents a somewhat impoverished southern variant of the Hassunan assemblage, in an area where the optimum conditions of the piedmont zone were thinning out.

It is pertinent at this point to note that we have been wrong (R. J. and L. Braidwood, 1953) in suspecting that the absence of the standard and coarse types of Hassunan pottery in the available reports on Baghuz and Samarra itself is due to selectivity on the part of the reporters. In our visit to Baghuz in early March of 1955, we collected potsherds in considerable bulk and completely at random and such other artifacts as we could find. It is quite clear that the coarse and common pottery which attends the handsome Samarran painted pottery at Baghuz is in no sense Hassunan. What holds for Baghuz may very well hold for Samarra itself. Thus we are no longer justified in suspecting that Baghuz and Samarra may simply represent further variants of the "standard" Hassunan assemblage, with only the spectacular painted pottery so far reported.

Gird Ali Agha

Three soundings[3] exposed a total area of approximately 45 square meters. It was not possible to make a sounding at the very crown of the mound, for this is occupied by a cemetery—undoubtedly Islamic but no longer used by the people of Girdemamik village. The soundings were made just west of the stone-covered outlines of the graves, overlooking the sweep of the Zab. There was no significant trace of artifactual material other than that which makes up the apparently consistent prehistoric village assemblage to be described. Virgin soil was encountered in two of the soundings and is probably nowhere more than 1.50-2.00 m. below the surface.

The largest sounding (24 square meters) exposed a sequence of at least three "floors" or compacted earth layers with flecks of charcoal and other signs of living activity. Virgin soil was not reached in this trench, which contained traces of irregular pits or depressed areas. The margins of the pits, being relatively near the surface, were not easy to delineate; these pits apparently were not so nearly vertical-sided as those noted in the basal level of Matarrah. At Ali Agha one of the systems of pits or depressions—and of depressions within depressions—was sufficiently exposed to suggest a breadth of at least 4 meters. That they imply pit-houses is not at all certain. Traces of post-holes and positive evidence of tauf walling were not noted. Arrangements of small flat river boulders appeared, in one case as the lining of a basin-shaped hearth (Pl. 13A). All in all, there was no clear-cut manifestation of architectural activity in the restricted portions of Ali Agha

[3] Miss Broman supervised the soundings, and much of this description is drawn from her field notes. Caldwell's study of the pottery has also been utilized.

which we exposed. The shallow pits may represent some kind of farmyard activity rather than "architecture."

Pottery-making was certainly practiced by the original inhabitants of Ali Agha, although their product has a relatively primitive aspect (see p. 66 and Pl. 15:18). A simple coarse ware—thick in cross section, chaff-tempered, and lightly fired—predominated, but a finer simple ware also occurred. The usual form was a shouldered jar or bowl with the dougle-ogee profile characteristic of the lower Hassunan levels. Trays, the same in profile as the normal Hassunan husking trays but without the intentional inner roughening, were present. Applied lugs or knobs of clay appear below the rims of some jars, including a few cases of molded "eyes." Only two incised sherds and one or two small sherd bits with possible traces of painted decoration appeared.

Objects of clay form a small category. It consists of several pierced sherd disks (spindle whorls?), a finger-modeled spindle whorl, a few bits of apparently human figurines, fragments of rods, a ball, a cone, and a few beads. Broman believes that the figurines resemble those of Jarmo but that no animal figurines are indicated by the fragments.

Apparently again in the Hassunan tradition, the Ali Agha flint industry is very poor. The tool types are mainly rough flake scrapers, and neither well struck blades nor blade cores occurred. A few larger celtlike chipped pebbles appeared, as well as pebbles flaked possibly as tools for chopping. Small blades and bladelet fragments in obsidian occurred in some quantity, however, and included the transverse "side blow blade-flake" of Jarmo type.

The ground stone category is very meager and consists mainly of fragments of coarse boulder mortars and probable pestles. There is one fragment of a flat-based stone bowl. Two polished celt fragments were found on the surface.

Bone objects include a spatulate blade fragment, several awls, and a flattened barrel-shaped bead.

Several bits of red ocher appeared. The plant impressions in lumps of clay and in sherds and the animal bones have not yet been studied in detail.

A flexed burial, in poor condition, encountered at the edge of the largest sounding was not completely exposed and was presumed to belong to the Islamic cemetery.

The soundings at Ali Agha were too restricted to reveal the general character of the original settlement. The lack of positive architectural traces is somewhat puzzling. There was general agreement that the pottery resembles that of both uppermost Jarmo and the basal levels of the Hassunan phase; Broman's impression of the flint and obsidian tools and the figurines confirms this general comparative positioning of the assemblage. Given the possibility of some regional variation in technology, the uppermost Jarmo, the Ali Agha, and the basal Hassunan manifestations may have flourished at about the same time. It is not necessary to hold as we once did (Braidwood et al., 1954) that Ali Agha represents a full chronological phase to be intercalated between the other two.

Qalat Jarmo

As well as may be judged from present surface indications, the extant portion of the original village covers approximately 3.2 acres (1.3 hectares) or about 13,000 square meters. In Wright's opinion (see p. 27) as much as a third of the original area of the village on the northwest may have been eroded away by the wadi (Pl. 8B, Fig. 6). The areas exposed by the expedition[4] total about 1,370 square meters, in some cases to depths of only a meter or less. The larger operations of the first and second seasons plumbed well into

---

[4]The field work was supervised by Adams during the 1950/51 season and by Miss Broman during the 1954/55 season; their field notes have been utilized for the following description. Adams' study of the pottery of the 1950/51 season has been supplemented by the studies of Matson and Caldwell, which have also been drawn on here. We are indebted to Miss Broman for the notes on the clay figurines, to Linda Braidwood for the flint and

the mound, over an area of 350 square meters, and 130 square meters of virgin soil were exposed, at a depth of about 7 meters below the crest of the mound. If we combine the profile of a step trench on the bluff face (operation A) with the six floors exposed in the largest operation (II), the lines of about sixteen floors or compacted levels with living debris may be counted. In our beginning operation (I), the surface of which was significantly lower than the crest in elevation, only eight major "floors"—one or two of which had subdivisions or minor renovations—appeared above virgin soil. Operation II was taken only to its sixth "floor" below the surface; the thickness of this occupational debris was less than half the total thickness observed in the adjacent operation A.

As the third season began, we rashly assumed that we had adequately sampled Jarmo in depth. Hence, we decided to attempt an exposure of the village plan in breadth in the uppermost levels. Our experience indicated that it would take our normal staff and a crew of fifty diggers approximately ten successive digging seasons to strip the whole surface of Jarmo at a safe pace and then only to a depth of about 2 meters at most. To exhaust the mound completely would certainly take over twenty-five digging seasons. Unfortunately, archeologists may not use bulldozers on sites of this type! For various reasons, both economic and strategic, stripping all of Jarmo was out of the question. A short cut was necessary.

The short cut we devised was to plot a 5 x 6 meter grid over the whole mound (Pl. 8, Fig. 6) and to dig test pits 2 meters square in as many of the grid units as time and money allowed. The co-ordinates of the grid were laid out to intercept the architectural elements that we knew in operations I and II at a 45° angle (cf. Pl. 13B). Surface indications suggested that about 360 of these grid units might encounter occupational debris not tested in the exposures of our earlier seasons. We managed to dig 151 test pits during the spring of 1955. The depths to which they were taken varied with the features encountered in them; the average depth was about 1.75 m., but one test in the southern center of the mound was taken to virgin soil, about 4 meters below the surface at that point.

Unfortunately, what this test-pit system showed us most clearly is that there are no short cuts for examining what goes on underground. The intermittent sections have still to be studied in detail, but it appears that the extrapolation of completely meaningful sections which we had hoped for will be impossible. The underlying strata of archeological sites may pitch and toss in ways which their present surface contours seldom suggest; the conventional lecture-hall analogy of archeologists that the layers in a mound are like the layers of a cake is a vast oversimplification. In Jarmo, the pitching and tossing seemed to be excessive in some portions of the mound.

What our test squares suggest, in gross, is indicated by the plot plan (Fig. 6). A cluster of squares marked by stippling (e.g. squares S 13, R 14, P 17, N 18, etc.) shows the surface occurrence of a zone of fine gray ashy material which pitches downward toward the west to run under level 6 of operation II. A cluster of squares marked by stippling in a different pattern (e.g. about H 9) stands for a peculiar area which, to a depth of 2 meters, contained no architectural features but, rather, a compacted and tough orange-buff silt, with occasional concentrations of varved bands of fine silt—evidently the remains of successively dried-out mud puddles in depressions. (Wright observed the same phenomenon while examining the interiors of recently ruined mud-brick structures south of Kirkuk.) Below the 2-meter depth, the test pits in this area yielded traces of architecture and concentrations of potsherds. Potsherds had appeared near the surface in modest numbers in operation I and in quantity in the western portion of operation II. Within the area closely tested by pits, potsherds were found to be concentrated near the surface in only three scattered points (about K 23, X 16, and L 12, the last being part of the concentration in the western portion of operation II). The test pits about T 16, U 15, and V 14 yielded traces of several layers of cracked limestone pebble paving immediately under the surface.

---

obsidian tools, to Adams for the stone bowls, and to Hattula Moholy-Nagy for the smaller ground stone objects.

Jarmo was not, however, a secondarily disturbed site; the stratigraphic irregularity clearly depends on its original make-up. Save for a handful of iron horseshoe fragments and nails, an occasional brass rifle-bullet casing, and bits of modern bottle glass, the Jarmo assemblage is consistent within itself. Moreover any suggestion that the four near-surface concentrations of potsherds point to a significantly later occupation (of four scattered houses) does not stand up to examination. There are the occasional concentrations of consistent and similar sherds of coarse pottery at depths of over 2 meters, as at the base of the compacted-silt area about H 9. There is also the fact that all other artifact categories (e.g. the flint industry) which occurred in the four areas of near-surface pottery concentration are consistent parts of the total Jarmo assemblage. Actually, pottery made its appearance in the latter part of the duration of the Jarmo village; it is not found at depths of more than 2.25 m. below the surface, or lower than level 5 in operation II.

The total duration of Jarmo need not have been long. We learned in neighboring villages that fifteen years is probably a generous average allowance for the life of a casually built house with sun-dried mud walls and mud-finished roof. If _each_ of the sixteen floors mentioned above means a separate architectural renovation (which each probably does not), the total duration might still be only about 250 years _minimum_.

Finally it should be noted, before we describe the Jarmo assemblage, that some of the soils in both the piedmont and the foothill zone show the effects of leaching and the formation of little limestone concretions. This is a feature in the history of the formation of one type of soil with high lime content and has to do with the penetration of rain water through the humus, the leaching-out of at least some of the carbonates, and their redeposition in little nodules or concretions. The zone of water penetration and concretions was well marked at Jarmo, and some of our other sites showed it as well. At Jarmo, the zone of concretions penetrated to approximately 1.50 m. in the normal soil of the occupational debris. Wright, incidentally, believes there are too many variable factors involved in this process ever to make it useful as a precise chronological indicator. At Jarmo it seemed to shatter the original consistency of the earth of the _tauf_ walls to the depth of penetration of the limestone concretions. This was also the approximate maximum depth of penetration of the deeper-rooted plants, such as large thistles. Hence, the only signs of architecture that we were able to trace above a depth of approximately 1.50 m. were the presence and alignments of stones which had been used as wall foundations or pavements (Pl. 13B) and the hard-baked areas of hearths or ovens. Below this depth, the possibility of tracing mud walls (_tauf_) increased rapidly.

The houses of Jarmo were built of _tauf_, often on rough field-stone foundations. There is no exact English equivalent for the Arabic word _tauf_. The French word _pisé_, often used in the archeological literature, is inexact in that it implies the pressing of rather fluid mud between built forms. The Spanish-American usage _adobe_ covers either simple sun-dried mud or sun-dried mud-brick walling. In Iraq _tauf_ walls are still used, generally as garden or courtyard walls, and forms are not employed; nor does ancient _tauf_ show traces of the impressions of forms. A _tauf_ wall is built of a mud mix of sufficient fluidity so that the lowest "course" may be molded with the builder's hands, with a vertical face on either side, to a height of about 3 or 4 inches without slumping. Having laid the first "course," the builder simply waits a day or so for complete sun-drying before he adds the second "course," after which he must wait again, and so on. The mud mix contains straw or grass to prevent cracking, just as does that used for preparing the later sun-dried mud bricks (_libn_).

The tracing of a _tauf_ wall in archeological context is a delicate operation. The wall stub usually is preserved to a height of not over 2 or 3 feet. It is surrounded, as one finds it, by the _tauf_-disintegration product of the upper portions of the same wall system (as well as earth debris from the roof construction), which tumbled down when the building went into ruin. The _tauf_-disintegration product is of the same general color and texture as the wall stub itself. But the disintegration product does not have the vertical cleavage planes which were the original faces of the wall itself, and it does not show its horizontal bedding lines in proper position. The horizontal bedding lines appear at the top of each

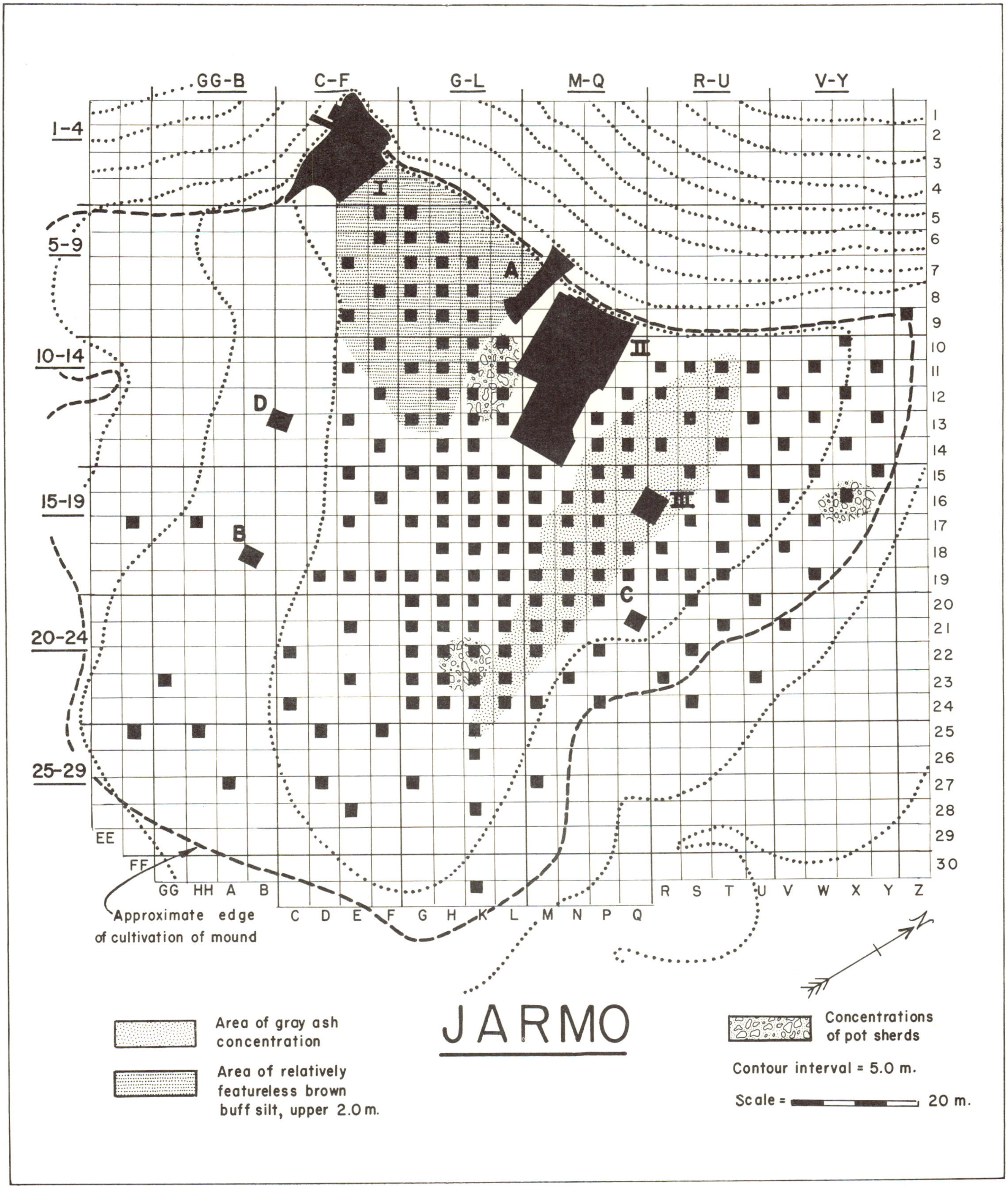

Fig. 6. Jarmo plot plan

"course" and are probably due to some kind of capillary rise of finer mud particles to the surface of each "course" as it dries. The bedding lines show up as horizontal lines of finer and lighter (or sometimes darker) bands of mud, about half an inch thick.

The well trained pickman uses a light single-tined pick to "feel" with light taps for the vertical cleavage planes of wall faces. At the same time, he watches carefully for the mold marks of the disintegrated straw reinforcement and for the horizontal bedding lines. Tauf walls are identifiable, and they do fit over the foundation stones which underlie them, although some of our Iraq Petroleum Company guests insisted that we were simply manufacturing earth walls as we dug!

A representative Jarmo house is the southernmost one of the complex in level 5 of operation II (Pl. 14A). It was stone-founded and tauf-walled, rectilinear in plan, oriented approximately 15° west of north. To the east (as far as our exposure went) was an open area; immediately adjacent to the north (and probably to the south) were other houses. A walled courtyard (no doubt unroofed) appeared to flank the house on the west, along with some open space. The northern and southern boundary walls of the house were separate from those immediately adjacent; party walls were not used.

The interior of the house was divided into seven rectilinear spaces; it was not clear whether all of these were actually rooms, for the tauf partitions may not all have extended to the ceiling. A long room (5.6 x 2.2 m.) ran north-south along the east front of the house; a narrow hallway along the south front gave access to this room, and there may also have been a doorway through the east wall (near the southeast corner). There was a fragment of a tauf curtain wall, which apparently was added over the reed flooring to separate the northern and southern halves of the long room. The arrangement of four "rooms" north of the hallway, along the west side of the house, was compact, and each "room" was very small (ca. 2.0 x 1.5 m.). One of these "rooms" included the oven, which was fired from the courtyard on the west, the two "rooms" north of it were probably bins for the storage of grain, and the "room" to the east may also have been for storage. Means of circulation within this complex was not clear; it is possible that the partitions were low and that the complex could have been crawled into from the hallway on the south. If so, some of the heating and drying effect from the oven would have been transferred to the whole house. Cooking was no doubt done in the courtyard on the west; several fragments of querns for the cracking or grinding of grain appeared on its simple earth floor. It has been suggested (Braidwood et al., 1953, p. 526) that such ovens were for the purpose of parching or "popping" grain, rather than for bread-making, but there is no direct evidence of popping.

The interior floors of Jarmo houses were generally composed of a thin layer of clean packed silt on a bed of reeds. The use of reed bedding for earth floors was commonly noticed below the line of leaching.

It would be reasonable to assume that the central partition in the house described above (separating the long room on the east from the oven-storage complex) rose to become the ridge-bearing point for a simple low gable roof, framed with rafters of saplings which bore a sheathing of reeds or brush into which mud was puddled and packed to form the roof surface. Such, at least, is the present practice in neighboring villages.

The details of an oven of tauf were better seen in the more intact remains of part of a house in operation II 6 (Pl. 14B). Here again the oven, which appeared to have been completely domed over with tauf, was fired from the adjoining room or (more probably) courtyard through a small scoop-shaped opening almost at floor level. The chimney was semicircular in section (through the flue) and was incorporated in the tauf wall directly above the scoop-shaped opening of the fire door. The floor of the oven proper was slightly higher (ca. 25 cm.) than that of the fire door and sloped gently up toward the back of the oven. Both floors consisted of a surface layer of fine silty clay, which had been burnished and fire-hardened, over a thin foundation layer of coarser earth and gravel well mixed with straw. Such floor surfaces apparently cracked readily, since oven remains showing a number of refloorings were encountered. The heavy straw tempering used in these floors yielded Helbaek some of his best grain impressions.

The fragmentary house in II 6 (Pl. 14B) shows two other interesting features. The outer face of the doorway into the oven room was provided with a recessed jamb, presumably so that the door itself might fit snugly into the recess. A flat stone set into the rear wall of the room had a slit in the tauf above it. Apparently this was a narrow window with a stone sill, although it was perhaps not in an exterior wall.

Although both of the following elements were missing from the doorway mentioned above, door framing at Jarmo apparently involved the construction of a rough door (of crudely dressed boards or a skin-covered frame?) on a vertical swivel-post with elements to receive the swivel-post at top and bottom of the opening. There are examples in place to show that the bottom of the post swiveled in a normal mortar-like stone door socket. The upper end of the swivel-post was held by a long stone, most of which must have been bedded horizontally into the tauf walling at the top of the jamb but with its protruding portion drilled to receive the swivel-post (Pl. 20:4). Such stones also have been found adjacent to doorways; the drilled ends were carefully finished and even decorated, while the butt ends were left rough.

In spite of its incompleteness, the picture of Jarmo architecture is clearly not one of fumbling beginnings in a new craft. The plastic potentialities of tauf as a building material seem to have been well understood even by the people of the earliest levels, and the architecture which we exposed revealed no particular advances during the occupation of the site.

Our attempts to arrive at a notion of the overall village plan, even in the uppermost levels, have so far been frustrated (see p. 39). The complex in II 5 clearly shows that houses were built in contiguity at least on two sides. But the open areas on the other sides may have been broad; we have no firm suggestion of anything approaching streets. We have guessed (Braidwood and Reed, 1957) that the total number of houses in the Jarmo village probably did not exceed twenty-five and that the village population amounted to no more than 150 people.

In some of the lower levels of operation I we located simple oval depressions in the floors which we first called "baked-in-place pottery basins." While these may in fact have been receptacles, they may equally well have been prepared clay-lined hearths of the type which even today is usual in simpler Kurdish and Arabic houses. Some of the "basins," however, contained rough stones which might have been used hot as "boiling-stones." These fired clay-lined depressions must have been prepared in much the same way as the ovens described above, although the latter apparently were domed over; on this score there is probably no point in separating the two types too strictly. In sum, there appears to be no evidence that these ovoid depressions, whether they were receptacles or not, are to be viewed as an evolutionary forerunner of portable pottery vessels.

The clearest record of portable pottery vessels comes from the western portion of operation II, of the 1950/51 season, and the following brief description is based on that occurrence. The potsherd bulk acquired in the 1954/55 season (see pp. 63-66) will amplify but not essentially change the following generalizations. In the 1950/51 season, a total of 204 potsherds (representing, Adams believes, no more than about 35 vessels) occurred in our exposures of floors 5, 4, and 3. The count on floor 5, the lowest at which pottery occurred, was only 65 potsherds. The pottery from floors 5, 4, and 3 is easily distinguished from that of floors 3, 2, and 1 on the basis of fabric, surface treatment, and decoration (with typological overlap on floors 3 and 2). Adams does not, however, consider the two groups separate wares and sees evidence of continuity of gross manufacturing tradition as well as of difference. The Jarmo pottery is handmade, vegetable-tempered, buff to orange-buff in color, and frequently exhibits a darkened unoxidized core on a clean break.

More than half of the group of earlier potsherds shows outside surfaces burnished, often over a red slip or painted decoration. The simple linear painted patterns often show oblique arrangements of blobbed lines (Pl. 15:12-17). On several potsherds scratches run underneath the painted lines. In its own simple fashion, the earlier Jarmo pottery shows technical competence in potting, and it is not at all supposed that it represents the fumbling beginnings of a new craft.

The uppermost floors of the same operation yielded approximately 12,000 potsherds, but these seem to be from less competent examples of the potter's art. The fabric is both coarser and softer than that of the earlier group, the surfaces of the vessels seem to have received less attention, and there is little trace of painted decoration (Pl. 15:1-11). There was a general tendency to thicken the body walls of all form and size categories, although absolutely larger vessels did now occur also. Plastic or incised decoration now appeared, also a peculiar type of pierced lug handle. And while Adams does not see a complete change in ceramic tradition separating the earlier and later Jarmo pottery, both Caldwell and Matson stress the commonality of the potting tradition of the later Jarmo pottery with that of Ali Agha and basal Tell Hassunah (see Pl. 15:18). While the fabric of the later Jarmo pottery appears to be inferior to that of the earlier lot, it has been suggested that the difference might depend in part on the effects of soil chemistry in the uppermost 1.50 m. of Jarmo (see p. 40) since the time of its occupation. This is an aspect of the detailed study of the pottery that is now in process, along with considerations of the dominance of certain types of forms and sizes of pots in relation to their possible uses, their degree of permeability to liquids, and so on. One interesting observation is that in the upper levels tall-bodied and larger pottery vessels appear to replace the earlier tall-bodied stone vessels. But low plates or saucer-like forms in stone persist, probably because the production of broad open types of profiles called for more sophistication in potting than the Jarmo potters commanded. Adams is not completely convinced that the replacement is direct, however, and certainly sees no evidence of a wholesale replacement of stone bowls by pottery within the range of Jarmo.

The Jarmo assemblage does not appear to have been rich in clay objects of forms which clearly suggest specific and immediate utilitarian purposes. Beads of clay were common enough, in simple spherical, barrel, flattened elliptical, and flattened diamond forms, and double-pierced "toggle" beads also appeared. A large and carefully made paw-shaped object was perhaps a bitumen-dauber. A clay cone with a carefully worked spiral incision on its base may have been used as a stamp seal for wet clay, but we found no impressions of the type.

It is in a less immediately utilitarian category of forms that the people of Jarmo have left the clearest trace of their understanding of the plastic qualities of clay. Broman has finished her final study of over 5,000 pieces of figurines of animals and human beings (Pl. 16) and of forms of even less conceivable function such as balls and cones. Objects of this general category appeared throughout the range of depths in Jarmo.

Most of the figurines are small, not very carefully shaped, and very lightly baked. In rare cases the entire surface is covered with red ocher. To the degree that the site has been adequately tested, some change may be observed from the basal to the upper levels; for example (1) horned animals appear to occur only in the upper levels, (2) the human figurines become very complex in the upper levels, and (3) "double-wing bases" (Pl. 16: 14-15) seem to occur only in the upper levels. But these are details within the development of the general category, which was certainly the product of a single tradition in modeling.

The flint and obsidian industry of Jarmo (Pls. 17-19) is a blade-tool industry that shows relatively little change throughout the life of the settlement. A goodly proportion of the tools are made of obsidian. In the lower levels the obsidian supply seems to have been somewhat more limited than in the upper levels. However, the tendency toward re-chipping and reusing obsidian tools and the relatively small number of worthless chips would indicate that at no time did the Jarmo inhabitants have enough obsidian at hand to feel free to waste it. Throughout the levels, microliths, in flint and especially in obsidian, consistently predominate over larger tools.

The Jarmo tool kit is fairly simple, but on the whole the tools are neatly made. Among both the large tools and the microliths, simple unretouched blades used "as is" are overwhelmingly predominant. Traces of bitumen are found on some of the unretouched blades as well as on some of the retouched tools.

Among the large tools, blades retouched along the edge (and occasionally at the end) and sickle blades are most common. Neatly made round flake-scrapers, neat end scrapers on blades, borers, and notched blades also are present, but in smaller quantities.

Among the flint microliths, tiny blades with nibbling retouch at the edge and less frequently at the end are in the majority. Notched blades, borers, and sickle blades are present throughout, but in small numbers.

The chipped obsidian is almost entirely microlithic (cf. Pl. 18B). Only a few larger blades are found in the lowest levels; more are found in the upper levels (mainly unretouched but a few with edge retouch) but still in small quantities. As regards the great bulk of microlithic tools, bladelets with nibbled retouch at one end are most common and those with edge retouch are numerically second. Notched blades are rare. Curious but distinctive "side blow blade-flakes" (made from obliquely struck transverse blade sections with subsequent retouch) are fairly common in the upper levels. More noteworthy still is the presence, in the upper levels only, of rare triangles and trapezes in both flint and obsidian, forms most familiar from earlier sites.

The chipped stone industry is fairly impressive as regards bulk. Over 100,000 pieces of flint and obsidian (including waste chips) were found in the 1950/51 season alone, with obsidian accounting for about 40% of the total.

The Jarmo objects in ground stone (Pls. 20-21) suggest a greater variety of activities than we are yet able to comprehend from any other category. In celts, fair-sized fully ground types with axlike bits predominate, although there are examples with chipped bodies and ground bits. These were probably hoe blades, but they may have served as axes also. Large pierced balls such as are often called digging-stick weights, loom weights, or maceheads are rare. The variety of sizes and shapes among querns (Pl. 20:5-6) and rubbing stones (metate and mano) and among boulder mortars and pestles (Pl. 20:1-3) is considerable. The presence of such objects is usually taken to suggest at least the cracking of grain for porridge, if not the grinding of flour for bread (see p. 42). Helbaek's tentative identification of acorns (p. 47) also may suggest a use for these objects, although Dahlberg's observations on the human teeth poses a question about their use for food preparation (see p. 47), and some of the smaller examples may have been used for grinding other substances. Bits of ocher were common, and stone palettes also occurred.

Aesthetically, the stone-bowl industry was highly satisfactory. The bowls were made predominantly of marble and often have crisply outlined profiles and thin finely polished walls. Apparently the bowl-makers often selected their marble with care and so worked it that the natural veining of the stone added to the decorative effect by yielding horizontal bands or oblique lines of varying colors. Most common are inverted truncated conical forms with flared lips, subspherical or ellipsoid forms with a variety of lip treatments, and low carinated bowls (Pl. 21:12-16). The truncated conical form was most common in the deepest levels but tended increasingly to be replaced by other forms—usually smaller and more open—in the upper levels. Adams reckoned that the fragments (over 1,000) found in 1950/51 alone must have pertained to at least 350 separate vessels and that the investment in man-hours involved in their production by hand was most impressive. The people of Jarmo apparently valued their stone bowls highly, for many fragments show drill holes made for repairing cracks.

Spoons, more common in bone (see below), were made in ground stone, and there was a variety of tools for odd purposes. Pierced spheres of "macehead" size, grooved abrading-pieces of the sort sometimes called shaft-straighteners or bead-polishers, whetstones, fine-grained polishers, and pierced disks of "spindle-whorl" size all occurred, but not in impressive numbers. Another interesting tool is a large drill bit in the form of a symmetrical "waisted" pebble; Moholy-Nagy noted that its curved lower surface exactly fitted fragments representing the preliminary drilling stage in the production of stone bracelets (see below). A model bit mounting with a simulated stone bit bound by thongs on the end of a wooden shaft was found to be practicable for use with either a bow-drill or a stone-weighted crank-drill. Stone door pivots are described above (p. 43).

Ground stone was well evidenced at Jarmo in the "decorative" as well as in the immediately utilitarian categories. Cylindrical, barrel, and flattened biconical beads were common; collared barrel beads occurred, also a cylindrical bead with spiral "rope" incision.

Pendants are usually simple but include several examples with incised decoration. Since we are not able to comprehend their use, we list here the considerable number of small finely ground pestle-shaped objects (Pl. 21:9-10) and stone balls which the site yielded, as well as some smaller stone disks, "buttons," "nails," etc. Objects classified as bracelets (Pl. 21:1-6) were especially well made. They are usually of marble and ovoid or round in cross section, though the outer faces are sometimes channeled, concave, or even spirally grooved. These objects must have been popular, for fragments, suggesting at least 225 complete specimens, appeared throughout our operations. Objects suggesting finger rings occurred in ground stone as well as in bone.

There are several examples in finely ground stone (as well as one or two in coarsely ground stone and one in rough clay) of a peculiar type of object. In observation of the two best examples (e.g. Pl. 21:11) Dr. Cornelius W. Vermeulen, Professor of Urology in the University of Chicago School of Medicine, offers the opinion that these objects are "highly suggestive in size and form of the distal segment of the adult human penis. The glans penis is well shown along with the penile corona and the remains of the foreskin following circumcision. It is interesting to note that the deeper drillings on the proximal face of the objects are in the location of the urethra as it courses through the ventral portion of the penis while the larger dorsal depression could be accounted for as the cavity formed by the terminations of the corpora cavernosa. If the object be, indeed, a representation of the distal penis, its configuration almost certainly indicates circumcision." Some of the objects of this type are smaller than life-size, and all show central drilling, as if they were intended to be mounted upright on small sticks. They also have at the base a peculiar stepped groove, the purpose of which is not apparent.

The most common items of worked bone are awls. These may be short or long, broad or narrow, with smoothed or natural articular butts. Some are of broad thin spatulate form and may not have had pointed ends. Simple bone hafts, made by drilling a large hole into the long axis of a phalange, were common. Bone pins and needles occurred; the latter were sometimes drilled at the very end and sometimes a centimeter or so below the end. There were simple rings, made by cutting long bone transversely, and grooved ferrule-like sections of long bone which may simply have been incompleted rings. Thinner cylindrical bone beads also occurred. Three other types of bone objects are somewhat unusual: (1) well made spoons with either short pierced (Pl. 21:8) or long and sometimes spirally grooved handle, (2) points (Pl. 21:7) made of a section of long bone with the round shaft left complete at the butt end and obliquely trimmed at the opposite end into a rounded somewhat gougelike point, and (3) bulbous off-center bead-pendants which recall those of the Natufian (Garrod and Bate, 1937, Pl. XII 2:2).

Pierced tablike objects were produced in shell, usually with twin drill holes giving the effect of eyes. Snapped sections of dentalium shells were probably used as beads, and there was a handful of small pierced gastropod shells. Random examples of unworked riverine clamshalls were probably used as spoons or scrapers.

In addition to impressions of reed bedding for floors (see p. 42) there were impressions of woven matting or baskets. Unfortunately, none of the impressions that we reclaimed were large enough to show either the edges or the general form and size of the mats or baskets. The simple over-and-under weave of some of the impressions suggests matting; the twined appearance of others suggests basketry, and this suggestion is strengthened by the fact that some of these impressions actually consist of a thin layer of bitumen (see p. 49), as if some attempt at waterproofing was made. Bitumen-coated basket-trays are still used in Chemchemal. Bitumen was also often found adhering to flint blades, and its use as an adhesive for hafting was clear in the case of a four-element curved sickle of flint. There was no evidence of the material of the haft itself, but we assume that it was made of wood. Broman noted clear impressions of very fine fabric on two small clay balls. The fibers used in the fabric have not yet been identified.

Few if any clearly intentional burials appeared in the Jarmo exposures. In most cases we suspected accidental death due to roof cave-in, and in no sense were a standardized burial position and Beigaben manifested. There was probably a cemetery somewhere outside the immediate village precincts.

Much of the Jarmo raw material (worked and unworked) still awaits study, but such available identification and interpretation as may have either cultural or ecological significance are presented in the following sections.

The human skeletal material was in no case well preserved. Otten's and Barth's casual field observation indicated a generalized Mediterranean physical type. The single skull fragment studied in detail is a facial skeleton (J II S 4) examined by Professor J. Lawrence Angel of the University of Pennsylvania, Baugh Institute of Anatomy. To Angel "the general impression is a face showing Iranian as well as Mediterranean traits. . . ."

A study of a number of human teeth was undertaken by Dr. Albert A. Dahlberg of the Zoller Laboratory of Dental Anthropology at the University of Chicago. The teeth of the Jarmo people were of medium to small size and completely modern in type. They show even milling and no marginal enamel fracture; apparently there were not gross coarse particles in the diet which would cause excessive erosion or cracking. Since the teeth available to Dahlberg do not represent a very large number of individuals, the full implication of this evidence is not yet clear. It may, however, bear upon the original use of the querns and rubbing stones and the boulder mortars and pestles (see p. 45).

Helbaek, in a letter (Nov. 11, 1951) which remarked on the whole variety of food-plant finds, wrote that "it will take years and much work to make an organized picture of all these surprising details." His study goes forward, and some of the details are indicated in chapter viii. It is interesting to note here that some individual examples of the two types of Jarmo wheats bear close resemblances to their respective present-day wild counterparts (*Triticum dicoccoides* and *T. aegilopoides*), while others seem to be intermediate forms approaching either *T. dicoccum* or *T. monococcum*. Helbaek takes this suggestion of wheat crops of a mixed character to mean that Jarmo cannot represent the very first steps in agriculture, even if human selection of the best seed grain had not yet been carried far. The Jarmo barley shows a close conformity with the wild species, *Hordeum spontaneum*, but had a tough axis; in genuinely wild barleys the axis is more or less brittle. Contrary to expectations that very early barley would be six-rowed, the Jarmo barley was two-rowed. Helbaek believes that barley first came into cultivation as a result of its presence as a weed in cultivated wheat fields. As to noncereal food plants, Helbaek mentions (p. 115) "the field pea, lentil, and blue vetchling," although it may not yet be clear whether these were already under cultivation or simply the result of food-collection. Two items (mentioned in his correspondence) indicate that food-collecting was still of importance at Jarmo; these are the remains of pistachios (Pl. 28D) and acorns.

The other botanical information available from Jarmo derives from the identifications of woody charcoal by Professor Elso S. Barghoorn of the Botanical Laboratories of Harvard University. Because of the character of the preservation of the samples, Barghoorn was able to make only genus, not species, identifications. Of fifty specimens examined, forty-five are of oak (some being from large trees), two of tamarisk, two of a leguminous tree (*Prosopis*, cf. mesquite), and one is unidentified.

Since Reed accounts in chapter ix for the present state of his study of the zoölogical remains, his list of fauna will suffice here. Only for the goat (No. 4) is there direct morphological evidence of domestication (see p. 131). This does not, of course, mean that some subsequently domesticated animals may not already have been herded or otherwise cared for at Jarmo. Reed observes, moreover, that the two "subspecies" of goat (Nos. 3-4) were probably practically identical, since domestication was almost certainly still in an early phase. The concentration of attention on animals as evidenced by the figurines is impressive but not explicit. A little figure with a curled tail (Pl. 16:2) is considered doglike by Reed (see p. 128).

1. An equid (probably *Equus hemionus*, the onager)
2. Gazelle (*Gazella subgutterosa*)
3. Wild goat (*Capra hircus aegagrus*)
4. Domestic goat (*Capra hircus hircus*)

5. Sheep (Ovis orientalis)
6. Bovid (Bos [?] primigenius)
7. Red deer (Cervus elaphus)
8. Roe deer (Capreolus capreolus)
9. Pig (Sus scrofa)
10. Bear (Ursus arctos)
11. Wolf (Canis lupus)
12. Fox (Vulpes vulpes)
13. Leopard (Panthera pardus)
14. A small unidentified cat (house-cat size)
15. Badger (Meles meles)
16. Beech marten (Martes foina)
17. Unidentified rodents
18. A few small unidentified birds
19. Tortoise (Testudo graeca)
20. Unidentified fish
21. Fresh-water crab (Potamon potamios)

The largest group of bones of animals that Reed feels confident were hunted wild consist of pig, sheep, and gazelle. This naturally bears on the question of hunting and on the lack of normal flint or obsidian projectile points in the Jarmo chipped stone industry. If the bow was known and used, arrows might have been tipped with single or composite microlithic points of types so far unrecognized as such.

The yield of snail shells, especially in the deeper layers, was so great that we accounted for the unbroken specimens by number of cubic-foot boxes. The species has been identified by Dr. Fritz Haas, Curator of Lower Invertebrates, Chicago Natural History Museum, and Dr. Joseph C. Bequaert, Museum of Comparative Zoölogy, Harvard University, as Helix salomonica, a large land snail. The much less usual riverine clamshells have been identified as Unio tigridis. The study of the ecological role of these invertebrates is being undertaken by Dr. Stuart A. Harris and the Rev. Mr. H. E. J. Biggs.

The petrological study of the Jarmo stone artifacts has not yet been completed. Wright observed that most of the raw materials appear to come from boulders in the wadi below the site, which were weathered out and transported away from the ridges to the east. The range of occupation at Jarmo marks the earliest appearance of obsidian in quantity in the known Iraqi sequence. The occurrence of obsidian, a volcanic glass formed under special circumstances, is relatively restricted. The probably pertinent mother lodes nearest to Jarmo are two Turkish clusters, those in the Lake Van area, about 250 airline miles to the north, and those near Aksaray, about 650 airline miles to the northwest (Kökten, 1952). No other lodes have been reported save for more distant occurrences in Turkey and those of the Aegean and Ethiopia, and it is very doubtful that any of these would be pertinent. The extent of carrying trade which the quantity of obsidian at Jarmo suggests is impressive. It assures us that trade and communications over considerable distances had already been established and that truly isolated regional cultural developments are hardly conceivable. Traces of obsidian (in far lesser quantity) in the Zarzian or even earlier horizons may also imply absence of regional isolation but are more difficult to assess.

Four of nine possibly bitumen samples tested in the laboratories of the Iraq Petroleum Company[5] in Kirkuk proved to contain bitumen, and there were traces of oil in at least one other sample. Moreover, one of the four bitumen samples was of a fairly pure asphalt, a fact which restricts its source to three of the known bitumen seeps in this area. One of these (in the Sagirma Dagh) is only about a dozen miles from Jarmo. The other samples

[5]This was only one of many kindnesses extended to us by the I.P.C. In this particular case, we were indebted to Mr. D. E. Bunyan of the Petroleum Engineering Department, Mr. Leo Damesin and Mr. H. V. Dunnington of the Geological Department, and Mr. J. W. Boyd and Mr. P. R. Rainsford-Hannay of the Chemistry Department.

were less pure and could have come from a number of seeps in the general Chemchemal-Kirkuk district. In the instances of the sickle-blade hafting and a basket- or mat-impressed sample (p. 46) the bitumen was part of a matrix of earthy matter.

An overall interpretative assessment of the Jarmo yield seems to point toward two opposite extremes. Helbaek's and Reed's studies tend to stress the still only very partial achievement of domestication and the dependence on food-collecting which must still have persisted (i.e., hunted animals, snails, some wild food plants such as acorns). Another aspect of the "primitiveness" of the assemblage is the survival of older traditions in flint-tool preparation; especially enigmatic is Linda Braidwood's observation that some seemingly older tool types occurred in the upper levels only (p. 45).

On the other side of the coin, the relative sophistication shown in architectural construction and in secondary constructional features such as ovens and the general excellence of the work in finely ground stone seem to point toward a tradition of familiarity with settled life and some freedom from the constant pressure of the food quest. This freedom would seem to be especially marked in the stone-bowl category (with its implications of time spent in their production). Probably the clay figurines should be listed here as well.

The tools which to us are comprehensible parts of the food quest lend themselves logically to interpretations at either end of the bipolarity suggested above. Thus celts (axes, adzes, or hoes?) and milling stones occurred, albeit less well made, on the typologically earlier sites of M'lefaat and Karim Shahir and were as reasonably employed by food-collectors as by food-producers. Sickles were common for the first time (in our sequence) in Jarmo, and it may be assumed that they were used in reaping grain, although presumably their sheen could also have developed from the cutting of reeds. The several types of celts and milling stones and the care taken in their preparation probably represent the most impressive aspect of all the artifactual items which may have been included in the food-quest complex.

We are inclined to minimize the implication which might be drawn by some from the absence of portable pottery in the lower levels and its presence in the upper—in the face of the overall consistency of the Jarmo assemblage from bottom to top with its own implications of inherent cultural continuity. The sherds from levels 5, 4, and 3 of operation II are obviously early but good examples of the potter's craft. We do not see on Jarmo the fumbling beginnings of this craft. They may not, of course, be very far back.

Finally, there are two as yet imponderable features. One is that at Jarmo we see the first instance in our sequence in Iraqi Kurdistan of the pairing of pottery with a typologically elaborate flint industry, in contrast to the previously known situation in which early pottery is found with essentially characterless flint artifacts, as at Hassunah, Matarrah, Ali Agha, and Banahilk. The typologically elaborate flint industry did reach the piedmont, however. Harris (see p. 12, n. 1) made surface collections of flint tools along the rim of the plain south and southwest of Kirkuk; his interests at the time did not include pottery. At Tell Urwell and Tell Raseien, 6 miles from the embouchure of the Tauq Chai onto the piedmont, he found Jarmo-like flints. Furthermore, Jarmo-like flints persisted at least until Hassunan and Samarran pottery reached the intermontane valleys; Linda Braidwood observed them in the Tell Shimshara collections in the Danish National Museum in Copenhagen in August of 1948 (see p. 6). The factors at play here are still unclear as regards geographical distribution, relative chronology, and cultural affinities. It will be of great interest to learn whether the full assemblages at Tell Urwell and Tell Raseien do or do not include such characteristic Jarmo features as the figurines, the ground stone objects, and the pottery.

The second imponderable feature concerns a possible reflection of certain other as yet unassessable factors. In 1949, after she had classified the stone, bone, and clay objects of both Matarrah and Jarmo in the field, Linda Braidwood (R. J. and L. Braidwood, 1950) was struck by the dynamic "feel" of the Jarmo materials in contrast to those of the later Matarrah. From this admittedly subjective observation she went on to suggest that it was "as if the Jarmo craftsmen had been in a phase of productive intensity and creativity, whereas the Matarrah craftsmen were simply producing—in a rather spiritless way, as if they had reached a peak and then leveled off." We might wonder, further, whether such phases of intensity seem generally to characterize periods of great cultural acceleration and change. Is this not, perhaps, an earlier example of what Frankfort (1951, p. 16) saw for the emergence of civilization as ". . . the outcome of a sudden and intense change, a crisis in which its form—undeveloped but potentially a whole—crystallizes out . . ."?

The primitive aspects of the Jarmo assemblage, while quite natural, perhaps give a sense of the primitive which may be more apparent than real. We suspect that Jarmo was in other respects already "over the hump" and that it exhibits an early (but not the earliest conceivable) aspect of the settled village-farming community. Was there, in fact, a phase or two of proper "villageness," with simple agriculture and animal domestication, earlier than Jarmo but coming after the very basic level of incipient cultivation which we suppose the assemblages of the Karim Shahir type suggest? On the basis of the available evidence in Iraqi Kurdistan we believe that such a phase or phases existed. Questions such as this give importance to the Palestinian evidence. The major cultural theme of this general time range might be pictured as one of ever-increasing success in regional adaptation and specialization, and we can no doubt learn much by viewing the regional cultural foci comparatively, as if they were separate experiments. Nevertheless it is illogical to expect that any human culture ever existed completely in a vacuum, and the image of "separate experiments" must not be overdrawn.

Kani Sur, Khora Namik, Kharaba Qara Chiwar

Material from these sites in the general vicinity of Jarmo (see p. 27) is represented only by surface finds. The selection from Kani Sur seems to have remarkably close counterparts at Jarmo, including fragments of marble bracelets and stone bowls. The same is true of Khora Namik, where traces of a Jarmo-like ground stone industry appeared in bowl fragments, possibly a stone ball, and a pestle fragment. Microlithic obsidian bladelets appeared in some quantity; there was a flint blade with sickle sheen, and the remainder of the flints are probably best assignable to the Jarmo phase but are actually quite generalized.

The larger and much more impressive site of Kharaba Qara Chiwar, overlooking a stretch of the Tauq Chai where it is still perennial, may refer to a horizon somewhat intermediate between those of Jarmo and Karim Shahir. Here, four of us in slightly less than an hour collected 320 worked flints, seven pieces of ground stone, and one obsidian flake. The count of blades and blade cores ran high, and about one-third of this yield was microlithic. The cores, the nibbling produced on end scrapers by wear rather than retouch, and the lack of sickle-blade sheen and (essentially) of obsidian suggest an industry closer to that of Karim Shahir than to that of Jarmo. A chipped celt with polished bit and a grooved pebble abrading-piece of schist also suggest Karim Shahir, but a "waisted" pebble and especially a fragment of a small finely ground pestle-shaped object recall Jarmo, as do a few large neat blade cores. There were also two quern fragments and a rubbing stone, common to both sites.

Tell M'lefaat

We took advantage of the inner face of the tank-trap trench on the lower western flank of the mound to project a test pit (sounding II) up in the direction of the crest of the hill. This yielded only talus-wash material and some signs of casual later occupation. Two soundings were put in near the crown of the mound itself. The consistency of the soil seemed to encourage moles; their holes were numerous and proceeded even to depths of over 2 meters. There was a modest scatter of sherds of wheel-made pottery of several late periods on the surface—not surprising on a little hill overlooking an important ford—and several odd wheel-made potsherds occurred at some depth, no doubt having tumbled down the mole holes. It is surprising that M'lefaat is, after all, so relatively undisturbed, when one takes its position into account. The general run of surface material and the artifacts from our soundings give every appearance of making up a consistent assemblage.

Sounding I, somewhat off the crown of the mound on the river slope, exposed approximately 20 square meters and was taken to a depth of 2.15 m. below the surface at one end, although its average depth was not over 1.50 m. Virgin soil was about 1.90 m. below the surface. In sounding III, slightly off the crown to the northwest, an area of approximately 40 square meters was exposed to a depth of about a meter, and virgin soil was not reached. In sounding I, two phases of what was probably a small pit-house were encountered. In sounding III, two well marked floors, with concentrations of stones, were present, and at one point the profile showed two intervening black layers and a pebble layer between the two floors. It is clear that the site of M'lefaat was settled long enough for architectural renovations and changes to have been made.

The original pit exposed in sounding I was somewhat irregularly ovoid in plan (ca. 3.55 x 2.70 m.). A hearth depression appeared in its southern end. The floor of the pit was about 1.54 m. below the surface at this point. Subsequently, at a depth of 1.25 m. below the surface, the floor was enlarged toward the north and west to almost 4 x 3 meters. The lower portion of the older pit had been filled in, and the whole was "floored" with coarse stones. The sides of these pits were reasonably vertical up to about 80 cm. below the surface. No details could be traced above this level, which was the base of the limestone concretion zone. How deeply the pits had been cut below their own original ground surface and how they may have been roofed were not apparent.

In sounding III traces of architectural activity were even more ambiguous. The area was full of random stones, some coarse and cracked (perhaps by fire) and some smoother. Quite a few fragmentary boulder mortars and querns occurred. On the first floor, encountered at a depth of slightly over half a meter, about a third of the circumference of what had apparently been a circle (ca. 4 m.) of small rough stones appeared in one corner of the sounding. This circular stone "wall" was not over 15 cm. thick, rather too thin to suggest the foundation for a wall of room height. Between the well marked first and second floors were two discontinuous areas of pebbles, which clearly had been purposely laid. Practically nothing could be made of the scatter of stones at the level of the second floor unless it was a cluster of large worn flagstones, which—with various pebble scatters and random groupings of larger stones at the same relative level—marked an occupation horizon.

About two dozen shaped but fragmentary bits of at least semifired clay appeared. Several of these were unmistakably fragments of figurines or of rods or balls. There was a simple cylindrical clay bead. Since such objects are known to be in context at Karim Shahir (see below) as well as at Jarmo, there is no reason to suppose them intrusive at M'lefaat.

The M'lefaat chipped stone industry was predominantly of flint, obsidian being restricted to six examples found *in situ* (including a pyramidal bladelet core) plus five from the surface. Pyramidal bladelet cores and polyhedral flake cores were very prevalent in flint. Backed bladelets of microlithic size run to pointed tools, and there are also notched bladelets, bladelets with nibbled retouch, and a series of concave-ended bladelets and end scrapers. Normal-sized blades appeared, but not many scrapers (and these predominantly on flakes) or burins (most of them made on bladelet core fragments). The industry appears to be very similar to the industries of Karim Shahir and Gird Chai (see below).

In ground stones M'lefaat yielded a fair proportion of usually fragmentary boulder mortars, pestles, querns, and rubbing stones, as well as ground and polished celts. Smaller ground stone objects include a fragment of a finely ground and polished rod, a "waisted" pebble, a shallow bowl fragment (from the surface), and two balls.

The site yielded several bone awls or awl fragments. There was a pierced pendant of clamshell, rectangular with rounded corners; several other bits of clamshell also appeared. These objects, plus a lump of ocher and the very ephemeral ghost of a mat impression (just below the first floor in sounding III) complete the inventory of M'lefaat.

The animal bones have not yet been studied.

Broman and Howe are impressed with the general similarity of the M'lefaat flint industry to the industries of Karim Shahir and Gird Chai. But Gird Chai does not appear to have a ground stone industry to parallel that of M'lefaat, and there are evidently some differences between the ground stone industries of M'lefaat and Karim Shahir. For example, celts were predominantly pecked, ground, and polished at M'lefaat but chipped and only bit-polished at Karim Shahir. Marble bracelets like those of Karim Shahir did not appear in the restricted M'lefaat soundings. Such differences might be reflections of the local availability of proper stone or of some cultural or temporal variation, but it seems too soon to generalize on the differences in the face of the similarity of the flint industries.

In December of 1957, Dr. Ralph Solecki and Dr. Rose L. Solecki most generously went over their materials from the Shanidar cave and the Zawi Chemi Shanidar open site (see p. 5) with the Braidwoods and Howe. We all agreed that the Zawi Chemi Shanidar assemblage fits into the general range of M'lefaat and Karim Shahir. With its impressive yield in heavy ground stone, the Zawi Chemi Shanidar assemblage appears to approach that of M'lefaat perhaps somewhat more closely than that of Karim Shahir, but, again, this may be due to any of the factors noted above.

Karim Shahir

Excavations in 1951 at the open-air hilltop site of Karim Shahir exposed some 500 square meters in one major operation (Pl. 22A) and seven minor exploratory trenches. The latter were widely distributed over the crown of the site and were relatively unproductive. The main operation, expanded inward from along an eroding bluff edge, accounted for roughly 65% of the total area exposed and was dug to depths ranging from a few centimeters to nearly 4 meters (in one restricted area). A narrow step-trench down the bluff face at one spot penetrated the underlying silts to over 10 meters below the top surface; it was dug primarily for geological reasons.

The occupation, densest along the bluff on the east side of the hilltop, was represented by one thin layer, in general just below the present humus. It was at, or close to, the surface near the northern edge and usually about 20 cm. below elsewhere. Its effective base was nowhere more than about 30-40 cm. below the surface, although some of the smallest artifacts and other debris as well as a number of pits occurred at various depths down to about 2 meters. It is entirely possible that cultivation and some erosion have disturbed the upper centimeters of the original deposit, while slumping and erosion along the bluff have certainly removed an unknown amount of the original site.

Remains of the settlement consisted of a widespread, chaotic scatter of assorted stream pebbles which not only were out of natural context and had obviously been carried up to the site but also were intermingled with some 30,000 artifacts and great quantities of friable and not too well preserved faunal debris. The stones were spread openly in some places and irregularly concentrated into a sort of closely set pseudo-pavement in others (Pl. 22A). Aside from the distribution of introduced pebbles and a number of rock-littered pits, some with traces of fire, there were no vestiges of any discernible structure or other formal architecture. Further signs of fires scattered here and there in the apparently unplanned expanse of stones were evident in small quantities of charcoal and in numerous fire-cracked and discolored rocks and bones. This site may represent only an intermittent or seasonal aspect of a horizon which also displays indications of perhaps more permanent settlements (see p. 158).

Extensive excavation at Karim Shahir furnished a relatively plentiful sampling of the local tool kit. The chipped flint industry—exclusive of the plentiful unworked debris, little-used pieces, and cores—was made up primarily of over 70% of notched blades and flakes; about 4% of very characteristic microlithic backed bladelets and fragments variously worked to points or ends retouched at an angle; 2-3% each of such types as delicately nibbled blades and flakes, end scrapers made mostly by use, microlithic end scrapers consisting of minute traces of use on flakes and blades, and crude side scrapers; roughly 1% or less each of poor burins (predominantly simple with a few angle and other types), fabricators and the smaller drill forms combined and including a few characteristic double-backed microlithic bladelets coming to an almost needle-like point. Further categories include several dozen crude rounded or discoid scrapers, a handful each of certain steep scrapers, pointed bladelets, rare blades and flakes with traces of sickle sheen, and a very few extremely dubious geometric microliths. Artifacts of obsidian were virtually absent.

Besides these smaller finished flint tools, the occupation layer yielded considerable flint-knapping debris and numerous cores and hammerstones. The more than 1,300 pyramidal pebble and other cores exhibit a skill, uniformity, and quantity not found in the cave sites or, indeed, in the early mounds so far. The majority are blade and bladelet cores, and, as one might expect, the industry as a whole reflects this characteristic too.

Nearly three dozen chipped celts (Pl. 22B), some with remnant patches of pebble cortex and some with traces of slightly ground and polished areas, came to light, as did rubbing stones, grooved stone abrading-pieces of schist, and used pebbles, as well as a few boulder mortar, quern, and pestle fragments (Pl. 23:1-7). A very few simple ground and polished stone pendants and beads (Pl. 23:9-14) and some plain marble bracelet and ring fragments (Pl. 23:15-16), simple bone tools, some bone beads, and small pierced shell beads and plaques also occurred. All these ornaments, but especially the bracelets and rings, are generally comparable with similar but much more varied classes at Jarmo.

Although pottery was entirely absent, two tiny lightly baked clay figurines (e.g. Pl. 23:8) bear definite resemblances to certain specific examples of one special group among those found at Jarmo. One of the figurines from Karim Shahir was found near the center of a circular area of red ocher in a pit.

Until Reed's faunal study is complete, only Barth's tentative field identifications are available.[6] Of these, potentially domesticable forms are sheep and/or goat, pig, and cattle. In addition there were deer, gazelle, wolf, marten, fox, and a canine, as well as small undetermined mammals, birds, and much turtle. Among the considerable quantites of snail shells identified by Bequaert, *Helix salomonica* predominates.

Helbaek's study of the Karim Shahir botanical evidence is not yet complete. Ten samples of charcoal were sent to Barghoorn. Seven of these were of *Selkova*(?), a tree of the *Ulmaceae* closely related to elm, two of tamarisk, and one was of the mesquite-like legume *Prosopis*. Only samples from what we considered "reliable" findspots were submitted to Barghoorn, but any sample of a bit of charcoal from so shallow a site as Karim Shahir is somewhat suspect. It is interesting that *Selkova*(?) did not appear in either the Jarmo

---

[6] The reason for the incompleteness of the study of the Karim Shahir animal bones is as follows. Upon our return from Iraq in 1948, we succeeded in soliciting the kindhearted interest of Professor Bryan Patterson of the Chicago Natural History Museum (now of the Museum of Comparative Zoölogy, Harvard University), although Patterson's own specialization is vertebrate paleontology. The collection was transferred to the Chicago Natural History Museum for Patterson's attention as he found time available. On our way to the field in 1950, we were invited by Professor Richard Pittioni to send the bones to Professor J. W. Amschler of the Institut für Tierzucht of the University of Vienna. In correspondence, Patterson urged us to take advantage of Professor Amschler's great competence and interest. As a consequence, the 1948 collection was forwarded to Amschler from Chicago, and the 1950/51 collection (from Jarmo and Karim Shahir) was sent directly to Vienna from Iraq.

When Reed joined the staff in September of 1954, he visited Vienna and spent several days in conversations with Amschler and in going over the collections; Reed paid another visit to Vienna upon his return from the field in 1955. In 1956 came the unhappy news of Amschler's death. Through his efficient secretary, Fraülein Helly Kaluza, we arranged for the bones to be returned to Chicago. Unfortunately, the Karim Shahir bones were not part of the shipment, and the matter must rest until Reed can again visit Vienna. Reed feels certain that Barth's identifications are essentially correct en masse but has questioned his expression of proportions as given by Braidwood, 1952a.

or the Palegawra samplings and that Zohary (1950) notes it as being rare in Iraq today.

Noteworthy at Karim Shahir is the presence or absence of certain traits with very interesting implications for interpretation. First, there is the association of chipped celts, a limited number of querns, pestles, and rubbing stones, some ground and polished ornaments, rare clay figurines, and a significant proportion of domesticable animals. Next, one notes the absence of obsidian and pottery and the presence of a chipped flint industry that appears "archaic." This combination of the old with at least some of the new hints, we believe, at a position for Karim Shahir on the threshold of the transition.

The category of ground stone artifacts, both large and small, utilitarian and nonutilitarian, first makes a marked appearance in our area at Karim Shahir—as well as at M'lefaat and Zawi Chemi Shanidar. Here we appear to have the earliest positive evidence, for the hilly-flanks zone as now known, of a whole new technology, that of the preparation of stone tools and receptacles by grinding, pecking, and polishing. True, there were already hints of this new technology in the Palegawra cave (p. 58) and layer B of the Shanidar cave (Solecki, 1955, p. 410). The products of this technology, especially as they are large, coarse, and bulky, have certainly not received the attention due them from archeologists in the Near East; adequate techniques for their classification and study can hardly be said to have been devised, although such artifacts no doubt have much to tell us. At Karim Shahir, M'lefaat, and Zawi Chemi Shanidar we presumably see them at or very near their naissance at least in this portion of the hilly-flanks zone; we have no comparative material and cannot yet do much more than guess at their implications.

The situation is somewhat analogous as regards clay figurines, and here there is even less material to form a basis for speculation.

The Karim Shahir chipped flint industry seems less a part of the Jarmo tradition than an attenuated and possibly only seasonal continuation of some aspects of the presumably earlier Zarzian stone-working tradition found near by in caves, shelters, and perhaps even outdoors (see p. 57). Karim Shahir shows technical and typological change with greater specialization in some respects but deterioration in others. Thus, the normal-sized backed blades, the better-made burins and scrapers, and the various geometric microlithic forms known from Zarzian sites are essentially absent; but various microlithic backed bladelets and the double-backed needle-like bladelet drills have been developed with specialized shapes and details; and the rare, not always clear-cut, burins as well as the much more plentiful scrapers are in general very poorly made, the latter more often by wear than by any obvious retouch or preparation. Fabricators and smaller drills as well as notched and used flakes and blades are each significant items in both the Karim Shahir and Zarzian chipped flint industries, and to these one may add the grooved stone abrading-pieces of both sites. It is noteworthy, too, that this rather fully documented chipped flint industry at Karim Shahir bears a broad typological and morphological resemblance to the limited assemblages collected from soundings at Gird Chai and M'lefaat, situated in lower territory farther north, and to the material at Solecki's recently discovered open-air site of Zawi Chemi Shanidar (see p. 52).

From the point of view of our central problem—the understanding of the establishment of the settled village-farming community—Karim Shahir is just as important as Jarmo. In fact, the phase which Karim Shahir represents—combining typological survival and degeneration with a first few strikingly new elements—is probably the more important, and it is unfortunate that the bases for interpretation are relatively restricted. With the materials of the general aspect of those from Karim Shahir, M'lefaat, and Zawi Chemi Shanidar, we come face to face with the difficulties of specifying—on artifactual grounds alone—any activities within an era of incipient cultivation (see pp. 5, 181-83).

Gird Chai

The crown of the mound, in full view of the Zab, was tested by five small trenches, plus a narrow cut down the bluff facing the river. The total area exposed was approximately 45 square meters, to an average depth of about a meter. Because of the appearance of intrusive pits in most of the trenches and fairly recent wheel-made pottery and tobacco-pipe fragments in all of the operations, the site was abandoned after five and a half days. Part of one trench was taken down to sterile soil at 1.35 m., to which point late potsherds were present. We encountered no floor or feature which we thought could be assigned to the original site of the blade-tool and microlithic industry. Larger pit structures, such as the probable pit-house at M'lefaat (see p. 51), may or may not have existed on the site; certainly no outlines were apparent in our clearances. The later intrusive pits were not all put down at once and showed clusters of interpenetrating circles.

The flint industry of Gird Chai appears to be very close to those of Karim Shahir and M'lefaat.[7] Pyramidal bladelet cores appeared in quantity. Microlithic backed bladelets are pointed at one end and obliquely truncated at the other. Some simple bladelets are notched, and all tend to show varying degrees of use and/or retouch. Since the main source of material seems to have been small flint pebbles, even the normal flakes are small (and were used without further preparation after having been struck off the core). Only three burins appeared, two being on bladelet core fragments. There were only eight pieces of obsidian from the test and five from the surface.

Strangely, although rubbing- and grinding-stone fragments, chipped celts, a "waisted" pebble, and possible pestle fragments appeared on the surface, there was little evidence in situ of ground stone. The chipped celts recall Karim Shahir rather than M'lefaat.

In view of the disturbed condition of the site, nothing trustworthy can be anticipated from the animal bones. The site would appear to have been thinly (probably a single layer) occupied by people whose tradition of blade-tool and microlith preparation was close to that of both Karim Shahir and M'lefaat. Since the site was on a ridge overlooking the Zab River, with rolling fields behind it, it is easy to understand its subsequent occupation in considerably later times.

Turkaka and Kowri Khan

These two small open-air sites, investigated during our survey in the Chemchemal plain in 1951, are represented by surface collections. As both sites are covered with loose sod and were searched only on one or two occasions, their complete range of artifacts, especially microliths, may not yet be in hand. Nevertheless, given the apparent absence of obsidian and pottery, the artifacts now known from these two sites make it clear that their flint industries cannot be simply equated with that of either Karim Shahir or Jarmo. They have one or two particular forms and some basic unspecialized artifacts in common with those sites, but they also contain certain other artifacts that are more characteristic of the Zarzian and, partly, even of the earlier Baradostian (see pp. 153-57).

At Turkaka the collection of over 1,600 artifacts, exclusive of unworked debris, comprises very rare backed bladelets, which may turn up in greater numbers in careful excavation; a number of neatly made end, thumbnail, and discoid scrapers in that descending order of frequency, along with some scrapers produced by wear on blades, flakes, and cores; rare but fairly well made steep scrapers and burins of the simple, angle, and especially polyhedral varieties; abundant microlithic and normal-sized notched blades and flakes, as well as others marked by less wear; and cores which are rarely truly amorphous but rather predominantly rough and irregular pyramidal pebbles with only occasional neat parallel bladelet scars. A striated and polished pebble also was found.

Most of these types, and especially the careful shaping and quality of work on certain scrapers and burins, are characteristic of the Zarzian industry. This quality and the special scraper and burin forms are missing, so far, in the chipped stone from Karim Shahir, M'lefaat, and Gird Chai. Notched and used pieces are common to either tradition. On the

---

[7]The traces of architectural activity and the larger ground stone objects at M'lefaat most clearly differentiate it from Karim Shahir, as we now know the sites.

other hand, Turkaka lacks the normal-sized backed blades and geometric microliths such as are found in the Zarzian. However, its microlithic backed bladelets suggest either Karim Shahir or some phase of the Zarzian tradition. Various scrapers formed by wear seem more at home in a Karim Shahir than a Zarzian context.

Subject to much more detailed investigation, the Turkaka assemblage suggests either a phase between the Zarzian and that of Karim Shahir, M'lefaat, and Gird Chai or else a simplified open-air and, perhaps, only seasonal version of some aspect of the Zarzian tradition as found in Zarzi, Shanidar, Palegawra, and the lesser caves and shelters described below. The only bases of comparison at present are morphological and typological, and these will be quite unsatisfactory until Turkaka is known in something approaching its entirety so that its tool kit can be compared in detail and quantity with the other tool kits.

From Kowri Khan there was an admittedly small yield of less than 500 worked or used pieces of flint. It contained rare neat end scrapers and a significant quantity of excellent clear-cut burins merging typologically, via straight and twisted polyhedral burins, into a series of steep scrapers. A good number of both normal-sized and microlithic irregular end scrapers formed by use turned up along with a few poor irregular discoid and thumbnail scrapers. Mixed with relatively coarse, irregular, pyramidal pebble cores were a few with bladelet scars. Some unworked microlithic bladelets also occurred. The microlithic cores and bladelets hint at possibly greater numbers in existence at the site, but so far no especially elaborate microlithic bladelets have been found there. Missing as yet also are neatly retouched discoid and thumbnail scrapers, backed blades, and geometric microliths.

This industry, with diminutive neat end scrapers, steep scrapers, polyhedral burins, and some microlithic bladelets and bladelet cores, suggests a portion of the Zarzian tool kit. In addition there is an overall lack of quality in workmanship, displayed especially in the commoner end scrapers and rare thumbnail and discoid scrapers, formed largely through use, that might suggest the Karim Shahir range. On the other hand, the strong emphasis on polyhedral burins brings to mind the even earlier Baradostian industry (see p. 154). Another interesting factor is that, in contrast to the predominantly buff soil of the locality, a grainy gray crust adheres to some artifacts. This, with the slightly rolled appearance of a few other tools, suggests that there may be a near-by source of this industry *in situ* under circumstances resembling the stream-bed occupation at the much earlier site of Barda Balka (see pp. 61-62).

In the face of undoubtedly incomplete surface collections it is hard to decide convincingly just where Turkaka and Kowri Khan belong. The two assemblages correlate roughly with each other typologically, although that of Kowri Khan seems cruder and poorer on the whole and as yet lacks specific microlithic tools. Burins, especially the straight and twisted polyhedral varieties, are present on both sites; steep scrapers and well made end scrapers as well as plentiful end-scrapers-by-use appear at both; notched and slightly used flakes and blades are plentiful, and pyramidal pebble cores are the rule at both places. Each assemblage seems to lack normal-sized backed blades and geometric microliths. Only in the presence of definite discoid and thumbnail scrapers and of rare backed bladelets at Turkaka alone do the two sites so far seem to diverge from one another. Nevertheless, if we assume that the two are essentially similar, are they to be considered literally as representing an outdoor and perhaps somewhat simplified seasonal version of the Zarzian tradition in caves? Are they one special variant of several to be viewed as on a single plane displaying roughly contemporaneous cave and open-air sites? Or do they constitute a separate stage in a sequence of development between Zarzi and Karim Shahir? Our only means of dating so far is by techno-typological and morphological comparison, and, on that basis, the weight of evidence seems to favor aligning them with the generalized Zarzian range. More knowledge of the stone industry at these two sites and of that in the caves and additional open sites is needed before we can arrive at a reliable picture of the situation at this juncture in prehistory. One always hopes, too, for a multiplicity of evidence from faunal, geological, and direct stratigraphic data and perhaps from radioactive-carbon samples.

Our materials from M'lefaat backward, especially those from Turkaka and Kowri Khan, may hint at a way of life (of still uncertain duration) in which both caves and open-air sites were utilized for relatively extended habitation. Obviously, such alternating settlements may have been season bound, and the tool kits for good-weather activities may not have been the same as those for poor-weather activities. The popular belief that "men of the old stone age" always lived in caves and were, in fact, "cave-dwellers" undoubtedly stems from the classic prehistoric region of western Europe, although most professional prehistorians have realized since the early 1930's that in vast areas of central and eastern Europe late Pleistocene man dwelt in open-air sites and have also realized why Childe (1950) might justifiably entitle an article "Cave Men's Buildings." The conventional assumption of a rather abrupt change in southwestern Asia from cave-dwelling to the use of open sites has tended to remain popular, the change-over being assumed to have been more or less coincident with the transition to food-production. Prehistorians concerned with the archeology of late Pleistocene times have tended to seek their sites in caves or, for earlier Pleistocene times, in terms of transient sites within the broad geological contexts of natural features in the open air. Archeologists specializing in the latest (post-Pleistocene) prehistoric or earliest historic ranges of time have thought only of permanent open sites.

At this point in our present sequence we appear to witness, in Iraqi Kurdistan at least, traces of possibly alternating aspects of the same general industrial tradition, coming from both caves and open sites. The evidence, so far, is too incomplete and too inconclusive, from both the caves and the open sites, to allow us to arrange it in a clear and convincing sequence. We do not feel bound, however, to consider all materials from cave deposits earlier than all materials from open sites, in any possible chronological arrangement.

Our central problem forces our attention on a middle ground which lies between the conventional foci of attention of the older scholarly traditions in prehistoric as against historic archeology, conventionally contrasted as concerned with cave-dwellers versus village- or town-dwellers. But a tendency toward more persistent open-site living may have begun well back in the Pleistocene (in some areas we know it did), or, more likely, some open-site living may always have obtained. A marked trend might be expected to have set in as cultures began to swing free of prime dependence on natural subsistence and as they developed specific artifactual means of producing their subsistence. The advance of this trend entailed changes and responsibilities which the settlement patterns and catalogues of artifacts reflected directly; by Jarmo times no doubt there was year-around fixed settlement in one place. But at what point in the archeological record do we first see the trend toward fixed settlement, as distinguished from transient open-site living by food-collectors such as undoubtedly always obtained? Our evidence hardly allows us to be specific. The important thing now is that we face the issue squarely rather than hide it under the conventional easy contrast of cave-dweller versus village-dweller. Fortunately, the evidence for facing the issue squarely is also beginning to appear at the other end of the hilly-flanks zone as Natufian open-air occurrences at Jericho, Mallahah, and Nahal Oren become available.

Ishkaft Palegawra

Our next industrial horizon has been found to be fairly widespread in the caves and shelters of this region and is apparently the last strictly stone-age manifestation of any significance in them. Whether it was completely antecedent to the archeological horizon represented by some of the aforementioned open-air sites is a matter to which we have just alluded and to which we shall return. It is a distinct stone-working tradition and may properly be called "Zarzian" after the cave site where an earlier and a later superposed special microlithic phase of this generally diminutive flint industry were first excavated (Garrod, 1930, pp. 1-23; 1957, pp. 444-46). It is characterized throughout at Zarzi by various backed blades and bladelets, very rare single-shouldered points, many notched blades, and various neat burins, end and round scrapers, both normal and microlithic in size, and in the later phase by the addition of geometric microliths, notably triangles and a few lunates.

At the shelter of Palegawra, overlooking the Bazian valley from the south slopes of the Baranand Dagh, Howe excavated materials including an excellent sample of what is probably an exclusively late Zarzian phase (Braidwood, 1951c, pp. 13-14; 1952a, pp. 23-24, 26-27) strongly marked by geometric microliths (Pl. 24, 2d row). During the two campaigns of 1951 and 1955 virtually all the deposit inside the small chamber was removed but that of the entrance platform and beyond was left intact. An area of about 30 square meters was dug to bedrock at a depth ranging from a few centimeters at the walls to nearly 2 meters in one place near the threshold. The work revealed two major bodies of archeological material concentrated roughly into two separate superposed occupation horizons. These had become considerably intermingled because of disturbances of cave-living and movement of artifacts through a somewhat loosely packed and rocky deposit.

The upper and later of the two major horizons comprised largely Uruk, Ninevite V, and later materials, including fragments of an Islamic glazed bowl. They appeared to be concentrated at a depth of 0-40 cm. but were found below this in places. Fragile, fragmentary, and much disturbed burials and scattered human bones were encountered between 15 and about 60 cm. These may be either contemporary with the bulk of the older pottery of the upper horizon or more likely of a more recent date. Save for somewhat deeper ashy pits, which in some cases cut through the burials, this layer may perhaps be considered as having a maximum thickness of 60 cm.

Tending to be localized about the base of the upper layer were a few distinctive stone artifacts that suggest items already noted from Karim Shahir, Jarmo, and other sites in their ranges. Such were a small number of delicate microlithic double-backed bladelet drills, certain obsidian artifacts, ground and polished marble bracelet fragments, hammerstones, fragmentary boulder mortars, and a fragmentary chipped and polished celt.

The lower and earlier major horizon was at a depth of 60-130 cm. and yielded the great bulk of the Zarzian material, over 4,000 artifacts exclusive of debris. As at Zarzi itself and other known sites of this horizon, the flint industry at Palegawra was marked as a whole by important numbers of backed blades and microlithic bladelets (Pl. 24, top row), various end, round, and other scrapers (Pl. 24, 3d row), both large and small, by smaller numbers of coarse side scrapers, simple, angle, and polyhedral burins, various drills and fabricators, and by microburins and an assortment of microlithic geometric forms including triangles, trapezoids, rare lunates, and rarer rectangles. On some of the trapezoids the converging ends are markedly concave. Large numbers of notched and otherwise used blades and flakes were found. The pebble cores include clearly pyramidal blade- and flake-scarred varieties (Pl. 24, bottom row) as well as a good number of amorphous subspherical ones. Simple pointed bone tools, beads and pendants of shell, tooth, bone, or stone, and a grooved stone abrading-piece also occurred. A sizable chipped and polished celt (mentioned above) from a depth of 80-100 cm., a quern fragment from below 1.00 m., and scattered but definite traces of obsidian debris and distinctive implements suggest either disturbances or a very late phase of the Zarzian. But very occasional small plain or painted wheel-made sherds at these depths—obviously displaced from the upper layer—suggest disturbance throughout this horizon. However, the obsidian implements include a stubby backed blade, a thumbnail scraper, geometric microliths, microburins, and notched blades. These types begin to echo some of the relatively complex flint forms present at the same depths, although the majority of the obsidian counterparts were found at the top of or just above the main bulk of the Zarzian material.

Animal bones were well preserved in some quantity. According to a brief preliminary study by Reed they include:

1. An equid (probably *Equus hemionus*, the onager, most common of the ungulates)
2. Gazelle (*Gazella subgutterosa*)
3. Wild goat (*Capra hircus aegagrus*)

4. Probably wild sheep (Ovis orientalis)
5. Large bovid (probably Bos primigenius but possibly Bison)[8]
6. Red deer (Cervus elaphus)
7. Roe deer (Capreolus capreolus)
8. Pig (Sus scrofa attila?)
9. Wolf (Canis lupus)
10. Fox (Vulpes vulpes)
11. Medium-sized cat, very probably lynx
12. Hedgehog (unidentified but most probably Erinaceus europaeus)
13. Numerous unidentified small rodents
14. Numerous unidentified small birds
15. Tortoise (Testudo graeca)
16. Toad (probably Bufo viridis)
17. Unidentified fish

Berquaert has supplied identifications of fresh-water crab (Potamon potamios), fresh-water clam (Unio tigrides), and land snail (Helix salomonica). Reed considers it strange that, even though bones of cattle and sheep and/or goats were not very numerous at Palegawra, not a scrap of horn core was found. This may be due either to chance or to some human utilization of horns.

Helbaek has not yet studied the possible botanical samples from Palegawra, but Barghoorn identified fourteen charcoal samples. Eleven were of oak, one was of tamarisk (a large tree), one of poplar (very probably Populus euphratica), and one of a conifer (probably Juniperus). These seem to suggest a climate at the subhumid-semiarid borderline, probably not greatly different from that of the present.

The Zarzian occupation layer at Palegawra is a single unit and yielded a generous sample. Regardless of the various debatable pieces, this horizon is certainly late by virtue of the varied geometric forms which are distributed throughout its extent. Its chronological position with respect to other late Zarzian assemblages having geometric microliths is so far merely a matter of typological and morphological argument. The proliferation of geometric forms, some with exaggerated shapes, the presence of various somewhat crude scrapers marked by wear rather than retouch, and the increase in distinctly pyramidal blade cores over amorphous ones might indicate a later stage than that represented at the Zarzian sites where these traits have not been noted. At least they indicate a difference, and that in the direction of types found at Jarmo and Karim Shahir.

Ishkaft Barak, Ishkaft Hajiyah, Ishkaft Babkhal, and the Zarzian Horizon

Except at Palegawra, for the most part we found unsatisfactory traces of a generalized Zarzian horizon. These turned up in soundings at the shelters of Barak and Hajiyah, along the ridge of the Berat Dagh between Aqra and the Greater Zab (Braidwood et al., 1954, pp. 124-26, 130-31), and again at Babkhal, close to Havdian near Ruwanduz (ibid. pp. 127-28). At each site two or more trial trenches exposed totals of between 20 and 30 square meters and reached virgin soil or bedrock at depths usually ranging from a few centimeters to about 1.50 m.

At Barak portions of a Zarzian accumulation, comprising barely 100 implements, appeared to be partly in situ outside the chamber, but all ancient deposits except consolidated high-level wall remnants had somehow been removed from inside. At Hajiyah certainly the front of the chamber lacked any ancient deposit, and the Zarzian material of less than 200 worked pieces, exclusive of debris, was found only on the talus slope, where it proved

[8] Half again as large as a Hereford cow and much larger than a male American Bison bison; the Jarmo bovid (see p. 48) would seem to be much smaller than this earlier one from Palegawra.

to be greatly disturbed and mixed with later pottery. At Babkhal, an almost open shelter against a cliff base (see p. 30), inconclusive traces of generalized Zarzian, totaling about 250 worked pieces, lay in a thin and partly disturbed veneer of material near or at the surface over a Mousterian deposit (see below). A possible reason for the disturbed and cleared-out condition at these sites is noted on page 30.

Although these three samples are small and from disturbed sites, it is noteworthy that each for the most part lacks not only geometric microliths but also the usual backed blades and quantity of notched pieces. They are marked simply by various burins, scrapers, microlithic bladelet tools, and the usual cores. Thus, entirely on morphological grounds, they may represent a separate Zarzian phase, though this possibility needs the confirmation of better sampling and fuller stratigraphic relationships. Moreover, these three minor samples of a possible generalized Zarzian in caves and shelters resemble to a striking degree the collections from the open-air sites of Turkaka and Kowri Khan (see above).

With Solecki's ample sampling of the Zarzian of level B at the Shanidar cave (Solecki, 1955 and 1957) our catalogue of occurrences for this industry is complete. Underlying the Zarzian of Shanidar B, and evidently separated from it in time (see p. 154), is the Baradostian industry of level C (ibid.). This generalized upper paleolithic blade-tool industry has so far been found at this site only.

Ishkaft Babkhal, Ishkaft Spilik, and the Mousterian Horizon

We recorded technically rather advanced Mousterian deposits at Babkhal and Spilik (Braidwood et al., 1954, pp. 127-28; Braidwood, 1956b). Since this industrial horizon was already known from several other caves and shelters in Iraq and neighboring Iran, our soundings were merely confirmatory.

Our exposures were modest in size. At Babkhal, two test trenches opened up a total of about 25 square meters and penetrated to depths ranging from a few centimeters to a maximum of 1.40 m. The Mousterian horizon occupied the bulk of the deposit excavated to bedrock and underlay the shallow zone of Zarzian noted above. At Spilik, a hasty sounding 2.50 m. square did not reach bedrock but, below recent deposits, showed Mousterian occupation at a depth of 2 to 3 meters, below which we did not have time to explore.

At Babkhal, where the undisturbed portions of this horizon yielded some 150 artifacts, exclusive of debris, the industry was marked by triangular points on flakes and flake-blades ranging in size from medium to very small (Pl. 25, top row). Some points were elongated and narrowed to drill-like proportions. Numerous side scrapers (Pl. 25, middle row), a few burins, and various used flakes occurred. The flat and only moderately invasive retouch was delicate and often minute. The medium to small cores (Pl. 25, bottom row) were mainly discoid but included a few roughly spherical ones. Selected stream pebbles were probably the ultimate source of all these artifacts. Judging from the small, and only occasionally diagnostic, quantity of material extracted from Spilik, the same Mousterian horizon is represented there. Faunal remains, rare and badly weathered at Babkhal, were more plentiful and well preserved at Spilik, and there is hope of fuller data when studies are completed.

Although burins and flake-blades occur in these samplings, as at the type site, Hazar Merd (Garrod, 1930), and in Shanidar cave, layer D (Solecki, 1955 and 1957), there is at present no convincing evidence that the blade-tool tradition as such had made its appearance in Iraqi Kurdistan by this time.

Telegraph Pole 26/22 and Serandur

There exists the possibility of a generalized relatively crude Mousterian horizon, as yet chronologically and stratigraphically unfixed, in this area of foothills. Slim, largely techno-typological evidence, suggests that it is, perhaps, earlier than the technically more advanced Mousterian found in caves of the region and that it followed the industry of Barda Balka type discussed below. It is equally possible that this grosser open-air variant of Mousterian was contemporaneous with the cave Mousterian of the region noted above or else with the earlier materials of Barda Balka. Garrod originally noted two occurrences of rolled Mousterian implements associated with gravels near Kirkuk (Garrod, 1928, pp. 270-72; 1930, p. 13). In 1950 and 1954 we found two instances of mixed surface collections of flint which included coarse Mousterian types of artifacts. Neither site is favorable for isolating an early Mousterian horizon since both have admixtures of typologically later tools and some relatively fresh and little-weathered material, but each seems worth noting because of the definite association of coarse Mousterian types with gravel scatters to streams.

First, at telegraph pole 26/22 a typologically mixed assortment was collected from a flint- and gravel-littered surface. The Kirkuk-Sulimaniyah highway there emerges from gravel hills and descends via a constricted lateral wadi onto the broad main valley. Besides undiagnostic used flakes and fragments, some relatively fresh-looking material, coarse pyramidal cores, rare blades, and a handful of small end scrapers and steep scrapers on pyramidal cores, we found a number of weathered coarse discoid cores and large flake artifacts including a side scraper. These suggested an older, possibly Mousterian, type of workmanship. Although these forms might be equally at home in a Barda Balka type of industry, no pebble tools or hand axes were found here.

Second, at Serandur we found discoid cores and broad flakes of Mousterian types. These were well dispersed amid gravel litter on two spurs rising about 25-30 meters above the Bastura River bed. Both relatively fresh and more rolled examples occurred along with typologically later material such as neat pyramidal cores, end and rare rounded and steep scrapers; but the degree of weathering and rolling and the characteristic gross appearance of some of the large flakes and cores suggest the possibility that products of an early Mousterian industry had been lying about somewhere near and were dispersed into slope deposits of gravels on these low spurs.

Barda Balka, Cham Bazar, Eski Kelik

At Barda Balka in 1951, four of a number of meter-wide test trenches, exposed a total area of about 20 contiguous square meters in one place and revealed tools of a special food-gathering or typologically middle paleolithic industry in situ in certain late Pleistocene stream gravels (Wright and Howe, 1951; Wright, 1952). The artifacts obtained comprise hand axes, pebble tools, and flake tools (Pl. 26). This particular combination, as far as we know, is new for this quarter of the world. The nearest comparable material is in the Punjab in northwestern India (De Terra and Paterson, 1939, pp. 301-12; Movius, 1944, pp. 24-29) and in Tunisia (Gobert, 1950), but there are special problems connected with both of these occurrences (see pp. 150-52).

It was once customary to treat the core-biface or Abbevilleo-Acheulean tradition and the pebble-tool tradition—each with its attendant utilized flake tools—as separate and persisting habits in the preparation of chipped stone tools. There is strong evidence of such separation in certain great areas in earlier Pleistocene times, but there is increasing evidence that both traditions may also occur within one industry. The Barda Balka collection shows both traditions merged into one industry, which may tentatively be considered as middle paleolithic. It contains somewhat less than 5% of expertly made hand axes. These, on both large and small flint pebbles or flakes, display the various ovoid outlines, straight edges, and skillful flat bifacial flaking of generally Upper Acheulean type. In fact, certain very small hand axes and also a number of other specimens with flaking on alternate opposite faces suggest a late, possibly derivative, aspect of the tradition.

Intimately associated with the bifacial tools, however, is a significant proportion (ca. 10% of the total) of simple pebble tools. Virtually all on sizable limestone stream cobbles, these are in nearly every case flaked from only one face, either across the truncated half or around some or most of the circumference of the pebble, forming a class of tools usually known as choppers. Some specimens, more pointed but still flaked from only one face, seem transitional to hand axes in shape. On the very few bifacially flaked pebble tools the flaking is so little developed on the second face that they may probably be retained in the chopper class and not considered true chopping-tools. Two coarsely flaked stone spheroids of the size of oranges were, alas, found in slope-wash deposits, but they are almost certainly derived from the same gravel bed that yielded the rest of the material.

In addition to hand axes and pebble tools, the bulk of the industry (over 70% of the total number of implements, exclusive of debris and little-used pieces) consists of various sorts of medium and small irregular rough flint flakes and fragments. Of flakes with discernible striking platforms, most (75%) have plain platforms, either normal angle (45%) or wide angle (30%), and only about 25% are faceted. Worked pieces have been slightly or heavily used at various points and only in some cases perhaps deliberately retouched. Difficult to classify into clear-cut categories, the flake tools appear to be various forms of simple and technically poor scrapers. They, too, are intimately associated with the hand axes and pebble tools. They were produced from large, medium, or tiny cores which constitute about 10% of the total tool kit considered as an industry here. Made on pebbles or pebble halves, most of these cores (ca. 60%) have flake scars predominantly from one direction, more rarely (ca. 30%) radially disposed as in truly discoid cores, and the remainder are amorphous polyhedral forms.

The likelihood that several periods marked by different industries are here confused in a river bank is remote. The close-packed and intermingled occurrences of all artifacts and bones in these stream gravels suggest contemporaneity and little disburbance, since stream action theoretially tends to disperse rather than to concentrate. There are only very rare and minor cases of multiple patination, all on flake tools. Both hand axes and flake tools display the same order of freshness and patination. The more waterworn appearance of many of the limestone pebble tools was conclusively shown, by close observation of the position of individual specimens in situ, to be due to the relatively weaker, more soluble, composition of the limestone. Upturned faces, exposed to ground-water and other action, appeared leached and worn, while downturned, relatively protected, faces were encrusted and preserved fresh. Thus all three categories—flint hand axes, limestone pebble tools, and irregular small flint-flake artifacts—are considered as contemporaneous at this site.

Traces of fauna, completely intermingled with the tools, disclosed the presence of elephant, rhinoceros, ox, sheep or goat, and an equid which was possibly an onager (letter of July 16, 1952, to Braidwood from Dr. F. C. Fraser of the British Museum of Natural History) as well as snail (identified as Helix salomonica by Mr. Wilkins of the same museum).

Scattered surface finds suggest that this horizon is extensive. At Cham Bazar, somewhat downstream from Barda Balka, the same sorts of hand axes, cores, and flake tools, but as yet no pebble tools, were found weathering out from a remnant hummock of the same general gravel formation. On a slope immediately adjacent to Jarmo, located in the same valley and just east of these two points, two similar hand axes were collected from a surface scatter of the same gravel system weathering out from under silts. In another drainage area, farther north at Eski Kelik on the right bank of the Greater Zab, a single isolated Acheulean type hand ax was found not far from massive deposits of gravel.

As represented primarily at Barda Balka, then, this special middle paleolithic horizon is unique in this quarter of the Near East so far. It provides the first excavated occurrence of pebble tools in western Asia and a new and combined variant of the pebble-tool, core-biface, and flake traditions. It may eventually be found to be more widespread in southwestern Asia.

VI

SPECIALIZED CERAMIC STUDIES AND RADIOACTIVE-CARBON TECHNIQUES

Frederick R. Matson

THE CERAMIC YIELD OF THE 1954/55 SEASON

Qalat Jarmo

The Jarmo sherd yard was the pleasantest kind of field laboratory, for the relationship of men to clay, straw, dung, storms, crops, heat, cold, donkeys, and sheep was implicit, and ancient sherds in this setting challenged one to interpret fairly their scant evidence of the ways of local men over eight thousand years ago.

The pottery found at Jarmo presents several peculiar problems. It occurred in concentrated areas in the uppermost 2 meters of the occupational debris, and the wares of best quality are the earliest; the poorest pottery is in general the latest. The degree of weathering observed in the soil is reflected by the condition of the potsherds; the surface paint, for example, has almost entirely disappeared from the later wares. There are similarities between the pottery types found at Jarmo and those from basal Hassunah and Matarrah, but the local ceramic industry had its own characteristic qualities.

Almost 17 cubic feet of sherds were excavated during the 1954/55 season in the upper 2.50 m. of the deposits. Most of them came from square-groups (see Fig. 6) G-L 5-9 and G-L 10-14 (ca. 5 cu. ft. from each), contiguous areas between the wadi and operations I and II of the earlier seasons, which likewise yielded abundant pottery. Square-group V-Y 15-19, on the eastern slope of the mound, was a third productive area, yielding almost 2 cubic feet of sherds.

The greatest concentration of rims, lugs, bases and, carinated body sherds varied in depth in these three areas. In G-L 5-9 the diagnostic sherds were most abundant in levels 3-4 (100-200 cm.); in G-L 10-14 they occurred in levels 2-4 (75-200 cm.); while in V-Y 15-19 the concentration was found from the surface through level 2 (0-100 cm.). This variation in depth has interesting implications in the possible interpretation of the settlement pattern—longer occupation on the highest part of the site with the resulting accumulation of soil, or more rapid erosion of the slope.

All the pottery fragments were taken to the sherd yard each day and piled according to square and level. They were cleaned lightly, sorted according to texture and degree of firing, counted, and grouped for restoration of individual vessels when possible. All rims, bases, interesting body pieces, restorable units, special shapes, and sherds showing details of manufacturing techniques were taken back to camp, where they were further cleaned, examined with care, measured for diameter of rim and base etc., and drawn in profile. A generous sample of the several shapes and decorative details was selected by the Directorate General of Antiquities to supplement the collections from the previous Jarmo field seasons that are deposited in the Iraq Museum in Baghdad.

An approximate correlation of changes in pottery types and quality with the levels in the excavations can be seen, but until detailed studies have been made of both the sherds and the relationship of the levels in the several squares, only trends can be suggested. The following tabular summary refers to G-L 5-9 and G-L 10-14, where sherds were abundant.

Level	Trends
Surface through 1 (0-75 cm.)	Coarse chaff-tempered thick ware was dominant. It was very friable and usually was removed from the ground in small pieces.
2 (75-100 cm.)	Larger and less friable sherds, 5 x 5 to 10 x 10 cm. in size, were common. This ware was typically 10-12 mm. thick. Many fragments were from storage jars. Thinner specialized shapes began to appear.
3 (100-150 cm.)	Larger pieces with less weathered surfaces were abundant. Many sherds had a lime deposit that gave a glossy-appearing surface. Carinated bowls and cups and nose lugs of mugs were common. Ceramically this was the most interesting level at the site.
4 (150-200 cm.)	Many base sherds were found. They probably indicate the level at which the storage jars were buried in the soil or the ground level on which they stood.
5 (200-250 cm.)	A scanty scattering of small sherds occurred. Probably there was no extensive use of pottery at this level in the areas that were excavated in 1955.

The types of pottery characteristic of these upper levels may be listed according to approximate frequency of occurrence as follows:

1. Storage jars up to about 60 cm. in diameter. They tend to be globular with flat bases. It was obvious that the potters built up the walls around a flat basal slab. The lack of restorable jars such as those from basal Hassunah and Matarrah must certainly be kept in mind when we attempt to understand the uses of the Jarmo pottery. The friability or fragility of the thick ware with porous fine-textured body, susceptible to frost action and lime penetration, as opposed to the more durable storage jars made of the clay on the Mesopotamian plain is an important factor. It would appear that clay storage jars were less essential at Jarmo than at some of the more extensively developed early agricultural villages, perhaps because the greater rainfall made it more difficult to store the grain successfully in the ground.

2. Carinated deep cups ranging in diameter from 8 to 20 cm. with corresponding differences in wall thickness. Rim sherds of these cups were the most abundant of the special shapes at Jarmo, followed closely by the carinated shallow bowls (No. 3). Both of these shapes occur in basal Hassunah and Matarrah, but not so frequently as at Jarmo. These are natural shapes for potters to develop when they add a band of clay to form a vertical rim. It is not necessary to look for stone prototypes.

3. Carinated shallow bowls 20-40 cm. in diameter were characteristic of level 3 and occurred in level 2. Some of the sherds retain faint traces of red ocher surfacing. Lumps of red ocher were not uncommon at the site, but evidences of its use to decorate pottery were very scanty. The bowls are well made, and the surfaces are smoothly finished. There is evidence that the rim area was added as a separate strip at the carination.

4. Straight-walled mugs 10-20 cm. in diameter with slightly flaring rims and two or more nose lugs attached at the rim are unique at Jarmo. The long narrow vertical lugs have one hole, or occasionally two, drilled horizontally, and at first

glance suggest very simple faces with large eyes, as the term "nose lug" indicates. Over 50 whole and fragmentary nose lugs were found. It would be interesting to know why they have horizontally drilled perforations. They could have been for suspension but might have been "just for fancy," as the Pennsylvania Dutch would say. They do not suggest wooden or stone prototypes.

5. Less than 90 small sherds showed traces of red ocher on one or both of their surfaces when they were carefully examined. In many cases the term "fugitive red" might be appropriate. The soft friable nature of the fired clay and the apparent lack of burnishing in many cases, together with the eroding effects of ground water, frost action, and lime deposition, are factors which could have accelerated the removal of most of the surface red. The several lumps of red ocher found in the excavations show that the use of red pigment on pottery (and possibly for the adornment of human bodies, cloth, skin, or wood) was more common than a casual study of the sherds might indicate. Within this group of sherds about a tenth show traces of simple decoration of bands and diagonal lines, design elements that are common in the Hassunan pottery. Sayid Fuad Safar examined the few painted sherds when he visited Jarmo and classed them as like the Hassunan archaic painted ware. Burnishing, often just in streaks, occurs on about a third of the sherds of this group, but it is possible that weathering has removed the traces of this finishing technique from many pieces which have rough surfaces. Tests of the local Jarmo clay have shown that it can be burnished.

   A small vessel was made in camp from the local Jarmo clay, and the surface of the dried piece was readily burnished with the aid of a small smooth polished stone found in the excavations. A high gloss was developed. It would therefore seem that burnishing as a technique could have been more extensively used by the Jarmo potters, had it suited their purposes. This interesting factor will be more fully considered in the final report on the Jarmo pottery. Microscopic study of thin sections of the painted and the burnished sherds now under way could possibly show that they are imported pieces, but superficially they appear to be local products.

   Most of the sherds showing traces of red ocher came from the first three levels, level 2 containing a few more than the others. Only six occurred in level 4 and one in level 5. This distribution suggests that the use of red ocher on pottery was not limited to one level at Jarmo.

6. Two small crudely modeled animal heads with punctate eyes appeared to be basal corners of small vessels and are perhaps analogous to, although better made than, an object from Matarrah (Braidwood et al., 1952, Pl. IX 6). A peculiar shape found at Hassunah (Lloyd and Safar, 1945, Pl. X 1, lower right-hand corner) that suggests an ocarina or a penny bank may be of the same type.

The Jarmo pottery and clay are being studied in more detail for correlation of the physical properties of the local clay with the wares produced in the ancient village. Some decorative traits can be related to those used at basal Hassunah, Matarrah, and Gird Ali Agha, but in many ways the Jarmo pottery forms a distinct ceramic unit, which, if one is willing to assume that thin painted and incised wares are evidence of ceramic progress, is less developed than the pottery at the first two sites just mentioned. This assumption may not be justified if the properties of the available clays limited the potter. The differences may only reflect local cultural needs rather than chronological ordering of the sites. If the sites are contemporaneous, however, it is strange that a few good Hassunan painted or incised sherds were not found at Jarmo, since they do occur at Tell Shimshara in the hill country northeast of Jarmo (Ingholt, 1957). Cultural contact with settlements on the plain, however, may have been limited, although Jarmo-type flints have been collected on the plain.

The shapes of the better-made Jarmo ceramic pieces are not related to those of the

Samarran and Hassunan wares but find their best parallels in the Matarrah fine simple wares. The occasional use of burnishing and the carinated shapes could suggest that at Jarmo one sees an early and provincial stage of the Halaf ceramic tradition.

Gird Ali Agha

The occupants of the site made only thick utility ware, to judge from the test excavations. The walls of most of the vessels were 15 mm. or more thick and were built up of strips of clay 3-5 cm. in width. Some surfaces are ridged with finger impressions that were left when the potter was shaping the plastic walls, but most of the surfaces are smooth. The clay contained a small amount of chaff; the vessels were fired to about 600°-700° C. for no more than an hour, since many of the sherds retain a black inner core and firing experiments have established this time-temperature range. Local clay was available on the Greater Zab terrace, and samples of it were collected for study.

After the sherds were washed and sorted at the site, only 900 rims, bases, carinated body pieces, and unusual fragments were taken from the sherd yard back to camp for further study. Over half of this first selection was later discarded, and the remainder was divided equally between the Directorate General of Antiquities and the Oriental Institute. The ware seems to be related to the simplest aspects of the Hassunan ceramic industry. Five sherds with molded eye and eyebrow fragments similar to those found at Matarrah and one sherd that may represent an animal were the only decorated pieces excavated. The analogous material from Hassunah is more sophisticated and has painted as well as molded facial decoration. Small conical knobs which appear on nine sherds from Ali Agha are similar to those found at Matarrah and also to those on the large jars from the early levels at Hassunah. A few knobs also occurred at Jarmo. Horizontal lugs added just below the rim occur on eleven sherds from Ali Agha. The only other items of special interest are two solid feet, perhaps of braziers; a few thin sherds, some with traces of red ocher surfacing; nine spindle whorls shaped from sherds; two tiny pieces that might be Hassunan painted ware; a crude flat-based cup about 7 cm. in diameter; and several pieces of daub with reed impressions.

The role of ceramics at Gird Ali Agha thus seems to have been utilitarian. It is odd that no incised sherds or fragments of "husking trays" were found and that only the slightest suggestion of painted ware appeared. Perhaps the site represents a temporary Hassunan encampment or poor village where the only clay vessels needed were cooking pots and possibly containers for grain storage and water.

Tell al-Khan

The pottery obtained during the sondage consisted of Hassunan painted, painted-and-incised, and incised wares, husking trays of several varieties, fine plain ware, and coarse plain ware. Half of the almost 900 sherds that were sent back to camp for examination were decorated, and most of these were saved. In the preliminary study of the plain wares, almost all body sherds and some other pieces, which together constituted four-fifths of the plain wares, were discarded to reduce the bulk of materials.

The painted and incised designs and the vessel shapes are being analyzed and compared with the similar materials from Matarrah, Hassunah, Samarra, and Baghuz. Sherd and clay collections made at these sites during the 1954/55 season, as well as the published reports, will be used in this study. The major sherd collections from the original excavations have been studied in the several museums in which they are deposited.

There are many problems related to the manufacture, decoration, and use of Hassunan pottery in its manifestations at several sites that the sherd collections and the site reports will help clarify. For example, the relation of incised and painted designs and shapes, the degree of firing of the several ceramic styles, the methods of forming and finishing the vessels, the presence of trade wares, and the function of these several types of pottery within the culture at this stage of man's technological and social development are worthy of further examination.

POTTERY THIN SECTIONS

Slices 0.03 mm. thick can be prepared from sherds for microscopic study of their mineral content in the same way that thin sections are made from rocks and minerals. Light can pass through many of the minerals in a thin section when it is placed on the stage of a microscope, making it possible to identify the nature and shape of the individual mineral grains and rock fragments that are included in the clay matrix of the pottery. Thus a trained ceramic petrographer can study and describe the characteristic mineral inclusions in the clay and can learn something about its probable geological or geographical origin. Some of the specific problems the archeological analyst has in mind are:

1. Was more than one clay used for pottery production at the site at the same time or in different periods? A knowledge of the local clays available and some understanding of the geology of the area will help in the study. The pottery of the Amuq, or the Plain of Antioch, in south-central Turkey, produced in a mountain-ringed plain, was fashioned from several different clays depending upon the ware and the period of manufacture.
2. Should some wares be considered as imported to the site on the basis of the mineralogical differences found in the thin sections and the differences in the physical appearance (shape, decoration, texture, etc.) of the sherds? It is at times possible to identify foreign wares in this way even though the basic shapes and decoration would be approximately at home in the local milieu.
3. Was the clay purified before it was used so that it would be less sandy?
4. Were the surfaces of the vessels worked, burnished, slipped, etc.? The orientation of the elongated mineral grains and platelets near the surface and the detailed microscopic appearance of the surface will serve as clues in such a study.

   The degree of firing of pottery can sometimes be judged by changes in the minerals in the thin sections, and the secondary inclusion of lime in the pottery during burial in the soil can be observed.

An extensive microscopic study is under way of sherds from Jarmo and the associated sites, and even in its initial stages interesting data are forthcoming. For example, the friable clay of the Jarmo pottery is exceptionally free of coarser mineral particles and contains fine bits of quartz, calcite, biotite, muscovite, flint, quartzite, feldspar, ocher, and plant fibers. A detailed description of this mineralogical texture will define the characteristics of the Jarmo clay. The thin sections show that sherds from Hassunah contain much coarser mineral inclusions and a different pattern of minerals; the Arpachiyah sherds are distinct in section, containing lumps of very pure clay; the Banahilk sherds are of clay of a different geological origin, and the grain orientations show that the surfaces of the vessels were carefully worked. This very time-consuming study includes analyses of sherds from most of the early ceramic horizons in Iraq and also microscopic examination of the raw clays that were collected at the many sites that were visited.

CLAY AND SOIL STUDIES

The work of the potters cannot be fully appreciated unless one is familiar with the problems they faced in collecting, purifying, working, and firing the clays that they used. Much can be learned from microscopic study, but the actual testing of the clays available at the sites is essential. For example, it has been shown through actual trial that the Jarmo clay can be used to produce well burnished pottery, yet this technique was quite unimportant at Jarmo. The cultural implications are obvious. Clays that shrink and crack easily as the vessels dry pose problems; other clays are too sticky or too mealy, and many, I find, can be worked very well without the inclusion of fine straw or chaff that is quite common in early pottery. A series of firing tests of each clay being studied will show the possible range of colors that may be developed with various rates of firing to increasingly high temperatures. The fuels used also pose problems related to color development, the gray, dark brown, and black surfaces often being caused by smoky fires. These problems have been discussed in detail elsewhere (Matson, 1955; Shepard, 1956).

A technically related problem is that of the nature of special soils that may be encountered in excavation—hearths, the fill of deserted rooms, dark ash layers that are sometimes rather extensive, reddish areas, etc. A geomorphologist is best fitted to study soil deposits, but a field study by a ceramic technologist with a simple microscope, sieves, water, and acid can help answer some of the questions. A series of Jarmo soils was subjected to such study in the field, and samples were brought home for more complete investigation.

Sherds and other fired-clay fragments often contain permanent impressions of seeds, chaff, etc. that are of much interest to botanists, and Helbaek has studied a great many such fragments. They have another use, however, in that they can give clues as to the presence of domesticated animals (Matson, 1956, p. 355). Much of the chaff seen in sherds is so fine that it hardly seems likely that it came from the threshing floor, but the very fine chaff left by dung beetles may be of the right order of size. Dung itself could have been mixed with a raw clay that was too mealy. I collected samples of chaff from dung beetles' leavings and from more direct sources. The effect of the digestive processes of ruminants and perhaps of other animals on the size of the chaff found in dung is a possible factor for explaining impressions of very fine straw in pottery.

RADIOCARBON DATING

One of the objectives of the Iraq-Jarmo Project in the 1954/55 season was the collection of charcoal and other charred materials from hearths and burned buildings in well defined strata in as many as possible of the excavated sites in the Near East (see p. 26). With luck, such samples can be used to determine the age of the level in which they were deposited if they are not too contaminated with modern organic materials and if they are large enough. Permissions to reopen trenches and other portions of excavations were most graciously granted by the responsible authorities in the several countries that we visited. In particular, Dr. Naji al-Asil facilitated the work in Iraq in a great many ways and we are most grateful to him.

The fifty-two samples obtained were carefully collected in clean glass jars and in polyethylene bags after they had been isolated as far as possible from modern organic contaminants such as surface layers of soil containing moss, lichens, rootlets, beetle wings, worm casts, mold, young scorpions, tobacco smoke, etc. Because of the great influence of modern carbon in the samples on the determinations obtained in the analyses, the laboratories in which the expensive time-consuming work is done have been experimenting to find better ways to eliminate this and other possible sources of error. A recent article by Barker (1958) best summarizes the present state of these studies.

Since most of the samples in our collection cannot be duplicated soon, and some never, I have felt it best not to submit most of them for analysis until the problems of contamination are better understood and controlled. Although this is an unpopular position to maintain when dates for the early levels at many of the Near Eastern sites are sorely needed, only the samples which are large enough for more than one analysis have been submitted to the overworked laboratories, where with great generosity the analysts have undertaken their dating. Each of the radiocarbon specimens is carefully sampled for microscopic study before it is sent to the laboratory, since a complete description of each specimen is essential if the radiocarbon determination obtained is to be interpreted responsibly. Knowledge of the stratum and soil conditions can be augmented by a microscopic study of each specimen. The Jarmo samples, for instance, contained abundant flecks of charcoal, limestone grains, shell fragments, siliceous skeletons of straw, rootlets, bark, ash, red and gray pellets of fired clay, and raw clay.

Recent papers (Braidwood, 1958a-b) summarize the data available at present, including three samples from Jarmo and one each from Hassunah, Matarrah, Mersin, and Byblos. Even though there might be some questions as to the complete removal of all contaminants, one can at least assume that the determinations obtained are minimum ones for the specimens. At present I favor the earlier cluster of determinations for Jarmo (at ca. 6750 ± 250 years B.C.), assuming that the later cluster (at ca. 4750 ± 300 years B.C.) reflects more modern organic material that resisted chemical removal. In areas where bitumen might conceivably be present, as in burned buildings of somewhat later date, such an assumption would be dangerous, for bitumen is rich in extremely old carbon.

The table given on page 70 lists the samples according to what are thought to be their cultural horizons as judged by the stratigraphic positions from which they were obtained. The radiocarbon determinations were made by Dr. Meyer Rubin of the U. S. Geological Survey.

RADIOACTIVE-CARBON SAMPLES OBTAINED DURING THE 1954/55 SEASON

Cultural Horizon	Site	
	Iraq	Lebanon, Syria, Turkey
Historical periods	Nimrud Nippur (Akkadian) Nuzi Warka (Ur III)	Tell Chagar Bazar Tell Brak
Protoliterate c phase	Ur Khafajah Sin Temple I Warka (Anu ziggurat staircase)	Tell al-Judaidah phase G
Uruk period	Tepe Gawra XII Grai Resh	
Ubaid period	Tell Uqair (shell) Tepe Gawra XVII Tepe Gawra XVIII Tepe Gawra XIX Warka XVIII	
Halaf period	Tell Arpachiyah 6 Tell Arpachiyah 8 Tell Arpachiyah 10 Gird Banahilk Tell Hassunah IX	Tell al-Halaf
Hassunah period	Tell Hassunah V (W-660, 7040 ± 200 B.P.) Tell Hassunah Ia (contaminated) Gird Ali Agha Tell Matarrah (W-623, 7570 ± 250 B.P.) Baghuz	Byblos A (W-627, 6550 ± 200 B.P.) Basal Mersin (W-617, 7950 ± 250 B.P.)
Pre-pottery stages	M'lefaat Jarmo (W-607, 9040 ± 250 B.P.) (W-657, 11,240 ± 300 B.P.) (W-665, 11,200 ± 200 B.P.) Palegawra (Zarzian)	Ksar Akil (Aurignacian) Yabrud (Acheuleo-Yabrudian) Ksar Akil (Levalloisio-Mousterian)

VII

CLIMATE AND PREHISTORIC MAN IN THE EASTERN MEDITERRANEAN

Herbert E. Wright, Jr.

ABSTRACT

In the Levant, geologic studies have been undertaken for the determination of the geologic age of prehistoric archeological deposits. This is accomplished either by correlation of a local paleoclimatic sequence based on geologic or paleontologic observations or by determination of the relationship of a deposit to the records of Pleistocene sea-level changes. Most of the well studied late Pleistocene archeological cave sites, like Mt. Carmel, Yabrud, and those of the Wadi Kharaitun, have little to offer in the way of reliable paleoclimatic indicators and cannot be related directly to marine features. Cave sites and open sites associated with marine terraces of the last interglacial time of high sea level along the coast of Lebanon provide the best archeological starting point. Those records of low sea-level stages during the last glaciation which have been submerged by the postglacial rise in sea level may be studied only in the subsurface. Pfannenstiel's analysis of the submerged coastal plain of Palestine falls into this category, but his correlation of the deposits with the glacial stages of Europe is dubious. Sand dunes deposited far on-shore during this time and not submerged by postglacial marine transgression contain buried soils and artifacts near Beirut, but the climatic significance and correlation of the deposits is problematical. Active alluviation of a coastal stream during the initial phases of a Levalloiso-Mousterian accumulation in the rock shelter of Ksar Akil, near Beirut, provides a good record of habitation during the last pluvial, but further definite climatic subdivision of the total deposit may not be justified.

For the post-Pleistocene, it is felt that the reports of climatic fluctuations for the whole Near East recorded by Butzer may not represent synchronous regional climatic trends over this broad area, although it is recognized that the climate may have changed from place to place and from time to time and may even have left a physiographic or paleontologic record.

Review of the background and current status of concepts of the climatic history of the Würm cold period in Europe leads to the conclusion that the subdivisions Würm I, II, and III should not be used in either Europe or the Mediterranean and that instead one should conceive of a single long period of increasing cold (with relatively minor fluctuations) and probably of increasing dryness, culminating about 20,000 years ago with maximum extent of the ice sheets. Climatological reconstructions for the Mediterranean should call for a single long pluvial period, but whether or not important fluctuations of regional extent (in either temperature or moisture) should be expected here as extrapolation from Europe is a matter of speculation.

The problem of late Pleistocene sea levels in the Mediterranean is examined with respect to the magnitude of the climatic fluctuations and thereby the volumes of the ice sheets in Europe at different times. Zeuner's claim for a phase of sea level higher than the present during the first interstadial of the Würm is considered unlikely on this basis, but of course it must stand or fall on the field evidence.

Inland from the Levant, the glaciation of the Taurus-Zagros Mountains gives the clearest record of late Pleistocene climate. Depression of the snow line of about 6,000 feet is postulated on the field evidence. In the foothills and lowlands there is some record of Pleistocene climates in the changing behavior of certain streams, particularly in the Chemchemal plain, where a site with Acheulian hand axes was buried by alluvium which was then deeply dissected before post-Pleistocene habitation of other prehistoric sites. On the flank of the limestone ridge above the Chemchemal plain are benches of slope breccia probably formed during an earlier Pleistocene pluvial period; similar breccia benches elsewhere in the foothills have caves containing Mousterian artifacts. In the deserts of Iraq and adjacent areas an extinct wadi system probably records a past pluvial climate, but dating or correlation with archeological stages is at the present impossible.

The evidence from depression of the Pleistocene snow line in the interior mountains implies that life zones, including woodland, were lowered into the lower foothills and piedmont above northern Mesopotamia and perhaps into the lowland itself. Return to warmer climates of the postglacial period was accompanied by the upward migration of life zones. According to radiocarbon dating, pollen chronology, and glacier activity in Europe, ice recession in the Alps started about 18,000 B.C. and accelerated after 8500 B.C. If ice recession and the climatic sequence were synchronous in the Zagros Mountains and the Alps, the cultural transition from food-gathering to food-producing in the Kurdish foothills (10,000 to 7000 B.C.) would fall at about the time of rapid climatic change. Cause and effect relationship between climatic change and the origin of agriculture must not—on the basis of present evidence—be inferred, however, because a wide range of ecological habitats suitable for domestication of animals and grains had probably long been available at lower elevations in the Mesopotamian lowland and piedmont through much of the preceding glacio-pluvial period.

INTRODUCTION

The climatic picture in the eastern Mediterranean during the time range of 10,000 to 7000 B.C.—a range which probably saw the inception of cultivation, domestication, and a modest agriculture in this region—has been inferred largely from the belief that the Pleistocene of the Mediterranean was marked by a relatively moist cool climate and that the postglacial period has experienced gradual warming and drying, perhaps with minor fluctuations. In fact, a case has been strongly argued for a close climatic control on the beginning of agriculture. The case was stated by Childe (1952, p. 25) in these words:

> In any case the conditions of incipient desiccation at which we have hinted would provide a stimulus towards the adoption of a food-producing economy. Enforced concentration by the banks of streams and shrinking springs would entail a more intensive search for means of nourishment. Animals and men would be herded together in oases that were becoming increasingly isolated by desert tracts. Such enforced juxtaposition might promote that sort of symbiosis between man and beast implied in the word "domestication."

For Europe, the glacial and postglacial climatic history has been carefully studied in recent years. Maps have been prepared showing the climatic and vegetation belts across Europe during the last glacial period (Poser, 1948; Büdel, 1951) and even eastward across Asia (Frenzel and Troll, 1952). The sequence of postglacial vegetational and climatic changes is recorded by the succession of plant fossils (especially pollen) in peat bogs, and the occurrence of a warm period about midway through postglacial time has been recognized for many years. The effects of climate on the development of prehistoric man in Europe have been explored (Howell, 1952), but the problems are concerned largely with the paleolithic of this region rather than with the later periods of incipient cultivation and the village-farming community. Agriculture was apparently introduced into Europe from the east, and by the time this event took place, perhaps just before 6,000 years ago, the major climatic fluctuation of the last glacial period had long since passed, although the minor fluctuation represented by the postglacial warm period ("climatic optimum") may have had some influence.

In the eastern Mediterranean the problem is different from that in Europe. We are concerned with an earlier time range for the beginning of food-production, perhaps 10,000 to 7000 B.C., a time so close to the end of the last glacial period (according to radiocarbon dating) that a more potent climatic control might have existed. On the other hand, the severity of climatic change may have been less in these lower latitudes. In northern Europe the reduction in temperature brought about the growth of the ice sheet. According to the usual climatological deduction, storm tracks which now bring moisture to central Europe were pushed south of the Alps, and the Mediterranean region, which is now marked by severe summer drought, experienced greater precipitation and lower temperature. The nature, intensity, and even the actual existence of these changes, however, must be based on geological evidence rather than climatological reasoning, and the geological record has not been well explored. Speculation about the effects of climatic change on the inception of agriculture is justified only after the fact of climatic change has been established.

Until the last few years, paleoclimatic information on the Near East has been confined largely to North Africa and the eastern Mediterranean coast and chiefly concerns the time range of the Pleistocene proper. Observations in the Syrian and Arabian deserts, in Mesopotamia, and in the Taurus-Zagros arc have been scattered. The recent excavations of very early village sites in the Zagros foothills of Iraq, however, make this area an especial objective of paleoclimatic studies, in so far as the problem of agricultural origins is concerned.

In the following discussion, the description of the paleoclimatic studies in the eastern Mediterranean for the time range of the beginning of agriculture is preceded by an examination of earlier (Pleistocene) climatic changes, which were presumably more pronounced. Comparison with European chronology involves a review of the basis for the European sequence. If any correlations can be made between Europe and the eastern Mediterranean for the Pleistocene, then some counterparts to the minor postglacial fluctuations in Europe might be anticipated more readily in the eastern Mediterranean record. The preliminary results of the geological investigations of the 1950/51 and 1954/55 expeditions of the Iraq-Jarmo Project are included where appropriate.

Attention may be called to the comprehensive survey of Pleistocene prehistory and chronology of the Levant by Howell (1959), who approaches the problem from the archeological side rather than the geological and is primarily concerned with the relations of the flint-tool industries from the most important sites in the Levant. As such, it complements the present paper, which deals more directly with the geological problems.

The writer is grateful to the Guggenheim Foundation, the Wenner-Gren Foundation for Anthropological Research, and the Oriental Institute of the University of Chicago for grants in support of the field investigations; to his colleagues of the Iraq-Jarmo Project staff, in particular Bruce Howe, for aid in the field and in the refinement of the manuscript of this paper; to Dr. Naji al-Asil, Sayid Fuad Safar, and others of the Iraq Government's Directorate General of Antiquities; and to the geologists H. M. Dunnington and R. V. Browne of the Iraq Petroleum Company and Dr. Louis Dubertret of Beirut.

THE PROBLEM

Climatic fluctuations in the eastern Mediterranean during the development of early man have been inferred from a variety of biological and geological evidences. For example, terraces around the Dead Sea and other inland lakes or basins imply greater rainfall or less evaporation. Alluvial terraces in the coastal streams of Lebanon and Palestine suggest periods of greater moisture. The fossil faunas recovered from the cave excavations have been interpreted as representing dry or wet periods. Layers of breccia and red clay in cave deposits may indicate periods of greater moisture.

The climatic causes for increased humidity in the Mediterranean area in the Pleistocene are based on valid climatological deduction, as summarized by Childe (1952, pp. 15-16):

> While Northern Europe was covered in ice as far as the Harz, and the Alps and the Pyrenees were capped with glaciers, the arctic high pressure deflected southward the Atlantic rainstorms. The cyclones that today traverse Central Europe then passed over the Mediterranean basin and the northern Sahara and continued, undrained by Lebanon, across Mesopotamia and Arabia to Persia and India. The parched Sahara enjoyed a regular rainfall, and farther east the showers were not only more bountiful than today but were distributed over the whole year, instead of being restricted to the winter. On the Iranian plateau the precipitation, although insufficient to feed extensive glaciers, filled the great hollows that are now salt deserts with shallow inland seas whose presence tempered the severity of the climate.

Childe's summary refers both to the actual occurrence of climatic fluctuations and an explanation for those which may be inferred from the evidence. More difficult, however, is the correlation of these changes with any detailed geological time scale, such as the time scale established for northern Europe on the basis of glacier fluctuations. On the Mediterranean coast the correlations may sometimes be made on the basis of the marine terraces, which themselves record the fall and rise of the sea that accompanied the advance and retreat of the continental glaciers. In the interior there is rarely such a connection, and the fluctuations inferred must be dated by other means.

THE LEVANT

Pleistocene

Mt. Carmel and the Climatic Trends of the Late Pleistocene

Paleoclimatic investigations in the eastern Mediterranean coastal regions have been confined largely to the Pleistocene because the climatic changes during this time were sufficiently pronounced to be recorded by relatively clear geologic and biologic phenomena. The status of climatic reconstruction for the coastal region was summarized by Zeuner (1945 and 1958a) in a synthesis directed ultimately toward archeologic correlation. It is significant that Zeuner's thesis of correlation rests principally on the relations at Mt. Carmel in Palestine, where Bate (Garrod and Bate, 1937, p. 141) had inferred fluctuations in climate from the stratigraphic alternation in abundance of gazelle (a grassland form) and deer (a woodland form) in the succession of prehistoric layers in the excavations and had described an abrupt break in the faunal succession at the second of the three humid phases inferred. Although Garrod and Bate (1937, p. 124; Garrod, 1956) felt correlation of the climatic fluctuations with the European sequence was premature, Zeuner (1958a, p. 231) placed the faunal break at the beginning of the Würm, as it is usually placed in Europe, and correlated the following two humid phases inferred from the deer maxima with Würm I and II.

The uncertainty of climatic cycles as inferred from the relative frequency of just two animal species has been pointed out by other zoölogists, especially when certain of the other faunal elements do not allow the same interpretation. The site is in hilly terrain in which both woodland and grassland exist near by; changing hunting habits of the cave inhabitants might result in correlated percentage changes of deer and gazelle. Microvertebrates that are not ordinarily dietary items (e.g. rodents) are more suitable for environmental studies.

A different interpretation of the Carmel sequence was offered by Vaufrey (1939a), who believed that the Würm climatic fluctuations in the Mediterranean were a matter not so much of temperature change as of a change from oceanic to continental climate. He pointed out that some of the large Würm mammals of western Europe persisted in Egypt and the Levant into historic times and reasoned that the pronounced climatic changes of the glaciated regions were not apparent in the east and the faunal changes retarded. In this view the late Pleistocene "faunal break" therefore was not necessarily synchronous in east and west, and Vaufrey preferred to correlate the entire Carmel sequence of industries (Upper Acheulean to Atlitian) with the two phases (moist followed by dry) of the Würm. Blanc had earlier (1938) inferred a single major shift from cold oceanic to cold continental climate for the last glacial period, using fossil evidence from the Italian coastal plain, and has recently (1957) reasserted this view. Recent workers in central Europe (Büdel, 1953) also describe an oceanic phase during glacial advance and a continental phase during glacial maximum, and Butzer (1957a) has applied the hypothesis anew to the Mediterranean. The humidity relations as well as the chronology of the late Pleistocene in Europe and the Mediterranean are complicated and are considered in detail below.

We deplore the lack of evidences at Mt. Carmel for climatic change independent of the deer-gazelle frequency curve. Although the sites overlook the sea, they have not been related to any coastal morphology that might record sea-level changes or climatic changes, and there has been no general climatic interpretation of the physical stratigraphy of the cave deposits. In a more recent analysis, Garrod (1951) has emphasized evidence for strong spring activity at one stage in the sequence. Perhaps new investigations in the area would reveal geomorphic features that could be related to the coastal sequence.

Interior Palestine

The criticisms of the first Mt. Carmel correlations have led to attempts to study other sites in the Levant which might lead to less controversial interpretations.

Neuville (1951) has described in some detail a number of caves of interior Palestine which he has excavated over the years and has offered climatic correlations based on the frequency of stone falls and stalagmites in the cave deposits. He uses the same climatic concept as do Vaufrey and Blanc and concludes that there was a single pluvial period (Würm) consisting of an oceanic phase marked by Levalloiso-Mousterian industry and a later continental phase characterized by blade-tool industries.

The Iraq-Jarmo group visited several of the Neuville sites on the Wadi Kharaitun, which leads down to the Dead Sea from near Bethlehem. The caves are well up on the rock walls of the wadi and bear little relation to the steep alluvial terraces along the valleys, although one site is actually located on a terrace. The wadies in this area descend so steeply to the Dead Sea that the terraces cannot be traced downstream, and in fact Neuville implies that the terraces are early Pleistocene and have been affected by tectonic movements as well as by climatically controlled changes in the level of the Dead Sea. It therefore appears that climatic correlations in Neuville's sites can find little aid in the local or regional geomorphology but must depend on the climatic interpretations of the rather nondescript cave stratigraphy. Such correlations are tenuous at best, and the most that can be hoped for is the broad identification of the last pluvial. Subdivisions of the last pluvial are not recognizable.

Ksar Akil

A coastal site which may prove to be the most useful in the Levant for climatic correlation as well as for the volume of its flint-tool yield is Ksar Akil, just north of Beirut on the coast of Lebanon (Ewing, 1947). Here is a site that can be related to the European chronology by means of the coastal geomorphology. The lower cultural deposits in the rock shelter (Upper Levalloiso-Mousterian) are interbedded with terrace sediments of a wadi that flows close by the base of the cliff. Similar terrace deposits on a wadi farther north along the coast are interbedded with dune sands that rest on the 18-meter last interglacial beach deposits and extend below present sea level. The dunes and therefore the interbedded fluvial deposits were formed during the marine regression of the last glaciation (Wright, 1951). The Upper Levalloiso-Mousterian and the following blade-tool industries at Ksar Akil are therefore correlated with the last glaciation. Three distinct stone layers or red clay beds (soils) in the sequence have suggested three pluvial maxima within the last glaciation, one near the end of the Levalloiso-Mousterian, a second in the Chatelperronian, and a third in the Gravettian, according to Ewing (1947). The faunal break, similar to that recorded at Mt. Carmel, occurred also here at the beginning of the Chatelperronian and serves as a check on correlations between these two sites and probably also the sites of

Neuville (1951) in interior Palestine. Acceptance of this suggested climatic interpretation at Ksar Akil, however, first must await evaluation of the relation of the intensity of soil formation in the rock shelter to intensity of occupance; the red layers may record times when the shelter was not inhabited and when soil could develop uncontaminated by cultural debris. Any nonoccupance might or might not be linked to climatic change. Studies of the flints, bones, and sediments of this site have not yet been fully published.

The relations at Ksar Akil prompted Garrod (1953) to reappraise the earlier Mt. Carmel correlations based on the deer-gazelle frequency curve, and as a result she reversed her earlier opinions about the relative ages of comparable upper paleolithic cultures in Europe and the Near East. The importance of Ksar Akil cannot be overestimated because of its long and relatively complete succession of archeological stages and its relatively distinct physical stratigraphy.

Strand Lines on the Coast of Lebanon

Of equal importance in the coastal region are the studies of the strand lines and associated cultures. A firm base for geologic and archeologic studies had been established by Wetzel and Haller (1945) in the Tripoli area of northern Lebanon. This work was concerned with the differentiation of Pleistocene marine terraces and associated sand dunes, river terraces, and slope deposits and with the correlation of the flint implements found therein. Similar studies have been made in the Beirut area by Dubertret (1946) and Fleisch (1956).

Among the critical sites in this area are those sea caves which mark the last high stand of sea level (+ 6 m.) of the last interglacial and which were apparently occupied soon after the marine regression commenced. Several such caves north of Beirut contain Mousterian and Levalloiso-Mousterian implements, suggesting that the cultures represented by these implements flourished here at the beginning of the time of the last glaciation (Fleisch, 1956). Younger caves or open stations occupied at lower levels as the sea regressed during the last glaciation have of course been submerged by the postglacial transgression, and the record of them is lost.

At the time of the last marine regression (last glaciation), the coastal area was subject to extensive sand-dune deposition, not only close to the shore of that time but extending inland to elevations not since submerged by the postglacial rise in sea level. Implements have been recovered from the dunes and intercalated red soils. The dune sands are now thoroughly cemented to *ramlah* (*kurkar*) and are well exposed in deep quarries south of Ras Beirut. In the dune deposits that were formed subsequent to the last high sea-level stage (last interglacial), two or possibly three buried soils can be found of which the upper one is by far the thickest and best developed. In fact it is overlain by only a few feet of uncemented sand, with the modern weak soil on top. The buried red soils were formed in the past by downward leaching of carbonate and by oxidation of the iron impurities of the calcareous sands. In the case of the major buried soil, the red zone extends downward in pipelike pendants 10-20 feet long. The buried red soils clearly represent times of stabilization of the dunes by vegetation, but the climatic significance of the stabilization is debatable. Although stabilization of dunes by vegetation in acid or semi-acid regions commonly implies a change to pluvial climatic conditions, in the case of coastal sand dunes such an inference is not safe. Dune activity may depend as well on sand supply, coastal configuration, etc.—factors which may have no direct climatic control. Thus at present south of Ras Beirut active dunes lie adjacent to a coastal area without dunes.

There is a further difficulty in climatic correlation of dune soils. Dune deposition is usually considered to result from marine regression, which brings about broad exposure of beach sands subject to wind deflation. Marine regression is correlated with times of glaciation. On the other hand, soil formation is generally correlated with pluvial climatic conditions and thereby also with times of glaciation. One or the other (or both) of these types of climatic correlation must be incorrect, or at least oversimplified.

It might be considered, however, that in the Beirut area the present dune activity is minor and local and that the major dunes of the past were related principally to sand supply and thus favored by a phase of lowering sea level and exposure of source areas. Conversely, during times of marine transgression the sand supply should be reduced, and the dunes might then be stabilized by the advance of the vegetation that had previously been restricted by blowing sand. The main buried red soil in the Beirut dunes might therefore reflect the transgressive sea of late glacial and postglacial times until the recent minor interruption and reactiviation of the dunes. Sea level reflects the extent of the ice sheets. For the last glaciation the maximum extend occurred at the time traditionally called Würm II or Main Würm (see pp. 78 ff.), culminating about 20,000 years ago. The main deglaciation and the main postglacial rise in sea level started about 11,000 years ago.

In the Beirut dune complex most of the flint tools were recovered from the main buried red soil. These include types ranging from Levalloiso-Mousterian to "Énéolithique" in Fleisch's terminology (1956). The concentration of implements and the mixing of types initially scattered throughout the sands may reflect a general lowering of the land surface by soil formation (solution of carbonate) after most of the flints had accumulated. On the other hand, some of the tools were certainly dropped on the soil surface at the time of soil formation and thus were added to those already in the sands. Internal stratigraphy of the main red soil is lacking, and a distinction between these two modes of emplacement of tools is therefore not possible. Just when the Levalloiso-Mousterian gave way to the blade-tool cultures therefore cannot be determined from the sand-dune sites.

The Lebanon coast, however, seems to hold the best hope for subdivisions of the last cold period, what with the combination of strand lines with their associated caves and open sites, the sand dunes and buried soils, and the site of Ksar Akil with its buried soils and rich content of flints and bones. All that can be stated at present with reasonable certainty, however, is that as the last cold period started and the sea withdrew, the Upper Levalloiso-Mousterian people took over freshly cut sea caves and the valley floor at Ksar Akil and dropped flints in the dune area south of Beirut. In time, perhaps during the first part of the last cold period, cultures which produced the Levalloiso-Mousterian industry were replaced by those which made blade tools; the latter persisted through most of the rest of the last cold period, including part of the marine transgressive phase which followed.

Coastal Plain of Palestine

Attempts to find other records of the events of the last glaciation in geologic context along the eastern Mediterranean coast prompted a study of the records of well-drilling from the coastal plain of Palestine by Pfannenstiel (1952). The sequence of interbedded marine, fluvial, and aeolian deposits to a depth of about 90 meters has been correlated with three substages of the Würm on the basis of comparison with artifact-bearing dunes found above sea level, comparison with Zeuner's correlation of the Mt. Carmel faunal sequence, and comparison with a rather similar subsurface record on the Italian coastal plain. The interpretation differs greatly from the earlier view of Picard (1943), who believed that the sediments represented practically all of the Pleistocene rather than just the Würm and were affected by crustal movements rather than by glacier-controlled fluctuations of sea level. Furthermore, Picard correlated the Pleistocene deposits of the Palestinian coastal plain with those of the Dead Sea area on a climatic basis.

Specifically, the Würm I horizon is placed by Pfannenstiel at -50 to -90 meters, the Würm II at -21 to -32 meters, and the Würm III at -2 to -7 meters, each presumably recording a pause in the general rise of sea level caused by temporary re-advance of the ice. This scheme resembles the sea-level assignments suggested by Zeuner (1958a, p. 133) for his Würm substages, but these assignments are reasonable only if the extensive Warthe glaciation corresponded to Würm I. And the present general agreement that the Warthe does not belong in the last glaciation (Woldstedt, 1954) leaves Würm I without much ice. The maximum extent of the ice (and therefore the maximum lowering of sea level) came late in the Würm II of Zeuner's classification (main Würm) rather than in Würm I. Furthermore, the Würm III sea level, if correlated with the Pomeranian moraines of northern Germany (Zeuner, 1958a, p. 133), must certainly have been lower than the -2 to -7 meters indicated by Pfannenstiel (or even the -30 m. indicated by Zeuner). For further discussion of sea-level changes see pages 84 ff.

Yabrud

One further recent investigation of importance in the Levant is that of Rust (1950) at the rock shelter of Yabrud, north of Damascus in Syria. The complexities of the Yabrud archeologic sequence and the problem of its correlation with the sequences of other Near Eastern sites prompted the Iraq-Jarmo group to examine the site to see whether there was a chance of the materials having been mixed by stream action. Rust's excavations took place more than 20 years ago, but the pit in the most important shelter (I) was well preserved, and the physical stratigraphy sketched by Rust could be identified. No evidence for stream activity could be found, except for the one thin sand layer near the base already noted by Rust; all the other material was normal rock-shelter debris, with angular unsorted fragments of roof limestone, flint, and bone in a matrix of ashy silt and sand. Whatever typological compromises may be demanded between Yabrud and Mt. Carmel or Ksar Akil must be made on the basis of the artifacts alone; Yabrud cannot be dismissed as a disturbed site. Unfortunately, no geomorphic features of the setting of the rock shelters are susceptible to climatic interpretation—or at least none appeared to the writer during a brief examination of the area, and nothing in Rust's description would suggest any. The lower half of the deposit in shelter I, containing implements of the Yabrudian and Acheuleo-Yabrudian industries, consists primarily of loose limestone rubble. This is interpreted by Rust (1950, p. 139 and Table 4) as a product of a relatively dry environment and correlated with the last interpluvial. The upper half of the deposit, bearing artifacts of industries labeled Acheuleo-Yabrudian, Micoquian, Yabrudian, pre-Aurignacian, Yabrudeo-Mousterian, etc. in a complicated sequence, contains breccia layers suggesting to Rust a moister climate and correlated by him with the last pluvial. The stratigraphy does not permit subdivisions of this generalized sequence.

The publication of Rust's monograph on Yabrud introduced a rival to Mt. Carmel as the most intensively studied prehistoric site in the eastern Mediterranean, and the complicated archeologic sequence has occasioned several extensive reviews, concerned primarily with typology but partly with correlation (e.g. Waechter, 1952; Bordes, 1955; Garrod, 1956; Howell, 1959). Garrod's 1956 paper was the second major review of her Mt. Carmel studies in relation to new investigations in the region, for she had earlier (1953) discussed the Ksar Akil sequence and treated afresh the relative age of the blade-tool industries in east and west. Her new review was occasioned in part by the analysis of Bordes (1955), who concluded that the Acheulian and Yabrudian of the eastern Mediterranean occurred as late as Würm II, the Mousterian and Levalloiso-Mousterian in Würm III—all much younger than in Europe, suggesting migration from west to east. This is an extremely young chronology, even younger than that of Vaufrey, who favored Acheulian in Würm I. On the basis of the Lebanese coastal stratigraphy, and without regard to the Carmel faunal sequence, Garrod supports a still longer chronology, with Acheulian in the last interglacial and Levalloiso-Mousterian as Würm I. Further discussion of the relation of the cultural horizons at Yabrud and other sites of the eastern Mediterranean to those at coastal sites or in Europe is beyond the scope of Garrod's review.

Problems of Chronology

The Würm Chronology of Europe

The relative age of comparable cultures in east and west is a prime concern in Pleistocene archeologic studies because the time factor controls concepts of migrations and evolution of cultures. It is central to the problem of the origin of late Pleistocene archeological stages. The fact that different archeological authorities can come to such different conclusions about the climatic chronology suggests that the climatic evidence either is not good or has been misinterpreted.

The present writer believes that the gross structure of the chronology will be established in time, that is, identification of the last pluvial and last interpluvial in the archeological sequence of the eastern Mediterranean, but is skeptical about attempts to identify subdivisions of the last pluvial and correlate them with Würm substages in Europe. The difficulties are numerous, and not least among them are changing concepts of the climatic subdivisions of the late Pleistocene in the glaciated and periglacial regions of Europe. We may no longer speak of (and probably never should have done so) a "standard Würm sequence" for Europe. The uncritical adoption of the magic units Würm I, II, and III is not justified, since it presupposes that such units are in fact standard and well defined and that they should necessarily be reflected in the Mediterranean. A summary of the background and basis of classifications of the last cold period must be presented before their application to the eastern Mediterranean can be considered.

The usual tripartite subdivision of the Würm in Europe stems from studies not in the Alpine glaciated regions (where the Würm River is located) but in the periglacial region of loess deposits and river terraces, with impetus in many cases coming from archeological investigations. Soergel (1919) was the first to draw together the geologic, paleontologic, and archeologic evidence into a comprehensive chronology. His pioneer work has served as the framework of reference for archeologists ever since its introduction, particularly after it was adopted by Zeuner (1945 and 1958a), who has both geologic and paleontologic repute and has the interests of prehistoric archeology at heart.

Although Soergel's work in the periglacial regions with the loesses, fluvial terraces, vertebrate faunas, and archeological sequence is still generally accepted, his attempts to establish a continent-wide Pleistocene chronology have had less success. The Soergel-Zeuner chronology leans heavily on the Milankovitch solar radiation curve, which shows three radiation minima for the time range considered by them to be appropriate for the Würm, namely about 116,000, 72,000, and 23,000 years ago for Würm I, II, and III respectively. Although this hypothesis for climatic fluctuations has not been disproven, it is utilized by few Pleistocene geologists. Emiliani (1955) adopted the Milankovitch curve for the interpretation of his paleotemperature analysis from oxygen isotopes in ocean-bottom sediments, but he utilized only the last two radiation minima for the Würm, rather than the last three as Soergel had done, and was forced to introduce an average time lag of 5,000 years for a close match (61,000 years ago for his Würm I and 18,000 for his combined Würm II-III). Refinements proposed by Broecker et al. (1958) in the method of extrapolation to earlier times will probably destroy the coincidence that Emiliani noted in the two curves for still earlier cold phases.

The climatic classification as built up by Soergel and Zeuner was based on the subdivision of the loesses of central Europe and supported by the grouping of periglacial terraces and glacio-fluvial terraces. The loesses are subdivided basically into an older loess and a younger loess. The younger loess rests on Saale till and outwash terraces in northern Germany; it is therefore considered to be younger than Saale (= Riss of Alpine region) and to represent the last glaciation. It is separated from the older loess by a deep weathering zone assigned to the last interglacial. The younger loess (last glaciation) is divided by a weaker soil zone into younger loess I and II, of which younger loess II may in turn be locally subdivided.

Soergel found that the lower two or three terraces along several streams in the periglacial area of central Europe are related to the younger loess, and they are similarly assigned by him to subdivisions of the last glaciation.

In the Alpine piedmont the "Niederterrasse" (low terrace), which on the Würm River served as the type for the Würm glacial stage in the Alps, is locally subdivided into three units. At the base of the mountains these terraces lead back to three fresh moraine loops, which are therefore termed the Würm moraines.

The occurrence of two or three subdivisions in the above features reasonably ascribed to the last glaciation (Würm) in these several regions led to the widespread use of the terms Würm I, II, and III by Soergel and others, although it was commonly admitted that the evidence for a Würm III substage was not always present.

The relative importance of the three substages has long been debated, as well as the correlation of substages from region to region. Recent application of new stratigraphic, pedologic, and paleontologic methods throughout Europe are now supplemented by radiocarbon dating. Many agreements in correlation have been reached, but other issues have been sharpened.

For the loess region much recent detailed stratigraphic work, particularly on the soils, has resulted in the refinement of the subdivisions in different regions and a finer understanding of the conditions at the time of formation of the deposits. Buried soils cannot easily be correlated from place to place because the character of the paleosol depends on the local topographic, climatic, and vegetational conditions and on the extent of the erosion or other modification of the soil prior to its burial. Facies of synchronous soil formation ranged from dry grassland soil on the east to forest soil on the west, even as now. Before burial by renewed loess deposition a soil may have been reduced in thickness by erosion or increased in thickness by solifluction. Careful analyses of soil structure, content of clay and lime, and other soil characteristics are required to diagnose the relations in each area. Probably because of these closer examinations the sweeping generalizations of Soergel for the entire loess region are now not so readily accepted, and the correlation of loesses and soils between northern France, southern Germany, Austria, and Czechoslovakia are by no means settled despite several recent comparisons (Bordes and Müller-Beck, 1956; Brunnacker, 1958; Brandtner, 1956; Prošek and Ložek, 1957). Because of the greater possibilities for complete preservation of the loess deposits in the drier climatic province of southeastern Europe, Lower Austria has been used as a type area for the classification of the loess sequence (Gross, 1958; Woldstedt, 1956). There the following sequence is used:

younger loess IIb
    Paudorf soil
younger loess IIa
    Göttweig soil
younger loess I
    Krems soil
older loess

The well developed Krems soil and associated paleofauna ("Banatica" snail fauna) indicate a warm climate—the last really warm climate of the region and therefore correlated with the last interglacial period (Brandtner, 1956). The Göttweig soil, on the other hand, is not nearly so well developed—the original structure of the loess has not even been destroyed—and the associated snail fauna ("Striata" fauna) and pollen (mostly pine, spruce, and nonarboreal forms) suggest a cool-temperate climate not much warmer than that of the preceding younger loess I. The "Columella" snail fauna and "Primigenius" mammal fauna of younger loess II suggest a climate increasingly colder, reaching a maximum of coldness after the weak Paudorf interval of soil formation.

Three radiocarbon dates for the Paudorf interval average closely at about 26,000 years ago (De Vries, 1958). Although Gross (1958), in his analysis of late Pleistocene C^{14} determinations of De Vries (1958), considers that the Göttweig interstadial persisted from 44,000 to 29,000 years ago, almost all the dates used for this conclusion come either from northern Europe or from caves in the south, from deposits whose relation to the Göttweig soil is really unknown. The only pertinent date from the loess region places the Göttweig soil as ending somewhat before 31,000 years ago, with duration undetermined except on the basis of a questionable date of 48,000 years ago for younger loess (De Vries, 1958) and on the basis of comparison with the postglacial soil of the region—only a speculation in view of the differing climatic conditions, etc.

Correlation of the loess sequence with the Würm moraines and glacio-fluvial terraces in the Alpine piedmont has been particularly controversial. Some have postulated that the innermost of the three moraines represents the earliest ice advance, corresponding to younger loess I (thus Würm I), and that after retreat (Göttweig interval) the ice advanced over this moraine to a more distant position (Würm II), destroying any interstadial soil or deposits that may have developed. The evidence for this sequence is somewhat elusive, however, and the three Würm moraines are more generally considered as representing a single climatic unit marked by minor fluctuations.

Because of the lack of evidence for important subdivisions in the Alpine piedmont, other authors (e.g. Büdel, 1953; Weidenbach, 1953), in following the principle that every loess presupposes a glacial-outwash plain from which it could be blown, have maintained that all the Würm moraines and Niederterrassen of Penck in the Alpine piedmont should be correlated with the last loess (younger loess II) and that the next-to-last loess (younger loess I) should be assigned to the next older terrace ("Hochterrasse"), called by them "young Riss" to follow more closely the original nomenclature of Penck. In this view the Göttweig soil would be correlated with the interglacial interval between young Riss and Würm and the Krems soil with the "interglacial" interval between middle-old Riss and young Riss.

This problem in nomenclature is commonly dismissed as an unnecessary complication. In the more usual classification (Gross, 1958; Woldstedt, 1956), younger loess II is still correlated in a general way with the three Würm moraines (main Würm), but younger loess I is assigned to a Würm I stage (early Würm, old Würm) in which the ice never reached the piedmont or at least never left any record. It must be emphasized, however, that physical connection between the well developed loess deposits and the moraines and outwash terraces is not well established. The terraces of the Danube River in Lower Austria to which the loesses of that region are closely related cannot be easily traced to the glacio-fluvial terraces of the Austrian Alps (Fink, 1956; but see Brandtner, 1956, p. 163).

Radiocarbon analysis has so far been directly applied to Würm moraines at only one locality. Peat from Würm till at Karrestobel near Ravensburg in southern Germany was determined as 28,840 years old (De Vries, 1958). However, there has always been general acceptance of the correlation of the outer Würm moraines with the outer Weichsel moraines (Brandenburg) of northern Germany, and of the latter with the outer Wisconsin moraines (Tazewell) of the United States, on the basis of morphological development and degree of subsequent weathering. The outer Wisconsin moraines are well determined at about 20,000 years ago. Therefore, to the extent that this trans-Atlantic correlation is correct, the Würm moraines in the Alps should be correlated with younger loess IIb after the Paudorf interval, for the latter bears an age of about 25,000 years. The snail and vertebrate faunas of the loesses indicate that maximum coldness was reached at this time—an expectable trend considering the fact that the ice reached its maximum then.

For northern Europe, Zeuner (1958a) assigns the Warthe, Brandenburg, and Pomeranian stadials respectively to Würm I, II, and III, but geologic study and radiocarbon analysis (Woldstedt, 1954 and 1958) have shown that the Warthe belongs with the Saale and that Würm I in the loess sense of Soergel (i.e., younger loess I) is not represented in the glaciated regions of the north. Thus, just as in the Alps, the ice sheet in northern Europe did not reach its maximum until near the end of the time of loess deposition of the last cold period. Accelerated study of buried peat deposits in Holland and Denmark outside the Weichsel border, by pollen analysis and radiocarbon determination, has encouraged attempts at identification of the Göttweig equivalents in this region. Work to date has led to the recognition of a complex of cold and cool-temperate stages postdating the presumed last interglacial and perhaps predating the Göttweig (De Vries, 1958). Although this area may hold as fine a record of the late Pleistocene as does the Austrian loess region and has the added advantage of peat deposits suitable for climatic analysis, most of the record is in the subsurface and not easily studied. It will be some time before a satisfactory climatic curve is established for northern Europe for the early part of the last cold period.

In conclusion, it is considered that continued use of the term "Würm", and especially the subdivisions I, II, and III as standards for climatic chronology beyond the Alps leads to much unnecessary confusion. Persons utilizing the terms often are not aware of their true meaning in the Alps or of the manner in which they have been distorted. Büdel (1953), who writes strongly on this point, states that the term "Würm I" has been used in ten to twelve different ways. Many others, including Zeuner (1945), have recommended restriction of the term "Würm" to the Alps, but it is firmly entrenched in the literature and in the minds of Pleistocene workers everywhere. The term "last cold period," which is used occasionally in the present discussion in place of "Würm" in its broad sense, is not satisfactory as a formal term because of indecisions about the status of interstadial and interglacial climates; the term "letzte Kaltzeit" as used by Freising (1957), for example, refers specifically to the time of younger loess II because he believes the preceding soil (cf. Göttweig) is an interglacial soil.

Despite the fact that glacial features are perhaps the most striking and best studied deposits of the Pleistocene, it appears that a longer climatic record in Europe is available in the loess region than in the glaciated regions. It is therefore suggested that local terms be introduced for the major loess deposits of the different regions of central Europe, the names to be selected from outstanding exposures that have been studied in detail. The terms "Göttweig" and "Paudorf" for the interstadial intervals of the loess region are already in general use for Austria and are convenient, even though they may not be based on the very best exposures (Brandtner, 1956). Comparable names for younger loess I, IIa, and IIb would be useful, and correlation with other regions could be expressed in tables rather than implied by the use of such general terms as "younger" and "older." It has already been mentioned that the subdivisions of the "loess recent" of northern France, for example, are not necessarily the same as the subdivisions of the "jüngerer Löss" of Austria. General classifications that combine terms from widely separated localities are potentially troublesome.

The modern work, primarily in the loess regions, suggests that the Würm in the broad sense (i.e., younger loess) is subdivisible into different climatic phases. The first part of the period was marked by decreasing temperatures and by loess deposition, but the extent of glacier expansion is unknown. Then came the Göttweig interstadial with somewhat milder climate, cessation of loess deposition, but no extensive reforestation. This was followed by increasing coldness and dryness in central Europe (with a short interruption for the Paudorf interval), culminating with the maximum advance of the glaciers. The glaciers then started a fluctuating retreat to produce the observed moraines, loess deposition ceased, and the climate soon improved enough so that forests re-invaded northern Europe (ca. 13,000 years ago). Unfortunately the new concepts of Würm climatic changes are not accompanied by agreement on terms, as shown by the following table. The writer finds it somewhat easier to use Gross's terms, although even here the all-important maximum ice advance is de-emphasized.

<table>
<tr><th>Glaciated Regions</th><th>Loess Region</th><th>C^{14} Time Scale</th><th colspan="2">Gross, 1958</th><th>Woldstedt, 1958</th></tr>
<tr><td></td><td></td><td></td><td colspan="2">late Würm</td><td>late Würm</td></tr>
<tr><td>Würm and Weichsel moraines</td><td>younger loess IIb</td><td>25,000 years B.P.</td><td rowspan="3">maximum Paudorf advance</td><td rowspan="3">main Würm</td><td rowspan="3">middle Würm</td></tr>
<tr><td rowspan="4">no record</td><td>Paudorf soil</td><td>26,000 years B.P.</td></tr>
<tr><td>younger loess IIa</td><td>31,000 years B.P.</td></tr>
<tr><td>Göttweig soil</td><td></td><td>Göttweig</td><td></td><td></td></tr>
<tr><td>younger loess I</td><td>> 48,000 years B.P.</td><td>old Würm</td><td></td><td>early Würm</td></tr>
</table>

Mediterranean Climates on the Basis of Climatological Theory

The foregoing discussion of the Würm chronology must now be applied to problems in the eastern Mediterranean in two respects—expectable fluctuations in climate and in sea level.

The relationship between climatic changes and their geologic record even in Europe involves much speculation. In the usual climatic reconstructions (Büdel, 1953; Flohn, 1953; Willett, 1950) the Würm is considered in its entirety without regard to possible internal temperature fluctuations, and it must be remembered that Büdel holds the view that the Würm equals only the main Würm of other authors, the old Würm (Würm I) being assigned to the young Riss. It is stated that a change in solar radiation produced a basic world-wide change in atmospheric circulation which resulted in a temperature depression of about 4°C. in most latitudes (Flohn, 1953). Southward displacement of the climatic and vegetational zones permitted the development of tundra with intensive frost activity, solifluction, and loess deposition in central Europe (Büdel, 1951; Poser, 1948). Depression of the snow line on the mountains resulted in the slow growth of ice sheets in Scandinavia and the Alps. Eventually the ice sheets reached their maximum extent, and their presence intensified the continental climate (cold, dry) in central Europe. Close to the ice sheets at this time the temperature depression may have amounted to 12°C. at the time of the maximum extent, elsewhere in central Europe about 8°C., and at lower latitudes about 4°C.

In this reconstruction the effect on the Mediterranean region can be treated as a fairly simple southward migration of storm tracks and lower temperatures. The subtropical high-pressure belt which now keeps summer rain from the Mediterranean was pushed to the south (Willett, 1950) or was weakened and broken into cells by the southward penetration of cold air masses from the north (Flohn, 1953). Meridional (north-south) circulation at any rate was thus strengthened at the expense of latitudinal circulation, and the Mediterranean region experienced a pluvial climate at the same time that central Europe had a glacial or periglacial climate. This is the modernized expression of the long-accepted picture of Pleistocene climate in the Old World (see quotations from Childe, 1952, on pp. 72 and 74 above). Flohn (1953), however, has made the important distinction that the climatic changes of low latitudes were parallel to but not caused by glaciation in Europe, and Büdel (1953) has emphasized on geological grounds that even in Europe the effects of the ice sheet were restricted.

Butzer (1957b) has derived additional support for this concept of Mediterranean pluvials by an analysis of meteorological records in the low latitudes of the Old World, in which he found that decreased precipitation in the Mediterranean region in A.D. 1911-40 as compared with the preceding 30-year period was accompanied by increased mean barometric pressure. This finding suggested that dryness is related to strengthening and expansion of the subtropical high-pressure cells and consequent northward migration of storm tracks, which are concentrated at the zone of junction of the polar and subtropical air masses—the situation generally postulated for the interglacial (interpluvial) intervals.

Reconstructions of Mediterranean climate on the basis of climatological theory become more difficult, however, if the Würm of Europe north of the Alps is considered in the broader sense to include the time of younger loess I and the Göttweig interstadial (see e.g. Gross, 1958) as well as younger loess II. For this we must postulate an early cool phase, and interstadial, and a later cold phase with maximum glacier expansion near the end. The extent to which the glaciers advanced during the early cool phase is unknown. Besides the temperature changes we must consider the humidity relations. Apparently on the basis of the snail faunas of the Austrian loess area, Woldstedt (1956) considers that the early Würm was relatively humid and that dryness reached a maximum at the time of maximum ice extent. He thus de-emphasizes the interruption of the Göttweig interstadial as far as humidity goes. Furthermore, in Austria and adjacent regions (Brandtner, 1956), each loess is marked by a relatively humid early phase (solifluction loess) followed by a relatively dry phase (pure loess). Thus the humidity curve of the last glaciation should show decreasing precipitation until the time of maximum glacial extent, with two fluctuations toward wetness for the times during(?) and immediately after the Göttweig and Paudorf interstadials. Dryness of central Europe during the glacial maximum is inferred also by Firbas (1939), who points out that the greater depression of the tree line than of the snow line can only be a result of deficient precipitation.

Butzer (1957a) attempts to apply these concepts of temperature and humidity changes to the Mediterranean and cites as evidence the climatic interpretation of various cave deposits. As a climatological explanation he postulates two basic patterns of atmospheric circulation during the cold phase of the Würm for both Europe and the Mediterranean rather than a single one as usually assumed in the simpler reconstruction described above (pp. 79 ff.; see Flohn, 1953). He implies a precipitation cycle independent of a temperature cycle. To explain the inferred high humidity at the beginning of the Würm in the Mediterranean he proposes that the general atmospheric circulation was changed by increase of meridional air flow, bringing storms and low temperatures to the Mediterranean. During the drier later Würm, however, he postulates a "slackening of the condensation cycle" (decrease in precipitation) without change in temperature. Finally, in this hypothesis, the Würm drew to a close by the return to the dominant latitudinal circulation of interglacial times, with summer storm tracks shifted again northward out of the Mediterranean. Presumably the precipitation cycle also changed (or will before the next glaciation!). To make this hypothesis fit such evidence as there is for multiple humidity changes in both Europe and the Mediterranean, it would be necessary to postulate not just one cycle but repeated cycles of temperature and humidity. Because of the difficulties in climatic interpretation and correlation of Mediterranean late Pleistocene sediments, the evidence for broad synchroneity of either temperature or humidity changes is really not sufficient to justify development of such a hypothesis.

Until such time as the humidity curve, the temperature curve, and the glaciation curve can be constructed with more confidence for Europe, it seems futile to attempt to predict what climatic conditions to expect in the Mediterranean. It appears reasonable that the last cold period in Europe should be considered essentially as a single event culminating in maximum coldness and maximum extent of ice about 20,000 years ago and that the interruptions marked by buried soils in the younger loess of different regions and by buried peats in Holland indicate only minor interruptions in the general climatic trend that were not necessarily synchronous from one region to another. Reference may be made to the oxygen-isotope curve for ocean-bottom sediments (Emiliani, 1955), in which the fluctuations during the last cold period are quite minor and are within the limits of error of the technique. With this view one might expect in the Mediterranean a definite climatic record of the last cold period as a whole, but evidences for fluctuations from place to place should not necessarily correlate with one another nor with anything in Europe. This is not by any means a new view but is an interpretation of the recent Pleistocene studies in Europe and is a plea against unrestricted climatic interpretation of archeological deposits.

Fluctuations of Sea Level

Sea level presumably reflects directly the extent of glaciation, but estimates of ice extent at different times during the last glaciation are difficult to make. The European glaciers apparently did not reach their maximum extent until near the end of the last cold period. If the North American glaciation paralleled the European, then sea level during the old Würm and much of the main Würm must have been only moderately lower than the present. It must have reached a minimum level late in the main Würm and then have risen rapidly during the late Würm fluctuating ice recession and in the postglacial.

The rate of rise of sea level during the late glacial and postglacial is a matter of some discussion. Radiocarbon analyses of wood buried in the Mississippi Delta deposits suggest that the sea had risen from its low level of the last glacial period to about 100 feet below modern sea level by about 10,000 years ago and that it reached essentially its present level about 5,000 years ago (Fisk and McFarlan, 1955). Another interpretation, based on radiocarbon determinations from the coasts of Texas, Louisiana, and Holland, shows a decelerating rise during the entire last 10,000 years; the relations before this time are not clear (Shepard and Suess, 1956).

At any rate, the inferred volume of the ice sheets for different intervals of the last glacial period render improbable the Würm sea levels postulated by Pfannenstiel (1952) for the coast of Palestine (see p. 77 above); sea level was lowest not in Würm I but actually much later, and the rise from the lowest level (-90 m.) occupied not the entire Würm but only the very end of the Würm. The gravel beds labeled "Würm II" (-21 to -32 m.) and "Würm III" (-2 to -7 m.) by Pfannenstiel must represent late-glacial and postglacial events, perhaps of no climatic significance.

High sea levels during the last cold period are also difficult to predict, because of uncertainties about the extent of deglaciation during interstadials. The principal interstadial inferred for the last cold period, the Göttweig, was marked by a cool-temperate climate in southern Europe, according to the evidence from the flora and fauna (Brandtner, 1956), but without the forestation characteristic of a full interglacial climate. The length of the interstadial is undetermined, although Gross (1958) postulates 15,000 years on the basis of the comparison of the thickness and degree of development of the Göttweig soil with the modern soil of the region. His supposed confirmation of this duration by radiocarbon dates is based on samples from Holland, England, and a Hungarian cave rather than on samples from the Austrian loess. At any rate, the implication from the paleontologic interpretation is that sea level may not have fluctuated a great deal at the time of the Göttweig interstadial and certainly did not reach or exceed modern sea level.

Zeuner (1953a), on the other hand, considers that sea level during the Göttweig interstadial did rise high and, in fact, cut a notch and terrace at 3-4 meters above present sea level at numerous places. In as much as marine terraces and associated deposits are in many cases the most reliable indicators for past interglacial periods as well as a means of distant correlation for Pleistocene events, this claim must be considered in context with other marine terraces and their use in Pleistocene correlations.

Gross climatic correlations between Europe and the Mediterranean depend in many cases on the identification of the break or transition between the last interglacial period and the last glacial period. An interglacial or interpluvial climate can sometimes be identified in the Mediterranean on the basis of the climatic requirements of soils, plants, or animals, but there are many questions about the expected nature of such an interpluvial climate. Correlation of the last interpluvial on the basis of the occurrence of an index fossil—a form with widespread distribution but limited time range—is also uncertain; for example, Vaufrey (1939a) has argued for nonsynchroneity of the "great faunal break" (p. 74 above). And of course correlation on the basis of archeological stages is to be abhorred as circular argument.

The most reliable basis for distant correlation, therefore, is probably the marine terrace and its associated sediment, for glacier-controlled changes in sea level are presumably world-wide and unaffected by local climates. Troubles immediately begin, however, with the correlation of marine terraces with Alpine glacio-fluvial deposits or the central European loesses, because these features cannot be reliably traced to the sea. There is a greater possibility in northwestern Europe, where the deposits of the Eem Sea are overlain by sediments assigned to the last glaciation (Weichsel) and themselves are younger than the Warthe drift of the next-to-last (Saale) glaciation (Woldstedt, 1955). There seems to be little doubt that the Eem represents the last interglacial period, on the basis of the contained Lusitanian (warm-water) fauna and of the flora of associated peat deposits as expressed in the characteristic pollen diagrams.

Unfortunately the Eem deposits do not terminate neatly in a marine cliff and terrace, and there is no physical connection between the definite Eem deposits of northwestern Germany and the marine terraces of southern England and western France, where the correlation of the 18-meter marine terrace (Monastirian I of Zeuner, 1954a and 1958a) with the last interglacial is based on relations to local loesses, solifluction deposits, fluvial terraces, and other climatic indicators (Zeuner, 1954a). In the Mediterranean region the 18-meter terrace is the first to bear deposits with the warm-water indicator Strombus bubonius. The next lower terrace (6-8 m., Monastirian II of Zeuner) is also referred to the last interglacial; this cannot represent a first Würm interstadial because the Strombus bubonius which it contains would have been exterminated by the early Würm cold-water phase, according to Zeuner. Furthermore, if the 6-meter terrace represented a Würm interstadial its formation would have been preceded by a deep regression corresponding to the early Würm glaciation, and no evidence for such regression has been found in the Mediterranean (Dubertret, 1946; McBurney and Hey, 1955) or in England (Zeuner, 1954a).

Although there is also no physical connection between the Eem deposits and the loesses, radiocarbon dating suggests that the Eem is older than all the younger loess (Würm) of central Europe (Gross, 1958; De Vries, 1958). Further, the Göttweig soil and correlative paleoflora, occurring between younger loess I and II, imply a climatic phase not so warm as an interglacial (Gross, 1958; Woldstedt, 1958). Consequently, as stated above, it is not to be expected that sea level during this interstadial phase would be so high as during the Eem (last interglacial) or so high as at present. It may be pointed out, however, that the possibility of some post-Eem warm-water marine deposits has recently been reported in the subsurface of Holland (Van der Heide, 1957), possibly corresponding to the first Würm interstadial. Further, Zeuner (1953a) believes that numerous examples of a 3-4 meter strand line in southern England and in the Mediterranean should be assigned to this interstadial, which he himself believes is a fully temperate interval. This strand line is his epi-Monastirian level, which is difficult to identify because it is not far below the last interglacial 6-8 meter level (Monastirian II of Zeuner) nor far above a possible post-glacial high level (1-2 m.). In the Mediterranean it reportedly does not carry Strombus bubonius, the presumed index for the last interglacial in this region (Zeuner, 1953a), and therefore should be assigned to a phase of the last glaciation. There is no good evidence for deep marine regression prior to this "epi-Monastirian" stand, however, and such regression is required if the usual concept of at least partial glaciation during the old Würm phase of loess formation is accepted. Zeuner refers to cut-and-fill relations of the Thames estuary terrace sequence as indication of regression at this time. The extent of the regression is undetermined, and a sea level only a few meters below the present one would have been enough to produce the observed terrace relations.

Such a possibility of a high sea level subsequent to what is usually considered the last interglacial (Riss/Würm, Eem, Monastirian I and II) recalls the classification difficulties as to what is Würm and what is Riss in the Alps (Büdel, 1953; Weidenbach, 1953; Zeuner, 1954a). One fears that the identification even of the last interglacial levels in the eastern Mediterranean coast is in jeopardy and that even on a climatic basis the presumed equivalent last interpluvial might be confused with a younger warm phase. Until the climatic and marine sequence in Europe for this time range is resolved, the correlations in the eastern Mediterranean must remain tentative.

Conclusions

If we accept the 18- and 6-meter strand lines of the eastern Mediterranean as representing the last interglacial period, all features younger than the 6-meter stand must be assigned to the last glacial period. This was a time of general low sea level (if we set aside consideration of the "epi-Monastirian" level), and most of the coastal deposits formed during it have been submerged by the subsequent rise in sea level. The difficulties in working with such submerged deposits have been considered above (pp. 77, 85) in connection with Pfannenstiel's work on the coastal plain of Palestine. Deposits not so submerged include the sand dunes of the Beirut region (pp. 76 f.) and the fluvial deposits of coastal streams such as that which flows past Ksar Akil (p. 75). In both cases the sediments are interrupted by buried soils. In the case of the Beirut dunes, the climatic significance of the main buried soil is suspect because of other possible controls on dune activity versus dune stabilization. In the case of Ksar Akil, the possibility of climatic control is better, but the purity of the red soil layers within the cave sequence may be the result of temporary nonoccupance of the shelter rather than climatic change. The matching of three red soils or rubble zones with Würm I, II, and III may be too easy, in view of the alternative possibilities for the interpretation of these strata and in view of the new concepts of Würm climatic trends in Europe. The internal physical stratigraphy of other archeological sites in the eastern Mediterranean is even less susceptible to accurate climatic interpretation, and we are left without any reliable local climatic subdivisions for the last pluvial.

Post-Pleistocene

The foregoing remarks pertain to the Pleistocene time range in the Levant. They are intended to show the current status of paleoclimatic and physiographic knowledge in this area, as based on more recent investigations. There is enough evidence to demonstrate that there were indeed climatic fluctuations in the eastern Mediterranean, but correlation with the late Pleistocene climatic sequence in Europe must still be tentative, when based strictly either on climatic indicators or on their relation to marine terraces. The fluctuations which have permitted the subdivision of the last cold period in Europe (Würm) into substages may be incompletely recorded in the eastern Mediterranean. It might be expected that the minor postglacial fluctuations established for Europe have little record in the east. The possibility, however, must be explored.

Archeological sites that record the transition from the levels of food-gathering to those of food-production have not been well investigated in the Levant, and physiographic studies have yielded few significant paleoclimatic data. The physiographic or paleontologic contrasts are either not very striking or not easily dated.

Butzer (1957c) has presented what amounts to a catalogue of claimed indications of climatic conditions for this time range for the whole Near East, ranging from northwestern Africa to Afghanistan. Climatic criteria utilized include not only physiographic features, many of which are feebly developed or subject to alternative nonclimatic explanations (e.g. lenses of stream gravels in alluvial silts), but also such events as floods and droughts mentioned in the Bible. Butzer has attempted to fit all the suggestions into a uniform chronology for the "late glacial and postglacial" for the entire region, involving six climatic phases that were relatively dry ("postpluvial") or relatively moist ("subpluvial"). But even with this large number of phases he was forced to subdivide two of them in order to accommodate some of the data, and in a few cases he had to admit that the climatic inferences in different regions could not be matched. On the other hand, he was confident enough to suggest a parallelism between four Near Eastern phases or subphases and four pollen zones from the postglacial of northern Europe (Preboreal, Boreal, Atlantic, and Subboreal) and to build upon this some climatological theory.

The difficulties in constructing such a detailed climatic chronology over this broad area are manifold. The Near East is not a uniform climatic or geomorphic province. Although North Africa is in the heart of the trade-wind belt, monsoonal effects are present close to the Indian Ocean and strong continental effects are present in the interior of Iran. Elsewhere mountain ranges, local large water bodies, and various geologic conditions affect the geomorphic and climatic characteristics. The behavior of the lower Nile may be affected by conditions in the high mountains of Abyssinia as much as by climatic or physiographic conditions in its lower reaches or by sea-level changes at its mouth. Similarly, the Tigris and Euphrates Rivers rise in the high mountains and plateaus of the Zagros-Taurus arc and flow through the desert of Iraq to the sea.

Apart from possible unreliability of the paleoclimatic evidence, the problems in dating are just as numerous, especially in the prehistoric time range prior to about 3000 B.C. Possible nonsynchroneity of comparable archeological-technological stages or levels in different parts of this broad region must always be considered. Certainly the existence of important barriers to migration (such as deserts) or of important refuge areas (such as mountains) encouraged diversification of cultures in prehistoric times, even as today. And if such broad and ill-defined terms as "neolithic" and "mesolithic" are used for correlation purposes the chronology loses much of its precision. The writer believes that the use of prehistoric archeological-technological stages or levels is no more reliable for long-distance correlation of the minor climatic phases of the post-Pleistocene than it is for correlation of the major climatic phases of the late Pleistocene.

Radiocarbon analysis has contributed much to control of the late Pleistocene chronology of Europe and America but has not yet been applied sufficiently to the post-Pleistocene problems of the Levant. Even the most concentrated series of analyses, devoted to dating a carefully selected group of closely related early agricultural sites in the eastern Mediterranean, produced widely divergent determinations (see p. 159), and great care must be taken to evaluate the purity of individual samples and the possibility of geobiochemical contamination prior to their collection.

The roster of post-Pleistocene paleoclimatic features in the Levant is meager. Wetzel and Haller (1945, p. 45) ascribe a black soil in some localities in coastal Lebanon to a moist period in the "mesolithic," but such black soils might form under local conditions of poor drainage without regard to regional climate. In Palestine at Mt. Carmel the Natufian occurrence had the stamp of aridity placed on it by Bate (Garrod and Bate, 1937) on the basis of the deer-gazelle ratio and of the microfauna (or lack of it). The difficulties with the frequency computations have already been mentioned (p. 74). Haas's analysis of the microfauna of the "neolithic" from near-by Abu Usba cave suggests a climate much like that of today with perhaps a little more rain (Stekelis and Haas, 1952). Jean Perrot (personal conversation) also doubts that there is evidence for significant climatic modifications in this region during the time range concerned.

Several features in the interior of Palestine have been attributed to postpluvial climatic changes, including depositional and erosional features along the Jordan River or its tributaries and also strand lines of Lake Tiberias and the Dead Sea (Picard, 1937; Butzer, 1957c). Few of these are even approximately dated, however, and for many of the Jordan valley features the possibility of nonclimatic controls cannot be eliminated.

Apart from these few suggestions, there are no grounds for postulating significant climatic changes in the Levant during the post-Pleistocene. In late cave sites and early village sites (R. J. and L. Braidwood, 1953) few reliable geologic or faunal studies have accompanied the archeological work, with the exceptions already noted, and there is no further information for evaluating the climatic settings.

Of the many claimed indications of Near Eastern paleoclimates cited by Butzer (1957c), probably the most realiable are from the Egyptian oases, where evidence for a "neolithic wet phase" was summarized by Huzayyin (1941) and Murray (1951). North Africa, however, and also East Africa, where the Makalian and Nakuran wet phases may fall into this general period, are beyond the area under consideration here.

We are left with few definite evidences for broad and synchronous climatic changes for the post-Pleistocene in the Levant. Although cycles of minor climatic change certainly must have occurred then even as they have in recent decades (Butzer, 1957b) and may even have left some local physiographic record, it is still premature to correlate such changes over great distances, certainly not from the Levant to Europe. Such climatic cycles as did occur, moreover, may have had only limited effects on the movements of man or the development of his cultures.

THE INTERIOR

East from the Levant, physiographic investigations have been lean, with little impetus supplied by prehistoric archeological excavations. Although flint artifacts have been gathered from many localities in the desert country (Field, 1956), there have been no excavations or related physiographic studies comparable to those carried on in the deserts of North Africa (Caton-Thompson, 1952). Flints were collected by Passemard (1926) from the terraces of the Euphrates River as it crosses the desert of eastern Syria, and a curious attempt was made to correlate them with Pleistocene sea-level changes 500 miles away. In the mountains of northeastern Iraq, the stone-age sites of Zarzi and Hazar Merd (Garrod, 1930) did not yield climatic data. On the geological side, however, Bobek (1940) described Pleistocene glaciation in the high Zagros Mountains in Turkey just over the Iraq border, and De Morgan (1926, pp. 96 ff.) mentioned glacial features farther to the southeast along the same range in Iran.

Similarly, there has been little work on post-Pleistocene climate. Brooks (1949, pp. 318-24) has summarized the meager evidence for post-Pleistocene climatic fluctuations in southwest Asia, on the basis of postulated human migrations which were believed to have been initiated by droughts and on the basis of changes in the level of the Caspian Sea. He correlated these changes with the postglacial climatic fluctuations of Europe. Within Iraq about the only significant physiographic event which has received archeologic attention is the growth of the Tigris-Euphrates Delta in lower Mesopotamia (De Morgan, 1924; Lloyd, 1947). This event has no important climatic side lights, and, in fact, its significance in the early history of Mesopotamia has been questioned (Lees and Falcon, 1952).

The recent work of the Iraq-Jarmo group was centered in the foothills of northeastern Iraq and was concerned with the transition from cave habitation to villages and the early development of farming. The writer attempted to work out the sequence of climatic and physiographic changes which might serve as a framework for the archeologic studies. During the 1950/51 season, activities were confined largely to the area around Jarmo in the Kurdish foothills. During the 1954/55 season the program was more comprehensive and involved a study of the Zagros area of Iraq, Iran, and Turkey, additional work in the foothills and plains of northeastern Iraq, and excursions into the deserts of Iraq, Syria, and Jordan.

The foothills of northeastern Iraq have never been the object of any consistent physiographic study, although geologists of the Iraq Petroleum Company have worked out the pre-Pleistocene geologic history in some detail and additional geologic work has been done recently in connection with dam-site location. Terraces along some of the major rivers have been measured, according to unpublished reports examined by the writer in the offices of the Iraq Petroleum Company, and a single occurrence of glacial deposits is described in an early report of the same company. This particular deposit, at Qarachitan at the southern base of Pir-i-Magrun, west of Sulimaniyah, proved, however, to be a landslide feature.

High Mountain Belt

The clearest records of climatic change in northeastern Iraq and adjacent Iran and Turkey are the glacial deposits of the Zagros-Taurus Mountains. The crest of the range stands about 9,000-13,000 feet above sea level. In Turkey there are many small glaciers in the high valley heads on the sheltered northeast side of the range at about 11,000 feet. Bobek (1940) determined that during the Pleistocene the snow line was lowered about 2,300 feet to 8,700 feet and glaciers reached down as low as 6,000 feet. The writer, however, found fresh moraines of the last glacial stage below 4,000 feet in the major valleys in the high Zagros Mountains of northeastern Iraq, scarcely 50 miles from the area studied by Bobek, and identified small cirques in protected locations at least as low as 5,000 feet. These new figures suggest a lowering of the snow line of about 6,000 feet for the last glacial stage instead of the 2,300 feet indicated by Bobek. The moraines mapped by Bobek must represent a retreatal phase rather than the maximum phase of the last glaciation.

A Pleistocene depression of the snow line amounting to 6,000 feet is much greater than that usually quoted for the Alps for the last glacial stage (Würm), where an average depression of about 4,000 feet for the Alpine border area corresponded to a decrease in mean annual temperature of about 8°C., if no increase in precipitation is assumed (Klebelsberg, 1949, pp. 683, 432). The reasons for the high figure for the Taurus-Zagros area are not clear, but they may be related to the precipitation regime. The local influence of precipitation on the growth of glaciers is indicated by the lower occurrence of small Pleistocene cirques (representing snow line) on the moist southwestern flank of the range rather than on the drier interior portion and the Iranian-Anatolian plateau. Prominent glacial outwash terraces extend downstream from the moraines but unfortunately become lost in the canyons which transect the higher foothill ridges. They cannot be followed individually to the Tigris valley.

The great depression of the snow line in this region in the Pleistocene was presumably accompanied by a large depression of the upper tree line. The upper limit of woodlands (just as the lower limit), probably controlled in part by deforestation by woodcutters and grazing animals, is now at about 6,500 feet. Its position during the Pleistocene must have been much lower, but undoubtedly the ameliorating effects of the desert lowlands were more potent here than in lowlands near temperate mountain ranges. A full discussion of Pleistocene glaciation and its climatic and biologic implications is in preparation.

Foothills and Lowlands

Caves

The Iraq foothills of the Zagros Mountains consist of parallel limestone ridges increasing in height toward the Iranian frontier. Although not high enough to have supported Pleistocene glaciers, the ridge slopes carried heavy mantles of limestone rubble which slid down from higher ledges probably under the influence of the greater moisture (and probably greater frost activity) prevalent during the glacial ages. Most of the breccia deposits seem to be older than the last glacial age. They are firmly cemented, and the benches are old enough to contain caves and rock shelters with artifacts of Mousterian and later flint industries. Ishkaft Barak and Ishkaft Babkhal, newly excavated by Howe (see pp. 29 f., 59 f.), fall in this category. Other traces of late Pleistocene occupation in caves in the limestone ridges have been excavated by Garrod (1930), Howe (pp. 57 ff. above; Braidwood, et al., 1954), and Solecki (1955 and 1957). Most of the sites present no stratigraphic or geomorphic relations susceptible to useful paleoclimatic interpretation, but Shanidar cave has some possibilities because of the radiocarbon determinations on its deposits.

Shanidar cave is located at an elevation of 2,200 feet above see level on the south-facing slope of a limestone mountain ridge whose crest is at about 6,000 feet. The following sequence, with radiocarbon determinations (in years before present), is given for the near-by open-air site of Zawi Chemi Shanidar (Solecki, 1955; Solecki and Rubin, 1958; see also p. 149 below) and the cave:

Zawi Chemi Shanidar, chipped and ground stone	10,870±300
Shanidar B (Zarzian), microliths, near top	10,600±300
near base	12,000±400
unconformity	
Shanidar C (Baradostian), blade tools, upper part	26,500±1,500 and 29,500±1,500
lower part	32,300±3,000, 33,630±400, and more than 34,000
Shanidar C-D contact zone (Mousterian)	50,300±3,000

Solecki (personal conversation) considers the unconformity between the Baradostian and Zarzian layers to mark a distinct hiatus when the cave was not inhabited, and the suggestion is supported by the gap in the C^{14} determinations between horizons just below (26,500 ±1,500 years B.P.) and just above (12,000±400 years B.P.) the unconformity. If glacier activity in the Zagros Mountains was parallel to that in the Alps, the hiatus would encompass the time of maximum extent of the Würm glaciers. If the snow line in the Zagros Mountains descended 6,000 feet to an elevation of 4,000 feet during the last glaciation, the upper tree line, now at about 6,500 feet, must have been depressed below the level of Shanidar cave (2,200 feet), rendering the cave less hospitable to occupance. The extensive surveys and soundings by the Iraq-Jarmo group in northeastern Iraq turned up no sites that would fill the apparent archeological gap between the Baradostian and Zarzian cultures of Shanidar cave (see p. 154). The entire region of ridges with their limestone caves may well have been inhospitable to man at the time of the gap because of prevailing climatic and ecologic conditions. Habitation of Shanidar cave by the Baradostian people at earlier times may reflect less severe conditions still within the last glacial period but prior to the time of maximum coldness and maximum extension of the ice.

Chemchemal Plain

In some of the broader and lower valleys within the foothills, a combination of regional uplift and climatic change during the Pleistocene resulted in a multiple sequence of erosion and deposition. The sequence in one such lowland was worked out during the 1950/51 season of the Iraq-Jarmo Project (Wright, 1952). The physiographic events were related to the archeological sequence by means of the paleolithic site of Barda Balka, the early village site of Jarmo, and some Assyrian potsherds found in a gully fill. The hand axes, pebble tools, and flake tools at Barda Balka—an unusual assemblage characterized by Howe (p. 61 above; Wright and Howe, 1951) as in part typologically Acheulian—occur at the base of a fluvial silt deposit that covers an extensive erosion surface termed the "Jarmo surface." Although it is difficult to differentiate climatic from tectonic controls on river activity in this foothill region, it is suggested that a period of tectonic (and climatic) stability resulted in the cutting of this broad pediment across the tilted Tertiary rocks of the Chemchemal plain. At or near the end of this period the site of Barda Balka was occupied.

A change in river behavior about this time resulted in the burial of the pediment by silts, generally 10-20 feet thick but locally 50 feet thick, derived from erosion of the limestone ridges several miles distant. The change in behavior of the rivers on the Jarmo surface from a graded condition to aggradation cannot easily be attributed to basin subsidence or other tectonic activity, because the aggradational surface cuts across the local rock structure. It is suggested that the deposition came about as a result of accelerated erosion on the limestone ridges consequent upon a pluvial climate, presumably during the last pluvial period (Wright, 1952). This was not the first cycle of pediment formation and burial that the region had experienced, for extensive remnants of a higher surface of the same type are preserved around the edges of the Chemchemal plain. Small benches standing still higher on the flanks of the bordering limestone ridges indicate yet an earlier cycle in the formation of the plain.

Subsequent rejuvenation of the stream system started a cycle of dissection, which has since converted the former smooth Jarmo surface into an area of intricate wadies separated by untouched remnants of the silt-covered plain. It is not known whether the rejuvenation was the result of a change back to an "interpluvial" climate or the result of tectonic uplift of the mountain axis and consequent steepening of river gradients. Considering the depth of the subsequent erosion, it seems likely that uplift was at least partially the cause. At any rate, dissection extended through the cover of silt and basal gravel and cut deeply into the Tertiary bedrock to a total depth of 150 feet near the major streams. Most of the dissection was completed by the time of occupation of the early village site of Jarmo (probably around 6750 B.C.; see pp. 159 f.) on top of the bluff of a deep gully, as is suggested by comparable degrees of soil development on a low terrace in the gully and on the occupation deposits of the Jarmo mound.

In the western part of the Chemchemal plain still another cycle of filling and cutting is shown by the relations along the principal wadi that cuts into the Jarmo surface. The wadi was apparently backfilled by alluvium during the first millennium B.C., because near the village of Sedan it contains Late Assyrian (ca. 750-600 B.C.) potsherds. The fill reaches a thickness of 30 feet and may be traced down the river part way through the broad ridge of Pliocene gravel which separates the Chemchemal plain from the broad Kirkuk plain. The episode of filling was ended by a wave of dissection, and the alluvium is now a well formed terrace along the entire wadi system. The cause of this Assyrian cycle of fill and cut is tentatively attributed to a relatively humid and a relatively dry climatic phase respectively, for the relations resemble very closely the arroyo cycles in southwestern United States that are climatically controlled. No other instances of such relatively recent cut-and-fill could be identified in the intermontane plains of northeastern Iraq, however, so that the features may possibly have resulted from some unidentified local condition rather than from a regional climatic cycle.

It is not uncommon to discover small gullies extending back into low terraces from the flood plains of larger rivers, and some of them even have small fill terraces. Such cut-

and-fill features, however, have no climatic control but result from lateral migration of the major stream on its flood plain, which causes truncation of the lower end of the small tributary and thus rejuvenation and dissection of the gully floor, followed by deposition as the major river migrates to the far side of the flood plain.

Terraces of Major Rivers

The Greater Zab River, the major transverse stream that heads in the very high Zagros crest, shows glacial-outwash terraces in its upper reaches, but the terrace fills are lost as the streams transect the limestone ridges in gorges. Where the Greater Zab tributaries flow in narrow longitudinal intermontane valleys between limestone fold ridges, terraces are prominent; but it is difficult to determine whether they are tectonically or climatically controlled. Thus in the valley of Shanidar cave, occupied by the Greater Zab River, several conspicuous terraces are present (Solecki, 1955). Downstream in the piedmont belt, this river and those that head only in the unglaciated ridges are marked by erosional terraces which may have no climatic significance. They may record merely local or temporary interruptions in the general dissection of the piedmont and foothills that have been going on since the epoch of massive Pliocene alluviation and deformation. Such terraces may be traced for some distance across the plains above Mosul, Erbil, and Kirkuk, and in places they broaden so much that their veneers of locally hardened gravel and silt are difficult to distinguish from the conglomerate and silt stone of the very gently folded Pliocene formations into which they are cut. The terraces or plains descend downstream but eventually terminate before the Tigris River is reached. Farther downstream on the Tigris itself patches of terraces occur with veneers of polished chert pebbles, sand dunes, undrained depressions, and other geomorphic features. One such depression next to the Euphrates River was studied by Voute (1957), who found that it at one time received floodwaters from that river.

The broad distances between the Kurdish piedmont and the lower Tigris, however, along with the gentle gradients, poor exposures, and inadequate maps, discourage studies of regional terraces in this area, and it appears unlikely that the river features of the mountain and foothill belt can ever be traced all the way to the Tigris River and thence to the delta and Persian Gulf for possible correlation with strand lines or other marine features (Wright, 1955). The history of the alluvial plain and the delta region is undoubtedly complex, as suggested by the remarks of Lees and Falcon (1952) on recent deformation near the delta edge and by the significant work of Jacobsen and Adams (1958) on historic changes in channel patterns on the alluvial plain. Here all the major forces acting on the regime of a large river system come together: upstream controls on the various major headwater streams (short-term and long-term variations in snowmelt and rain in the mountains), mid-stream controls on the Tigris and Euphrates themselves (desert rains, physiographic possibilities for flood-plain water storage, etc.), and downstream controls (sea-level changes, delta subsidence or regional deformation, activity of the Karun River that enters the Persian Gulf at the same point). Study of the Pleistocene and recent history of the delta region and related parts of lower Mesopotamia will require a major effort that should include investigation of the sediments by well borings in a manner comparable to that undertaken in other major delta areas and alluvial plains, such as those of the Mississippi and Rhine Rivers.

Other Features

The occurrence of early village sites in the lowlands only a few feet above the present flood plains of the major Tigris tributaries (e.g. Gird Ali Agha on the Greater Zab; see p. 26) indicates that these rivers have not cut down very much during the past 7,000 years within upper Mesopotamia. Most of the rolling plains transected by these streams have only a thin veneer of silt weathered and washed from the underlying Pliocene silt-stone or terrace deposits. Such minor and local erosional activity is undoubtedly common on sparsely vegetated slopes, and a sterile silt layer several feet thick in the midst of the cultural deposits at the low mound of Tell al-Khan (see p. 25) on a low terrace of the Khazir River probably was the result of local wash from near-by slopes.

The silt veneer on the piedmont plains superficially resembles wind deposits (loess) in its general homogeneity, color, and lack of good stratification. That it is not loess, however, is indicated by the local occurrence of lenses of sand and gravel, the higher content of fine silt and clay, the local stratification, and the relation to the Pliocene silt stone that is its source. Despite the fact that the piedmont area is subject to long-lasting dust storms originating in the desert regions to the south, the dust has apparently not accumulated as loess over the years, as indicated by the fact that none of the prehistoric sites that the writer has examined in all of northern Mesopotamia—some of them probably as much as 8,000 years old—has even a veneer of loess; ancient potsherds, stone tools, bones, and other cultural debris are present exactly on the surface. It is possible, as Wirth (1958, p. 39) suggests, that the source of today's dust is actually only the disturbed or cultivated areas, largely confined to the Tigris valley. Thus in earlier times when agriculture or grazing was less widespread dust storms may have been less common than they are today.

Soil formation on early village sites on the piedmont plains shows a perceptible development in the form of a slight accumulation of organic matter in the upper several inches, a barely visible clay accumulation in the underlying "B" horizon, and a horizon of calcium carbonate concretions below. So many of the mounds have been either cultivated (if low) or eroded (if high) that precise measurements of profiles would probably be misleading. An attempt was made to locate buried soils under the cultural deposits at several sites, but the best that could be found consisted of a weak zone of carbonate concretions. No inferences can be drawn at this point about either the time factor or the climatic factor in the formation of soils before and after the occupation of the different prehistoric sites.

In conclusion, it may be stated that in the belt of foothills and lowlands, including the valley of the Tigris River itself, evidence for physiographic changes during the Pleistocene is present in the form of river terraces, river diversions, and a few other features, but there is little direct evidence that these features are all climatically controlled or that they can be correlated with any outside chronology, with the possible exception of the features of the Chemchemal plain. The situation for the post-Pleistocene is no more hopeful, again with the exception of the Chemchemal plain.

Desert Regions

Lakes

In the desert regions of western Iraq and adjacent Syria and Jordan, search was made without success for records of Pleistocene lakes which might reflect greater rainfall and/or lower temperature (evaporation) in the past. Closed depressions do exist as a result of structural deformation, underground solution of calcareor gypsiferous bedrock, deposition or deflation of sand, or volcanic activity (Wirth, 1958). One such depression (Abu Dibbis) near the Euphrates River in Iraq, which now serves as a reservoir for floodwater from the Euphrates, was recently investigated by Voute (1957), who found evidence that it once carried a salt lake of its own attributed in part to greater inflow of runoff from the desert side. The date of the old lake is indeterminate, however. Many other depressions in the desert area contain water periodically after rains and have broad silt-floored valleys.

Wadies

Another desert feature which may have value as an indicator of past climates is the wadi system of western Iraq and adjacent Syria and Saudi Arabia (Wright, 1958). The terrain in this region is marked by broad benches leading upward from the Euphrates River to the desert wastes of the Arabian plateau. The broad low scarps between benches are dissected by subparallel wadies which lose themselves on the flat benches below, partly because of coverings of wind-blown sand.

The wadi floors are marked by transverse vegetation stripes which reflect broad shallow troughs an inch or so deep but several tens or hundreds of feet apart (Wright, 1958). Surface moisture accumulates in these shallow troughs to favor growth of grass and small herbs. The microrelief and vegetation patterns are so inconspicuous on the ground that Wirth (1958), in his broad study of the land forms and soils of the Syrian-Iraqi desert, apparently did not notice them and mentions only that the wadi bottoms are covered with vegetation. The patterns are almost spectacular on air photographs, however (Wright, 1958), and as striking as the patterned ground in arctic regions.

The microrelief of the wadi bottoms seems to be controlled by localized swellings of soil in clay-rich zones transverse to the wadi axis. The mechanism of formation is not fully understood, but it is not related to the flow of surface water. The vegetation, microrelief, and soil formation would probably be destroyed by any important flow of surface water along the wadi floors; in fact, in the downstream segments of some of the larger wadies the pattern is destroyed by the development of a narrow central trench.

The wadi system itself may be very old, for Wirth (1958) believes that the upper benches are old Oligocene and Miocene peneplains modified on the east by repeated Miocene marine transgressions. The wadi networks on the low scarps between benches may therefore have started formation as early as the Miocene. They were certainly occupied and modified by running water during the Pleistocene pluvial periods, but they now seem to be essentially extinct. Whatever precipitation there is in this area under the present climatic conditions (ca. 4-5 in. per year) must largely infiltrate or result in sheet-wash of negligible erosive or transporting power. There is no alluvium on the wadi floors but only sandy silt with scattered pavement of angular stones, all derived by weathering from the shallow underlying bedrock.

Soils

The soil under the desert pavement may be of some paleoclimatic significance. The pavement itself consists of wind-polished stones scattered either loosely or closely on a substratum of buff stony calcareous silt. The silt is the upper horizon (1-2 ft. thick) of a soil which extends downward into caliche subcrust with red clay matrix. This type of soil underlies the bottoms of the extinct wadies described above and was found as well over the lava area of the Jabal Druze in northeastern Jordan and in adjacent regions, where the rainfall is only a very few inches per year.

Wirth (1958) believes that the silty upper horizon of the soil is a result of disintegration of bedrock by formation of small calcite crystals resulting from rapid wetting and drying (solution and reprecipitation of carbonate) during the infrequent showers and that the calcareous subcrust results from precipitation of carbonate following deeper penetration of winter rainfall. He considers that such a soil can result from modern climatic conditions in this area. The writer believes, however, that the presence of the red clay matrix of the subsoil suggests more chemical weathering than can be accomplished under present moisture conditions and would rather consider these soils to be essentially a relic of a pluvial climate. Wirth would agree at least that the soils are quite old and that the formation at least started during the Pleistocene. At the archeological site of Khirbat al-Ambachi on the north edge of the Jabal Druze, south of Damascus, the writer found such a soil buried by a lava flow dated by C^{14} analysis as 4,075 years old (De Vries and Barendsen, 1954).

Dating

None of the Pleistocene lakes, wadies, sand dunes, soils, or other geomorphic features of the desert regions between the Levant and Mesopotamia has so far been dated with any precision with respect to any Pleistocene chronology—climatic, archeologic, or absolute. Numerous finds of worked flints have been reported over this area and adjacent Saudi Arabia by many people (e.g. Coon, 1957; Field, 1956; Rhotert, 1938; Waechter and Seton-Williams, 1938; Zeuner, 1957), and more careful search for major Pleistocene oases may produce more information (see p. 96). The occurrence of possible Acheulean core-bifaces near a spring at Azraq in eastern Jordan (Harding, 1958) may have potential in this connection. The important climatic and archeologic records in the North African oases may also serve as examples.

Conclusions

The potentialities for a reliable Pleistocene climatic chronology for the interior region, that is, the Syrian desert, Mesopotamia, and the Taurus-Zagros arc, are probably not so good as those for the coast of the Levant because of the absence of marine strand lines and associated deposits that provide a base for the local chronology. On the other hand, the glacial features of the high mountains are moderately well developed and have a better chance of being matched directly with comparable features in the Alps. Climatic effects in the foothills synchronous with the extension of mountain glaciers are of particular importance because of their relations to human habitation.

Geologic work in the mountains and foothills, however, has not progressed to the point where subdivisions of the last glacial or pluvial stage can be attempted. Even at their maximum extent the glaciers were quite small and were confined to the fairly narrow mountain valleys. No successive moraine loops comparable to those in the Alpine piedmont were found. If one adopts the current concepts of Alpine glacial chronology, as discussed in detail above, the maximum glacial extension occurred late in the last cold period (ca. 20,000 years ago), and during the earlier phases the ice may have remained far up in the mountains.

At the time of maximum glaciation in the Zagros Mountains, the snow line was apparently 6,000 feet lower than it is at present. Whether the tree line was depressed a comparable amount is not certain. In the Alps the snow line was lowered about 4,000 feet and the tree line even more (Firbas, 1939). However, the ameliorating effect of the desert lowland may have lessened the temperature reduction at low altitudes, as Mortensen (1957) suggests for subtropical mountains. It appears likely from the snow-line evidence in the Zagros Mountains, however, that the outer foothills and piedmont of this region (elevation 1,000-3,000 ft.) must have been wooded during the last glacial period. Whether trees extended out into the Mesopotamian lowland is undertermined at present.

Of particular interest in the present archeological problem is the climate during the transition from the terminal food-collecting stages to the time of the village-farming communities. The interval involved extends from perhaps 10,000 B.C. (on the basis of C^{14} determinations for the Zarzian level at Shanidar cave; see p. 147) to about 6750 B.C. (on the basis of the cluster of C^{14} determinations considered by Braidwood to be the most probable for Jarmo; see p. 159). How can we reconstruct the climate of this time on geologic evidence? From the local relations there is very little evidence. The very fact that Shanidar cave was re-occupied by about 10,000 B.C., after an inferred long period of nonoccupance, suggests that the upper tree line had risen again, so that the area was more hospitable (see p. 90). Other caves and rock shelters in the foothills were also occupied by the Zarzian people—Palegawra, Zarzi, Barak, Hajiyah, Babkhal (see pp. 57-60). One assumes, of course, that the Zarzian people would not have lived in such caves if they had been located in the relatively inhospitable habitat above the tree line; perhaps, however, they were only summer sites. It may be pointed out in this connection that at present in this region all permanent villages (which of course subsist on farming and herding rather than on hunting) are confined to elevations below the upper tree line, although such is not the case on the barren drier plateaus north of the Zagros Mountains in Iran and Turkey.

The only other local indicators of climate for this time interval are the snails of Palegawra and Zarzi, which suggest climatic conditions not greatly different from those of the present (pp. 169 f. below; Garrod, 1930). The wood and vertebrate remains from Palegawra imply similar climatic conditions then and now, although the possibility of importation from different life zones must be taken into consideration.

The rate of climatic amelioration in the Zagros Mountains after the glacial maximum, therefore, cannot be determined with any accuracy on the basis of the local evidence. In the Alps the retreat of the last ice is marked by distinct moraines that can be correlated from valley to valley, and the elevation of the snow line at each stage is calculated. In as much as no stadial moraines have been identified in the Zagros Mountains, such stages of ice retreat and climatic change cannot be worked out. Solely for the purpose of comparison, however, it may be mentioned that in the Alps the inferred snow line rose from about 4,000 feet below the present level at the glacial maximum in about 18,000 B.C. to about 3,000 feet below the present level for the Geschnitz stadial, which is generally believed to represent the moderate re-advance of the ice in about 8500 B.C. after the Alleröd warm fluctuation that is recorded in pollen diagrams all over Europe. During the postglacial warm period in the Alps (centering ca. 4000 B.C.) the snow line was reportedly about 1,000 feet above its present position (Klebelsberg, 1949, pp. 704-11; Gross, 1954). The tree line at each stage was of course several hundred feet below the snow line.

A supplementary method of vegetational and climatic reconstruction in the Alps, as also in northern Europe, is the study of late-glacial and postglacial peat and lake sediments in which the vegetational history is recorded by the pollen grains that are blown from the near-by vegetated terrain. Thus the distinctive late-glacial Alleröd pollen zone, first identified in Denmark, has been traced all over Europe and into the Alps, where its presence gives a clue to the correlation of late-glacial moraine stages between the Alps and the north (Gross, 1954). Similarly the postglacial pollen zones, changing in character from one vegetational province to another, have been traced from Scandinavia, where they were first identified, southward to the Alps.

Pollen studies remain as the major technique of paleoclimatic study untried in the eastern Mediterranean area. The difficulties are great because the modern flora is not well known, there are few good lake or swamp sites from which suitable samples can be taken, and those lakes that do exist do not have a base on dated material. The last difficulty might be overcome by radiocarbon dating of selected samples.

A few small lakes occur high in the glaciated Zagros Mountains of northeastern Iraq at elevations of 8,000-9,000 feet, well above the present tree line. These lakes have a firm base on glacial deposits of the last glaciation, although the absolute date is of course not known. Other suitable lakes or swampy areas may be found in the foothills or lowlands, but on undated materials. Several large lakes of tectonic or volcanic origin are present in the Levant, for example Amuq Lake, the Ghab Marshes, Lake Hulah, etc. Pollen analyses at such sites might show the extent of depression of the life zones from the mountains into the piedmont and lowlands during the last pluvial period. They should not only record the vegetational and climatic history extending well back into the Pleistocene but perhaps also reveal the vegetational disturbances caused by the inception of agriculture and grazing.

For the desert areas of the eastern Mediterranean, the prospects for a useful chronology depend on the discovery of an oasis situation in which there are well defined physiographic or paleontologic indicators along with archeological remains, plus materials for radiocarbon analysis. Oasis sites in Egypt (e.g. Caton-Thompson, 1952) have yielded information about possible climatic fluctuations. Comparable sites in the deserts of Iraq and Syria may some day be discovered, and the findings of Voute (1957) at the Abu Dibbis despression and those reported by Harding (1958) in Jordan indicate that there is some hope.

Studies in the interior of Iran have revealed a number of physiographic features which Bobek (1954) has put together in a historical-ecological survey directed toward showing the relationship between climatic change and early man. Bobek emphasizes that the Iranian plateau climatically is a part of the great Asiatic land mass, whereas the Mediterranean desert belt has more of an oceanic climate. During the glacial stages of the Pleistocene, according to Bobek, the Mediterranean deserts may have experienced greater rainfall, but the great interior of Asia was covered by an air mass even more stable than at present and the Iranian plateau may therefore have experienced lower temperatures but not increased precipitation. The expansion of Pleistocene lakes here is attributed by Bobek to the resultant decrease in evaporation rather than to greater rainfall. Dissected rubble deposits on mountain slopes are considered to be a result more of increased Pleistocene frost action than of increased precipitation. For the middle of the postglacial period, however, Bobek postulates a dry period in Iran on the basis of the occurrence of loess below shore lines of the Caspian Sea that are correlated with the last pluvial period. The subsequent forestation of the loess deposits suggests return to a moister climate. Additional evidence for a dry period comes from the occurrence of sand dunes bordering lake basins from which the sand must have been blown but which now contain water. Having set up this sequence, Bobek discusses the influence of the postglacial dry period on the inception of agriculture and herding and the effect of the subsequent moister climate on the development of nomadism.

Bobek's comprehensive study of the Pleistocene and recent paleoecology of Iran is important for his conclusions with respect to the early development of farming, herding, and other cultural trends—conclusions which have already been adopted in analyses of anthropological problems (e.g. von Wissmann, 1957). There is little doubt that there are valid paleoclimatic indicators on the Iranian plateau and bordering mountain ranges, but unfortunately not all of them can be dated easily, particularly such desert or semidesert features as lake strand lines, slope deposits, and sand dunes. In as much as Iran lies outside the area under consideration here, critical discussion of Bobek's thesis must be reserved for another occasion.

With regard to the effect of climatic change on cultural development on the outer flanks of the Taurus-Zagros Mountains from the Persian Gulf to Syria and Turkey, it should be emphasized that climate and thus vegetation, animal life, and other ecological factors important in human existence are closely controlled by elevation. Altitudinal zonation of all of these elements is very clear at present, and the life zones range with altitude from desert-steppe to steppe to woodland to alpine. Climatic change during the maximum of the last glacial period undoubtedly resulted in a lowering of the upper zones by several thousand feet and may have affected the lower zones as well. Early man may have been excluded from the higher mountains, at least in winter, but he had only to follow the life zones to lower elevations. The life zones included open woodlands that contained the domesticable animals and almost certainly the wild grains, just as they do today.

In later times, as the glaciers and life zones remounted the ridges, the variety and extent of preferred habitats may have been much the same as before, while the locations and the elvations changed. Although at present there is no means of dating directly the chronology of this climatic phase, comparison may be made with the climatic sequence in the Alps, which is based on radiocarbon determinations as well as pollen chronology and glacier activity for late-glacial and postglacial Europe. This Alpine chronology involves ice recession starting in about 18,000 B.C. and accelerating after 8500 B.C. If the sequence in the Zagros Mountains was synchronous with that in the Alps, then these times of rapid climatic change in the Zagros area involved the period (ca. 10,000-7000 B.C.) which saw the transition from a hunting, food-gathering economy, with habitation primarily in caves, to a village-farming economy. In view of the diversity of habitats available in both glacial and early postglacial times in the Zagros belt, however, it is not safe to infer that this important and relatively rapid revolution was necessarily brought about by climatic change. Favorable habitats for animal and plant domestigation had long been available, but man had not reached the technological level to exploit them. It seems to the writer that the gradual evolution of culture, with increasing complexity and perfection of tool technology, may have been a more potent factor in bringing about this economic revolution than was the climatic change at the end of the glacial period. By the same token, the paleoclimatic evidence in the Zagros region is not sufficiently precise to indicate that environmental changes during subsequent prehistoric times were great enough to have important regional effects on the further development of cultural levels. Future work in climatic reconstructions must be directed toward a search for sensitive paleoclimatic indicators that can be dated with some precision, so that the subtle relations between environment and culture can be worked out for this area for the time range of this important economic revolution.

VIII

THE PALEOETHNOBOTANY OF THE NEAR EAST AND EUROPE[1]

Hans Helbaek

INTRODUCTION

For more than a hundred years there has been a certain degree of co-operation between the botanist and the archeologist. Lignified and carbonized grain and wood found in archeological excavations have been identified, and thus a certain aspect of the dependency of man upon the plant world has been illuminated. In several respects, however, this co-operation was motivated by views which were too narrow. The archeologist usually thought in terms of artifacts when he was trying to picture man's past achievements, and the botanist put foremost the purely taxonomic interest in the plant material handed to him by the excavator. The realization that man and nature could not have been what they were without the profound influence of one upon the other is of quite recent date (Iversen, 1941). This fundamental interdependency cannot be understood unless the remains of plants are synchronized with the proper cultural levels. Discrepancies in dating make the whole picture meaningless. In the past dating was not always regarded with the same earnestness that it is today, nor were the dating techniques so well developed as they are now. The botanist was in most cases just a laboratory scientist who never saw a dig and who had to accept the observations of the biologically unskilled archeologist. In consequence, much of the literature on paleoethnobotany is quite useless because of wrong dates on the one hand and faulty identifications on the other. It is amazing that the first serious work in this field, Oswald Heer's "Die Pflanzen der Pfahlbauten," written in 1865, still towers as a monument of morphological skill and spiritual dash, unsupported as it was by previous experience in this field or background of reference.

During the last few decades, close teamwork between biologists and archeologists has made a fair start. Natural scientists go to excavations and make their own professional assessments, or they do their own excavating and at the same time become steeped in the scientific and technical background of archeology. Biologists go to the field to study prehistoric deposits in situ and to make ecological observations of present conditions. Only by such means will it be possible in the long run to build up the image of the true conditions of man's life in the remote past.

Essentially paleoethnobotany rests upon morphological and anatomical comparison of prehistoric plant remains with contemporary plants. The archeological botanical materials consist of carbonized plant parts, imprints of grain and seeds in pottery and sun-dried adobe, lignified vegetable material such as the food deposits in ancient Egyptian tombs, and, more sporadically, the silica skeletons of chaff and straw and the stomach contents of prehistoric corpses preserved in peat bogs (Helbaek, 1955a and 1958a).

Technically, the study of ancient plants is performed by macroscopic comparison as well as by microscopic analysis. The material of all the categories is procured by archeology, and its dating—of paramount significance—also depends upon archeology.

Any attempt to draw up a comprehensive history of the cultivated plants should natu-

---

[1][A basic bibliography of the sources used throughout this paper, as it refers to work done before 1953, is to be found in Helbaek, 1953a. Occasional references are made to more recent work.—R.J.B.]

rally begin with the transition between the food-collecting and the food-producing stages of human economy. Hitherto it has been difficult to get even tolerably near this critical point, and it must be realized that the actual turning point of the transition will never be demonstrable in full, either botanically or culturally. Paleolithic man did not suddenly resolve to give up his perambulations and settle down to tilling the soil and tending crops, immediately beginning to build the houses and make the specialized tools which permanent settlement implies. Probably some kind of nursing and protection of the wild food plants came first, without either actual specialized implements or sedentary life, while only eventually did the advantage of tillage and of permanent residence dawn upon the earliest farmers.

Hence, the first steps in the transition can hardly have left very clearly recognizable traces for the archeologist to excavate and interpret. At present, plant materials found in archeological sites which contain the earliest known traces of permanent dwellings are our nearest approach to evidence of the emergence of agriculture. The plant remains themselves may furnish some precise clues (pp. 102 f.), but an approximate analogy for the cultural stage just before permanent settlement began may perhaps be seen in the feeble agricultural achievements of certain present-day nomads. These people wander through the same tracts a few times a year and—in tiny depressions in the desert—grow small variform plots of wheat and barley, seemingly not watching them until the time of ripening.

The subsequent stages of early plant husbandry are also but fragmentarily illuminated. Our present knowledge of the history of cultivated plants is no more than an irregular patchwork whose gaps we try to fill by speculation. We have every hope of gaining a more thorough understanding of what happened in the developing stages, however, if continuous and intelligent co-operation is maintained between the archeologist and the botanist.

It has been my unique privilege to enjoy the opportunities of studying numerous freshly excavated plant deposits, covering many periods, from the historically important foci of western Asia, Egypt, the Mediterranean lands, Switzerland, western Europe, and Scandinavia. Further, the generosity of the American Philosophical Society, the Oriental Institute of Chicago, the Danish National Museaum, the Danish Carlsberg Foundation, and the Iraq Government's Directorate General of Antiquities and its Economic Development Board has enabled me to travel widely in the Near East to study the ecological conditions prevailing in the lands where agriculture was first developed. The following attempt at sketching the migrations and development of the most important crop plants of the ancient cultures in Hither Asia, Egypt, and Europe is based largely upon my personal understanding as affected by the impressions that I gained during these recent experiences. (It should be noted that I use the names Kurdistan and Mesopotamia to refer to northern and southern Iraq, respectively.)

HISTORY OF THE CEREALS

Wheat

Cytologically the cultivated species of Triticum, the wheat genus, are classified into three groups: the diploid group with 2 x 7 chromosomes, consisting only of einkorn; the tetraploid group with 4 x 7 chromosomes, including emmer, hard wheat, rivet wheat, and several others; and the hexaploid group with 6 x 7 chromosomes, comprising bread wheat, club wheat, and spelt.

Irrespective of genetical views, however, einkorn, emmer, and spelt are often placed together on purely morphological grounds in a group called the "glume wheats." As opposed to all other wheats, these three have retained some of the characters typical of the wild species, such as a rather fragile axis (rachis) and stiff, close-fitting glumes which do not release the kernels during threshing. In all other wheats the kernel is loose within the spikelet at maturity and is easily detached and separated from the chaff. These other wheats are called the "naked wheats."

WHEAT

genus Triticum

	diploid (2 x 7)	tetraploid (4 x 7)	hexaploid (6 x 7)
Wild forms	T. aegilopoides	T. dicoccoides	
Glume wheats	einkorn (T. monococcum)	emmer (T. dicoccum)	spelt (T. spelta)
Naked wheats		hard wheat (T. durum) rivet wheat (T. turgidum) etc.	bread wheat (T. vulgare) club wheat (T. compactum) etc.

Consequently, in carbonized grain and in imprints of grain in clay the glumes of the glume wheats very often occur associated with the kernels, thus ensuring positive identification even when the grain is puffed and misshapen or the imprint of the kernel is ambiguous. In deposits of naked wheat no glumes or internodes are normally found, but, as the kernels of all the tetraploid naked wheats are slender and those of the hexaploid naked varieties are squat and rounded, it is possible to discriminate between these two groups. On this basis alone, however, the actual species itself cannot be distinguished. Spelt has a kernel of intermediary type, which varies so much when it is carbonized that, without the guidance of spikelet parts, its remains are in many cases difficult to specify.

It is, of course, impossible to ascertain the number of chromosomes in carbonized grain, but, since today the squat kernel is typical of the hexaploid group, it is warrantable to assume that prehistoric kernels of this shape also belonged to this group. The length of the internode, and the consequent density with which spikelets occur on the axis, is a character that fluctuates in parallel fashion in the hexaploid and tetraploid groups. Thus there is in the hard wheat (tetraploid) group a fluctuation of density corresponding to that between the lax spelt ear and the very dense spike of club wheat, both of the hexaploid group. It is worth noting that the blunt kernels that have been found in prehistoric deposits associated with determinative spike elements have proved to be of the dense type, that is, club wheat.

The Triticum sphaerococcum, Indian wheat, which John Percival claims for several Mediterranean finds, is the usual European type which generally is named club wheat. It should, on the other hand, be understood that when no spikelet parts are found, the term club wheat may, theoretically, include the lax-eared bread wheat as well.

Emmer

The wheat which occurs associated with the artifacts of early village-farmers from western Asia and Egypt to Britain and Scandinavia is principally emmer, Triticum dicoccum Schübl. The innumerable wheat occurrences from Egypt dating from predynastic villages to the time of the Roman Empire are almost exclusively of this species, which for all time levels appears as a highly developed cereal. Even in the earliest predynastic villages it is distinctly different morphologically from any wild species (Caton-Thompson and Gardner, 1934; Lauer, Laurent-Täckholm, and Aaberg, 1950).

The distinguished Russian plant geographer Vavilov (1926), whose extensive plant collections in Asia and eastern Africa transformed the basis of the modern approach to the genetic and geographic origin of cultivated plants, propounded the theory that the place in which a cultivated plant occurs in the greatest diversity (the multiplicity center or the gene center) should be considered the place of its origin. Vavilov identified the present gene center for emmer in Abyssinia, and this circumstance, together with the early occurrence of emmer in Egypt as a highly important food plant, led to the belief that the species was first cultivated in Abyssinia. During early predynastic Egyptian times it was supposed to have spread from upper Egypt, in part across the Red Sea to Yemen, in part northward along the Nile and through the eastern Mediterranean littoral to Syria, whence it would have branched out to Mesopotamia in the east, on the one hand, and to Asia Minor in the northwest and on to Europe, on the other. Since the tetraploid wild wheat Triticum dicoccoides Koern was not present in Abyssinia, Vavilov simply rejected it as the progenitor of cultivated emmer (T. dicoccum).

Contrary to Vavilov's views, I am convinced that emmer spread to Abyssinia from Egypt at a time when it was still being grown in Egypt. The archeological evidence substantiates this conviction (see below). The present Abyssinian emmer is of the same main variety as the ancient Egyptian one. Apart from this we have no factual knowledge regarding its history in Abyssinia. The commercial contact across the Red Sea from Yemen during the last two millenniums may well account for the introduction of emmer from Abyssinia into Yemen and from there to India. Obviously, Abyssinia, with its extreme climatic diversities, constitutes a natural barrier to the further distribution of the species, and this very circumstance is undoubtedly the reason so many different varieties developed in the area. The varietal multiplicity in a species has, fundamentally, no dependence on a very long factor of time, although multiplicity certainly is dependent on ecological conditions; it is an aspect of the adaptational process.

In discussions of the history of plant husbandry, a migration route from Egypt to Spain along the North African coastlands has often been propounded. This is a sheer postulate with no foundation in fact. In my opinion, agriculture in North Africa, including Egypt, came with settlers from across the sea, from a variety of points of vantage on the eastern and northern shores of the Mediterranean. It is still an open question whether the region between Egypt and northwestern Africa was consistently settled in earlier postglacial times. Culture contact and traffic across the Straits of Gibraltar were probably already pendulum-like and thus present an isolated problem.

At present the wild T. dicoccoides is generally acknowledged as the progenitor of emmer, and thus we must look for the place of original cultivation of emmer within the distributional area of the wild species, which extends from Palestine and Syria to the Zagros Mountains of the northern foothills of Iraqi Kurdistan and Iran. As a matter of fact, this is exactly the area in which the first traces of initial cultivation have been established archeologically. The present evidence happens to come from northeastern Iraq, but it is quite likely that domestication will prove to have started in several places within the whole distributional range of T. dicoccoides.

When we consider the fact that all the emmer so far described and recorded from early villages is of a comparatively uniform and highly specialized type, we realize that it cannot have derived from crops of the first few generations of deliberately cultivated plants, not even from the first hundred generations. Some time must have elapsed since the wild wheat was first taken under cultivation to account for the form in which we first see emmer in the general run of sites representing the early village-farming community. In a really early stage of cultivation we would expect to find cereals of varied and wild types. Furthermore, we should be entitled to interpret the presence of cereals approximating wild types as indicating cereal cultivation in its initial stages. Recently such a find was actually made at Jarmo. A series of grain imprints in clay lumps revealed spikelets of a wheat (Pl. 27A, C) very close to the present wild T. dicoccoides (Pl. 27B) and much larger and coarser than the oldest emmer known so far. Some of the carbonized grains (Pl. 27D) from the same layers of Jarmo very closely resemble the wild wheat in size and appearance and are quite different from the developed "neolithic" emmer found in other localities.

There seems to be no reason to doubt that at Jarmo we are faced with the earliest stage of plant husbandry yet discovered, an assumption that is strongly supported by the relatively primitive appearance of the cultural remains as a whole. However, that even Jarmo does not represent the very first steps in the agricultural economy is suggested by the fact that its wheat spikelets seem to belong to a crop of a conspicuously mixed character, some of them being large and coarse, others more delicate and bearing more resemblance to the typical cultivated emmer. Evidently, human selection had not been carried very far, and one gets the impression that the early steps in the morphological change caused by cultivation were accomplished comparatively quickly. It is probable that the mutation rate was accelerated by forcing the wild plants to grow below the limits of their natural habitat, that is, in altitudes and localities more suitable for tilling the soil and utilizing the rainfall than were the steep slopes where the wild T. dicoccoides usually grows.

Supported by theoretical conclusions as well as by this excavated evidence, we may now conclude that emmer was brought to the west from northeastern Iraq and possibly from other places within the distributional range of the wild prototype by the so-called "great neolithic migration," whether or not this expression should be understood as inferring an actual long-range movement of populations. At the eastern end of the Mediterranean the flow divided, and in one way or another emmer spread southward to Egypt and northward to Asia Minor and Europe and eventually reached northwestern Africa. Some part of its transmission was undoubtedly by sea. Incidentally, at some early time agriculture also made an eastward move which eventually resulted in agricultural settlements in the Indus Valley and Chorasmia south of the Aral Sea, for instance. On its way east, however, it seems that emmer shortly found unsuitable ecological conditions and was ousted by the hexaploid wheats in Afghanistan and India (until its probably recent introduction in India; see p. 102).

We have already noted that emmer occurs abundantly in the predynastic deposits of Egypt; it is also found in early horizons in Iraq, Palestine, Syria, and Asia Minor. All along the Danube, the first peasant farmers cultivated this cereal. The most spectacular European discovery of "neolithic" emmer was made in 1854 in the Swiss Lake dwellings. Only after its identification in Switzerland was emmer acknowledged as a prehistoric cereal of Europe. Since the time of Oswald Heer's identification, it has been gradually realized that emmer spread to all parts of the continent that have so far been investigated. Moreover, it is now clear that this spread was accomplished by the earliest village-farmers and that emmer probably served almost everywhere as the principal food plant. In no tolerably large "neolithic" find does the supremacy of emmer seem to be in any way contested, except in Switzerland itself; there, on the other hand, the Michelsberg culture seems to have relied largely on club wheat (pp. 104 f.). The emmer plant thrived even in the then subboreal climate of northwestern Europe, a region where it would hardly produce a profitable crop today (Helbaek, 1953b and 1954).

Since emmer is present wherever we encounter the primary levels of the food-producing stage in central, western, and northern Europe, it will undoubtedly prove to be present in southern Europe also, when relevant material is uncovered. During the succeeding or "Bronze Age," its supremacy was encroached upon from various sides; in northern Europe by barley in particular, in southern Europe by club wheat as well as barley. Club wheat seems to have replaced emmer to some extent in Asia Minor, Syria, and Palestine during the second millennium B.C. Evidence for the situation in Iraq is not satisfactorily clear at the moment, but at least one find, of the early second millennium at Bazmosian in Kurdistan, consists mainly of club wheat. Samples of club wheat now in Egyptian museums seem to indicate that the cereal was either grown in or possibly imported into Egypt in the late first millennium B.C. On the barbaric fringe of northwestern Europe, however, emmer still lingered on long after the birth of Christ; in Denmark it lasted until the third century, in Gotland, Sweden, until the fourth, and in northern Britain until the sixth century. Even today, it is cultivated to a certain degree in central Europe, Spain, Morocco, Russia, and the Balkans, as also in Transcaucasia, Iran, Yemen, Abyssinia, and India. Its cultivation in India is considered a fairly recent phenomenon, for no old Indian name is known for the plant (which incidentally is an argument of doubtful value). This area would be an extension of the Abyssinia-Yemen line. However, future finds of grain from the early Indus Valley cultures may cause us to modify our views on this point.

Other Tetraploid Wheats

Cytologically, emmer is grouped with a number of naked wheats, all of them tetraploid. It is believed that these species were derived from emmer by mutation or interbreeding among extreme varieties. They display a great diversity in morphological and physiological features, approaching emmer on the one hand and the bread-wheat group on the other. Even though archeology has not yet contributed to an understanding of the history of the naked tetraploid wheats before their occurrence in Egypt in Greco-Roman times, these species deserve mention. According to the theory of their phylogeny, the naked tetraploid wheats would have emerged somewhere in the area of emmer, possibly in the region between the Mediterranean and Transcaucasia. A great number of varieties are cultivated in this area even today. Only one member of this group, hard wheat (*T. durum* Desf.), has gained a position of importance in world economy. It occupies the summer-dry steppe regions all over the world where bread wheat cannot thrive. Another member of this group is rivet wheat (*T. turgidum* L.), which is grown in western and Mediterranean Europe and as far east as Transcaucasia. It has been claimed that these two species occurred in various prehistoric contexts, but no evidence has yet been offered to substantiate the claim.

Hexaploid Wheats

A further development of emmer is reflected by the bread-wheat group of hexaploid naked wheats. These varieties, comprising the dense-eared club wheat (*T. compactum* Host.) and the above-mentioned Indian wheat (*T. sphaerococcum* Perc.), as well as the lax-eared bread wheat (*T. vulgare* Vill.), were at one time supposed to have emerged in central Asia, where a multiplicity center has been identified by Vavilov. Again it should be pointed out that the diversity within this center is due in all probability to the position of central Asia as an ecological outpost for the hexaploid wheats rather than to a particularly long duration of the grain in these regions. Their actual center of emergence is to be sought farther west in Asia. Their origin has been ascribed to chromosome aberration in emmer, but Percival suggested that goat-face grass (*Aegilops*) was involved in a hybridization with emmer. If this is true, the area of origin for the bread-wheat group would be in regions where *Aegilops* and emmer occur together, as in the uplands which stretch between the Caspian and Mediterranean. The emergence and beginnings of cultivation of the naked hexaploid wheats are by no means clear. Whatever view is taken of their phylogeny, they certainly emerged in Asia.

The overall picture of the early occurrence of club wheat is as follows. One imprint is recorded from Jamdat Nasr in Mesopotamia at about 3000 B.C.; slightly earlier, stray club-wheat kernels have been found with emmer at Merimdah Beni Salamah and al-Omari in Egypt. Strangely, we have no finds of club wheat immediately following in lowland Mesopotamia and Egypt. Club wheat is found sporadically in Kurdistan in the middle third millennium B.C. It does not turn up as a cultivated species in Iraq until about 2000 B.C., but then a deposit of the Hurrians at Bazmosian in Kurdistan (unpublished) contains so much club wheat that it must be considered as having been of major importance to these people. Later in the second millennium B.C. and at the beginning of the first, club wheat occurs in bulk in Turkey, Syria, and Palestine (Helbaek, 1958b), and at the end of the first millennium it again turns up in Egypt (Helbaek, 1955b). The latter grain, however, may well have been imported. Thereafter, the tetraploid naked species take over in the areas in question, both in the mountains and on the plains.

In contrast to the situation in the Near East, club wheat is among the earliest cereals established in certain areas in Europe (Helbaek, 1954). In Switzerland and Denmark it is recorded together with einkorn and emmer for the earliest agricultural settlements (2700 to 2500 B.C.), and in the central European Michelsberg culture it was the most important cereal toward the end of the third millennium B.C. (Guyan, 1954). From then on, it occurs sporadically but continuously over most of Europe but seems to have been of only minor importance, most often occurring as a weed in the emmer field. The evidence seems to show that in Spain it was fairly common during the second millennium. Club and bread wheats replaced emmer over most of lowland Europe in the beginning of our era.

The conclusion to be drawn from this pattern seems to be that the hexaploid wheat emerged sporadically in very early times, possibly with the beginning of agriculture when T. dicoccoides was subjected to greater mutation and hybridization by the forcible change of ecology. It may well have emerged intermittently at various places in which it could not thrive in its initial form under the given conditions. It may have established itself as a definite species with full powers of propagation within the limits of cultivation only under certain specific conditions. One of these conditions seems to be the factor of altitude; club wheat never thrived in irrigated lands but occurred for the first time as an established cultivated plant in mountainous areas. Also, its very appearance in Asia Minor, Syria, Palestine and, especially, Kurdistan suggests an increase of rainfall during the second millennium, even though this is not a commonly accepted view. It is difficult to understand this sudden appearance and subsequent practical extinction of a species in a given area without presupposing some kind of change in climatic situation. Moreover, present-day evidence shows that club and bread wheats are species which prefer summer rains.

Today, it is mainly in Asia that dense-eared wheats are grown, but club wheat is still cultivated in mountainous central Europe along with other old-fashioned cereals.

Spelt

Spelt (T. spelta L.) represents an unusual mixture of genes. It is hexaploid, but we have noted that morphologically it belongs with the glume wheats, having its kernels jammed into a sturdy spikelet structure. Even so, it has a mode of articulation of the spike which differs from that of the other glume wheats. It breaks at the upper end instead of the lower end of the internode, a peculiarity which it does not share with any other Triticum but which it does have in common with some of the Aegilops (goat-face grass) species of the Near East, a genus closely related to Triticum.

A hundred years ago the first prehistoric spelt was excavated in "Bronze Age" deposits in Switzerland, and further finds were eventually made in that country and in neighboring regions of Germany. Recently it has been identified in first millennium B.C. contexts, for example in Poland (Wasylikowa, 1956), in Alsace, in England (where it was also important in the Roman period), in the "Late Bronze Age" and "Roman Iron Age" of Denmark, and in the "Late Iron Age" of Gotland in Sweden. In 1954 the writer found it in abundance in deposits of the early second millennium B.C. (or "Early Bronze Age") in northern Italy and in the later pre-urban tombs in Rome.

The Romans are known to have appreciated spelt to such an extent that they organized Germanic settlements in northern Italy in late imperial times. Furthermore, Germanic tribes migrating to remote parts of Europe carried the cereal to such out-of-the-way places as Asturias and the Banat in historic times. It is curiously characteristic of spelt that it seems to have remained attached to those ethnic groups with which it moved from central Europe. Apart from Asturias and the Banat, spelt is today grown only in Switzerland, southern Germany, and the Eifel-Ardennes region. In spite of constant reference to the species in Russia, Turkey, and elsewhere, there is no evidence of its cultivation beyond the above-mentioned localities.

It is very difficult to explain the phylogenetic origin of spelt. We first see it both north and south of the Alps in the first half of the second millennium B.C. Even taking the recent discoveries into account, however, we may assume that there is still much to be learned about its actual distribution in the past, in both time and space. The resemblance between the carbonized remains of emmer and spelt is the great stumbling block to a trustworthy recognition of spelt. Hence, claimed recognitions of spelt by casual observers only confuse the issue, and frequently its carbonized remains have been passed off as those of emmer.

On the basis of its prehistoric distribution as known a few decades ago, only one opinion was possible as to the origin of spelt: it emerged in the Alps, and this happened in about 1500 B.C. Phylogenetically this could have come about by chromosome aberration in club wheat or by hybridization between emmer and club wheat. At present this concept can hardly be improved upon. However, it is interesting to note that speltlike wheats can be produced experimentally in more than one way. An interesting explanation was offered by John Percival; he suggested producing spelt by crossing emmer with Aegilops, and this experimentally derived explanation has the advantage above all others in that it accounts for the specific mode of articulation in spelt. The feasibility of Percival's hypothesis was borne out by subsequent experiments. In an interesting paper two American geneticists (McFadden and Sears, 1946) report on a series of experiments on hybridization between Triticum dicoccoides and Aegilops squarrosa. It is outside the scope of my paper to discuss genetical research as such, but it may be pointed out that the ensuing conclusions do not entirely tally with paleoethnobotanical findings up to the present. In fact, it is a recurrent shortcoming of the geneticists that they disregard the time factor; they sometimes propose cultivated plant development in areas where no agricultural activity is demonstrable for the pertinent archeological time range. Vavilov's suggested gene centers and consequent emergences in Abyssinia and central Asia (see pp. 102, 110) and Aaberg's "wild" barley center (see p. 110) are cases in point. McFadden's and Sear's experimentally derived explanation of the emergence of spelt in the Near East is another case in point. Their explanation has the disadvantage that it presupposes emergence of spelt in southwest Asia, while the known prehistoric occurrences of the cereal are confined to Europe, as is also its present cultivation. Furthermore, it gives a phylogenetic priority to spelt over and above the naked hexaploid wheats. This is not in agreement with facts established by paleoethnobotany in southwestern Asia.

The word "spelt," which seems to be of Germanic origin, spread to Latin and all western European languages. Because of the general external similarity of einkorn, emmer, and spelt, the name "spelt" has been applied almost arbitrarily to any one of them, thus creating a most deplorable confusion in both the literature and statistics. Modern plant geography has done a great deal to clear up this matter, but even quite recent works on cereal geography may be rather unreliable because of this ambiguity. Erman and Grapow (1925) give ancient Egyptian words for "spelt," which are quite misleading since this cereal has never been found in Egypt.

Einkorn

All the species described above are believed to be more or less direct progeny of T. dicoccoides. Only one cultivated species, einkorn, cannot be related to this pedigree. This species (T. monococcum L.), the only cultivated wheat which is diploid, is evidently a descendant of the wild T. aegilopoides Bal., which is related to the genus Aegilops of the Near East.

Although morphologically attached to emmer and spelt, having the same sturdy spikelet construction and rather brittle axis, einkorn is quite independent in biological behavior. Whereas among most of the Triticum species it is very easy to produce fertile hybrids, it is next to impossible to cross einkorn successfully with any other wheat. Owing to this circumstance, it has been left out of most phylogenetic theories.

One variety of wild einkorn is distributed in the Balkans. Another reaches from Asia Minor to Palestine and northern Kurdistan. Wild einkorn grows together with wild emmer (T. dicoccoides) in the eastern and southern fringe area of its distribution, and it is rather difficult even for botanists to discriminate between the two in a mixed growth. It is conceivable that the first agriculturalists did not pay much attention to the slight difference in size between the two wheats, and thus einkorn may have been at first grown unintentionally together with emmer and only later selected in itself as a crop; the selection may have happened in Cilicia, where einkorn seems to have thrived unusually well in antiquity.

Even allowing for the difficulty in discriminating between carbonized kernels of the two species, one gets the impression that einkorn was always a cereal of minor importance, at least outside Turkey, and that in northern and western Europe it was never grown as an individual crop.

The earlier (third millennium B.C.) levels of Troy in western Asia Minor mark one of the few localities where einkorn—together with emmer—is reported to occur in quantity. Owing to our difficulties in identification, however, the relative importance of einkorn has not been established. It is associated with emmer in numerous "neolithic" sites along the Danube, in central and western Europe, and in Denmark. It occurs sporadically throughout the second millennium B.C. or "Bronze Age" and even persists as late as the fourth Christian century in Gotland in Sweden. Its present area of cultivation is confined to Turkey, with small secondary areas in the Balkans, central Europe, and Spain.

The discovery of einkorn at Troy, combined with knowledge of a center of multiplicity of the wild varieties in Asia Minor, inspired the idea that einkorn was first cultivated in Asia Minor. This idea, however, does not stand up to recent findings. In the first place, the Troy grain was found some seventy years ago and cannot be considered as satisfactorily investigated. Secondly, the Troy occurrence dates from the middle to the late third millennium B.C. and can hardly be regarded as indicative of the origin of a species which, at approximately the same time, had already spread to northern Europe (Helbaek, 1954). Thirdly, the occurrence of the species has now been established farther east for a much earlier time. Carbonized grain found at Jarmo and dated to about 6750 B.C. undoubtedly belongs to this species. Thus einkorn already accompanied emmer in the Jarmo occurrence, and its cultivation is now demonstrated long before the time of Troy. Various authors have claimed the presence of einkorn in prehistoric and early Dynastic Egypt, but their identifications have been definitely disproved (Helbaek, 1953c and 1955b). And, from my recent investigation, it does not appear to occur in the lower Mesopotamian irrigation agriculture.

BARLEY

It is an important fact that the two great Old World cereals, wheat and barley, occur together in practically all early grain deposits in Mesopotamia and Egypt. Barley was introduced into Europe along with wheat. The very first traces of agriculture, even in northern Europe, bear evidence of barley cultivation.

The barley genus (*Hordeum*) is classified into two main groups, the two-row and the six-row types, which are further divided into lax-eared and dense-eared forms. Whereas normally the paleae are united with the surface of the kernel, there are varieties of all the cultivated forms in which the kernels are free; these varieties are termed "naked." It should be emphasized that in the hulled forms the pales are attached to the surface of the kernel itself by fusion of the cell tissues, as opposed to the glume wheats and oats, in which the kernels are held mechanically within the flower by the stiff glumes or pales. No threshing, however violent, can remove the pales of hulled barley, but in ancient carbonized material the pales have very often disappeared as a consequence of heat and wear. Six-row barley bears three florets per internode, all of which are bisexual and capable of developing fruit. In two-rwo barley only the median floret is complete and develops a fruit, while the two lateral florets are unisexual (male) or sterile. Thus only one row of kernels develops on each side of the spike. The table on page 108 gives the very simplest systematization of barley, as pertinent to this discussion.

The two principal forms of six-row barley—the dense-eared, erect *H. hexastichum* L. and the lax-eared, nodding *H. tetrastichum* Kcke.—are reported to be equally old in the Egyptian finds, although the latter form is more common. In the so-called "neolithic" deposits of central Europe, the dense *H. hexastichum* seems to be predominant; but in other finds of the third millennium B.C., as for instance in Denmark and Britain, the lax *H. tetrastichum* has been identified, whereas the dense-eared barley has not been recognized. In a British find of the first half of the first millennium B.C. and in another of the early

Christian period (6th century), both lax and dense forms occur, but all other evidence shows only the lax-eared "bere." On the whole, however, one cannot form a true picture of the ancient distribution of the dense-eared barley on the basis of the literature alone because many authors claim its identification without offering proper documentation. Although *H. hexastichum* L. is mentioned as the most common form, my experience suggests that dense-eared barley was much rarer than "bere," except in the mountainous areas of central Europe and Turkey. Dense-eared barley is today grown only in restricted areas in Europe, that is, in the Alps, central Sweden, and the Färoes.

BARLEY

genus *Hordeum*

Wild two-row, hulled barley
(*H. spontaneum*)

cultivated two-row barley, hulled and naked
(*H. distichum*)

plains ? — mountains ?

cultivated six-row, lax-eared barley, hulled and naked (*H. tetrastichum*)

cultivated six-row, dense-eared barley, hulled and naked (*H. hexastichum*)

Two-Row Barley

Two-row barley is reported from a number of deposits in the Orient and Europe, dating from the earliest traces of agriculture onward. Here again, the documentation is in several cases far from satisfactory. Attempts have often been made to establish the presence of the species on the evidence of kernels alone, but it would seem necessary to have also the internodes, for instance, and preferably the reduced lateral florets (see below). Probably two-row barley did not arrive in Europe until classical times; Theophrastus mentions the species for Greece in the third century B.C., and according to Columella it was grown in Italy 300 years later. In northern Europe we see no sign of it until the second millennium after Christ.

In lumps of *tauf* from Jarmo numerous two-row barley imprints were found; many carbonized parts of the inflorescence of two-row barley were recovered also (Pl. 28A-B). The Jarmo grain is of the hulled type, long and slender, and tapers evenly toward both ends. As in the wild species, the pales are not wrinkled. In three of the carbonized kernels part of the internode and one of the lateral florets are preserved *in situ*, and the imprints also show the lateral florets. Several carbonized fragments of the axis, with long parallel-sided internodes, were recovered, and occasionally the stalks of lateral florets are preserved in these fragments.

It is a conspicuous feature of the Jarmo barley that in two instances the axis fragments consist of three internodes together, indicating that the axis was not brittle. After carbonization at the site and after excavation millenniums later, then transport and handling in the laboratory, a brittle axis would not show unbroken joints. In contrast, a dry present-day spike of wild barley, even if not fully mature, breaks into pieces when touched. Considering the fact that the hulled Jarmo grain shows a close conformity with the wild species *Hordeum spontaneum* Koch, the toughness of the axis is important, since in all genuinely wild barley the axis is brittle. The most interesting points of correspondence of the Jarmo barley with the wild *H. spontaneum* are that the lateral florets are pedicellate, not sessile as in cultivated varieties, and that the pales are not wrinkled. Not the slightest trace of a six-row barley was found at Jarmo. In another of the Iraq-Jarmo Project's sites, Matarrah, the same type of long straight barley grain is universal, and the imprints also all show the two-row spike.

Hitherto it has often been correctly noted that we have not encountered cultivated cereals corresponding in their more detailed characters to the wild species. This fact has been taken as indicating a long span of time between the actual beginnings of cultivation and such available earliest village-farming communities as have provided the first traces of agricultural products. In the case of Jarmo, however, we are now confronted with a cultivated barley which is morphologically very close to the wild form native to the locale of the prehistoric site. Straight-line wild progeny of the natural ancestors of the carbonized Jarmo barley still grows today in the fresh dirt of the dump heaps of the excavation. The features which distinguish the Jarmo barley from the wild barley are simply the greater volume of the kernels and the tougher axis of the ancient spikes. Thus, in the present state of our knowledge, the earliest barley appears to be of the two-row type.

I should like to emphasize that it should already have been possible, by means of archeological material, to trace the survival of the Jarmo barley and its derivatives and perhaps to ascertain its connection with modern two-row forms. But the evidence has not been conserved, nor have excavators realized the full potential for paleoethnobotanists of the imprints of plants in clay or of fragmentary bits other than carbonized kernels alone. It is very desirable that closer attention be paid to conservation and that careful and full documentation of the conclusions based on prehistoric cereal material be published. We especially urge excavators to take the utmost care in the recovery, removal, and packing of carbonized specimens of plant material, so that we may have more parts of the plants than simply the kernels alone, and under no circumstances to permit unidentified grain to be burned in the radiocarbon laboratories. It is too important for that.

The Problem of the Origin of Six-Row Barley

The cultivated as well as the wild barleys form a comparatively uniform morphological group. In spite of this circumstance, it has been extremely difficult to reach agreement upon certain views regarding the origin of the cultivated species.

The problem of two-row versus six-row barley assumes a central position in the study of the phylogeny of the cultivated genus *Hordeum*. The wild two-row barley of the Near East (*Hordeum spontaneum*) was originally described and named by the German botanist Karl Koch in 1848. Koch propounded that it was the progenitor of certain cultivated two-row forms. The French systematist De Candolle (1883) suggested that the *H. spontaneum* might possibly account for both the two-row and the six-row forms of cultivated barley, but at the same time he suggested a hypothetical wild six-row form, now extinct, as ancestor of the six-row group. Koernicke, the great German botanist, considered *H. spontaneum* as the wild prototype of all cultivated barleys—a logical conclusion on botanical grounds. Subsequent speculation has wavered between the Koernicke view and the hypothesis of De Candolle. In fact, a steady flow of papers on the subject has appeared representing every conceivable hypothesis and combination of hypotheses. Before the Jarmo finds, the earliest barley available from archeological contexts usually came from Egypt and Switzerland. The fact that this barley was exclusively of the six-row form seemed to make Koernicke's clear-cut view unacceptable. The finding of two-row cultivated barley in very early context at Jarmo now supplies evidence for the soundness of Koernicke's concept.

If two-row barley had been available from ancient sites when discussion of barley's origin began, the geneticists would have had a much easier task. *H. spontaneum* is an extremely tempting possible progenitor and is available in the exactly pertinent region. Furthermore, the difficulty of explaining the later development from two-row into six-row barley would not have proved insurmountable, since intermediate forms as well as radiation experiments (Nybom, 1954) clearly demonstrate the joint possession of genes by the two groups.

The problem before the Jarmo finds was to show a likely wild six-row species, but, unfortunately, this could not be done. Some scholars resorted to De Candolle's postulated six-row species, taking it now to be extinct and assuming that it acted either alone or in combination with H. spontaneum as the prototype of all the cultivated varieties. The recent discovery of an allegedly wild six-row species, described by Aaberg under the name of H. agriocrithon, seemed to substantiate this line of reasoning. But Aaberg's species has not been proven to be truly wild, and, furthermore, it is encountered in eastern central Asia far away from the area where all evidence indicates that the food-producing economy had its initial stages. Aaberg's barley attracted some attention because of its brittle axis. Now, though it is established that all wild barley has a brittle axis, it cannot be taken for granted that a cultivated barley could not, under certain conditions, regain this primitive physiological feature. The brittle axis is the single exceptional trait of Aaberg's barley. It comes from a general region where a great number of independent barley types have been developed by cultivation, such as the naked H. coeleste and the trifurcate forms. (These take the prize for freakishness among the barleys; instead of awns, the lower pales develop inverted sexless flowers.) In other words, Aaberg's barley comes from one of the ecological border regions. This is demonstrated by the fact that while wild barley in central Asia does not flourish above an altitude of 6,000 feet, the naked cultivated forms are grown on the mountain sides up to some 12,000 feet.

According to Vavilov's gene-center theory, the homes of the cultivated barleys would be in the mountains of Abyssinia and of southeastern Asia. The discovery of the Jarmo cereals, however, supports the concept that agriculture began within the rain-watered upland area—the arc from the Zagros-Taurus Mountains to Syria-Palestine—which had a common distribution of the wild forms of both wheat and barley. Cultivation spread in its initial phases only within the continuum of the same rain-watered upland habitat, where the plants might stay within their natural ecological conditions. When cereal cultivation encountered barriers of a climatic-ecological nature its progress was brought to a halt. Further spread was possible only if and when mutant types of the cultivated plants developed which allowed adaptation to new environments.

This was strikingly demonstrated by an investigation I was able to make in 1957/58. A considerable bulk of pottery and deposits of carbonized grain originating in the area from the Khabur in northern Kurdistan to Ur in southern Mesopotamia were examined. It became evident that in the northern foothill country the two-row barley was grown exclusively until later Halafian times, after which a sporadic sprinkling of the six-row form occurred. Even today, however, the barley of these northern regions is mainly (if not exclusively) two-rowed. On the other hand, in the area south of Baghdad and Aqer Quf, no traces of two-row barley could be identified for any time prior to the Islamic conquest, whereas good morphological evidence abounded for six-row barley. The two-row barley of the north was adapted to the fairly late (April-May) rainfall of the cooler Kurdish foothills. It seems probable that some mutant of this two-row form was six-rowed and that it proved more adaptable to the very hot dry spring irrigation conditions of alluvial southern Mesopotamia. The occurrence of six-row barley in late Halafian Kurdistan might be understood as evidence for a return of seed grain from the irrigated areas on the plain. So much the more so, since the grain deposit in question was accompanied by pottery showing definite Ubaid influence in decorative style. On the whole, it is useful to keep in mind that movements of peoples or of cultural items have rarely been one-way affairs. In order to understand the occurrence of cereals in the remote past, one must reckon with the possibility of two-way movements, even if the movement in one particular direction was more strongly oriented. It is no wonder that in early Islamic times the two-row barley came down into southern Mesopotamia, since the people involved interchanged ideas and products over the whole huge area under their domination. But today the six-row barley is again dominant in the south.

From the beginning in Mesopotamia the six-row barley is exclusively the lax-eared nodding variety, while in Cilicia the dense-eared erect six-row barley appears at about the same time or perhaps even earlier. The date of the grain from Mersin is not quite certain, but it can hardly be later than the colonization of the alluvial Mesopotamian plain. On the basis of the evidence available at present it might be suggested that the dense-eared form is another mutation of the wild two-row barley which came about under the influence of lower temperatures and higher rainfall, perhaps in the mountains of Cilicia. There is as yet no proof for this concept.

While the barley grown in Egypt during the third millennium B.C. and later was of the lax-eared six-row form, a Fayyum find of the fifth millennium exhibits an intriguing diversity. It comprises both dense and lax six-row spikes as well as a whole range of irregular deficient two-row spike types. While the classical (i.e., H. spontaneum) type is not available, many of these spikes had their glumes arranged in the manner of six-row forms whereas most of the lateral florets were crippled or highly rudimentary, or lateral florets were lacking altogether. The impression gained from examination of the grain which I carried out in 1959 is that the Fayyum barley is an example of the species in a state of vigorous mutation in consequence of its fairly recent introduction into the Nile valley. The positioning of the glumes seems to indicate that the spikes with abnormal development of the lateral florets are in reality deficient six-row ones. In the course of time this situation was simplified by natural selection, and the lax six-row form proved to be the only one suited to the cultivation methods and ecological conditions of Egypt.

Naked Barleys

As in the case of southwestern Asia, a climatic barrier might be suggested in prehistoric Europe. This suggestion is based upon the early predominance of naked barley in northern Europe. This variety of barley occurs today only in Abyssinia and central and eastern Asia; it seems not to occur in the nuclear area of the Near East. The suggestion of a climatic barrier pertains to certain other plants also, for example the large-seeded legumes which were able to penetrate into the European borderland only after the climatic deterioration of the first millennium B.C. The change to higher humidity seems to have brought about the extinction of the European naked barley, except in the extreme ecological conditions of the Alps.

The prehistoric naked barley of Europe constitutes a problem of far-reaching importance. To substantiate the inference of an isolated mutant emergence in Europe, the geographical and chronological distribution of European prehistoric barley must be painstakingly mapped. If the mapping invalidates this likely inference, we will be faced with the necessity of demonstrating a continuous route for the movement of the barley from eastern Asia or Abyssinia to Europe and, furthermore, of proving that these regions and the intervening lands were, in fact, settled before the third millennium B.C. Both lines of approach presuppose meticulous research and exhaustive documentation. Unfortunately, the available literature indicates that this requirement could hardly be satisfied at the moment. Sometimes naked barley has even been illustrated under the name of wheat; moreover, numerous reports of naked barley are obviously based only on damaged carbonized grain of the hulled variety. The occurrence of naked barley in prehistoric Europe is satisfactorily documented so far only for Britain, France, Belgium, Holland, Germany, Poland, and Scandinavia, but its occurrence has been claimed for practically every area where paleoethnobotanical work has been done.

Naked barley has also been claimed for western Asia and Egypt. In Iraq and Syria I was able to examine thousands of grain imprints in clay, ranging in time from the earliest villages down to the first millennium after Christ. I have also observed numerous deposits of carbonized grain from Iraq and Syria, as well as from Palestine and Cyprus (some having been sent to my laboratory in Copenhagen). Large quantities of carbonized and uncarbonized cereals were made available to me for examination in the Egyptian museums. I am not convinced that a single instance of naked barley occurs in any of this material. Recently I did see an example of the variety in prehistoric Turkey.

Thus it may be maintained—as regards the Vavilov southeastern Asiatic and Abyssinian gene-center theory for barley—that the cereal did not travel along the route normally suggested for the "great neolithic migration," and at present we know of no possible alternative route.

One of the most amazing experiences of the paleoethnobotanist traveling in the Near

East is the omnipresence of the wild barley H. spontaneum. It grows in the mountain forest, on the coastal plain, and along the border of the desert. He finds it along the wadies, in the shade of rock outcrops in semidesert areas, and as a weed in the fields of every conceivable cultivated crop. In May and June, the violent dust storms scatter its copiously armed spikelets over vast stretches, where they rest till the autumn showers start their germination. It is impossible to imagine circumstances in which the first farmers could have cultivated a plot of wheat that was free of wild barley. Today this is of no consequence, because the wild barley ripens and scatters its seeds before the field crops are ready for harvest. But at the time when the primitive wheat matured simultaneously with the barley, the mixture mattered a great deal. Little by little some individuals of both species would have developed tough axes—which happens sporadically in the wild state but is, of course, most detrimental to natural distribution—and year after year these individuals would have yielded increasingly larger portions of the grain which the earliest farmers were now consciously caring for. Consequently, the seed grain of both species would have been characterized by increasing dominance of the tough-axis genes, and the spikes with brittle axes would have been wasted as a more summary reaping technique developed. Thus the primary selection would have been a purely automatic one, dependent upon this natural quality in the cereals more than on human intent. Since the wild wheat does not commonly occur as a field weed, it must have been the principal object of earliest cultivation. It is reasonable to suggest that, at least in the beginning, barley was a secondary consideration. Had barley, and not wheat, been the prime consideration, cultivation could have started anywhere within the distributional territory of wild barley, from Turkestan to Morocco.

To judge by archeological finds, wheat and barley were certainly the earliest cereals cultivated. They occur together in all the sizable early grain deposits now available from southwestern Asia, Egypt, and Europe. We know of no instance of an early village-farming community based upon only one of these cereals.

Millet

From the late third millennium B.C. onward, kernels of broomcorn millet and Italian millet are encountered in European archeological sites. The two species often occur together, but broomcorn millet seems to be the more common of the two in "neolithic" contexts, where it has been identified in the Ukraine, in Thrace, along the Danube, in Switzerland, Germany, France, and Denmark. In "Bronze Age" deposits it occurs in Rumania and Holland also. Many imprints of it have been found, especially in Holland, increasing in number during the first millennium B.C. Even the Romans used broomcorn millet in Italy as well as in the central European provinces. Strangely enough, it has not been found in Britain, although great quantities of cereal material of the first millennium B.C. are available and have been investigated. In Denmark, millet has been encountered in deposits as late as the first few centuries after the birth of Christ.

The evidence for the cultivation of broomcorn millet in the ancient Near East is extremely slender. Recently, I found one kernel imprint in pottery of about 3000 B.C. from Jamdat Nasr. It next appears in a rather large deposit of the seventh century B.C. from Nimrud. The next occurrence noted in Iraq is in the Diyala region and dates from the ninth century after Christ. Since broomcorn millet is an important plant in more easterly parts of Asia and has been grown in China since preliterate times, its apparent scarcity in western Asia is possibly due to the fortuitous nature of archeological evidence.

Italian millet seems to have preferred the southern European climate. It occurs mainly in finds of both "neolithic" and later dates from Italy, France, and central Europe. However, a recent find, from the middle of the first millennium after Christ; at Bornholm in the Baltic shows that the species could endure colder climates, but it is uncertain whether it was cultivated there or subsisted as a weed.

Morphologically, Italian millet is related to the wild species known as green millet (Setaria viridis Beauv.). This is naturally distributed in western Asia and along the Mediterranean and occurs as a weed all over Europe, even in England and as far north as Finland. Whereas it seems probable that green millet is the progenitor of Italian millet, the claim that this species is the progenitor of broomcorn millet also is more questionable. The Abyssinian wild species (Panicum callosum Hochst.) displays a strong morphological likeness to broomcorn millet, but this matter has not yet been examined with sufficient detail. Again the geographical considerations are ambiguous; the complete absence of millet in Egypt leaves us with the same gaps in the record of the relatively well documented area between Abyssinia and Europe as in the case of naked barley.

In our own day, both broomcorn millet and Italian millet are grown in Europe to a minor extent and only in the south and east. In India and the Far East, on the other hand, they are of considerable importance as food grains. In ancient Chinese texts, broomcorn millet is mentioned as one of the cultivated plants connected with certain rituals, a circumstance which suggests the remote antiquity of millet in Chinese agriculture.

Rye

Each of the cereals discussed above has a very long history as a servant of man. The first millennium B.C. saw the introduction of two new species of cultivated European plants. These were rye and oats, which were weed grasses with brittle axes. As in the case of barley, these plants gained a predominance of tough-axis genes through man's unintentional interference and the automatic selection by the harvesting process. Under certain circumstances, rye and oats presently overwhelmed their host crops in the ecological competition. Neither of them emerged as cultivated plants in the nuclear area of the Near East, although wild oats are and always were widely distributed in the area and wild rye is native to Turkey and Afghanistan.

Rye (Secale cereale L.) appears for the first time in eastern and middle Germany in the early first millennium B.C. It does not seem to have been very common. In Britain it is found sporadically in the second and first centuries B.C., but it was evidently simply a fortuitous admixture to the grain imported from the continent by the newly arrived "Iron Age" tribes. In its first occurrence in Denmark, just after the birth of Christ, rye had rather the character of a weed. At the same time, however, it was being regularly cultivated in areas under Roman influence in central Europe, Hungary, and Britain. In Roman Britain it now proves to have been grown as a separate crop, but its use seems to have declined up until medieval times, when it regained some importance. In Denmark and northern Europe, on the other hand, its cultivation has increased steadily since the "Late Iron Age." The Romans transferred it to Italy, Greece, and Turkey, where it never gained particular importance. On the other hand, it is today a crop of major importance in the cold-temperate zone reaching from France and northern Europe across northern Asia to the Pacific.

It is noteworthy that wheat and barley have developed a multitude of different morphological types, which are adapted to the most varying vegetational conditions. Rye, on the other hand, is both remarkably monomorphic and not particularly versatile, as is shown, incidentally, by its present distribution. These traits are due mainly to the fact that the species is wind-fertilized and practically self-sterile, features which have the effect of producing an average and rather unvarying type of cereal.

The homeland of wild rye is in western and central Asia, with its center in the more easterly portion of this area. In Afghanistan and adjacent regions, certain varieties of rye grow as weeds in the cereal fields. The varieties are grouped under the name S. montanum Guss. They differ very much as to brittleness of the axis and thus cannot be considered completely unaffected by human activities. The rye prototype must have been a purely brittle species. In 1926 a plant of this description (S. ancestrale Zhuk.) was found growing wild in Turkey and Afghanistan. Apart from being brittle and extremely hairy, this wild form corresponds in its main features to the Asiatic weed rye as well as to the cultivated cereal, and a species like it may well be the progenitor of both. At present the ancestry of rye is the subject of much genetic research. It would, however, take us too far afield to discuss the several possibilities emerging from these experiments.

Rye presented itself for cultivation, so to speak, when man began to shift it away from its natural environment. It surreptitiously entered cultivated soil in the Asiatic wheat fields, in places where it was inferior to wheat for ecological reasons. But, as wheat cultivation moved farther north, or into higher altitudes, the resistance of the wheat declined at the same pace that the hardiness of the weed rye became established. Step by step rye took over the fields as wheat was removed from its optimal surroundings. In the winter-cold regions of Europe the farmer had no choice but to exploit the species which was able to follow his migrations, and which, by now, had a fully tough axis. This transformation did not take place in the Near East, Asia Minor, or the Danube basin, and we must postulate a route for rye into central Europe during the first and second millenniums B.C. The details of this diffusion are not yet clear to us, but the path probably led from the Aral-Caspian region along the steppes of southern Russia.

In summary, it would seem that when the practice of agriculture began its spread from the nuclear Near East (the hilly flanks of the Zagros-Lebanon arc), the eastward portion of this spread—which was eventually to reach the Indus Valley—passed through the area of distribution of wild rye. Here, rye became an associated weed in the wheat fields. A later migration in the opposite direction, but along some as yet unknown route, eventually delivered the rye-infested wheat to Europe. When it reached the more northerly latitudes of Europe, which were unfavorable to wheat but climatically and ecologically propitious for rye, the rye was finally brought into cultivation.

Oats

Because of their circuitous mode of introduction to cultivation, both rye and oats may be called secondary cultivated plants. Oats also invaded the cultivated field as a weed and were distributed with agriculture into areas where climatic conditions restricted the development of the older cultivated cereals—especially wheat—and at the same time enhanced the competitive qualities in the wild oat. Thus at some point in these regions oats would have been selected for separate cultivation, natural selection being supplemented by human endeavor.

The first occurrences of oats in Europe are inconspicuous and scattered—a fact which may mean simply that at present we know too little about them. In Switzerland, Germany, and Denmark oats appear at the beginning of the first millennium B.C. No cultivated oats are reported from western Europe at this time, although various species of the genus frequently occur as weeds in finds of spelt wheat of the late first millennium B.C. in Britain. Evidently, the oats were introduced together with the wheat from inland continental spelt-growing districts in connection with the La Tene expansions which took place during the latter part of the first millennium. The earliest British finds of pure oats, from Scotland, previously published as being of Roman date, have proved to belong to the Middle Ages, and the introduction of the cereal as a separate crop apparently should be credited to the Anglo-Saxons. This conclusion is based upon the fact that not until Anglo-Saxon times do imprints of oats appear regularly in pottery.

The "Iron Age" finds of oats in the Baltic islands are difficult to appraise because of the presence of the wild oat Avena fatua L. in large proportions. With the pales burnt off, the kernels of this species are frequently indistinguishable from those of the cultivated A. sativa L. The wild oat occurs spontaneously in eastern Europe and was an obnoxious weed in grain fields of adjacent regions.

Large finds of carbonized cultivated oats in Denmark show that during the early first millennium after Christ the cereal attained some significance. From then on it probably became an increasingly important food and fodder plant all over northern and eastern Europe.

Oats were never grown in the Near East, although several weed species of the genus extensively infest the grain fields. Oats are mentioned by Greek and Roman authors of the second century B.C., mainly as a fodder plant but occasionally as a substitute for bread grain in times of distress. Pliny informs us that the cereal was much enjoyed by the Germans for flat buns and porridge, and archeological finds show that the Romans themselves utilized oats in their central European provinces.

Even if the first cultivation of oats took place in Europe, two different phylogenetic lines may be distinguished. The A. strigosa group or bristle-pointed oat, grown exclusively in western Europe, is a descendant of a diploid form (form hirtula Lag.) of the Oriental-Mediterranean A. barbata Thell, which is naturally distributed in the Iberian Peninsula. The more universally cultivated A. sativa is undoubtedly the progeny of A. fatua, which is indigenous to eastern Europe, western Asia, and northern Africa and which, as a weed, has been distributed over most of the world outside the tropics. A. sativa is grown in Europe, temperate Asia, North Africa, and America.

NONCEREAL PLANTS

The cereal grains discussed above were man's most universal and basically important sources of vegetable food, at least within the greater area where the Western cultural tradition had its inception and development. But many other species were grown in the same general area, although at various times they were confined to certain regions. The genetic antecedents of these noncereal plants are not very well known, and the reports of their prehistoric occurrences are sporadic, but it seems worth while to consider them in a summary way. Paleoethnobotanical material from the Near East is being recovered and investigated at an increasing rate, and improvement of our knowledge seems to be within view.

Large-Seeded Legumes

The large-seeded annual legumes—for instance the horsebean, pea, vetch, vetchling, chickpea, and lentil—appear in early horizons in the Near East. They seem at times to have attained an economic value almost as great as that of the cereals; they were, in fact, mostly grown together with the cereals. At Jarmo we find the field pea (Pl. 28C), lentil, and blue vetchling. The same three plants are also encountered in Egypt from early predynastic horizons. Such plants were carried along with grain agriculture into the Mediterranean and Danubian countries by the early farmers, and eventually they spread farther north, peas and beans reaching northern Europe at about the time of the birth of Christ.

Flax

Flax (Linum usitatissimum L.) was of great importance in the Near East until its fibers were replaced by cotton and its oil (linseed oil) by sesame. It was cultivated in the fifth millennium B.C. (Halaf period) at Tell Arpachiyah and Tell Brak in the Kurdish foothills, a region where the wild Linum perenne Mill., which may be considered the wild progenitor of cultivated flax, is naturally distributed. Within the same millennium it was grown at Ur on the plain. For this general period it is known from Hamah in the Orontes valley and the Fayyum in Egypt. The seeds and imprints of seeds found in the irrigated areas are considerably larger than those found in the rain-fed uplands of Kurdistan; apparently the development of the larger-seeded race is associated with forced existence of the species beyond its natural habitat and consequent different cultivation methods. The size culminates in carbonized linseeds, found in Late Assyrian Nimrud in Iraq, which have a maximum length of 5.3 mm. and thus were some 6.2 mm. long in the fresh state (shrinkage by carbonization is calculated at ca. 15%; see Helbaek, 1959).

Together with wheat and barley, linseeds occur in the earliest agricultural level (early 3d millennium B.C.) in mountainous Switzerland, at Egolzwil. The species appeared in England and Holland slightly later, and shortly after 2000 B.C. the plant was grown in Spain and northern Italy.

While the seeds grown in irrigated lands are larger than those of the Kurdish uplands race, the maximum seed size is practically the same all over the rain-fed area from Kuristan to Switzerland and England, namely 3.8-4 mm.

It may be supposed that flax reached central and western Europe from the Near East via the Balkans and the Danube. From the middle of the first millennium B.C. onward flax appears in Poland, eastern Germany, and Denmark, but the seeds of this race are up to 25% longer than those of the early central and western European race. It is propounded that at some early date flax was brought with agriculture into Russia from the Balkans and that here it developed an independent race which eventually was circulated via eastern Europe by a branch of the Hallstatt movements of the first millennium B.C. (Helbaek, 1959).

The origin of flax has been discussed by several authors during the last hundred years. Heer (1865) suggested L. bienne (under the name L. angustifolium) as progenitor because of the distribution of the species as he knew it along the Mediterranean and thus fairly near to Switzerland. Neuweiler (1905) suggested L. austriachum for the role because this species is distributed within Switzerland itself and because its seeds correspond to the "neolithic" cultivated seeds much better than do those of L. bienne; this possibility is, however, excluded for anatomical reasons (Helbaek, 1959). Vavilov based his concept upon his main theory that a conspicuous multitude of forms in a cultivated plant within a given area is in itself proof that the plant was domesticated in that area. Having established a center of multiplicity for flax in India and Afghanistan, he identified that region as the center of emergence for flax. The lack of a possible progenitor in southern and central Asia, however, belies this concept; in my opinion the multiplicity may be reasonably explained by the fact that the region is a border zone to the distribution area of cultivated flax (see p. 102). I am convinced that L. bienne is the progenitor for the following reasons. The species occurs in the wild state in the region where incipient agriculture has been established archeologically; the seeds of the ancient cultivated plant remain within the same dimensional order in all ecologically comparable areas from Kurdistan to England; there is morphological and anatomical conformity in plants and seeds respectively; L. bienne has the same chromosome number (30) as L. usitatissimum; and, finally, it is the only wild species which produces fertile offshoots in hybridization with L. usitatissimum.

Fruit

The fruits of trees and shrubs were, of course, utilized long before the appearance of agriculture. It is evident that the idea of their domestication occurred to the peoples of the Near East long before it did to the Europeans and that the process of diffusion of fruit culture was much slower than that of the annuals.

The vine grape occurs very early in Egypt (predynastic) and Syria. Since it is not indigenous in Egypt, it must be regarded there as an imported cultivated plant. Probably its cultivation began in the mountains around northern Mesopotamia and in Syria and Palestine, where the plant grows wild and whence it followed grain agriculture all over the eastern Mediterranean and Aegean regions. During the first millennium B.C. it was carried to Italy, possibly by the Etrurians, and viticulture began in Europe, its most important world center today. Indeed, the wild vine was already distributed in mountainous Europe, and its grapes were being exploited on a fairly large scale by "neolithic" and "Bronze Age" times in central Europe. But, since the prehistoric finds do not occur beyond the possible natural-distribution area, this exploitation must be regarded as the product of food-gathering rather than of cultivation. In places where grape pips occur most frequently in prehistoric sites, they are found mixed with remains of other juicy fruits which were certainly not cultivated, such as bittersweet nightshade, elderberry, cornelian cherry, blackberry, and raspberry. Such occurrences evidently are refuse of wine-making.

The remains of apples and pears are commonly encountered in European prehistoric finds, these being certainly due to collection from wild trees. In the Near East, on the other hand, orchard husbandry had already been highly developed in the fourth to third millenniums B.C. The remains of dates and olives bear witness to this fact. In my mind there are two probable reasons for the fact that orchard husbandry began much earlier in the Near East than it did in Europe. In the first place, a multitude of attractive fruits such as those mentioned above as well as figs, almonds, pistachios (cf. Pl. 28D), walnuts, etc. occur naturally in the Near East, principally in the uplands. In the second place, growth rate for woody plants is much faster in the Near East. Thus the advantages of orchard husbandry were much more obvious, and less patience was required for bringing a tree or vine to a profitable and reliable level.

CONCLUSIONS

Our knowledge of the very early stages of the domestication of the food plants associated with the rise of the Western cultural tradition is still very sketchy. As far back as the evidence now goes, wheat and barley occur together as the earliest cereals. The evidence from Jarmo, the earliest excavated village site of the prehistoric sequence in Iraq, indicates the presence of (1) morphologically transitional types of emmer, some closer to T. dicoccoides than to the hitherto recognized emmer from the post-Jarmo phases of early village-farming communities, (2) carbonized kernels of T. monococcum, einkorn, and (3) two-row barley (H. distichum s.l.) closely resembling the wild H. spontaneum but obviously with a tough axis. Because wild forms which may reasonably be considered progenitors of these grains have a coincident distribution in the rain-watered hill country of the Zagros-Taurus-Lebanon arc, it may be assumed that Jarmo is within the ecological zone where the earliest experiments in cereal domestication were made.

The Vavilov theory, and its derivatives, which postulates the origins of domestication of these cereals in Abyssinia or eastern Asia, is not substantiated by the present archeological evidence. The cultivation of wheat and barley was diffused rather from western Asia to Europe along one or another of the routes of the "great neolithic migration." Exact details concerning these routes are still somewhat vague, especially for that important later route which apparently passed through South Russia to Europe, coming through the Caucasus or to the east and north of the Caspian.

Discoveries of relatively old six-row barley in Egypt and Europe have led to the assumption that this form of the grain was the earliest barley domesticated. Since a wild six-row progenitor was not available in the pertinent area, this assumption led either to exaggerated phylogenetic theorizing or to suggestions of possible progenitors in areas well removed from the archeologically demonstrable foci. The recovery of the very early two-row barley at Jarmo disposes of the assumption itself. The earliest occurrence of six-row lax-eared barley coincides with the agricultural colonization of the alluvial plain of Mesopotamia, which was presumably undertaken by peoples from Kurdistan who grew only two-row barley. It is propounded that the major selective factor leading to the establishment of the six-row mutant barley in the south was the ecological change from the rain-watered northland to the hot artificially watered alluvium of the southland. The exact explanation of the appearance of naked barley in northern Europe is still to be discovered.

It is postulated that the earliest farmers, on the flanks of the Zagros-Taurus-Lebanon arc, first cultivated the wheats. Barley—naturally present as a weed in the early wheat fields—came gradually into cultivation as it developed tough axes. Rye and oats probably became consciously cultivated crops in the same fashion, but this development took place in the more rigorous ecological situations of the northerly latitudes or high elevations in Europe and at a much later time. Millet first appeared at about 3000 B.C. in Mesopotamia, but its early history is not yet well understood.

In the Kurdish foothills, where the wild flax (Linum bienne) is native, evidence is found of cultivated flax in the fifth millennium B.C. Contemporaneous and later material from the irrigated plains of Mesopotamia, Syria, and Egypt reveal seeds of greater dimensions. It is propounded that this better development is associated with the ecology and cultivation methods of the plains. Flax is found in central and western Europe from the middle of the third millennium B.C. onward, and it shows the same seed size as the Kurdish flax. Coming by an eastern route, flax appears in northern Europe about the middle of the first millennium B. C. It is believed that all cultivated flax descends from the Near Eastern branch of the wild winter-annual species Linum bienne.

Unfortunately, I am unable to form an opinion of the present state of paleoethnobotanical research and interpretation within the Soviet Union, especially as regards eastern Europe. This is a serious but unavoidable deficiency, since detailed knowledge of the vast region of the Urals, Transcaspia, the Caucasus, and the Carpathians is of critical importance to our understanding of early husbandry in general.

An adequate notion of the history of cultivation of the leguminous plants and of orchard husbandry and viticulture is only now beginning to come into focus. Western Asia seems to have had a critical role in the domestication of these food plants also.

Paleoethnobotanical research has the broadest possible significance for our understanding of the great acceleration in cultural activity that attended the appearance and development of food-production. The fruitful potentialities of co-operation between the archeologist and the paleoethnobotanist have been demonstrated both in the laboratory and in the field. It is the archeologist's responsibility to recover and preserve the botanical material with painstaking care, to establish its culture-historical context and date, and to submit it for expert scrutiny. The paleoethnobotanist must himself occasionally check actual field activities, make his own judgments of pertinent ecological situations (ideally in company with other natural scientists), collect contemporary botanical material for comparison, and observe contemporary agricultural practices. I have observed that plant material of one kind or another is always encountered—if not recognized—in the excavation of prehistoric sites. Even ashes and carbon detritus, among which carbonized grain is usually found, are invaluable; these often contain crushed particles of the spikelets of cereals which are so profitable for precise determination. Obviously a handful of remains of the actual plants associated with ancient man far surpasses pages of phylogenetical theorizing.

IX

A REVIEW OF THE ARCHEOLOGICAL EVIDENCE ON ANIMAL DOMESTICATION IN THE PREHISTORIC NEAR EAST

Charles A. Reed

ABSTRACT

A critical analysis is presented, from a zoölogist's viewpoint, of the archeological literature on the origins of animal domestication for the prehistoric periods of Egypt and southwestern Asia. In general, with regard to the contribution of archeology to the solution of this problem, we must say tekel, "Thou art weighed in the balance and art found wanting." Too often the animal bones have been shoveled upon the refuse heap, and the contribution their study could have made to the reconstruction of a culture has been unrealized.

Such times, it is to be hoped, are past.

Even when the bones were salvaged, the identifications and the consequent interpretations of the data were often seriously in error.

A careful sifting of the published evidence has led to rejection of many generally accepted claims concerning the presence of domestic animals in the prehistoric Near East. Hence I have attempted an outline of the known facts (Fig. 7) upon which we can build in detail in the future. While it is believed to be firm as to fact, this outline is appallingly incomplete, and we must conclude that possibly most species of domestic animals were actually present, and important to the cultures of the people possessing them, for two or three thousand years prior to the time for which we have unimpeachable evidence of their domestication. The outline does, however, clear the way to future understanding by pointing clearly to the periods of human cultural evolution for which data concerning the origins and roles of domesticated animals are as yet missing or incomplete.

Following is a summation of conclusions.

1. The dog was presumably the first animal domesticated, being known in southwestern Asia from skeletal remains in a relatively early pre-pottery level at Jericho and from figurines of approximately the same period at Jarmo. Very possibly these dogs antedate those from northwestern Europe of the Maglemosian culture. In Egypt, dogs are not known until the Amratian period, about 5,700 years ago. The wild ancestor of the dog is still disputed; the wolf, the jackal, and the wild pariah have been suggested, but to date no agreement is near.

2. Domestic goats, derived from the wild Asiatic *Capra hircus aegagrus*, are found both at Jarmo and in pre-pottery levels of Jericho. Present evidence indicates that the goat was the second animal, and the first of the food-producers, to be domesticated. Goats are not known with certainty in Egypt before the Amratian period.

3. Domestic sheep, derived from *Ovis orientalis* of southwestern Asia, are not certainly known prior to their depiction on Protoliterate cylinder seals and stone vases from Warka, probably some two millenniums or more after their original domestication. Sheep were introduced to Egypt as domestic animals by early Gerzean times, or possibly earlier. The generally assumed importance of wool in the early history of sheep domestication is discounted.

4. The oft-accepted claim for a southeastern Asiatic origin for all domestic pigs needs thorough re-investigation; since wild pigs of the same species, *Sus scrofa*, occur

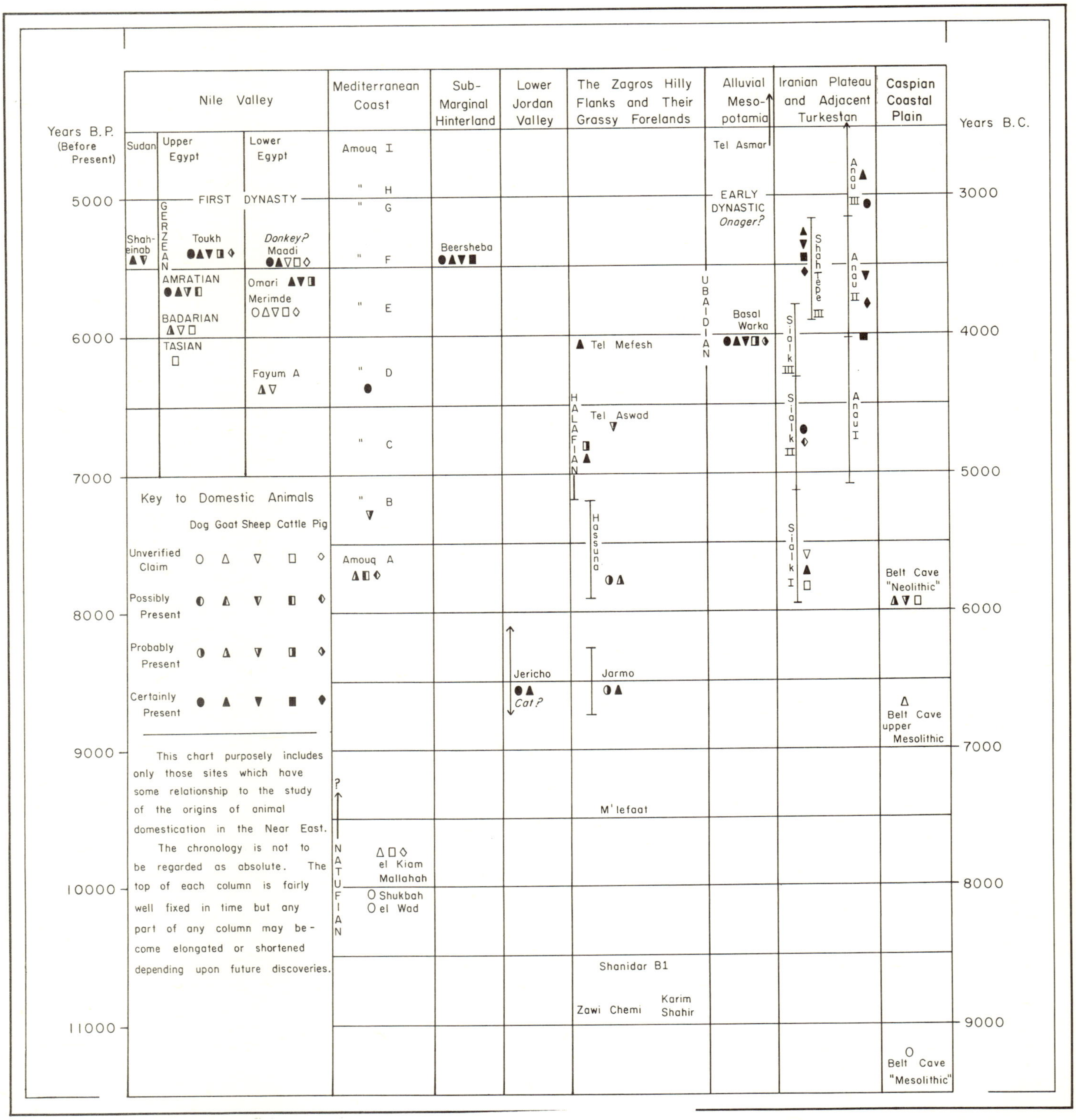

Fig. 7. Chronology of the known history of animal domestication in the prehistoric Near East

across northern Africa and throughout most of Eurasia, it seems probable that domestication of this animal could have occurred several times in several places. Domestic pigs are not certainly known in southwestern Asia prior to the second half of the fourth millennium B.C. and not in Egypt prior to the Dynastic period (in spite of numerous claims for an earlier status there), although they probably were present earlier in both regions.

5. Domestic cattle are probably derived from wild Bos primigenius and could have been independently domesticated in Egypt and southwestern Asia. In the latter area, contrary to oft-repeated claims, there is no proof of them prior to about 3500 B.C., although they were very probably present considerably earlier. In Egypt, although they are usually stated to have been present throughout the fourth millennium B.C., from the time of the Badarian culture onward, there is no proof of their presence prior to the Dynastic period (ca. 3000 B.C.).

Other domestic animals are not considered in this review, since (with the possible exception of cats in prehistoric levels at Jericho) the time of their domestication was undoubtedly later than the periods here considered.

INTRODUCTION

This is an exploratory chapter, leading toward a study of the origins and early phases of animal domestication, with particular reference to Egypt and southwestern Asia. While my own studies in the field (1954/55) were largely restricted to the hills and mountains of northeastern Iraq and particularly to the prehistoric village-farming community of Jarmo, and while the site of Jarmo is here our central point of reference, yet neither Jarmo nor any other archeological site exists by itself. Thus, with the animals as with the human cultures, a historical continuum must be considered if the zoölogical data are to be placed in perspective.

Knowledge of the beginnings of animal domestication in Egypt and southwestern Asia is perhaps less satisfactory than is our knowledge of the origins of the food plants. This situation is due not to lack of interest, nor to lack of published opinions, but to lack of careful studies. I intend to explore, in this chapter, why we really know so little of this interesting subject. Secondly, I intend to sift from the literature what seems to me to be trustworthy evidence, so that we can say definitely what we do know of the animals associated with agricultural beginnings in the Near East.[1] In so far as the still incomplete study of the animal remains recovered in the various sites of the Iraq-Jarmo Project allows, I shall add information to what I already trust of the knowledge of the different species as gleaned from the literature.

The chronological period covered is limited to late prehistoric time, history being defined narrowly as beginning with the first written records that can be read now. Even within this prehistoric period I shall stop somewhat short of the time of the beginnings of written history, for my major purpose is to establish the first appearance and early distribution of the dog and of each of the four major food-producing animals (goat, sheep, cattle, pig) that were first domesticated by the prehistoric peoples under consideration. The only other animals that might have been considered here are the donkey (probably present somewhat before 3000 B.C. in Egypt), the Syrian onager or half-ass (domestic by the same time—3000 B.C.—in southern Mesopotamia), and the cat (reported as domestic in Jericho [Zeuner, 1958b] of the 7th millennium B.C.). If there were domestic cats at this early date, it is probable that the situation was temporary, for domestic cats as we know them seem to date only from historic Egypt of about 2000 B.C.

The other domestic animals (zebu, water buffalo, camel, horse) that often, although erroneously, are considered to enter into the life of late prehistoric peoples in the Near

---

[1] The unfortunate and very recent military and political usage of the term "Middle East" (Pearcy, 1959) for the area here considered as the Near East is deplored and otherwise ignored.

East actually arrive as domesticants subsequent to the period of this survey.

The time range covered begins with the uppermost Pleistocene, the known animals of which are used as a reference in some instances, and ends around 3300 B.C. By this latter time the dog and the four basic food-producing animals are rather certainly integrated into all the more advanced farming cultures of the areas under consideration.

In making this survey, I have been helped tremendously, and my preliminary work has been considerably shortened, by Dyson's (1953) summary of the same subject. Dyson concluded that all the available archeological evidence points to southwestern Asia as the area of domestication of the four basic food animals. On the basis of the data assembled by Dyson, and of other recent archeological evidence from central Asia, von Fürer-Haimendorf (1955) strongly discounted the old notion that animal domestication began in an early stage of pastoralism. Although the dog may have first appeared with pre-agricultural hunters, the basic food animals always are found in a context with early village-farmers. Correspondingly, von Fürer-Haimendorf wrote that domestication of the horse and the reindeer came relatively late and had no influence on the earliest agricultural communities or on their immediate historical derivatives.

One of Dyson's basic points, which I reiterate here, is that domestication of any species could have occurred only in the natural area where the wild ancestor lived. Thus neither sheep nor goats were domesticated in Africa, for there is no evidence from the late Quaternary that true wild sheep or goats lived there.[2] Further, even within a general geographic area, animals and man must associate in the same ecologic range before domestication can occur. Thus goats, which live in hills and mountains, could not have been domesticated by desert or plains peoples, nor could the plains- and/or desert-dwelling dromedary have been domesticated by mountaineers.

A stumbling block in the earlier speculations concerning the domestication of the basic food animals was the riverine-oasis (or propinquity) hypothesis, popularized by Childe (1928 and subsequently) in his various surveys of prehistoric cultures. The fundamental idea of this theory is that as desiccation began in the early post-Würm period and continued throughout the early Recent period man and his potentially domesticable animals were forced into symbiotic associations of mutual benefit along river banks and around oases. It is true that there is considerable evidence, adduced from studies in geology, botany, zoölogy, and archeology, that during a time coincident with the late Würm and early post-Würm in Europe there were periods with more precipitation across the now-desert areas of northern Africa than occurs today (Alimen, 1957; Butzer, 1958).

The general tendency of most prehistorians has been to enfold southwestern Asia into the conclusions reached on the basis of North African data, but Wright (chap. vii above) has indicated that the evidence is far from clear and that the probability of a marked climatic change in the late Pleistocene or post-Pleistocene in southwestern Asia is unlikely.

Childe and other prehistorians who have espoused his theory seem never to have taken into account the fluctuating nature of alternate periods of precipitation and desiccation but, instead, have based their thoughts on the simpler conclusions of an earlier day (Brooks, 1926), namely that there had been a continuous post-Würm drying-up of northern Africa. Actually, the only period of increasing desiccation that might have corresponded with a period of animal domestication was during the seventh millennium B.C. (the last part of Butzer's "Postpluvial IIa"), two thousand years or more before the first known appearance of domestic animals in North Africa. By the time domestic animals did reach North Africa (Fayyum A, ca. 4200 B.C., is the earliest known site) the "Neolithic Wet Period" had set in, and, as evidenced by rupestrian art, herdsmen and their flocks spread quite rapidly over grassland areas that are now complete desert. The cycle toward the present desert

[2] Pomel's claim (1898) for native dwarf goats in the Algerian prehistoric must be doubted on the basis of Arambourg's statement (1929) concerning the uncertainty of the levels from which the specimens came. It is certainly possible, therefore, that Pomel was describing introduced, although still prehistoric, domestic goats.

conditions then began, to be completed by about 2500 B.C. On the basis of present evidence, therefore, it would seem impossible that any period of increasing desiccation corresponded with any origins of domestication in North Africa.

In southwestern Asia little is known of the correspondence of the climatic cycles of the present desert areas with the better-known fluctuations in North Africa. There is considerable evidence, however, that the hills and mountains were much less affected by any trends toward desiccation than were the lower-altitude deserts (Shalem, 1950 and 1953, for the Levant; Wright, 1955 and chap. vii above, for Iraq; Bobek, 1954, for Iran). In the mountains, the forests persisted, although with some shifting of the tree lines (see p. 90 above). The forest animals, however, would have moved with the shifting temperature and floral zones in order to maintain themselves in their natural environments and thus would have been little affected. Even if there was a slow upward post-Pleistocene retreat of the forest edge at its lower boundary with the grasslands, there was compensation due to advancing timber line at higher altitudes.

Even in the lowland areas one cannot assume that domestication would necessarily have occurred as man and the wild animals became crowded together into river valleys and oases. The definite dependence of most wild animals upon a particular environmental niche is obviously not realized by prehistorians who talk of the riverine-oasis theory of animal domestication. In actuality, with increasing desiccation, environmental life zones of forest, brush cover, and grasslands would retreat upward with the lifting precipitation gradient wherever there was a rain-creating elevation. Where such elevations were low or lacking, the plants determining the various life zones would die and the animals dependent upon them would become extinct; there would be no "crowding-down" into river valleys and oases of animals which—contrarily—could only, however slightly in each generation, be living at ever higher elevations. The animals eventually left in river bottoms and oases would be those that had already lived in such environments.

Further, it is my belief that pre-agricultural man in a desiccating (and thus deteriorating) environment would, quite logically, kill and eat anything he could; he would be an exterminator, not a conservator via domestication.

Lastly, much of the apparent Near Eastern desiccation, which so thoroughly impresses all visitors to that area (and particularly the supposed desiccation other than that of the true desert), has been in major part due to the destruction of the natural environment (forest, grass, soil) by man and his domestic animals, especially the goat. Once destroyed, that environment would take centuries to recover if left alone, but it cannot be left alone as long as the present population pressure of man and goat remains upon it.

In conclusion, there seems to be no evidence for the riverine-oasis theory of domestication and much against it. The primary difficulty is that the ecologic distribution of goats and sheep (probably the first two food animals to be domesticated) is such that these animals would never have been limited to oases or desert river banks. The whole concept was based on insufficient data, with regard to both climates and animals, and should now be abandoned.

DOMESTICATION

This is not the time to enter extensively into the problem of how and why animals were first domesticated and why some species were domesticated and others not. These questions have been considered in as much detail as present evidence allows by Zeuner (1954b and 1956) and myself (1959), with discussion of the natural sociability and herd instincts of man and all the animals domesticated by him (with the notable exception of the cat, which species perhaps has become adapted to the human environment but not domesticated). Zeuner and I both stress the symbiotic relations that could have arisen under natural conditions between man and certain other species, which must have been pre-adapted to domestication by a socialization that was due to natural selection.

Zeuner believes (and I concur) that when, in an area which contained such socially pre-adapted animals, human culture had evolved to a certain degree of complexity (and probably in a certain direction also) domestication followed almost automatically. He strongly discounts any concept of long-time purposeful behavior by primitive man in the incipient stages of domestication but believes instead that the seemingly age-old habit of pet-keeping of the young of wild animals by women and children led to taming and eventually to the keeping and breeding of the adult animals. In a primitive hunting and food-gathering society such pet-keeping may have continued for a long time with nothing more happening. The basic factor leading to the higher degree of intergroup co-operation that we know as domestication was, it seems to me, the development of incipient cultivation, which was associated with increased human population and more sedentary life.

An interesting side light on pre-adaptation for domestication is that the available physiological evidence suggests that social mammals produce, from their adrenal medulla glands, more epinepherin (adrenalin) than nor-epinepherin (nor-adrenalin), whereas carnivorous animals that hunt and live more solitarily produce more nor-epinepherin than epinepherin (Funkenstein, 1955). Such biochemical backgrounds relevant to the problem of the origins of domestication have only begun to be studied but open a wide field for future research.

There is a vast literature on domestic animals and their origins, but there has been little first-class research in the Near East. Much of the current literature depends upon old sources, oft-repeated and perhaps changed in the repeating. Many of the original identifications of animal bones in archeological context may have been erroneous, since there were (and are!) few comparative collections and the necessity for careful work was not always realized. Even identifications that were once accurate may now be out of date because of changes in taxonomic technicalities, but such changes remain largely unknown to the archeologist, so that animal names that are actually synonyms may sometimes be treated as if they belonged to separate species. One sees identifications of species or even subspecies on the basis of a fragment of a tooth or a few broken bones, and then conclusions are published from such difficult and possibly erroneous identifications. One also sees published lists of names of animals found in archeological excavations—with no indication as to the person making the identifications (a suspicious circumstance in itself)—followed possibly by conclusions as to distribution or domestic status based on such casual lists. Erroneous and sometimes quite impossible identifications get into print, to be repeated in subsequent references.

Much of the literature by prehistorians on both domestic and wild animals, as published in site reports and reviews, reveals incredible naïvity and shows no knowledge of animal distribution, ecology, taxonomy, or phylogenetic relationships. There is often a ridiculous oversupply of named species, particularly of domestic animals, which indicates complete disregard of all genetic and ecologic concepts implied by the word "species" and complete disregard of the International Rules of Zoölogical Nomenclature. It is strange that authors who name each morphological variant of prehistoric goat, for instance, as a distinct species would not think of so considering the much more diverse breeds of living dogs (Reed, 1957). If a zoölogist were to write of archeology, blithely confusing burins with projectile points and Egyptian with Chinese materials, the situation would be comparable. Published statements about animals easily creep into secondary and semipopular literature, there to be accepted as facts. One such instance was the published report that a beaver skull was discovered in a certain excavation in prehistoric Egypt. One then met with "beaver" in subsequent reviews, and indeed will probably continue to hear of it in the future, although the skull was actually that of a dog (Moustafa, 1955).

There is a delusion among most archeologists, dating back to Rütimeyer (1862), that bones of domestic mammals can be separated from those of their wild relatives by "feel," the domestic animals presumably having light spongy bones. This may be true of a penfed pig or a stall-fed cow (I don't know), but I know that I cannot make any such diagnoses on the basis of my osteological collections from southwestern Asia (also Zeuner, 1954b, p. 376). One does not sort or identify bones by "feel"; identification is usually a difficult anatomical problem, requiring a good comparative collection and considerable experience.

Worst of all, the archeologist has often paid no attention to the animal bones from his excavation; they have been cast onto the dump. Or, if he saved them, he has had trouble finding a zoölogist who could or would identify them. Adequate comparative collections of skeletons are very rare (although some special collections for special animal groups or special areas may be exceptionally good); the curators of such collections and other museum zoölogists are busy people, to whom the identification of an odd lot of broken bones is an onerous chore with few rewards zoölogically; and rarer than dinosaur eggs are the really good comparative osteologists who have knowledge of ecology and animal distribution and who have worked with archeologists and share their interest in cultural evolution. But dinosaur eggs are known, as are such archeological osteologists; certainly Miss Dorothea M. A. Bate was among the best of such rare individuals, and others of competence quoted in this essay are Romer, Gaillard, Duerst, Vaufrey, and Amschler.

Too often, however, a busy zoölogist (or his even busier graduate student who cannot protest) receives the bones from an archeological site which he has never visited, perhaps in a part of the world he has never studied, and responds after several months (sometimes years) with a list of Latin names of genera and species which are usually meaningless to the archeologist. The bones are usually then discarded, discouraging all future questions as to the validity of the identifications. Certainly, under such circumstances, it is difficult for the zoölogist to know what the presence or absence (the latter important point being usually overlooked completely) of certain animals can mean to the archeologist in the latter's attempt to reconstruct human cultures. Not often does the archeologist know enough of ecology, animal geography, animal behavior, etc. to ask the proper questions of the zoölogist. Thus little of interpretive value emerges from such nonco-operative and incomplete studies.

Once understood, the unfortunate errors of the past need not be repeated; there is obviously need for much closer co-operation between zoölogists and anthropologists of all types, both in the field and at the interpretative level, and each must be educated to know what questions to ask the other and what validity to ascribe to the answers (Taylor, 1957).

The primary duty of the archeologist is to reconstruct the cultures of the past and to show the influences of the older upon the younger. If he does not work toward this end he is but a glorified pot-hunter. To accomplish this purpose he needs the services of all the natural scientists: botanist, zoölogist, ecologist, geomorphologist, soils expert, climatologist, etc. Each of these men must himself feel a vital interest in the total problem; he must become something of an anthropologist and see his data not only in their biological and/or physical context but also in relation to ancient and modern human cultures.

Specifically, the biologist should study the total ecology of the area in which a culture developed, know the plants and animals and their requirements and micro-environments, and make good comparative collections with as complete data as possible because it is only through such collections that the biological materials salvaged from excavations can be identified.

Mere identification is not enough, however. With regard to animals, it is expected that the zoölogist can differentiate wild from domestic individuals (sometimes!) and thus reconstruct something of the hunting, herding, and food habits of the ancient people. Further, if he has sufficient evidence, he should be able to tell something of the age groups and relative numbers of the domestic animals involved and thus calculate the composition of the herds. Perhaps the butchering techniques can be determined, following the methods worked out by White (1952-55). A stratified site involving a considerable time period may reveal genetic changes in the domestic animals, and thus something can be learned of the selection factors that led eventually to the differentiation of breeds.

I cannot overemphasize the importance to the zoölogist involved in such studies of actually working at the archeological site and of seeing the bones *in situ*. Furthermore, the zoölogist, particularly if he has had paleontological experience, can remove and prepare the bones for shipment more competently than can the archeologist. Beyond these values, there are the possibilities of making a comparative biological collection in the area of the ancient culture and of experiencing and analyzing the environment. Lastly, there is the highly valuable experience of becoming one of the anthropologists, jostling their elbows and ideas in excavation pit and dining hall and around the campfire. It is to be hoped, too, that the idea-flow is not all in one direction.

Since even the worms and insects from an excavation may contribute to the understanding of the past (Dobson and Stachell, 1956; Bradley, 1958), the archeologist who disregards the biological factors is closing the door on his effort to reconstruct the culture he is studying.

Dogs

The ancestry of the domestic dog (Canis familiaris) is still not certainly known, in spite of a vast literature on the subject. In general three groups of possible ancestors have been suggested: (1) the wolf (Canis lupus); (2) the golden jackal (Canis aureus); (3) a group which includes some or all (depending upon the author) of the following: unspecified "wild dogs," pariah (pi) dog, dingo (Canis dingo or Canis familiaris dingo), a subfossil "wild dog" from Russia (Canis poutiatini), and Canis matris optimae (the latter thought to be an early domestic derivative from some other member of the group). Diphyletic origins (different authors disagreeing on which two groups were involved) also have been suggested. Many writers assume one or another type as the ancestor without reference to (or often, seemingly, without knowledge of) the other possibilities.

The Wolf as Ancestor

On the basis of careful osteological studies of wolves and of the early dogs from the European Maglemosian, Degerbøl (1927) concluded that the Maglemosian dogs of northwestern Europe, at least, were wolf-derived. Furthermore, wolves and dogs of the larger varieties interbreed readily and produce fertile offspring; the wolf can be easily tamed when caught young (Murie, 1944); and all the individual and social behavior of the dog can be traced back to the wolf (Scott, 1954). Additionally, Lawrence (1956) has shown that there are no clear-cut cranial characters by which the smaller subspecies of C. lupus of southwestern Asia can be distinguished from large domestic dogs but instead that there is definite overlap in all the characters regarded as reliable for the separation of dogs and northern wolves. Lawrence's work does not prove that all dogs were necessarily derived from the small wolves of southwestern Asia but does accentuate the close anatomical resemblances between dogs and those small wolves. Finally, the diploid chromosome number of the wolf, although not determined with absolute certainty, is thought to be 78, the same as that of the dog (Matthey, 1954).

The Jackal as Ancestor*

Lorenz (1955) is the major proponent of jackal-ancestored dogs, although he assumed interbreeding of the more northern varieties with wolves. The only evidence presented by Lorenz, however, is his assumption that the breeds of what he terms "aureus-dogs" behave like jackals, in contradistinction to the behavior of the remaining, larger, northern-type "lupus-dogs." Unfortunately, Lorenz presents no behavior study of jackals to substantiate his claims, nor do I know of such a study. The jackal can, however, be readily tamed (Arkell, 1956).

Arguing against a jackal ancestry is the dissimilarity in detail of the surfaces of the upper molars in dogs and jackals and also the fact that the diploid chromosome number of dogs is 78, whereas that of Canis aureus is but 74 (Matthey, 1954).[3] Matthey strongly advo-

---

*The problem of the jackal as the ancestor of the dog would no longer seem to be a live one, for Lorenz, the chief advocate of this theory, has withdrawn his support from it (verbal communication before the Ethological Conference held in Cambridge, England, September, 1959).

[3] A difference in chromosome number does not automatically result in the failure of production of fertile hybrids between two species, but one would certainly expect on the basis of known facts that gene flow would be curtailed thereby (Hamerton, 1958).

cates, on the basis of this evidence, re-examination under controlled laboratory conditions of the commonly accepted idea that the hybrids resulting from dog-jackal crosses are fertile. I know of no such experiments to date, but they could easily be accomplished in areas where jackals are native. (An admittedly incomplete survey of the literature on dog-jackal hybrids by myself has failed to turn up evidence of a fertile hybrid.)

In her discussion of the Natufian "dog" from Mt. Carmel (see below), Bate (Garrod and Bate, 1937) obviously was thinking of a jackal-type dog, although she made no claim that all dogs were so derived.

A "Wild Dog" as Ancestor

Primarily on the basis of a study of skeletons of "neolithic" dogs of Europe, Dahr (1937) declared that the morphological differences between those dogs and the wolf were so great (particularly for the skull) that the wolf could not have been ancestral. Instead, a "wild-dog" (*Canis poutiatini*) found associated with late paleolithic cultures in Russia was claimed as the ancestor. The dingo of Australia, the pariah dog of North Africa, the Balkans, and southern and eastern Asia, and a wild dog of the Tengger Mountains of Java are supposedly recent representatives of this population.

The "wild-dog" theory in one variant or another has had much support. Some of this would seem to be emotional, on the part of dog-lovers who abhor wolves and whose attitude is fostered by the survival in our culture of Medieval European folk tales of the wolf. However, the theory also has several serious supporters (see Sauer, 1952; Vesey-Fitzgerald, 1957; Bodenheimer, 1958; *ILN*, 1958). As Bodenheimer remarks, what is needed is a thorough study of the neglected pariah, still found throughout much of the Eastern Hemisphere but almost unknown zoölogically because of the general assumption that it is but a half-feral domestic dog.

Diphyletic Origins

Such ideas are common; only a few examples will be mentioned here. Whereas Lorenz (1955) regarded most dogs as jackal-derived, with wolf genes entering into only some of the larger northern breeds, Hilzheimer (1932 and earlier) regarded only the Egyptian greyhound as jackal-derived, with the other breeds descending from wolves. The latter concept has recently been presented to general readers as fact (*ILN*, 1956). (The same journal, two years later [*ILN*, 1958] blithely presented the pariah-dingo type as the dog ancestor!) Duerst (1908) conjectured that some dogs were derived from the pariah-dingo species and others from wolves; one of the types of breeds (salukis and greyhounds) that he specifically excluded from the pariah-dingo group is just as definitely included in that group by Bodenheimer (1958).

Recommendations for Research

The literature on the ancestry of the dog is so confused, and the published opinions of many authors are so *dog*matically asserted, that continued rehash of old ideas is fruitless. Instead, both review and new research are needed: review of all the fossil evidence by a specialist in canid osteology and new research, from the serological and gene-frequency viewpoint, of the dog, wolf, jackal, and pariah-dingo groups. Controlled breeding experiments and cytological studies of gametogenesis of the F_1 hybrids are also necessary. Behavioral studies would be most desirable (although admittedly time-consuming).

The Domestic Dog in the Prehistory of the Near East

It is claimed that the earliest dog, earlier even than the Maglemosian dogs of northwestern Europe, is the large heavy-boned canid from Belt cave in northern Iran (Coon, 1951, p. 44), which has a C^{14} determination of 11,480±550 years B.P. (Ralph, 1955). This animal is said definitely to be a dog and not a wolf, but its status as a possible domestic animal must remain uncertain until the necessary anatomical studies are made.

In her presentation of the evidence for what is generally accepted (although perhaps erroneously) as the earliest known dog (*Canis familiaris* cf. *matris optimae* from the Natufian of Mt. Carmel, Palestine), Bate (Garrod and Bate, 1937) supported the idea of the relationship of early domestic dogs with jackals. She definitely compared her subfossil skull with those of the large Egyptian jackals (Canis aureus lupaster), which may be native to Palestine also (though Bodenheimer, 1958, is skeptical). Her discussion, it must be stressed, far from treating of the doglike characters of the Natufian skull, deals extensively with its multiple resemblances to the above-mentioned Egyptian jackal, so that one gets the impression that the Mt. Carmel canid may well represent a true wild jackal.

Bate (1942) also reported a Natufian "domesticated" dog from the cave of Shukbah, Palestine, on the basis of unfigured jaw fragments; the largest and most important piece is of a lower jaw, which part was unrepresented on the Mt. Carmel specimen, so that direct comparison of these Palestinian canids is impossible. Comparison of the Shukbah specimens with a jackal is not reported, but this certainly should be done.

It is interesting, and perhaps revealing, that in the Natufian levels of both Mugharat al-Wad and Shukbah all the remains of Canis are ascribed to "dog" but that no remains of jackals or wolves are mentioned. Since these two animals (and possibly also "wild-dog" pariahs) undoubtedly occurred wild in Palestine during Natufian times, any Canis from that period should logically be assumed to belong to one of these wild species until it is proved to be domestic dog. Such proof has not yet been forthcoming.

Romer (1938) shows how confusion between bones of dogs and jackals may lead to erroneous ideas as to the antiquity of the dog, which had been reported from several "paleolithic" sites in Algeria. He believes that all such instances were due to hopeful misidentification of jackal bones. His findings should be a warning to all investigators who apply the word "domestic" to any familiar-looking bones.

In my opinion the earliest valid specimens of the domestic dog in the Near East are from one of the lower "plaster floor levels" at Jericho (Tell al-Sultan). These animals, reported by Zeuner (1958b) on the basis of dentition and jaw fragments, were obviously neither jackals nor wolves but definitely dogs. Furthermore, even the limited sample showed considerable size variation, indicating at least two breeds. On the basis of dental details Zeuner excluded the jackal as ancestor of these dogs, which he therefore concludes are wolf-type dogs (as he considers the dingo also, a viewpoint opposed to that of Bodenheimer, 1958).

Dogs have been reported from Jarmo (Braidwood, 1952a), and they were probably there, but all bones of canids which I found at the site in 1955 are thought to belong to either foxes or wolves. It must be presumed that foxes and wolves were eaten, even if rarely, and their bones tossed into the trash. The best evidence for the dog at Jarmo is not biological but cultural; some of the figurines are of very doglike animals (Pl. 16:2) with jaunty upcurled tails unknown to any wolf. If the Jarmo people had dogs, one would expect to find their skeletons, intact or semi-intact, mixed with the bones of the other animals in the debris. If dogs were eaten, the bones would certainly be present, broken but mixed with the bones of the other animals in the debris. If we think that dogs were present but do not find the bones, then we must assume that they were not eaten but that their bodies were disposed of elsewhere. Was it because the dog was held in such esteem, or such loathing, that its carcass was not allowed to lie in the village?

Stekelis (1951) casually mentioned the dog as being found associated with the Yarmukian culture in Palestine; he considers the Yarmukian as "midneolithic." The general opinion, however (R. J. and L. Braidwood, 1953; Albright, 1954) is that the Yarmukian is not particularly early. If it is as late as Jericho VIII (as suggested by the Braidwoods, 1953) or even somewhat later (as suggested by R. J. Braidwood in personal communication), it would correspond generally with the Ubaid period in Mesopotamia, by which time (Lloyd, 1948; Tobler, 1950, p. 50 and Pl. 37b) dogs are not only definitely known but at least one specialized breed, generally identified as the saluki, had become established. On the evidence of the skull published by Tobler and the actual appearance of a dog as seen on a cylinder seal from a later level at Warka (Frankfort, 1939, Pl. IVa), this breed was somewhat heavier than the modern saluki but definitely specialized in the same general direction of a lean short-haired hunting dog.

Early knowledge of the dog in Egypt is quite lacking, in spite of considerable casual assumption to the contrary. As mentioned above, bones of the large North African jackal can easily be mistaken for those of the dog, and we cannot accept identifications if this factor has not been considered. Three dogs are stated to have been found at Merimdah Beni Salamah (Junker, 1929, p. 219), but no descriptions or photographs are published, nor even a suggestion as to whether the material consisted of complete skeletons or scraps of bone.

There has been no claim for the presence of the dog in the neolithic Fayyum or in the Tasian or Badarian materials; the bones found have seemingly never been studied in detail and thus may be jackal in each case. No dogs were found in the Sudanese site of al-Shaheinab, a millennium or so more recent (by radiocarbon determination) than Fayyum A; lack of dogs at this site is particularly interesting, for it was permanently occupied and domestic goats were already present (Bate in Arkell, 1953).

The earliest valid evidence for the dog in Egypt is from Amratian times (Massoulard, 1949, p. 167 and Pl. XXXII), and again, as at Jarmo, this is cultural, not anatomical, evidence. Four fearsome-looking dogs, with teeth and jaws exaggerated, are painted on a pottery bowl (the famous "Golenischeff bowl"); each dog has an upcurled tail, and all are led on leashes by one man, so that we can definitely consider them to represent domesticated dogs. Furthermore, they represent a distinct breed, resembling greyhounds (Hilzheimer, 1932, so names them) or possibly, if we allow for some artistic license, salukis. The Golenischeff bowl is not an isolated instance, for other bowls with painted dogs are known from the Amratian (Kantor, 1953). Probably before this time, however, as mentioned above, saluki-like dogs were already known in the Ubaid period in Mesopotamia.

In contrast to Hilzheimer's idea that early Egyptian dogs, particularly the "greyhound" just mentioned, were derived from the jackal, Moustafa (1955) stressed the wolflike appearance of the skeletal remains of predynastic canids, believed by him certainly to have been domesticated, from Maadi and Heliopolis. He did not mention any resemblances to jackals, nor seemingly did he consider such a possibility.

Perhaps the fact that the true wolf (Canis lupus) is unknown in Africa has influenced some people to the belief that early Egyptian dogs were domesticated from the large local jackal. The other alternative, of course, is that wolf-derived dogs, as Moustafa would seem to believe, were introduced into prehistoric Egypt and from there spread over other parts of Africa.

In conclusion, we can say only that until there are more detailed reports on the canids from Belt cave and Mt. Carmel we can only look critically at the material presently published on the "domestic dog" from southwestern Asia and northeastern Africa. The assumption has been that the dog was the first animal to be domesticated, which certainly seems valid for western Europe. But is it necessarily true elsewhere? Without more detailed study of the bones, one can only suspend judgment concerning the presence of the domestic dog in the early cultural periods to which it is usually assigned; indeed, the animal appears only once with complete certainty (at Jericho) prior to the Ubaid period, probably some three to four thousand years after its first domestication. Such discrepancy between supposition and knowledge, however, serves to accentuate the state of our ignorance.

Sheep and Goats

The greatest obstacle to an analysis of the origin and spread of prehistoric domestic sheep and goats is my complete disbelief in the validity of most of the published identifications. Sheep and goat skeletons are extraordinarily similar and, except for phalanges, metapodials, certain parts of the skulls, and horn cores, cannot usually be distinguished. Hildebrand (1955) has shown that even with series of whole bones of domestic sheep and goats, and statistical analyses of certain key measurements, a separation often cannot be made. Such detailed techniques have never been used, to my knowledge, on osteological materials from Near Eastern archeological sites. To illustrate further the difficulties, Dexter Perkins (unpublished data), as a result of two years' intensive study of skeletons of wild and domestic Ovis and Capra at the Museum of Comparative Zoölogy, Harvard University, is convinced that many of Hildebrand's identifications are valid only for domestic sheep and goats.

In addition to these considerable difficulties, the unwary or inexperienced investigator may easily include in the sheep/goat group many bones of other, similarly-sized Bovidae such as various gazelles and antelopes; even some bones of some deer could be included. The ibex and the true goat can probably be distinguished only on the basis of skulls or horn cores, and both goats (Capra) and sheep (Ovis) can be confused with the Barbary "sheep" (Ammotragus) which occupied, into early historic times, most mountainous and hilly country of North Africa from the Red Sea to the Atlantic.

Where basic identification as to genus can present such difficulty, the further problem of distinguishing remains of wild animals from those of domestic animals cannot always be attempted, particularly on the basis of a few broken bones. Often the best that can be done, particularly in the absence of skulls or horn cores, is merely to create a sheep/goat group of bones that cannot be further identified. Such a procedure, although the only honest one under the circumstances, is satisfying to neither archeologist nor zoölogist; future research should include an attempt at further clarification—perhaps by serological means—of this difficult but important problem.

Goats

There is only one population, the bezoar or pasang (Capra hircus aegagrus), of true wild goat in southwestern Asia. Any domestic goat originating in this area must thus be derived from this particular wild ancestor, since there is no evidence that the ibex (Capra ibex), which also occurs in parts of southwestern Asia, was ever domesticated. There would seem little necessity of proving that the earliest known domestic goats, those of southwestern Asia, were derived from the local wild goats, were it not that Adametz and Niezabitowski (1914) found a screw-horned goat, "Capra prisca," in supposedly late Pleistocene deposits of Poland and advanced the claim that all screw-horned goats are necessarily derived from this supposed European species, now extinct. This view, for which the only evidence was the association between the twisted horn cores and the supposed antiquity, has found wide acceptance on the European continent but not elsewhere. Schwarz (1935) believed that the type specimen of "C. prisca" is a modern domestic goat, that it was found associated with domestic horse, and that the deposit is Recent and not Pleistocene. Pilgrem (1947) complicated the problem further by calling "C. prisca" an ibex, which is impossible on the basis of the shape of the horn cores; whatever the situation may be, the skulls described by Adametz and Niezabitowski were from true goats. Whatever the status of "C. prisca" may be, it is unreasonable to think that a mid-European Pleistocene(?) goat (which, indeed, may never have existed) could be the ancestor of domestic goats of the seventh millennium B.C. in southwestern Asia, where there is no evidence that such wild screw-horned goats ever existed. Furthermore, the earliest domestic goats from southwestern Asia were not screw-horned but scimitar-horned (Zeuner, 1955).

There must have been a period in the early domestication of the goat, as with other species, when the domestic form was identical morphologically with the wild, and discovery today of bones of such animals in an archeological excavation presents difficulties of identification. Relatively soon, however, genetic mutations occurred in the domestic herds, and, even if the herders did not select such mutant animals for breeding, at least they were not selected against, as seemingly they are in nature.

In goats, such mutations seem to have affected the horns and their bony cores, particularly of the males. In wild goats the horns are scimitar-shaped, as long as a meter in an old male, and embossed with bumps on the front. After death, the keratin of the horn disintegrates unless it is kept absolutely dry, so that it is invariably only the bony core that is recovered archeologically. The cores are some two-thirds as long as the external horn sheaths, have a sharp keel anteriorly, and are irregularly quadrangular in section (Zeuner, 1955, Fig. 12). Changes toward an almond-shaped cross section, or flattening of the medial surface (Reed, 1959), are presumptive evidences of domestication. Twisting of the cores indicates that the goats were "screw-horned," as most modern domestic goats are; this condition is unknown in wild Capra hircus. The earliest domestic goats in southwestern Asia were all scimitar-horned, but this type was generally replaced by screw-horned goats by the "Bronze Age" (Zeuner, 1955).

The claim for the earliest domestic goats is by Vaufrey (1951) for the Natufian III-IV levels of al-Khiam in the Wadi Kharaitun, which descends toward the Dead Sea from near Bethlehem. The supposed domestic status was not determined from the bones themselves but was deduced from the fact that remains of goats suddenly appeared in these Natufian levels but were not found earlier. The implication is that the animals had been introduced by man and were thus necessarily domestic. Further argument for the possible domestic status of these goats, not mentioned by Vaufrey, is that known wild goats are not recorded from the area, which actually falls within the former range of the Nubian ibex (Capra ibex nubiana); it can be argued that, considering the close relationship of goat and ibex, it is unlikely that their ranges could overlap without interbreeding occurring, with the consequent formation of a hybrid population intermediate in its characteristics between goat and ibex. True wild goats (Capra hircus aegagrus) did occur, however, during "upper paleolithic" times on the coast of Lebanon, where their bones have been found in the cave of Antelius (von Fritsch, 1893; Zeuner, 1955) mixed with ibex remains. Here, at least, the range of the two species once overlapped; presumably behavioral differences and/or habitat preferences kept the two groups of animals sexually isolated and preserved the identity of both species. We actually know very little of the detailed distribution of either goat or ibex in Palestine during Natufian times; certainly we cannot use that little as a basis for argument.

Morphologically the goat from the Natufian of al-Khiam is identical with Capra hircus aegagrus (Vaufrey, 1951, Pl. 20:3). Domestication would not, of course, necessarily alter the morphology, particularly in incipient stages, but without other evidence the appearance, however sudden, of a goat identical with the wild goat cannot be accepted as proof of domestication. The "domestic" goat has not otherwise been found associated with the Natufian assemblage.

Zeuner (1955) found three horn cores of goats in the lower pre-pottery levels at Jericho. Two of these were female cores, which are surprisingly similar in wild and domestic goats, but the single male core was shaped so differently from that of the wild bezoar (being almond-shaped in cross section instead of quadrilateral) that Zeuner unhesitatingly proclaimed it to be from a domestic animal. He has since found several other specimens of domestic goats at Jericho (personal communication), thus verifying his earlier identification.

I am convinced that the goat remains found at Jarmo are mostly of domestic animals, a conclusion based primarily upon a study of the male horn cores. Few of these cores are from wild goats; not only are they shorter than those of most wild males, but the cross section is typically different from that of the wild Capra hircus aegagrus (Pl. 29Aa; Zeuner, 1955, Figs. 12-13, 18-20). Some of these cores from Jarmo (Pl. 29Ab) are almond-shaped in cross section, similar to the Jericho specimen (Zeuner, 1955, Fig. 6) but not so narrow. More usually, however, the Jarmo horn cores have the internal surface flattened (Pl. 29Ac) or tending even more toward the shape of the cores of modern Kurdish domestic goats (Pl. 29Ad). Furthermore, many of these Jarmo cores show some tendency toward twisting, which the typical wild-goat horn core does not (Pl. 29B). The twist is always homonymous (the right horn twisting to the right and the left one to the left; Lydekker, 1913) and thus normal for domestic screw-horned goats.

These Jarmo horn cores not only show clear evidence of domestication but also indicate the simultaneous presence of numerous transitional stages between the wild-type morphology and that of later times. Unfortunately, nothing is known of the genetic factors responsible for the characters of caprine horn cores, but the Jarmo cores alone indicate that flattening can occur independently of twisting and that the characters which we call "flattening" and "twisting" are probably each controlled by numerous genes (i.e., multiple factors), each gene being additive and by itself having relatively slight influence. The goats of the Jarmo flocks, thus, were undoubtedly quite variable as to the shapes of their horns, with regard to both the degree of internal flattening and the degree of twisting, although neither character was as well expressed as it is in some modern breeds. Presumably, then, the Jarmo herders made no conscious selection for the isolation and perpetuation of individual morphological characters, at least with regard to horn shape, in an attempt to produce what we would call a "breed."

Domestic goats are thus known to have been present at Jericho and Jarmo about 8,500 years ago. What other areas may have had domestic goats at that time, and exactly when and where goats were first domesticated, cannot be determined yet. About five hundred years later, however, goats and sheep which were "probably domestic" were present at the southern end of the Caspian Sea, where rather scanty remains of both species have been found in the pre-pottery "neolithic" levels of Belt cave (Coon, 1951). Two C^{14} determinations for these lowermost "neolithic" levels have an average of 7790±330 years B.P. (Ralph, 1955). These goat and sheep bones await detailed study, and further discussion now would be premature. Whatever the final decision may be, however, I suspect that I will have trouble following Coon's reasoning in assuming that the later "neolithic" goats were milked and that the sheep were wool-bearing. These things may have been true, but I do not understand how such conclusions can emerge from the type of evidence available.

Since we find domestic goats at Jarmo and Jericho some 8,500 years ago and most probably at the southern end of the Caspian by half a millennium later, we would expect these animals in most of the later village-farming communities in southwestern Asia. Evidence, however, is meager or lacking for many sites, usually because the data were not noted or recorded. But there are a few records. In the Amuq sequence (R. J. and L. Braidwood, 1960), Amschler found domestic goat in the earliest phase (Amuq A) and domestic sheep in the next phase (Amuq B). Both species were relatively rare in these early levels; in later times remains of goats increase, but sheep (according to Amschler's unpublished list) remained rare throughout the subsequent phases.

The Halafian site of Gird Banahilk (see pp. 33-35) in northern Iraq yielded remains of domestic goats with the same type of straight upright horns that were found at Jarmo. The "chalcolithic" site of Khirbat Bitar in Palestine, with a C^{14} determination of 3325±150 B.C., had a domestic goat, and the single horn core found shows the homonymous twist, but the domestic goats from the approximately contemporaneous site of Ain Gedi, on the west side of the Dead Sea 40 kilometers south of Jericho, still show the straight type of core (Shimon Angress; personal communication). An Ubaid level at Tell Mefesh, in the Balikh valley of what is now northeastern Syria, yielded a goat with sharp-keeled, twisted horn cores (Mallowan, 1946, p. 128); the latter characteristic marks its domestic status. Somewhat later in southern Mesopotamia, the head of a domestic goat is carefully depicted in the earliest protoliterate texts from Warka (Falkenstein, 1936) and wild and domestic goats, both easily recognizable, are portrayed on cylinder seals of the same general period (Frankfort, 1939, Pls. III-IV). It is certain that by this time the domestic goat is an important animal in the general economy of southwestern Asia.

It is interesting to note that domestic goats are reported from the upper layers only of Anau (Duerst, 1908, p. 380), whereas domestic sheep are found in earlier strata. One would suppose that the goat, as a domestic animal, reached the oases of western central Asia at a relatively early date, but the published evidence from Anau is against such a supposition. One might suspect that in his discussion of "goat-horned sheep" Duerst was confusing horn cores of sheep with those of goats, but (1) he traced the changes in successive strata from early wild-type _Ovis vignei_ to a later domestic, two-edged, flattened (goat-like) type, (2) he reported on one sheep skull bearing such goatlike cores, (3) he carefully distinguished the morphology of the cores of goatlike sheep from those of true goats, and (4) in supposedly living descendants of Swiss turbary sheep (which had similar two-edged horn cores), reared by Duerst himself, the growth of the flattened goatlike horns could be studied. It seems definite, thus, that flattened horn cores superficially similar to those of goats were found on sheep in the upper parts of level II at Anau. While later (McCown, 1954, Table 1) than the bulk of the materials discussed in the present paper, "goat-horned sheep" serve as a warning that the study of domestication may be even more complex than seems possible.

For example, I seriously wonder whether Vaufrey in his study of the bones from the prehistoric levels of the Iranian site of Siyalk was not misled by Duerst's "goat-horned sheep" into identifying straight-horned domestic goats as wild sheep, Ovis vignei (Vaufrey 1939b, pp. 196-97, Pl. 32). The cores described and photographed are certainly not those of wild sheep, and I strongly suggest that they belonged instead to early domestic goats. Siyalk I and II, the levels which yielded these cores, are comparable in general typology with the Hassunan-Halafian range in Mesopotamia, and by this time domestic goats were undoubtedly widespread and common in southwestern Asia.

There is at present no acceptable evidence for the presence of a true native goat in Africa, although, considering the late Quaternary emigration of several of the larger Eurasiatic mammals (ibex, true cattle, red deer, bear) into North Africa, there is no reason not to expect the goat there, too; indeed, because of the versatility of goats I would expect them in Africa by the end of the Pleistocene. However, the only evidence that suggests the presence of native wild goats in Africa, that of Pomel (1898), is dubious, for Arambourg (1929) has stated that the age of the strata from which Pomel's dwarf goats came is undetermined, and there is a distinct possibility that Pomel's goats (which, curiously, he named as sheep) were early domestic goats of the Algerian "neolithic."

Present evidence indicates, thus, that the goat was introduced as a domestic animal into Africa; but the time of such introduction is unknown, for the archeological record of the period of food-production in Egypt begins suddenly with the relatively late Fayyum A (C^{14} determination of 4145±250 B.C.; Arnold and Libby, 1950), which is more than two thousand years later (if the C^{14} determination even approximates the date) than the domestic goats of Jarmo and Jericho.

At Fayyum A (Caton-Thompson and Gardner, 1934, p. 34) eight "cases" of sheep or goats are listed, but no actual data are presented. We have a hint, however, that possibly both species were represented (and, if so, both should be domestic); Arkell (1953, p. viii) mentions that at the time of her death Miss Bate planned to compare the goats and sheep from al-Shaheinab with those from the prehistoric sites of the Fayyum. Fayyum A, then, may be the earliest Egyptian (and thus African) site at which the domestic goat occurred.

With similar caution we must regard the reports of goats from the various Badarian sites (Brunton, 1927, 1929, 1937, 1948; Brunton and Caton-Thompson, 1928), since no osteological data are presented; the best published evidence would be the numerous "multicolored goat-skins" from Mostagedda if we could be certain that these actually were goat skins. (Again we have the hint [Arkell, loc. cit.] that Miss Bate had planned to study the goat remains from Badari, Mostagedda, and Matmar. Surely, then, there must be available remains of goats from these sites to be studied, and it is a pity that no one has done so.)

Probably somewhat later than the Baderian period, at the site of Merimdah Beni Salamah on the western edge of the Nile Delta there were supposedly sheep and goats (Junker, 1929, p. 219), although again the evidence is not stated; indeed Menghin (in Junker, 1933) considered the presence of the goat at Merimdah to be uncertain.

In the Amratian up-river cemetery sites of al-Amrah (Randall-MacIver and Mace, 1902), al-Mahasna (Ayrton and Loat, 1911), and Abydos (Peet, 1914), probably contemporaneous with Merimdah, goats are quite definitely reported, the identification for Abydos having been made by a zoölogist. If goats were definitely present in Amratian times as far south as Abydos, they must have been present throughout the length of Egypt then and subsequently; they are, for instance, stated definitely to have been present at Maadi (Menghin in Junker, 1933), where ibex also is distinguished.

The dwarf goats (Bate in Arkell, 1953) of the "neolithic" site of al-Shaheinab (with radiocarbon average determination of ca. 3300 B.C.), near Khartum in the Sudan, occupy an interesting position in the history of domestication, for they indicate something of the rate of spread of a domestic Asiatic species into areas south of Egypt and also show that selection, either natural or artificial or both, could produce a dwarf breed by this relatively early date. Actually there were two dwarf races in the Egypt-Sudan area at this general time, for Bate (Arkell, 1953) found that the dwarf goats from the Gerzean site of Tukh

(Gaillard, 1934) in southern Egypt were not of the same variety as the dwarf goats from al-Shaheinab. The Shaheinab goats were seemingly in the van of the southward spread of domestication in Africa, for no record of the dog was found and the evidence for sheep is questionable, although Bate (Arkell, 1953) in her conclusions lists a sheep as definitely present.

There remains the interesting problem of the relations of the dwarf goats from al-Shaheinab to other African dwarf goats, a problem which Miss Bate would certainly have studied had she lived longer. (She died in 1951, with much work unfinished.) She suggested (Arkell, 1953) that there are possibly relationships of the al-Shaheinab goats with those of Algeria (Pomel, 1898) and the modern dwarf Nilotic goat. The thorough osteometric study of the Nilotic dwarfs (Chang and Landauer, 1950) presumably was published too late to be utilized by Miss Bate in her study of the al-Shaheinab goats, but such comparisons are definitely needed, considering the possibility (or probability?) that in this way a genetic continuity of more than five thousand years can be traced for one or more of the breeds of dwarf goats in northern Africa.

Arkell (1953, p. 105) has argued for an origin from Tebesti for the general cultures represented by Fayyum A, Tenere, al-Shaheinab, and the Khartum neolithic. Of all this I am not competent to judge, but in correlating this supposed movement of cultures with a possible derivation of the dwarf goat of al-Shaheinab from Pomel's questionable "native" dwarf goat of Algeria (Arkell, 1956) he went beyond the available evidence.

Sheep

The problem of determining the origin of the domestic sheep is much more difficult than is that of the goat, in part because mammalogists are hopelessly divergent as to the taxonomy of Eurasiatic wild sheep of the genus *Ovis*. A large number of species and subspecies have been named, often on the basis of inadequate material, and the problem is further complicated by the fact that for many of the populations satisfactory collections can no longer be acquired because of dwindling numbers or complete extinction of many groups (Harper, 1945).

Lydekker (1893 and subsequently) divided the potential ancestors of domestic sheep into the following groups: the European mouflon (*Ovis musimon*) of Corsica and Sardinia, the Asiatic mouflon (*Ovis orientalis*) of Cyprus and southwestern Asia, the urial (*Ovis vignei*), which ranged from eastern Persia north into Turkestan and east into Tibet, and the argali (*Ovis ammon*) of Siberia. Several other species (the number and the names differing slightly in different publications) and the Canadian bighorn (*Ovis canadensis*) rounded out his analysis of the genus. Other influential authors (Ewart, 1913; Hilzheimer, 1936) have followed a practically identical taxonomic scheme, which, indeed, has become extremely popular. Anthropologists, led by Childe in his many books, have generally followed Lydekker and these other authors with absolute fidelity, so that their ideas have almost become a creed.

Lydekker's views were not the only ones, however. Sushkin (1925) summarized fifty years of Russian research and presented a much more complicated picture (undoubtedly too complicated for such a large mammal as a sheep, but taxonomic "splitting" was the fashion in his time). The various viewpoints, however, reflected not merely differences among taxonomic splitters and lumpers; when the Russians used the species name *orientalis*, for instance, they meant something quite different than did Lydekker and his followers when they used the term. Sushkin's and other classifications have been summarized by Carruthers (1949, Appendix I) and need not be repeated in detail here.

Within a quarter of a century, the Russians had swung to the opposite view from Sushkin's extreme splitting; Tsalkin (1951) regarded *Ovis* as consisting of but two species, *O. canadensis* and *O. ammon*. Thus he regarded all the Old World sheep that have concerned anthropologists as but subspecies of the single species *ammon* and considered the detailed anatomical differences which students of domestication have studied in tracing the phylogeny of different domestic sheep as of only subspecific value.

In the same year that Tsalkin's work appeared, Ellerman and Morrison-Scott (1951) published their classification, which is generally regarded as the definitive work in English on the subject. Although working at the British Museum (Natural History), with much of the same material that Lydekker had, they cut across his classification in several ways, the primary difference being that the Ovis vignei group is included within Ovis orientalis (even the common names of "Asiatic mouflon" and "urial," invariably sharply distinguished by anthropological writers following Lydekker, being listed as synonyms!).

It is not by whim that I mention the classification of sheep in such detail. From the contrasting ideas presented, it is at once apparent that the devotion of anthropologists to Lydekker's views is probably untenable. Secondly, we may never know the true taxonomic pattern of the Old World sheep, because the necessary ecologic picture of isolation versus natural gene flow between populations, upon which modern concepts of taxonomy are based, has been badly disrupted by near-extermination of many populations (Harper, 1945). Future research in ovine taxonomy must concentrate on gene-frequency analyses of genetically determined characters (particularly biochemical units; see Evans, 1956) as correlated with intensive time-depth studies of the sheep bones from numerous archeological sites.

There is no proof, so far as I could ascertain on the basis of field studies, that the identifiable remains (metapodials and horn cores) of sheep found at Jarmo in the spring of 1955 are from domestic animals. The bulk of the sheep/goat bones from Jarmo may well belong to goats, an opinion based upon the greater number of goat horn cores. The relatively fewer bones of sheep probably represent wild animals. Certainly sheep seem to be no more numerous than gazelles, and no one has suggested that the Jarmo gazelles are domestic or even potentially so.

There is a popular delusion that wild sheep are always mountain animals and that their bones in the debris of a foothill village necessarily indicate domestication. In North America this idea is fostered by the common name "mountain sheep" applied to the native Ovis, but before these animals were driven to near-extermination in the higher mountains they were often found in foothills. In Asia more than in America, many of the populations of sheep lived on rolling hills or even on plains (Hilzheimer, 1936; Carruthers, 1949, p. 165), although it is the sheep of the more inaccessible mountains, such as Ovis ammon poli of the Pamirs, that typically comes to mind when one speaks of "wild sheep." There are still wild goats and wild sheep living on hilly ridges within a few hours' walk of Jarmo. The sheep have been identified as Ovis orientalis, and two have been collected by the Oriental Institute for their skeletons. These sheep are now near extinction, but when Jarmo was occupied 8,500 years ago they may very well have ranged down to the village and perhaps to lower altitudes.

If domestic sheep have not been identified from Jarmo or from the pre-ceramic levels at Jericho and if one retains reservations (as I do) about the domestic status of the early Belt cave sheep, pending further study of the few remains (Coon, 1951), then when did the first domestic sheep appear? Unfortunately, there is no definite answer to this important question.

Presumably domestication of sheep had to occur in Asia, since wild Ovis is not known in Africa after the Pleistocene and in post-Pleistocene Europe was limited to Sardinia and Corsica. Thus the elaborate effort of Gaillard (1934) to argue for a primary Egyptian origin of domestic sheep was quite futile. If we assume, as I think we must, that sheep were first domesticated in southwestern Asia and if we follow the classification of Ellerman and Morrison-Scott (1951), then it can be stated simply that the first domestic sheep were derived from wild Ovis orientalis. The subsequent possible contributions of other populations to the gene pool of domestic sheep has been argued endlessly but need not concern us here.

The literature on the supposedly earliest sheep from different ancient cultures leads to no definite conclusions, but as usual the secondary summaries ignore the tentative identifications and the unanswered questions. Thus Vaufrey (1939b) tentatively identified an upper jaw with six teeth from Siyalk I as of domestic sheep. His caution was commendable, for there is no proof of domestication; the jaw could even be that of a goat. Ghirshman (1954, p. 29), however, later wrote confidently of the practice of stock-breeding as based upon the discovery of bones of domestic sheep. One certainly needs to be more skeptical.

Amschler identified domestic sheep in phase B and subsequent phases of the Amuq sequence (see p. 132), but the Amuq collection is to be studied anew and we will withhold judgment until the second analysis is completed.

Neither at Hassunah in Mesopotamia nor in the Fayyum A levels in Egypt can we be certain that sheep were present, for the published reports cautiously and rightly do not distinguish between sheep and goats. Both sheep and goats are mentioned as being present at Merimdah Beni Salamah in Lower Egypt (Junker, 1929, p. 219) and at the somewhat later site of Maadi, some 50 kilometers to the southeast (Menghin and Amer, 1932, p. 52). One cannot know, however, the accuracy of these identifications, since no study of the bones themselves has been presented; we do not even know what bones were found, or how many. Menghin (1934) did, however, mention that among the bones at Maadi the domestic goat was distinguished from the ibex, which occurred wild at that time in the Red Sea hills, so that presumably some careful study of the bones was made.

In various publications, Brunton for the Badarian in Egypt and Mallowan for the earlier Halaf period in southwestern Asia assume the presence of domestic sheep. But nowhere can I find for any of the Badarian material (Brunton, 1929 and 1937; Brunton and Caton-Thompson, 1928) that anyone has definitely identified sheep, which must be carefully separated not only from goats but also from the wild ibex and Barbary "sheep" (Ammotragus) present at that time in the near-by Red Sea hills. Similarly, for the various Halafian sites I cannot find proof that domestic sheep were present. I do not consider the animal figurines from Arpachiyah (Mallowan and Rose, 1935) diagnostic, and the animal bones are hardly mentioned. Bate (Mallowan, 1946, p. 124) identified sheep, from levels considered Halafian by Mallowan, at Tell Aswad in what is now northeastern Syria; they are mentioned as "apparently domestic," and this is as near as we have come to establishing domestic sheep in the Halaf period. Mallowan (1946, p. 114) has these "apparently domesticated" sheep producing wool and draws other cultural and economic conclusions not verified by the evidence of the bones.

Sheep were not identified in the preliminary sorting of animal bones from the Halafian site of Gird Banahilk in northern Iraq (Reed in Braidwood et al., 1954), although domestic goat was present there. Even if found, Banahilk sheep might well be wild individuals from the adjacent mountains.

By the time of the Amratian culture in Upper Egypt, sheep are reported as being present at Abydos (Haddon in Peet, 1914, p. 6) and Armant (Jackson, 1937). It is, however, somewhat uncertain that the animals described were actually sheep. Haddon suggested that she was unable to distinguish between horn cores of sheep and goats; and Jackson, while describing the bones from Armant as of sheep (in a seemingly competent manner), made no mention of goats, which were probably in Egypt in Amratian times (see p. 133 above). One wonders at the absence of goats at Armant and, if they actually were absent, why their absence was not mentioned.

Wool (see pp. 137 f.), which certainly implies sheep, has been reported from various Gerzean sites in Egypt, and we may very tentatively accept a date contemporary with early Gerzean for wool fibers from al-Omari. If we are correct, this would seem to be the earliest known evidence for sheep in Egypt, but by this time (see p. 138) we already have evidence of Mesopotamian sheep at Warka.

Whatever may be the uncertainties concerning sheep in Egypt in Amratian times and earlier, they are definitely known from osteological remains from the Gerzean site of Tukh in Upper Egypt (Gaillard, 1934). Sheep remains from Tukh were less numerous than the supposed ones from Armant, but Gaillard has done more with the materials available to him; his is a careful anatomical and historical study of a sheep he calls Ovis longipes palaeoaegyptiacus. This specialized breed was particularly long-legged for domestic sheep and had elongated spiral horns which projected laterally from the head. The breed persisted as the dominant type of sheep in the Old Kingdom and has been beautifully portrayed in bas-reliefs, so that we know it well.

Gaillard's argument that these sheep, as a specialized breed, are not known outside Africa is certainly incorrect, for their presence had already been noted in Sumer (Lutz,

1923, p. 23 and references there cited), and I find the identical long-legged, long-maned, spiral-horned ram on a cylinder seal from Warka (Frankfort, 1939, Pl. IIIa). Hilzheimer (1941) has discussed these hairy, spiral-horned Mesopotamian rams in some detail; he found them first depicted in early levels at Warka, and they seemingly persisted throughout Sumerian times. Thus this breed is known in Mesopotamia for almost two thousand years, and it may well be that this "sheep with the long legs" was first bred in Asia and from there introduced into Egypt.

A re-analysis of all the available bones of sheep and supposed sheep from early sites in Egypt and southwestern Asia is needed before any definite statements can be attempted on the origin and spread of Near Eastern domestic sheep. Actually about all we know now is that domestic sheep were possibly present in Belt cave by the early sixth millennium B.C. and in Amuq phase B (probably a few hundred years later). We can say they were probably present in the late Halafian period (as represented at Tell Aswad) and are known with certainty only from Warka in Mesopotamia, Anau II (Duerst, 1908) and Shah Tepe III (Amschler, 1939) in Iran, al-Omari in Egypt (Greiss, 1955), and Beersheba in Palestine (Josien, 1955). By this time (4th millennium B.C.) sheep-rearing was obviously widespread, and it is distressing that we can say so little of its prior history.

Wool

It is sometimes naïvely assumed by prehistorians and other nonzoölogists that sheep were domesticated for their wool. Actually, wild goats and wild sheep have similar hairy coats with woolly underfur, the degree of woolliness depending upon species and/or subspecies and upon the season. A macroscopic examination of the skins of wild *Ovis* and wild *Capra* preserved at the Chicago Natural History Museum would not indicate any greater degree of woolliness in the sheep. Indeed, a careful inspection of a May-killed *Ovis orientalis* from near Jarmo showed no trace of wool, whereas wild goats (*Capra hircus aegagrus*) from the same area killed at approximately the same time still preserved part of their winter wool.

This evidence would seem to indicate that, to a prehistoric people just entering into a pattern of animal domestication, goats offered as good a hide (and one probably as warm) as did sheep. Furthermore, no prehistoric people could have foreseen any possible changes in the predominantly hairy coats of the animals (either goats or sheep) which were being domesticated. If, as I believe, goats were domesticated prior to sheep, then man already had at his disposal one animal with a naturally woolly underfur and probably would not have domesticated another wild species in a search for "woolliness," when the second species was not noticeably woollier than the first.

There may well be genetic factors, as yet undiscovered even in this day of intensive research, which allowed domestic sheep to increase the degree of woolliness whereas the goats did not, but the first domesticators could have had no prior knowledge of such factors.

It is my belief, thus, that neither sheep nor goats were domesticated for their wool per se (although the fact that the hides of both species were woolly, and thus warm, was undoubtedly appreciated). If they were domesticated *for* something, it would have been for factors familiar to early hunter-cultivators, that is, meat and hides. Not until some time after domestication could there have occurred the idea of other uses (e.g. milk), and only after the natural and random appearance in the sheep of an increase in woolliness could that character have been recognized and selected for.[4] Indeed, throughout history some

---

[4] The problems involving selection for "woolliness" in sheep are not simple genetically, in as much as there are two types of skin follicles: primary follicles for the hairs and secondary follicles for the wool fibers. The transitions from wild sheep to primitive domestic sheep and then to the various modern breeds of woolly sheep have involved, first, the loss of the coarse hairs and their replacement by wool fibers in the primary follicles (so that both types of follicles produce wool) and, second, differential selection for rela-

types of domestic sheep have persisted as hairy breeds.

It is curious how the human mind, even the so-called scientific mind supposedly trained in logical thinking, seizes upon the familiar and projects it into the past. Thus it has been with wool; the presence of sheep bones in cultural debris has usually been considered valid evidence for a wool industry, because wool has played such a large part in the history of Western civilization. In like manner, since the Kurds today make string and rope from the strong hair of their long-haired goats, one could argue that the presence of goats in a past culture is evidence for a rope industry. For various reasons, however, "rope" produces a different emotional flavor in the mind of a historically trained Westerner than does "wool," so that such an assumption is never made.

Actually, since the qualities inherent in wool (as we have come to know it) are not automatically apparent to the inexperienced, the change in pelage from hairy to more woolly may have occurred several times and been lost again because it was not preserved as a pure genetic strain in the early flocks. Indeed, we have no way at present of knowing when or where the qualities inherent in wool were first recognized and utilized by man, for wool is peculiarly subject to deterioration, more so than almost any other fiber (Crowfoot, 1954), and thus is rarely preserved archeologically. The use of wool cannot be assumed from the presence of spindle whorls or looms, for the earliest known cloth, from Fayyum A of Egypt (Caton-Thompson and Gardner, 1934, p. 46), is definitely linen, and the scraps of cloth recovered from the Badarian graves are also of a plant fiber. Spindle whorls, as those from Jarmo, are known earlier than the cloth from Egypt, but wild flax grows at Jarmo and elsewhere, so that perhaps the Jarmo people were already spinning linen thread. (Indeed, Broman reports impressions of very fine fabric on two clay balls from Jarmo; see p. 46.) Perhaps, on the other hand, these very early "spindle whorls" were actually used for some other purpose entirely and had nothing to do with spinning.

Not only is the time of the first appearance of wool unknown, but the time of the earliest archeological record is disputed. Crowfoot (1954), in her thorough review of the subject, did not mention discovery of wool in Mesopotamia and discounted all claims that had been made for its presence in prehistoric Egypt. In contrast, both Lucas (1948, p. 24) and Fairservis (1955) accepted the validity of a "piece of brown and white woolen knitted stuff" from a tomb at the Gerzean site of Nagadah (Petrie and Quibell, 1896, p. 24). The latter mentioned the possibility of intrusion of the wool but stated their reasons for believing it to be as old as the burial with which it was found. More recently, Greiss (1955) has identified wool fibers from an excavated room at al-Omari, near Hilwan in Lower Egypt. Since al-Omari has been thought to date to the time between the occupations of Merimdah Beni Salamah and Maadi, it is considered contemporary with early Gerzean (Kantor, 1954, Fig. 1); at present, and until we know more about them, the fibers from al-Omari may tentatively be accepted as the earliest known traces of wool.

By this time (probably not later than 3500 B.C.) there was a breed of wool-bearing sheep (in addition to a hairy breed) in the Protoliterate of Mesopotamia (Hilzheimer, 1941). Unfortunately, we cannot state with certainty whether the sheep known from their bones to have been present elsewhere at approximately this time (Beersheba, Shah Tepe II, Anau III) were hairy or woolly.

Pigs

Evidence for the time and place of the first domestication of the pig also is sadly lacking, and, again, the lack is at least partly due to neglect of the excavated bones.

---

tive numbers, sizes, and positions of the two types of follicles, as well as for the length and quality of wool fibers produced (Ryder, 1958 and personal communication). Until the 20th century, with its accumulation of knowledge of genetics, such selection proceeded mostly by accident (although occasionally by purposeful trial and error) without knowledge of the many factors involved.

With one minor exception (Sus salvanius of Nepal, Sikkim, and Bhutan), the wild pigs of Eurasia and northern Africa are today regarded as belonging to but one species, Sus scrofa (Ellerman and Morrison-Scott, 1951, p. 344). Any pigs domesticated in these areas, therefore, are derived from this species, a fact that is almost universally recognized by application of the identical name, Sus scrofa, to the domestic pigs.[5] The wide distribution of wild pigs makes particularly important the careful study of all bones found, if one is to separate wild from domestic specimens, but within the range of the present review such care has been shown only by Duerst (1908), Gaillard (1934), and Amschler (1939).

Many people think of Old World wild pigs as animals limited to swamps and marshes, but as an omnivore with wide ecologic tolerance the wild pig is successful in marshes, in deciduous forests, or on forestless plains and hills where only sparse bush or tall grass serves as cover. They do not, however, range over wide individual territories, and they do require water, so that they will be found in desert and semidesert country only near springs or streams. I have seen fresh pig tracks near timber line in virgin forest in northern Iraq, but near Jarmo pigs survive in limited numbers in grassy wadi bottoms. The pig is a versatile animal.

When met face to face, an adult wild pig—either boar or sow—seems a most unlikely beast for any mere human to attempt to domesticate. Actually, however, the striped young of wild pigs, two of which we kept in camp at Jarmo in the late spring of 1955, are appealing little animals that tame easily. We did not keep these pigs beyond the age of about two months, but a tavern-keeper in France (Life, 1955) kept a wild boar until it was adult, and the animal followed him around the city like a dog. Other European experiences are strikingly similar (Altmann, 1957; Rosselli, 1957). This domestic behavior, contrasted with the ferocity of a wild boar, demonstrates an amazing and unexpected plasticity in the personality of the pig. It seems that if approached with food when young, the pig is found to be psychologically pre-adapted for domestication (as undoubtedly are many other "wild" animals).

Such psychological pre-adaptation for domestication, in correlation with the wide natural distribution of Sus scrofa, suggests that pigs could have been domesticated several times in different parts of their range, as indeed Amschler (1939) believed happened at Shah Tepe. One must, I think, keep such possibilities in mind, and there should thus be a complete re-investigation of the oft-repeated claim of Klatt (1927; see Sauer, 1952, for a summary) that all domestic Sus are derived from one subspecies (Sus scrofa vittatus) of southeastern Asia. If this claim is true, domestication would have been much earlier than the archeological evidence indicates, for domestic pigs would have had to be moved westward, presumably quite slowly, to reach the Near East and most of Europe in prehistoric times. It is particularly difficult for me to imagine domestic pigs being moved in prehistoric times from Asia (by way of either Sinai or the Hadramaut) into Egypt. Since wild pigs were common in the swamps of the Nile, it would seem more logical to imagine (until evidence to the contrary is forthcoming) that the domestic pigs of that ecologically isolated area originated from the local wild population.

Vaufrey (1951) suggested that perhaps there were domestic pigs at the Natufian site of al-Khiam in Palestine. However, only a single phalanx of Sus was found, and, in spite of the fact that pig remains were not found in earlier levels, the presence of a single bone is not sufficient evidence to suggest the possibility of domestication. At that time wild pigs lived a few miles westward on the forested side of the Judean hills, even if the Wadi Kharaitun itself was too dry for them.

At Jarmo remains of pigs were more numerous than those of cattle and perhaps as numerous as those of sheep, but examination in the field yielded no evidence of domestication. Indeed, the large size of the pigs would argue for the wild status.

---

[5]In the literature on domestication, however, with pigs as with other animals, one finds an amazing oversupply of named "species," all of which are actually either subspecies or merely local populations of Sus scrofa.

Perhaps the earliest known evidence of domestic pigs is to be found in the Amuq sequence, for Amschler's unpublished notes report them in the earliest phase (A). Indeed, he listed very few of the rather numerous remains of pigs as wild. If domestic pigs were present in Amuq phase A (ca. 5750 B.C.), one would expect them in Mesopotamia in the Hassunah and Halaf periods. Although pig bones were found at Hassunah (Lloyd and Safar, 1945), in the Hassunan and Halafian levels at Nineveh (Mallowan, 1933, p. 178), and at Tell Aswad (Mallowan, 1946, p. 124), so little information is given that no conclusions as to domestication are possible. At the Halafian site of Gird Banahilk in the mountains of northern Iraq, bones of pigs are extremely numerous; however, there is as yet no proof of domestication, and wild pigs are still fairly numerous in the area.

In the Ubaid period of Mesopotamia there is, to my knowledge, no osteological evidence for domestic pigs. The cultural evidence cited by Van Buren (1939, p. 81) I find unconvincing, for a study of the sources cited does not prove to me that the figurines portrayed are necessarily representations of domestic pigs. In general, it seems to me, the evidence for the domestication of pigs in the Ubaid period is not so strong as that for dogs, goats, and sheep. This conclusion does not mean that pigs may not have been ubiquitously present in Mesopotamia during Ubaid times; indeed, if Amschler was correct in his identification of them in Amuq phase A, one would expect them in the Ubaid period.

Pigs were introduced quite suddenly, as if already domesticated, in Anau II (Duerst, 1908), which is typologically equivalent to (and probably roughly contemporaneous with) the Uruk period of Mesopotamia. At Anau there was no prior (and little subsequent) evidence that wild pigs were hunted, although undoubtedly they were locally present. At approximately the same time, or perhaps a little later, we find domestic pigs in Shah Tepe III (Amschler, 1939), where the evidence indicated that they were domesticated from local wild pigs and thus not derived by introduction of the vittatus subspecies of southeastern Asia.

We can say generally, I think, that certainly by the second half of the fourth millennium B.C. domestic pigs were widespread in the farming cultures of southwestern Asia. They were not reported at Beersheba (Josien, 1955), nor would they be expected at such a marginal subdesert site.

Domestic pigs have been reported from several prehistoric sites in Egypt, on the basis of figurines or bones recovered from excavations. Newberry (1928), for instance, accepted domestication as fact, but the figurine that he believed proved domestication is only semirecognizable as a boar (Quibell, 1900, Pl. XXII 8) and in itself provides no more evidence for domestication than do the other figurines (calf, monkeys, pelicans, fish, scorpion) illustrated on the same page. The published evidence concerning the excavated bones is no more diagnostic than that of the figurines, for there is always the exasperating probability that bones of wild pigs are involved. In each instance the Nile swamps are immediately adjacent to the site, and we know that wild pigs were present in these same regions until they were finally exterminated about 60 years ago.

Menghin (in Junker, 1933) assumed that pig-breeding played an important role in the economies of both Merimdah Beni Salamah and Maadi and contrasted this importance in Lower Egypt with the lack of pig-keeping in Upper Egypt during the same periods. But nowhere in the excavation reports on Merimdah (Junker, 1929-30, 1932-34, 1941) and Maadi (Menghin, 1932a-c and 1934; Menghin and Amer, 1932 and 1936) have I found the slightest evidence to suggest that the pig bones were from domestic animals. Pig remains were reported to be numerous, but no census as to number of bones or age-groups of the individuals was presented, nor were there any anatomical studies which might have shown effects of domestication. Huzayyin (1941, p. 300) found ". . . no reason to consider the abundant bone remains of Merimde as being those of hunted wild boar . . .," but until there is some evidence to the contrary there is no reason to believe them anything else.

At the Gerzean site of Tukh (Gaillard, 1934), the remains of a small pig were exceedingly numerous, and the bones of juveniles or subadults were said to be in the great majority (although no census was published). In the absence of complete skulls, domestication could not be proved, but the implication in favor of it was strong. Gaillard found that these small, presumably domestic, pigs from Upper Egypt resembled Sus scrofa palustris, from the Swiss "lake-dwellings," more closely than they did any other pigs with which he compared them; he seemingly did not have, however, skeletons of wild pigs from Egypt for comparison.

Surprising as it will be to Egyptologists, we must conclude, then, that, although domestic pigs may well have been present in prehistoric Egypt, we have no proof of their presence prior to Dynastic times, when we know them first in the written record of the Third Dynasty (Newberry, 1928).

Cattle

Prior to historic times long-horned wild cattle (Bos primigenius) were distributed through the forested areas of Europe, southwestern Asia, and North Africa. They are known from the Nile valley in the late Pleistocene (Gaillard, 1934). Whether or not a second wild species, the short-horned Bos longifrons (=brachyceros), was found over all or most of these areas has been much disputed for more than a century, without conclusion. Zeuner (1953b) and Koby (1954), arguing from the paintings in Lascaux cave in France, think B. longifrons is merely the female of B. primigenius. However, the paleontological records of some areas, such as the Pleistocene of Britain (Reynolds, 1939), indicate the presence of the long-horned but not the short-horned type, and it is doubtful that all the Pleistocene British cattle were males or that only males were fossilized. In any case, several races of large and small wild cattle have been described (Dyson, 1953); in at least one region, eastern Algeria, the identifications were erroneously based on size differences due to age, the more worn teeth from older animals being attributed to "small cattle" (Romer, 1938). Romer's careful work indicates the extreme care that must be taken with problems that devolve upon factors of racial, sexual, and age variations.

In Iraq, in addition to the large wild cattle that are known from Jarmo (see below) and shown in Assyrian hunting reliefs, there was also, at least in the northern mountains during the late Pleistocene, a population of small wild cattle hunted by the people who lived in Shanidar cave. Unfortunately, the excavation (Solecki, 1955) yielded no skulls or horn cores of cattle, and, until the badly fragmented material has been studied in more detail (a study being undertaken by myself), little can be said except that the cattle were surprisingly small and that no remains of large cattle were found. I mention the Shanidar cattle only to indicate how little we really know of the details of the distribution of the wild populations to which we must look for the ancestry of our domestic cattle.

In Egypt the prehistoric archeological problem with regard to cattle is more confused than is usually realized. Both long-horned and short-horned cattle (possibly males and females of the same species?) have been reported associated with the Sebilian[6] materials in the Nile valley in what Gaillard (1934) considered uppermost Pleistocene. In any discussion of early cattle in Egypt the possibility that these wild animals were present must be considered, but this possibility has usually been disregarded. In addition, Gaillard distinguished one species of buffalo in the uppermost Pleistocene and another, related to the Cape buffalo of South Africa, at the Upper Egyptian site of Tukh amidst village debris of Gerzean times. Bate (in Arkell, 1949, p. 24) thought that Gaillard's Pleistocene buffalo was a large antelope,

---

[6]In the original description of the "Sebilian," Vignard (1920) classified his lithic materials, in part on typological grounds and in part by reference to what he considered three low terraces, into a three-part scheme. In conversation with Robert and Linda Braidwood in 1958, Butzer—who had then recently visited Vignard's site—expressed dissatisfaction with Vignard's proposed terrace scheme. We must, I think, agree with McBurney's carefully considered opinion: ". . . the accounts of this much quoted locality are so completely lacking in the type of information required of present-day investigations, that it is virtually impossible to draw any reliable conclusions from them . . ." (McBurney and Hey, 1955, p. 261).

but she herself found a different Pleistocene buffalo (Homioceras) in the Sudan (Bate, 1951) and in Cyrenaica (McBurney and Hey, 1955, p. 282). The buffaloes are important, for it is practically impossible to distinguish cattle from buffaloes on the basis of isolated teeth or many of the parts of the postcranial skeleton. If Homioceras was present in Cyrenaica and the Sudan, it was presumably present also in the swamps of the Nile valley, and we do not know when it, or other buffaloes possibly present, became extinct in Egypt. A large strange bovid discovered by Brunton and Caton-Thompson (1928, p. 12) associated with Badarian graves in Upper Egypt may well have been such a buffalo; that no effort was made to preserve the skull of this unique and remarkable specimen is indeed a sad commentary on the archeological thought of the period.[7]

In southwestern Asia, the European bison (Bison bonasus) was certainly present throughout most of the forested areas, and the water buffalo (Bubalus sp.) was present in swamps and along rivers (Hatt, 1959). In any attempted identification of "cattle" from archeological sites, therefore, the possibility of the presence of these animals in addition to Bos, wild or domestic, must be considered.

Thus it is true for cattle, as for the other species discussed, that all the factors involved in the problems of first domestication have rarely been considered. Further, for the most crucial periods in cattle domestication (Hassunan and Halafian times in Asia; Fayyum A, Tasian, and Badarian in Egypt) material has not been found or has never been adequately studied or has been discarded without study.

Claim for the earliest domestic cattle has been made by Vaufrey (1951), who thought them "probably present" in the Natufian of al-Khiam in Palestine. The only evidence for any member of the Bovini, however, is a single fragment of mandible with two deciduous teeth; even if this piece is identifiable as Bos, there certainly is no evidence of domestication.

At Jarmo remains of cattle were found but, contrary to the impression given by Braidwood (1952a), were extremely rare. Only a few dozen pieces of as yet unidentified Bovini were salvaged from the excavations of 1948 and 1950/51. (One of these pieces, it is true, was a skull [ibid. Fig. 21], but, although successfully salvaged in the field, it seems not to have survived the trip from the United States to Vienna and back to the United States again [see p. 53, n. 6, above].) In three months in 1955, with over a hundred thousand bone fragments sorted, very few definite pieces of Bovini (one M^3, two M_2's, a partial horn core, and a few fragments of limb bones) were recovered. The limb fragments and isolated teeth are not actually determinable, but the horn core is certainly that of Bos.

The teeth were compared with those of Bos in Amschler's laboratory in Vienna and at the British Museum (Natural History) in London. The M^3 was matched in size and proportions by teeth of large modern cattle of the Ayrshire and Hungarian Steppenvieh breeds. The two M_2's, however, are somewhat larger than those of any modern cattle seen but are of the same size as those of Bos primigenius from the early Maglemosian site of Star Carr in northern England (Fraser and King, 1954). This early Maglemosian B. primigenius, in turn, is known to be smaller than earlier, late Pleistocene individuals from northern Europe.

The partial horn core from Jarmo has neither base nor tip, so that the total length and size of the original cannot be determined. Even so, it is almost as large (30.3 cm. in cir-

---

[7] If, instead of an animal skeleton, the object had been a delicate mosaic or a poorly preserved strip of cloth, it certainly would have been preserved and restored; archeological techniques of the time were capable of remarkable restorations. But the object was not an artifact; it was a skeleton—not even a human skeleton—and thus obviously little effort was made to salvage it. Arguments that the skull was too "crushed and broken to permit of removal" are feeble, considering the successful techniques evolved by vertebrate paleontologists decades earlier to meet just such conditions. The result of the neglect of this valuable specimen was that it was lost and destroyed. This bovid with its broken skull was a unique specimen; no other has been found in the Badarian, and how long must we wait for more Badarian deposits to be dug?

cumference) as cores of British B. primigenius measured at the base (Reynolds, 1939, p. 13) and thus probably larger than cores from any domestic cattle. Although the remains of the Jarmo Bovini are too fragmentary to be determinable, we suggest with caution that they could have belonged to a race of Bos primigenius. They were undoubtedly wild, to judge by the rarity of their remains; perhaps they were too wild and fierce for the Jarmo farmers to capture easily.

Coon (1951) has suggested that the bones of Bovini (stated by him to be Bos) from levels 5 and above in Belt cave in northern Iran were from domestic cattle. However, relatively few bones were found, no evidence for domestication is offered, and wild cattle and wild bison undoubtedly lived in the area and could have been hunted.

Two other doubtful records of approximately the same time (ca. 5500 B.C. or slightly earlier) are those from Amuq phase A and Siyalk I. Amschler's unpublished notes on the animal bones from the Amuq give no indication of his evidence for differentiating bones of wild and domestic animals, but Dexter Perkins, a graduate student from Harvard University who worked briefly with Amschler in Vienna shortly before the latter's death, has told me that differentiation was mostly on the basis of surface texture. Perkins, himself a mammalian osteologist, could not distinguish the supposed differences nor duplicate Amschler's results.

Ghirshman (1954, p. 29) has claimed that stock-breeding is indicated by the Iranian assemblage of Siyalk I (roughly comparable on typological grounds with the Hassunan-Samarran range in Iraq): ". . . for bones of domesticated oxen and sheep were found in the remains of Period I." The only evidence for this sweeping statement, when one examines the original report (Vaufrey, 1939b), consists of six "sheep" (possibly goat) teeth and two(!) teeth of Bovini. Vaufrey assigns the latter, without giving his reason, to Bos taurus. Certainly such specific assignment by Vaufrey and Ghirshman's subsequent discussion of the importance of stock-breeding have not the slightest validity; even if determinable as Bos, two teeth do not indicate domestication (as the name taurus specifically implies); indeed, such a minimum of evidence suggests extreme rarity of cattle in the region. Furthermore, cattle are not recorded from higher levels at Siyalk. This sequence of statements concerning Siyalk, from an earlier impossible specific identification to a later sweeping cultural conclusion, serves as a warning, since it is (unfortunately) a characteristic example of much of the archeological literature on domestication.

It has been generally assumed that the herding of cattle was important in the economy of the people of Hassunan and Halafian times in Mesopotamia. Certainly bulls were important in the emotional life of the Halafian people, as shown by their art and deduced for their religion (Mallowan and Rose, 1935), but no evidence has been presented to show that these animals were domesticated. At Hassunah (Lloyd and Safar, 1945), where a few teeth were the only remains of cattle discovered, there is no evidence for domestication, nor was such claimed. Later authors (e.g. Lines, 1953), however, have boldly listed "domestic cattle" as present at Hassunah.

Of the various Halafian sites excavated, bones presumably were not saved at Tell al-Halaf itself nor at Arpachiyah. Only a cow's horn (undescribed, unmeasured, unfigured, and obviously unwanted) and unnamed uncounted pig bones were found in the Halafian layers at Nineveh (Mallowan, 1933), and only at Tell Aswad are several oxen reported. Those "apparently belonged to domestic races" (Mallowan, 1946, p. 124), but no evidence is offered, and we are actually told only that some were larger and some smaller. The best evidence of a domestic Bos during Halafian times is a small carved head, probably of a cow (Mallowan and Rose, 1935, Pl. VIa:895B), from Arpachiyah. The horns, as well as can be judged from the small but clear photograph, are short and curve forward, quite as in some domestic cows today.

I mention these points with regard to Halafian cattle not so much because I personally disbelieve that the people were cattle-herders as to show the paucity of evidence indicating that they were. Bones of Bovini were found at the Halafian site of Gird Banahilk, but unfortunately there were no skulls or horn cores (Andersen in Braidwood et al., 1954). Since wild cattle undoubtedly lived in the region at the time (Shanidar cave being only a few miles away), it will probably be difficult to establish domestication of cattle for Banahilk until more complete osteological materials are procured.

When did domestication of cattle occur? As with the other animals discussed, we cannot say; as with these other animals, domestication probably occurred two or three thousand years prior to any proof of that condition now known. We can say with certainty that by 3500 B.C. or soon thereafter domestic cattle were present in Mesopotamia and north across Iran to Anau at the border of Turkestan. The beautifully clear delineations on cylinder seals from Warka and other early Sumerian towns testify to the role and importance of cattle (as well as sheep and goats) in the cultures of the period. From Anau II and Shah Tepe III we have the careful osteological studies of Duerst (1908) and Amschler (1939), respectively, which show the presence of cattle in these communities.

During the next five hundred years and until the advent of the Dynastic period there is little evidence of domestic cattle in Egypt, in spite of numerous assumptions and published statements to the contrary. Since wild cattle were native in Egypt from at least the late Pleistocene period into early historic times (Gaillard, 1934), mere recognition of cattle bones in early assemblages is no evidence for domestication. An "ox" from "neolithic A" and horn cores of Bos from Old Kingdom sites in the Fayyum may represent such wild cattle (Caton-Thompson and Gardner, 1934, p. 122), as may other random prehistoric and historic finds from Egypt, such as those from al-Amrah (Randall-MacIver and Mace, 1902, p. 21), Merimdah Beni Salamah (Junker, 1929, p. 219), and Maadi (Menghin and Amer, 1932, p. 52), that have no immediate proof of domestic status.

Brunton's assumption of cattle domestication for the Badarian people must be completely discounted. Again, as with the Halafian in Mesopotamia, cattle-herding may well have occurred, but there is so little evidence!

From the Amratian we have remains of cattle listed from three sites—Naqada, Mahasna, and Armant (Massoulard, 1949, pp. 167, 187), but there is no evidence of domestication presented. The cultural evidence of domestic cattle from paintings on bowls—so definite for the dog (see p. 129)—is here most indefinite. Several of the animals portrayed are certainly cattle, but there is no indication of domestication. There is, however, one bit of evidence—suggestive but unfortunately not conclusive—that the Amratian people had domestic cattle. The Amratian graves at al-Amrah yielded several clay figurines of cattle, some of which were mounted four abreast on a single base and one of which showed a remarkably large udder (Randall-MacIver and Mace, 1902, pp. 16-17 and 41, Pl. IX). These figurines lack the kind of evidence (halters, ropes, stall, mangers, fencing, etc.) that would indicate domestication, but their posing and detail do suggest (if the cautious zoölogist may be allowed to digress) an emotional flavor of familiarity—as if the people who made these rough grave-goods knew the models as household animals.

One other bit of cultural evidence suggests domestic cattle, in very late predynastic Egypt. A slate palette (Capart, 1905, p. 236) shows three rows of animals (sheep, donkeys, and bulls) walking head to tail. In conjunction with the picture on the reverse of the same palette, the scene is interpreted by Egyptologists (Dr. Helene Kantor; personal communication) as showing the collecting of tribute or booty by a king of Upper Egypt from some conquered Libyans, and the cattle and asses are presumably domestic, as the sheep certainly are.

We must be satisfied for the present with such cultural evidence for domestication of cattle in predynastic Egypt, since the skeletal evidence from Gerzean sites is no more conclusive than it is for prior periods. The numerous bones of unidentified "ox" reported by Jackson (1937) at Armant and those of "Bos brachyceros" at Tukh (Gaillard, 1934) do not in themselves prove domestication, particularly since Gaillard was careful to make the point that wild short-horned cattle still existed and were hunted at much later times. Even the subadult age of most of the cattle killed cannot be used as final evidence of purposeful control of domestic herds, for the gazelle bones from the same middens were also mostly from subadult animals. If one were to conclude on the basis of the evidence presented that the Tukh cattle were domesticated, would he not have to draw the same conclusion for the gazelles?

Regarding the origin of domestic cattle in the prehistoric Near East, we can only say that cattle have been of tremendous importance to man, particularly to the circum-Mediterranean peoples and cultures derived therefrom,[8] and we must regret that to date the evidence for the origin and very early history of this domestication has been (with few exceptions) so largely ignored by archeologists, who, even while discarding the bones, have not been averse to publishing their surmises as established facts.

---

[8]I am thinking here not only of the economic factors—hides, milk, and meat (with the obviously great importance to both the stability and the evolution of the human cultures involved)—but also of peculiarly emotional factors associated with cattle of the Mediterranean peoples and their derived cultures. One links, and I think logically, such "cattle cults" as that which we glimpse at the Halafian level in prehistoric Mesopotamia and those which we know historically from the Rig-Veda for the Aryan invaders of India, from the Hathor cult in Egypt, and from the "bull-vaulting" activities of Minoan Crete. Such cults in part have died but in part have spread and persisted, particularly in India of course. However, they are still manifest in Spain, where the ritual sacrifice of the bull serves as an emotional release for a whole populace, and in the highlands of East Africa, where (differing in pattern in different groups) the cattle are often more important as a cultural or prestige factor than they are economically.

X

THE BASIS FOR A TENTATIVE CHRONOLOGY

INTRODUCTION

In outlining our tentative chronology of the prehistory of Iraq, we point out the specific facts which allow us to place each of the many sites and their material remains in some sort of sequence and show which placements are strongly founded and which are weakly founded on the basis of present evidence. In some cases, the simple and direct superimposition of deposits allows us to say at least that one set of materials came before another. Such stratigraphy may involve purely local archeological deposits or may depend on broader geological arguments. In other cases, the relative dating must remain tentative because we can point only to a techno-typological comparison or a general morphological similarity between bodies of material at different sites. In some further instances we may cautiously use the evidence of absolute age furnished by radioactive-carbon dating tests performed on documented organic remains. All these sorts of evidences are used, singly or in combination. The order of presentation is now reversed, from earlier to later in time (cf. chaps. iv-v). Within certain limits we can be more precise in the assignment of real dates as we move later in time. Our tentative chronology is summarized in chart form in Figure 8.

For the earlier food-gathering horizons, the stratigraphic evidence of Pleistocene geology provides the basis for a local starting point. The artifacts of the early food-gathering or middle paleolithic site of Barda Balka are incorporated in a river-gravel deposit marking the base of the youngest of three major aggradation cycles observed locally in the Chemchemal valley. This position places the site stratigraphically at a point much older than all other archeological remains so far found in the same valley, since they can all be associated in one way or another with the geological phases following the last major aggradation cycle. Incidentally, these later remains are all obviously much later on typlogical grounds also. However, to prove that the Barda Balka hand-ax, pebble-tool, and flake industry preceded the Mousterian of the caves and open-air sites of Iraq, one must rely on stratigraphic sequences outside the immediate area. These, on the basis of repeated and well known occurrences, show generally Levalloiso-Mousterian flake industries stratigraphically following core-biface or pebble-tool horizons either in caves, as in Palestine and western Syria, or in open-air river-valley sequences, as on the Indian subcontinent, to take only the nearer examples. While stratigraphic evidence cannot yet be shown in Iraq, the industries which on typological grounds could make up such a sequence exist at Barda Balka in a geological sequence, at telegraph pole 26/22 and Serandur, neither yet associated with any stratigraphic sequence, and in the Mousterian deposits found in the lowest levels of several caves.

Subsequent food-gathering and food-collecting horizons form the sequence known locally in caves. A Mousterian industry is the lowest known such horizon in Hazar Merd, Shanidar, Babkhal, and perhaps at the yet unplumbed site of Spilik. The whole Zarzian horizon, regardless of possible different stages or phases within it, occurs stratigraphically above the Mousterian and is the uppermost and probably terminal food-collecting layer in the first three of these sites. At the Shanidar cave, an intermediate blade industry, the Baradostian, exists between the Mousterian and the Zarzian. Radioactive-carbon determinations on an absolute scale have been furnished by layer B of Shanidar for the Zarzian (W-179: 12,000±400 years B.P., W-667: 10,600±300 years B.P.) and by layer C for the Baradostian (L-335H: 26,500±1,500 years B.P., W-178: 29,500±1,500 years B.P., L-335I: 32,300

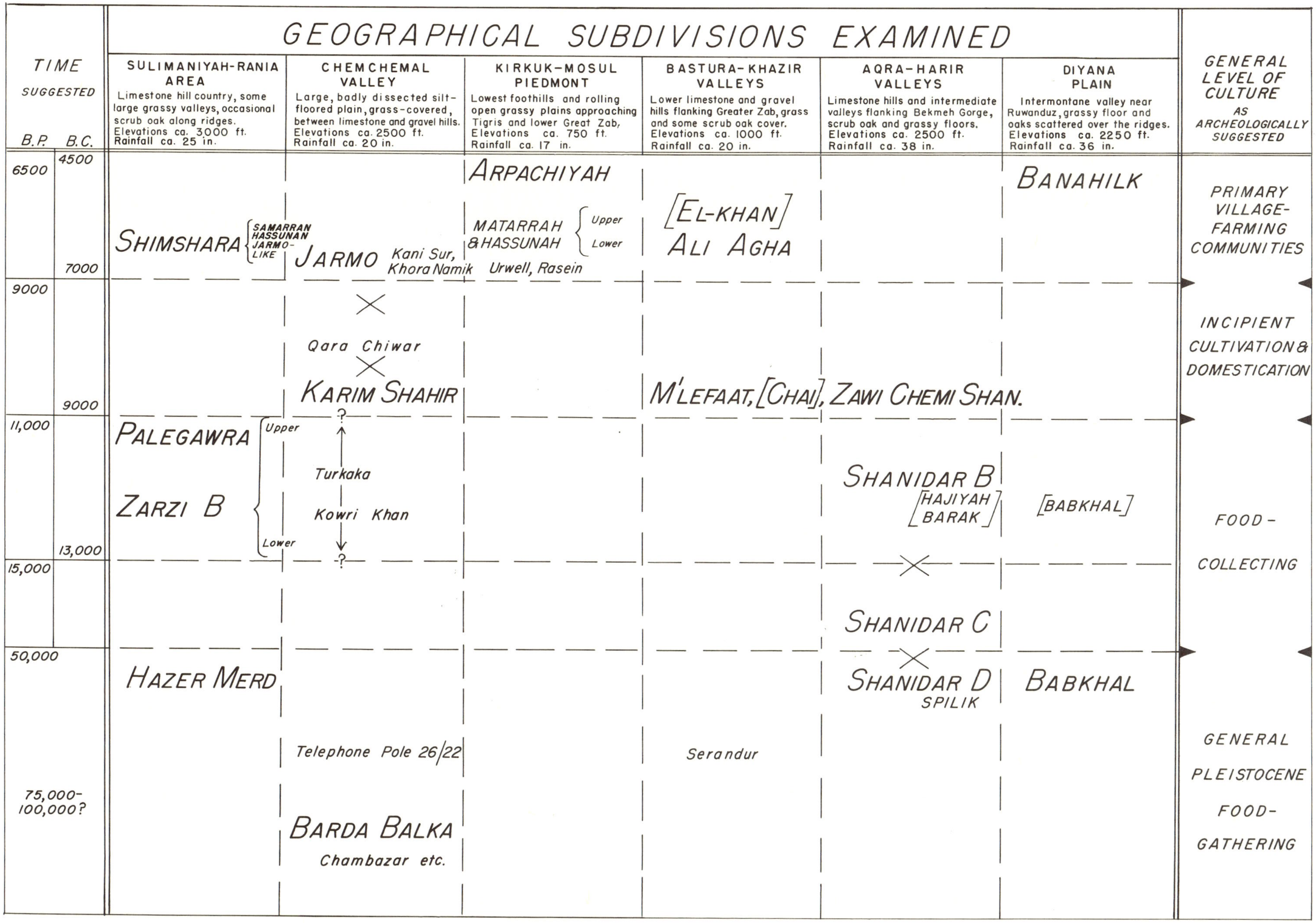

Fig. 8. A suggested chronological sequence of earlier prehistoric sites in northeastern Iraq

±3,000 years B.P., GRO 1494: 33,630±400 years B.P., W-180: older than 34,000 years B.P.). For the Mousterian of the caves, there are determinations from Shanidar reported as "from the borderline between layers C and D, more likely from D" (GRO 1495: 50,300 ±3,000 years B.P.) and Hazar Merd layer C (C-818: older than 25,000 years B.P.). There is as yet no radioactive-carbon determination for the Barda Balka horizon, which may in any case lie beyond the reach of this method.

Chronological subdivision within the interval between terminal food-collecting and established food-producing horizons is as yet weakly based. The open-air sites so far placed in this interval (Karim Shahir, Gird Chai, M'lefaat, and perhaps Turkaka and Kowri Khan) cannot yet be ordered in a sequence or related to any horizon clearly represented stratigraphically in caves or in the open air. The open site of Zawi Chemi Shanidar (see p. 52) also fits into this category on typological grounds. Its materials show considerable correspondence with those of Karim Shahir, Gird Chai, and M'lefaat and follow those of Shanidar B in time. A radioactive-carbon determination is available from Zawi Chemi Shanidar (W-681: 10,870±300 years B.P.). Subject to correction by future excavation, each of these open-air occurrences is viewed as a probably one-period occupation without evidence for any stratigraphic sequence or very long-range internal developments. Hence the placement of these sites is based largely on the techno-typological and morphological differences displayed by their respective features and archeological assemblages. These proceed from lack of discernible architecture to limited traces of structures and from assemblages essentially restricted to well made and varied chipped stone tools of latest paleolithic type to assemblages of less well made and less varied flint tools combined with small numbers of ground and polished stone implements and ornaments. Thus Karim Shahir, the first-found example of what we take to represent a community with some incipient cultivation (see pp. 181-83), has techno-typological elements in common with, and others in contrast to, the Zarzian on the one hand and Jarmo on the other. It appears to fall between these two major aspects of flint-tool preparation. The other sites shown on the general horizon with Karim Shahir in Figure 8 follow suit to a greater or lesser degree, depending on the type or intensity of traits, and may be placed before, with, or after Karim Shahir in time. Turkaka and Kowri Khan are on typological grounds positioned in Figure 8 as open-air counterparts of Zarzian cave assemblages, but they may have been nearer the general level of Karim Shahir. Besides lacking a stratigraphic basis, this portion of the proposed sequence in Iraq so far also lacks radioactive-carbon determination save for the single count from Zawi Chemi Shanidar.

From this point onward, the number of radioactive-carbon determinations or the overlapping fabric of the comparative archeological stratigraphy increases. The Jarmo phase is followed by the Hassunan, with Ali Agha perhaps representing a fairly wide-spread subphase between the two. Certainly the Samarran painted pottery style becomes an element of the developed Hassunan assemblage; the question of the existence of a separate "Samarran" assemblage is again an open one. Just how soon after, and by what means, the Halaf-

---

Notes on the chronological chart (Fig. 8). The relative positions of the site names are based on stratigraphy, comparative typology, and typological development. The dates in the left-hand columns refer to general time divisions as suggested by the available radioactive-carbon determinations. The names given in upper case letters are those of excavated sites (or of ranges within excavated sites) where the stratigraphic context appears to be reliable. The names within brackets in upper case letters are those of excavated sites (or of ranges within excavated sites) where the stratigraphic context is confused. The site names in lower case letters are those of unexcavated sites represented by surface collections. X is the symbol used for a postulated missing phase (or phases) suggested by breaks either in the general stratigraphy or in typological development. The rainfall figures at the heads of the columns are extrapolated from De Vaumas, 1955; the elevations are from the 1:253,440 map series of the Geographical Section, General Staff (2d ed.; 1942), save in certain cases where Wright had recorded altimeter readings.

ian assemblage followed the developed Hassunan assemblage is as yet unclear.

EARLY MIDDLE PALEOLITHIC FOOD-GATHERERS

On stratigraphic and typological grounds, the materials of Barda Balka (pp. 61-62) are the oldest so far known in situ in Iraq. Barda Balka has components of a stone industry traditionally considered as lower paleolithic and associated with early forms of the food-gathering economy. There is now geological and comparative archeological evidence to cast doubt on the chronological implications of the archaicness of this industry and to suggest that its seemingly early economy may have been of relatively long persistence at Barda Balka. Here the relatively fresh and unrolled pebble tools, flake tools, and Upper Acheulean type hand axes, as well as the poorly preserved animal bones, were all incorporated in a river-gravel deposit at the base of the third and youngest of a series of three major Pleistocene aggradation cycles. The first cycle comprises rubble benches high against the ridges; the second and third cycles are extensive spurs of gravel and silt beds, each comprising a basal gravel and overlying silt. The materials at Barda Balka, as well as the few hand axes and flakes from Cham Bazar and the two hand axes found near Jarmo (p. 62), were associated with the latest basal gravel. This third set of massive aggradation deposits has been particularly dissected by erosional processes of the last few thousand years and of the present, as established for the Chemchemal valley by the geological reconnaissance of Wright (1952). At Barda Balka, the physical condition of individual artifacts and the concentrated circumstances of both unrolled stone tools and fragile bones leave little doubt that these materials are broadly contemporary with the gravels themselves. The gravels, in turn underlying meters of silts, are the lowermost and earliest element in a single total cycle of gravel and silt deposit which Wright attributes to a third and youngest set of local pluvial conditions and tentatively equates with the last, or Würm, glaciation of more northerly latitudes. Thus, the gravels and their contained stone industry may be tentatively dated to the closing portion of the preceding Riss-Würm interglacial or, possibly but less likely, to the very start of the last glaciation. Entirely theoretical and hotly debated estimated dates used by geologists for the beginning of the Würm glaciation in Europe range from about 50,000 to 100,000 years ago.

As regards typological comparisons, an industry of flint hand axes, limestone pebble tools, and irregular small flint flake tools, distributed in three stratigraphic levels at Sidi Zin in Tunisia, is strikingly similar to that at Barda Balka. However, Sidi Zin (Gobert, 1950) is geologically undated and geographically quite distant. To find relatively comparable assemblages in tentatively dated geological contexts we must look farther into Africa and also eastward to the Punjab.

In eastern and southern central Africa, for example, especially in northern Rhodesia (Clark, 1959, pp. 79-88), the moot Hopefountain and certain early Rhodesian Sangoan industries bear considerable typological and morphological resemblance to the Barda Balka industry. The respectively associated gravels and ferricretes have been locally dated variously to a broad interval spanning the second half of the second pluvial and the early third pluvial. The so far largely unparalleled Hopefountain flake-tool and pebble-tool assemblages, a still uncertainly assessed manifestation of the later Chelles-Acheul tradition thereabouts, comprise a large proportion of very irregular simple flake tools and some core and pebble choppers as a rule, with hand axes in certain instances (ibid., pp. 79-83 and Pl. 8). Certain sites with the succeeding and commoner Rhodesian Sangoan assemblages yield hand axes, flake tools, and occasional pebble choppers and polyhedral spheroids (ibid., pp. 83-88 and Pls. 9-11). Thus, while the geological dating appears to be considerably earlier than that suggested for Barda Balka, the techno-typological and morphological comparison with these two types of assemblages in distant Africa at the transition from the Early Stone Age to the Middle Stone Age is close.

The lower paleolithic industries known from the Punjab also have types of implements which very closely resemble the material at Barda Balka. Again, the several characteristic elements are evidently not all found in precisely the close combination of the Iraq site. At numerous points in northwestern India and Pakistan various types of hand axes, cores, and flake tools are reported to occur together and are labeled Abbevillian-Acheulean, whereas pebble tools with associated cores and flake tools have been found at sites not yielding hand axes and are considered as representing a separate and parallel tradition, called the Soan (or Sohanian) industry in this quarter of the peninsula (De Terra and Paterson, 1939, pp. 301-12). Even at Site P-16 near Chauntra on the Soan River, where ". . . late Acheulian hand-axes in an unworn condition are associated with cores and flakes that are typologically similar to those of the Soan industry . . ." (ibid., p. 304), no characteristic Late Soan pebble tools, such as choppers, were found. While the fresh pieces were considered contemporaneous with the deposit, rolled examples indicated mixed increments from previous times (ibid., pp. 289-90, 310). Absence of pebble tools and, in this case, an arguable diagnostic role for cores and flakes in distinguishing Abbevillian-Acheulian from Soan assemblages seem to lessen the interest of Chauntra as an example of fused traditions. Chauntra is, however, a point of comparison for its late Acheulian hand axes and flake tools.

For the moment, if we exclude hand axes, the closest morphological and typological comparison for Barda Balka in the Soan sequence is in Late Soan A, for which several workshop sites have been noted in addition to numerous lesser finds. The types and relatively limited quantity of pebble choppers, the cores struck from one or two ends, the relatively great percentage of flake artifacts, and the marked but not overwhelming percentage among flakes of faceted striking platforms can all be matched at Barda Balka. On various geological grounds the Late Soan A industry, associated with the basal gravel of the Potwar loesslike silt on Terrace T 2, is considered to be of local third glacial age (ibid., pp. 272-74), and the implementiferous sandy silt on Chauntra is viewed as probably of local third interglacial age (ibid., p. 290). Current provisional correlations would assign the latter to the Riss-Würm interglacial, which, as geological time goes, is not too far from the date suggested for the Barda Balka material. However, the great bulk of the Punjab occurrences of both stone-working traditions are considered to be of third glacial and second interglacial age. An evolved Soan industry with diminutive pebble tools and flakes may be placed in the fourth glacial period. Thus, if one assumes that the geological attributions are fairly correct in both the Punjab and Iraq, the rather special Barda Balka occurrence appears to represent a late local survival or persistence of early regional traditions.

The Barda Balka assemblage seems special now because it combines late Acheulean type hand axes with apparently about the same types and relative quantities of pebble and flake tools and cores as are found in Late Soan A. Such a fusion of traditions has not been demonstrated in the Punjab for later stages and is excluded for the early stages of the paleolithic, according to the interpretation of the evidence to date. A question may reasonably remain in future work in the general area as to the extent to which the concept of separate and parallel development for Abbevillian-Acheulian hand-ax and Late Soan pebble-flake traditions will continue to be upheld for successively later stages.

Elsewhere in the Indian peninsula, in latitudes south of the Punjab and scattered from the center over to the eastern side south of the Ganges-Indus plain, there are sites where the pebble-flake Soan tool-making tradition appears to be mixed with the core-biface Madras-Acheul tradition so widespread over southern India. Although the Madras tradition has been found to include some pebble tools, too, this central borderline zone is seen as an area of mixture or contact between the two as yet distinct traditions. This concept has been briefly summarized by Krishnaswami (1953). However, hand axes in general greatly outnumber pebble tools in these allegedly mixed assemblages; the cleaver (not yet clearly established for Barda Balka) is a prominent type, and the local geological sequences, while studied in some detail, remain uncorrelated with the Kashmir-Punjab or any other dated sequence. Barda Balka, comprising a predominantly pebble- and flake-tool ensemble with some bifaces included and tentatively assigned to the very end of the last interglacial, may prove to be a relatively late westerly representative of such a contact zone, or its industry may provide a glimpse of some sort of continuity in stone-working traditions between India and Africa. Certainly, however, further work is needed before either the validity of these concepts or Barda Balka's role in them can be accepted. At any rate, in all three areas, similar-looking industries evidently developed in response to the needs of existence even though they may have started at different moments and lasted for different lengths of time.

OPEN-AIR SITES INDICATING A MORE EVOLVED MIDDLE PALEOLITHIC ASPECT OF FOOD-GATHERING

Following the earlier food-gathering horizon and its core-biface, pebble-tool, and flake industries, a subsequent period is marked especially by flake-tool industries which are broadly in the typological and technical tradition called Mousterian. One may view them as part of one great unit with the earlier material, representing only some progressive difference in kind or degree in an early food-gathering economy. Thus, a second general kind of primitive food-gathering horizon may occur.

Indeed, as a result of our reconnaissance, the surface materials from gravels at telegraph pole 26/22 and Serandur do nothing more than encourage further looking for better evidence of such a horizon. These finds simply suggest that Mousterian sites may exist thereabouts in the open air in association with gravels, river terraces, and valley deposits in general, as opposed to cave sites.

Should these occurrences truly indicate a valid horizon of open-air Mousterian sites, it may ultimately be shown that they can be associated with certain particular river terraces and that the industries are marked by standard, relatively large, simple broad flake tools with faceted or plain striking platforms and by coarse discoid and other flake cores. At present, the evidence is weak and rare, residing entirely in surface material which definitely includes typologically later artifacts, some of which even look unweathered and unrolled. However, in each instance there appear to be gravels near by which might be associated with some ancient stage of the local wadi or river, and there are unmistakable rolled and weathered relatively coarse artifacts. Also, the finer Mousterian types found in the caves of Hazar Merd, Shanidar, and elsewhere in this part of Iraq and in Iran have not so far been discovered among these open-air occurrences, that is, the long, narrow, delicate, triangular points on bladelike flakes, the occasional burins, and the small discoid or spheroidal cores. This further encourages the theory of a coarse, early, open-air Mousterian horizon and a delicate, later, cave Mousterian horizon in this quarter of the Near East.

In connection with the apparent absence of pebble tools and hand axes at these particular open sites one must bear in mind the possibility of this other stage between the Barda Balka gravels of late Riss-Würm or early Würm times and the lowermost cave deposits now available in the area. This alleged, earlier, coarser outdoor Mousterian is not fixed geologically or stratigraphically, and we know nothing further than the few artifacts picked up at three localities (telegraph pole 26/22, Serandur, and Garrod's Kirkuk gravels; see p. 61). The horizon must still be proven, and time must be allowed for it in any chronological sequence. On the other hand, one must not lose sight of the possibility that the outdoor sites may represent a cruder version of the more delicate Mousterian in caves and that these two sorts may be essentially contemporaneous, for some reason differing in their workmanship.

THE DEVELOPED MOUSTERIAN HORIZON IN CAVES

To date the caves and shelters of northeastern Iraq have produced nothing lower and earlier than a Mousterian industry of well made, shapely, sometimes diminutive tools. This represents a techno-typological advance over the various open-air industries noted above which are perhaps linked to presumably different and presumably earlier food-gathering horizons. Garrod first found the cave industry in the lowermost layer, C, of Hazar Merd (Garrod, 1930, pp. 25-37); Solecki next found thick deposits of it in the lowermost layer, D, of Shanidar (Solecki, 1955, pp. 416-21). We ourselves can report it (see p. 60 above) at the base of shallow unconsolidated deposits at Babkhal, not too far from Shanidar, and at some depth in a sounding at Spilik which did not reach bedrock (Braidwood, 1956b). In the base of layer C at Hazar Merd, Garrod found two hand axes (Garrod, 1930, pp. 30, 35, 37), but the industry in the nearly 4 meters of layer C was otherwise limited to typical Mousterian flake tools. A few hand axes are, in any case, not uncommon in the Mousterian of Europe. Coon found the same industry at the bottom of Bisitun in Iran (Coon, 1951, pp. 6-15, 33-36, 53-65, 91-92, 96-101); and in the cave of Jerf Ajla near Palmyra in Syria he found a generally Mousteroid but technically different horizon in the lower and middle levels (Coon, 1957, pp. 303-7). Radioactive-carbon determinations have been obtained from Hazar Merd layer C (C-818: older than 25,000 years B.P.), from Shanidar at the layers C-D contact zone, if not from D itself (GRO 1495: 50,300±3,000 years B.P.), and from a middle level at Jerf Ajla (New Zealand counter: 43,000±2,000 years B.P.).

A terminal date for the cave Mousterian in Iraq is perhaps, then, somewhere in the neighborhood of 40,000 or more years ago. If the middle paleolithic tradition revealed at Barda Balka proves to persist in this area down to a moment that just precedes the start of Würm, a moment broadly datable on geological grounds to an interval of 50,000 to 100,000 years ago, we can push the start of Mousterian traditions here back an undetermined amount into this interval. However, we should probably allow time for both the crude and the evolved Mousterian to run their respective courses in sequence or perhaps to some extent concurrently. Not over 50,000 years, and probably less, would be left for the duration of both the evolved cave Mousterian and the coarser allegedly open-air version. There is no way yet in Iraq to demonstrate the position in the geological sequence of these cave deposits with respect to any deposits outside the caves. Certainly any open-air site linked to river terraces or other such geological formations and having a Mousterian typological ensemble in any way comparable with that in the caves is yet to be found. Further perspective on the chronological position of the Mousterian in its various manifestations may be gained by looking beyond Iraq.

In addition to that in the Iraqi and Iranian caves already noted, the Mousterian tradition in general, with varying techno-typology, has been found, for instance, in the caves of Yabrud I (Rust, 1950, pp. 13-64 and Pls. 10-71) and Jerf Ajla (Coon, 1957, pp. 290-316) in western Syria, of Karain (Kökten, 1955, pp. 284-93) and near Mağracik in the Hatay (Şenyürek and Bostancı, 1956) in southwestern and south central Turkey, of Ksar Akil (Ewing, 1947, pp. 189-91; Wright, 1951, pp. 115-19) in Lebanon, and of Mt. Carmel (Garrod and Bate, 1937) and Umm Qatafa (Neuville, 1951, pp. 16 ff.) in Palestine. At Yabrud such general Mousterian alternated several times with hand-ax horizons; at al-Tabun on Mt. Carmel it was underlain by a hand-ax horizon and a still lower crude simple irregular flake industry; and at Ksar Akil, the only one of these sites so far placed geologically, the lowest Levalloiso-Mousterian levels rest upon deposits linked to a stream terrace attributed to pluvial conditions tentatively correlated to the Würm glaciation. Broadly speaking, then, such Mousterian assemblages might be held to fall within the Würm period. Extending this back to the Iraq area, Mousterian of one sort or another may well fill all the early Würm interval of undetermined length, in contrast to the Barda Balka type of material placed at its very beginning or just before.

THE UPPER PALEOLITHIC FOOD-COLLECTING HORIZON

The period of innovation marked by the appearance of various blade-tool industries following the Mousterian has traditionally been called the upper paleolithic. It is viewed here as representing a food-collecting horizon, as opposed to simpler food-gathering levels (see p. 179).

A single very important occurrence of such a blade-tool industry is Shanidar layer C, typologically and stratigraphically distinct from the underlying Mousterian of layer D and from the overlying Zarzian (a diminutive-blade industry) of layer B. The Shanidar C industry is marked especially by a high proportion of burins (including various polyhedric burins) and by perforators, fabricators, scrapers (including circular scrapers), points, notched blades, and used blades and flakes; it is essentially a blade industry, but the blades are of comparatively poor irregular quality. It has been named the Baradostian (Solecki, 1955, p. 415) because, although it contains some of the general features of an Aurignacian such as burins, scrapers, and notched blades, it is typologically more limited, crude, and simple and lacks entirely the steep or carinated scrapers so characteristic of the Aurignacian elsewhere. Available radiocarbon determinations of 26,500±1,500 years B.P. (L-335 H), 29,500±1,500 (W-178), 32,300±3,000 (L-355 I), 33,630±400 (GRO 1494), and older than 34,000 (W-180) span the layer from top to bottom.

We ourselves found nothing exactly like the Baradostian industry save for one possible aspect of the surface collection from Kowri Khan. There the startling quantity of one special tool type, the neat polyhedral burins, both straight and twisted, called to mind the same pronounced element in the Baradostian industry. Since this sort of burin may be present but not, as far as we can tell, especially prominent in the collections from certain other horizons with which we have been dealing in northeastern Iraq, it seems worth pointing out this one closely comparable element in the industries of Kowri Khan and Shanidar C—the one outdoors and unfixed stratigraphically, the other in a cave with absolute dates and fixed in a sequence. Since the Kowri Khan material is from the surface of an otherwise uninvestigated but probably shallow open-air site (pp. 56-57), its position in any sequence has yet to be fixed. Aside from its common bond with the Baradostian industry, which can only suggest a common need filled by a certain tool type, the Kowri Khan ensemble fits reasonably well into a broad conception of a Zarzian horizon, if we allow for morphological variation according to need, region, or time. The variations remain otherwise unexplained, and the Kowri Khan industry can only vaguely be placed in a sequence as possibly Baradostian or probably Zarzian.

The Baradostian industry of Shanidar C does much to fill the morphological and typological gap between the Mousterian flake-tool industry of Shanidar D, Hazar Merd C, lower Babkhal, and Spilik, on the one hand, and the late diminutive blade-tool Zarzian industry of Palegawra, Shanidar B, Hazar Merd B, Zarzi, upper Babkhal, and other minor sites, on the other hand. The latter sites are dealt with below. The X between Shanidar D and C on Figure 8 signifies the possibility of transitional aspects between the Mousterian and the Baradostian, which have not yet been located. Certainly fuller sequences exist to the west, but a conservative Monasterian tradition may have been retained in this quarter of southwestern Asia until the Baradostian appeared.

Between layers C and B at Shanidar there certainly appears to be something missing which may some day be found to intervene between the Baradostian and the Zarzian. There is still too marked a contrast between these two industrial traditions for one to have followed immediately upon the other. The simpler Baradostian has mainly burins, scrapers, notched blades, and a few drill-like tools. The more complex and diminutive Zarzian has all these types as well as steep and discoid scrapers, backed blades, backed and otherwise worked bladelets, and a number of microlithic forms. In a later phase of the Zarzian, several geometric microlithic forms are added. A theoretically intermediate and still undiscovered horizon might perhaps furnish a blade industry more advanced than the Baradostian and approaching the Zarzian in quality, taking on one or more of its types. Such a gradual development can be expected in northeastern Iraq if one judges by the fuller late sequence at Yabrud II and III and the upper half of Ksar Akil in the western portion of the hilly crescent. If a counterpart exists at all in the eastern portion of the crescent, it may be accounted for in new typological assemblages in Iraq, some of which may fortunately be fixed stratigraphically. Meanwhile, it is represented on our chronological chart (Fig. 8) by an X and is perhaps implied by the difference in radioactive-carbon determinations between the top of Shanidar C (26,500±1,500 and 29,500±1,500 years B.P.) and the bottom of Shanidar B (12,000±400 years B.P.).

THE ZARZIAN OR TERMINAL ASPECT OF THE FOOD-COLLECTING ERA

The sort of diminutive-blade industry represented in the Zarzian assemblage and containing various kinds of microliths, including geometric ones, has commonly been called either upper paleolithic or mesolithic, depending on typology, accompanying remains, stratigraphy, kind of site or on chronological position. This sort of assemblage is here considered as referring to a terminal aspect of the food-collecting era (see p. 180) and visualized as representing the end of the idealized pure form of a techno-typological continuum which had not been clearly affected by the new elements attending the appearance of food-production. This idealized continuum comprises the traditional upper paleolithic and mesolithic horizons in one grand developmental unit, hypothetically centered upon commonly shared but progressive food-collecting practices not yet well understood but probably reflected in the stonework remaining to us. Our way of looking at this industry in a still incompletely known area stresses its economic departure point rather than the more rigid traditional classificatory compartments into which the material might be put. In Iraq, this general stage of stone-working is found in caves and, we suspect, perhaps outdoors too.

The Cave Sites

Regardless of one or more theoretically possible industrial horizons interposed between the Baradostian and Zarzian industries, it is clear that the Zarzian not only follows Mousterian, as thin veneers at Hazar Merd (Garrod, 1930) and Babkhal (see p. 60 above) indicate, but also stratigraphically overlies both Baradostian and Mousterian at Shanidar. There layer B overlies layers C and D and contains a typical example of at least the late phase of the Zarzian, marked by geometric microliths. Since the work at Shanidar is still in process, it is not yet known whether the earlier phase of the Zarzian is represented there (Solecki, 1955, pp. 410-14). The proof of a division of the Zarzian into an earlier and a later phase comes from the rock shelter of Zarzi itself, where Garrod (1930, pp. 21-22) found that certain geometric microliths occurred only in the uppermost levels of the Zarzian layer. Since it is not yet known whether Shanidar B includes the earlier phase of the Zarzian, the radioactive-carbon determinations for Shanidar B (W-179: 12,000±400 years B.P.; W-667: 10,600±300 years B.P.) may indicate only the general placement of a later aspect of the industry. If the total duration of the Zarzian industry proves to have been relatively long, there may have been nuances of change in the environment. However, we have as yet only the most enigmatic clues, outlined in the paragraphs immediately following on both cave and open-air sites. Moreover, the general date tentatively suggested on the chronological chart (Fig. 8) for the lower limits of the Zarzian is quite arbitrary, although influenced somewhat by consideration of the marked gap in both time and typological development between the Zarzian and the underlying Baradostian horizon.

Further refinement of the later part of the Zarzian may become stratigraphically evident when more and thicker deposits are discovered but at present is suspected on the basis of techno-typological and morphological comparisons. At Shanidar B there is the occurrence of a bifacially backed microlithic lunate (Heluan type), a type which is common in the Natufian of Palestine (Solecki, 1955, p. 412 and Pl. 4a.). The Natufian, which has been adequately considered in the general literature, is described variously as "mesolithic," "pre-" or "protoneolithic," and "neolithic" (Garrod, 1932 and 1957; Perrot, 1957; Childe, 1952, pp. 28-29; Kenyon, 1959; McBurney and Hey, 1955, p. 250) and is taken to be a generally late horizon. At Palegawra (pp. 57-59) there is the proliferation of geometric microliths into a series including various triangles, lunates, trapezoids, and rectangles, some of the trapezoids having markedly concave converging ends, in common with Shanidar B (Solecki, 1955, Pl. 4c). This series is more elaborate than the elongated, or scalene, triangles and few lunates noted at Zarzi.

Aside from these obvious typological variants, there is the question of the degree and quality of retouch or edge wear and the not easily definable signs of degeneration in technique which become more prominent in the open-air sites. Do these things indicate a late, or at least a different, stage of this development? We cannot tell until we have more points of observation, preferably in stratified sequence. There are traces of obsidian in Shanidar B and at Palegawra, and two fragments are also reported from Zarzi (Garrod, 1930, p. 16). These occurrences of obsidian may be another sign of lateness but cannot yet be fully assessed in the light, for instance, of the virtual absence of obsidian at Karim Shahir, which is assumed to be later on other typological grounds. Moreover, some trace of obsidian does exist in pre-Zarzian horizons of Shanidar (Solecki, 1955, p. 412, and our informal inspection of material from layer D deposited with the Directorate General of Antiquities in Baghdad).

The occurrence at Palegawra of a fine large fully chipped celt and an oval grooved stone abrading-piece, the latter type found at Zarzi also (Garrod, 1930, pp. 21-22, Fig. 11), suggest affinities with some later developments. More work is needed to establish or exclude the existence of any prospective very late subdivisions of the Zarzian (see below).

The chronological significance of the generalized but apparently atypical and imperfectly sampled or disturbed Zarzian of Hajiyah, Barak, and Babkhal remains enigmatic (p. 157).

Meanwhile we are sure, on the basis of stratigraphy and typology at Zarzi itself, that the Zarzian industry has at least an earlier and a later phase. The latter is perhaps to be divided into subphases on the basis of various geometric microliths and other artifacts. We suspect that the differentiation may become more marked with further knowledge of such deposits as those of Shanidar B and Palegawra. In addition, on the basis of the radioactive-carbon determination for lower Shanidar B, we consider the Zarzian as a whole to have been in existence by 12,000 years ago and in all probability even earlier. It appears to have ended about 11,000 years ago, in view of the highest determination for Shanidar B and the determination for Zawi Chemi Shanidar. Attempts to collect unadulterated radioactive carbon samples from Palegawra have been unsuccessful, although one untested sample of the 1954/55 season provides hope.

Before leaving the Zarzian of the caves let us make one more significant observation. Regardless of the materials from open sites for which we suggest possible Zarzian affinities and regardless of intermittent traces of cave occupation from Zarzian times down to the very present, the Zarzian appears to be the last horizon in which the cave was a primary focus of human settlement in Iraqi Kurdistan. In virtually every case, the Zarzian material in caves is overlain or clearly disturbed by deposits containing pottery, often wheel-made. This sequence was noted at Zarzi, layer A, and Hazar Merd, layer A (Garrod, 1930, pp. 14 and 27-33), at Shanidar, layer A (Solecki, 1955, pp. 408-10), at Babkhal and Barak (Braidwood et al., 1954), and especially at Palegawra in the upper layers (see p. 58 above). Almost by definition, "layer A" in any cave is an uppermost zone of disturbance; in Iraqi Kurdistan it is usually the Zarzian which immediately underlies this disturbed layer. Any immediately post-Zarzian manifestations—if they occur in the caves—are mixed with traces of protohistoric and historic materials.

There is obviously, then, a long period imperfectly represented in the caves when developments between the Zarzian and the pottery-making horizons were taking place elsewhere. Some evidence for this interlude lies in sites like Karim Shahir and in Jarmo and the early village mounds of Iraq (see below).

The Open-Air Sites

Entirely on typological grounds the open-air and probably shallow sites of Turkaka and Kowri Khan (pp. 55-57) in the Chemchemal valley are provisionally assigned to the Zarzian horizon. The preponderance of their artifacts compares favorably, both typologically and technically, with the flint industries at Palegawra and other Zarzian sites. Their ensemble cannot be closely matched at Karim Shahir and the similar sites of Zawi Chemi Shanidar, Gird Chai, and M'lefaat. However, the absence of backed blades, except for a few backed bladelets at Turkaka, is puzzling. It seems significant for the alternative ideas that either these sites are closer to Shanidar C or our postulated transitional stage between the Baradostian and the Zarzian (see Fig. 8) or else that they represent some equivalent of a generalized Zarzian lacking the normal-sized backed blades that was so unsatisfactorily sampled at Babkhal, Barak, and Hajiyah (see p. 59). This hypothetical generalized Zarzian may or may not be contemporaneous with the standard cave Zarzian, but it certainly differs from the Baradostian in character and time. Such points might perhaps be partially cleared up by excavation at Turkaka and Kowri Khan. Their tentative placement as open-air equivalents of the cave Zarzian, either fully contemporary with it or somewhat offset in time, is only slightly favored over the following possible positions in a sequence: (1) subsequent to the cave Zarzian and representing a transition toward an assemblage like Karim Shahir etc. or (2) preceding the cave Zarzian and representing either a fully Baradostian industry, as perhaps in the case of Kowri Khan, or a transitional stage between the Baradostian and the Zarzian. Any dates for the hypothetical positions of the samplings represented by Turkaka and Kowri Khan are bounded by the radioactive-carbon determinations already obtained for Shanidar C and B, Zawi Chemi Shanidar, and Jarmo and by any which may be obtained for Palegawra, M'lefaat, Gird Chai, or other such sites.

Finally, an interesting possible side light on what may be some part of this entire Zarzian development comes from southern Turkmenistan in southern Russia. Okladnikov (1956) reports on a cave sequence at Peshtera Dzhebel, located east of the Caspian and just east of the railroad line between Krasnovodsk and Ashkhabad. There approximately 4 meters of essentially pre-ceramic deposit (layers 8, 7, 6, 5-6, 5a) underlie some 2.5 m. of neolithic and later material (layers 5 through 1). The five lower layers, of interest at present, contain a basic tool kit of notched and nibbled blades and bladelets, end scrapers, discoid scrapers (both large and small), and rough pyramidal cores. In layers 6, 5-6, and 5a this is combined with such additional microlithic forms as trapezoids and bladelets worked to diagonal or curvilinear ends. This industry lacks any backed blades but continues on up into layer 5, where a variety of pottery and chipped celts appear. Although layers 6, 5-6, and 5a each yielded a handful of sherds, which may or may not have been displaced downward from layer 5, the ensemble of chipped stone artifacts in layers 8 through 5a stands some comparison with a part of the Zarzian as observed in Iraq across mountain ranges to the southwest.

THE ERA OF INCIPIENT CULTIVATION IN OPEN-AIR SITES

Karim Shahir (pp. 52-54), a one-level site with no stratigraphic reference to any other archeological material as yet, can only be fitted into the chronological sequence on techno-typological and morphological grounds, with all that these imply regarding responses to total physical background and material needs. Its flint tool kit shares core types, notched and used blades and flakes, the general class of microlithic backed bladelets, fabricators, and drills specifically with that phase of the Zarzian industry which is found at Palegawra. The latter, on typological and, indirectly via upper Zarzi B, on stratigraphic grounds, may be considered a late phase. However, Karim Shahir lacks the normal backed blades, the well made burins, the well made end, discoid, and steep scrapers, and the geometric microliths of this phase of the Zarzian. On the other hand, it has numerous poorly made end, side, and discoid scrapers and a few poor burins which may represent retentions from the older stone-working tradition. As innovations, Karim Shahir has chipped celts, some with polished and ground bits, a number of ground stone ornaments, and two clay figurines. These, as well as the marked presence of querns, pestles, mullers, and grooved stone abrading-pieces, attest to other and perhaps new activities.

Hints of new activities may, of course, be seen in some of the Zarzian itself. Shanidar B and Zarzi both produced grooved stone abrading-pieces; Shanidar B also yielded mullers, and Palegawra yielded a single chipped celt, a grooved stone abrading piece, a quern fragment, and muller fragments along with a considerable number of poor scrapers and smaller numbers of burins and specialized backed and angled microlithic bladelets. Such ground stone and poor forms of chipped flint tools, in contrast to the remainder of more typically well made Zarzian types, suggest that the Palegawra assemblage might represent a development beyond upper Zarzi B and Shanidar B. Palegawra may be even further advanced in time toward such open-air settlements as Karim Shahir than is the microlithic late phase of Zarzi itself.

Such a possible development upon the late microlithic Zarzian industry may have had a seasonal open-air as well as a cave occurrence. In fact, even the limited knowledge of the industries at Turkaka and Kowri Khan leads to speculation as to whether these may not actually have constituted such a seasonal and open-air late Zarzian marked by selection of tools for seasonal jobs. Nevertheless, at Karim Shahir the partially degenerated and partially re-adapted and re-developed specialized chipped stone forms, combined with the numerous ground and polished tools and ornaments and the clay figurines, show that the Karim Shahir assemblage is definitely later than the Zarzian, whether in caves or in the open air.

Karim Shahir also may have been a seasonal site marked by tool selectivity for periodically recurring jobs and representing but a portion of the total artifactual tradition of its horizon. The absence of any sort of houses may or may not be significant, but in view of indications of such at M'lefaat (Braidwood et al., 1954) and Zawi Chemi Shanidar (Solecki, 1957), which both seem to contain approximately equivalent assemblages (e.g. in their chipped and in parts of their ground stone industries), the lack of "architecture" would seem to be a local Karim Shahir peculiarity. The rather intact appearance of some of the pseudo-pavements of stones at Karim Shahir (see p. 52) seems to rule out the possibility that the whole hilltop had been disturbed by plowing or other activity. Somewhat comparable "pavements" came to light in parts of the deeper exposures at Jarmo. The absence of pottery at Karim Shahir, combined with the occurrence of two tiny lightly-baked clay figurines and certain ground stone ornaments, suggests an affinity with the early levels of Jarmo, although the complete absence of obsidian at Karim Shahir suggests that it is certainly not contemporaneous with and presumably somewhat earlier than Jarmo. On the other hand, the limited techno-typological similarities in chipped stone at Jarmo are paradoxically all in the upper levels (cf. Linda Braidwood's observation concerning the Jarmo flint industry on pp. 49 f. above), but the geometric microliths of these Jarmo levels have counterparts in the upper Zarzian and miss Karim Shahir completely.

Gird Chai (pp. 54 f.) and M'lefaat (pp. 50-52) have chipped stone assemblages virtually indistinguishable from one another. These may, on the basis of our limited soundings, be tentatively compared with the Karim Shahir assemblage because of the general morphological and some particular typological similarity of their stone industry with that of the more fully excavated site. Pebble cores, poor scrapers, rare poor burins, notched and used blades and flakes, and distinctive microlithic backed bladelets show the common tradition. An essentially similar chipped stone industry is reported from Zawi Chemi Shanidar. The trace of simple architecture at Zawi Chemi Shanidar (Solecki, 1957) strongly recalls the ovoid or circular probably semisubterranean structure of M'lefaat.

Because of the exposed position of Karim Shahir, with its occupation level so near the surface and subject to extensive animal burrowing, no successful radioactive-carbon samples were obtained. The "probable true general date" for the era of incipient cultivation within the hilly-flanks zone of the natural habitat of the potentially domesticable plants and animals at first was put at about 9500 to 8000 B.C. (Braidwood, 1958a). This would include Karim Shahir, Gird Chai, M'lefaat, and Zawi Chemi Shanidar, and it is, of course, possible that the era lasted some hundreds of years longer, even within the hilly-flanks zone. The radiocarbon determination for the top of Shanidar B (10,600±300 years B.P.) and for Zawi Chemi Shanidar (10,870±300 years B.P.) appear generally to substantiate this dating for the era but incline us to lower it slightly to about 9000 to 7000 B.C. Still conformable are other determinations from Shanidar and Coon's "mesolithic" horizons at Belt and Hotu (cf. Braidwood, 1958a, Fig. 1), but then the earliest determinations from Jarmo (W-665: 11,200 ±200 years B.P., W-657: 11,240±300 years B.P.) must be ignored on the ground that they are too early.

The "probable true general date" for Jarmo is taken to be about 6750 B.C. (see below). Even if Jarmo were pushed back toward 7000 B.C., there would still—on grounds of comparative typological and morphological assessment of the two assemblages—be a gap in the record between the Jarmo horizon and that of Karim Shahir, M'lefaat, and Zawi Chemi Shanidar (see Fig. 8).

During the general range of time from about 10,000 to 6000 B.C. in regions of southwestern Asia which lie outside the hilly-flanks natural-habitat zone it is very doubtful that the era of incipient cultivation or the era of the primary village-farming community had yet been achieved. Regional variations such as the Jericho developmental sequence from indigenous extensively documented Natufian traditions upward into special non-ceramic and later levels may have existed, regardless of problems of relative chronology. At the moment the extreme interest of the Jericho sequence hangs upon which of several possible alternative explanations of its subsistence base will prove the most reasonable (see p. 182). On the other hand, some evidence for outlying conservative cultural pockets exists. Consider, for example, such radioactive-carbon determinations as those from the Belt cave which cluster at about 9520±550 B.C. and 6610±380 B.C. and those from the Hotu cave which cluster at about 9900±840 B.C. and 7230±590 B.C. (see Coon, 1957, pp. 170-72, 207-8, 211, where several determinations are grouped into average figures for each of several levels). Assuming that the determinations are acceptable, we believe that these "mesolithic" materials of the lush Caspian coastal plain pertain to a terminal aspect of food-collecting which persisted in the periphery during the time of the era of incipient cultivation and the era of the earliest villages in the hilly-flanks natural-habitat zone. In other words, the culture-historical principle of the "sloping horizon" (Willey and Phillips, 1958, p. 34) must be borne in mind when the radioactive-carbon determinations from all of the Near East are being assessed.

THE ERA OF THE PRIMARY VILLAGE-FARMING COMMUNITY

In contrast to the sites examined in the era of incipient cultivation—even those with traces of architectural activity such as M'lefaat and Zawi Chemi Shanidar—Jarmo is a proper "mound of many layers," a tell in the common Arabic usage. Such mounds are characteristic of the era of the primary village-farming community as well as of later eras. Even when they are first instanced, in the hilly-flanks natural-habitat zone, the successive layers of tauf houses indicate a persistence of occupation which the available sites of the era of incipient cultivation do not suggest. Archeologists have often attempted to translate the number of layers of architectural rebuilding or renovation or the absolute depth of accumulation in such sites into a direct expression of time duration. But Wheeler (1954, p. 29) correctly reasons that "objective calculation [of time] on the basis of depth is virtually impossible." Starting from the fact that the life expectancy of a modest tauf or libn house in present-day Iraqi Kurdistan is said locally to be about 15 years and its resultant debris product about 2 feet in height, we reckon a minimum duration for the approximately 27 feet of greatest depth of deposit at Jarmo at about 200 years (Braidwood, 1957, p. 75). The site may have been occupied a bit more than twice as long, but on this method of reckoning, at least, we doubt that it lasted more than 500 years.

There are now twelve radioactive-carbon determinations for Jarmo, which span a range from 3310±450 B.C. (C-744: 5266±450 years B.P;) to 9280±300 B.C. (W-657: 11,240 ±300 years B.P.), an inconceivable 6,000 years (Braidwood, 1958a). The first available radioactive-carbon determinations on Jarmo, from the Chicago counter, clustered about 4750 B.C., and Professor Zeuner's two runs appeared to substantiate the Chicago cluster. More recent runs by Dr. Meyer Rubin of the Washington counter and one run by Dr. Karl Otto Münnich of the Heidelberg counter produced the earlier determinations in the series. One cluster of earlier determinations from the Washington counter—taken with the Heidelberg determination—centers at about 6750 B.C. Mark well that this is consistent with several single determinations, at about 5750 B.C., for the next phase of the era of the primary villages from basal Matarrah, basal Mersin in Syro-Cilicia, and Tell Hassunah V. Modest as this net of determinations is, it corresponds reasonably well with a broad comparative archeological sequence and emphasizes the value of a widely based fabric of determinations from many sites. At present we assume that 6750 B.C. is the "probable true general date" for Jarmo, with a possible tolerance of at least 500 years in either direction and a possible duration for the site of Jarmo itself of up to about 400 years, although the phase represented by Jarmo may have lasted for a longer time.

The number of radioactive-carbon determinations available for Jarmo and the archeologically unrealistic span of time they cover emphasize the necessity for further investigation of the factors of what Wright calls the "geobiochemical" contamination of radioactive-carbon samples. It should be clearly understood that we do not lack confidence in either the principles of radioactive-carbon determination or the scientists of good will who man the various counters. A far more likely source of error, we believe, is the "geobiochemical" contamination of samples in situ and perhaps in their extraction and shipment. Until the sources of contamination are investigated and understood, so that allowances can be made for them, single radioactive-carbon determinations—and even clusters of determinations from single sites—must be used with the greatest reserve. Single determinations, or clusters, have true chronological meaning only as the contexts of the samples (the archeological assemblages with which they were found) make sense within the framework of a developing comparative archeological stratigraphy. To the degree to which the determinations within a sequence of assemblages and contexts conform to the framework of a developing comparative stratigraphy, the dates implied are acceptable. Otherwise, their acceptance must be held in abeyance. Such considerations come to mind in our assessment of the radioactive-carbon determinations for Jericho.

Recently, several very useful and thought-provoking papers have appeared from the hands of radioactive-carbon specialists (e.g. Barker, 1958; Olson and Broecker, 1959; Tauber, 1958). The authors consider the possibilities of "geobiochemical" contamination[1] and other sources of confusion and also clarify the implications of the statistical data. Thus Barker (p. 258) suggests that the usual single standard deviation tolerance expressed (i.e., the figure following the ± sign in any date formula) gives a range which is only fairly probable. Doubling the standard deviation results in a range which is probable, and tripling results in one which is highly probable. As the determinations are conventionally given in the lists published by the various counters (in terms of a single standard deviation about a suggested median "date"), the odds are only roughly two to one that the true date of the sample even falls within the range indicated by the ± figure. Doubling or even tripling the ± figure increases the expectation of accuracy but of course extends the range. The "date" figure in the lists merely suggests the place in past time about which the range is expected to lie.

Our chronological chart (Fig. 8) suggests a gap between the era of incipient cultivation as represented by Karim Shahir, M'lefaat, and Zawi Chemi Shanidar and the aspect of the era of the primary village-farming community which is exhibited by Jarmo. Allowance for a gap is prompted in part by the available radioactive-carbon determinations as we understand them (see above) and in part by the markedly different typological and morphological characters of the respective assemblages. Jarmo was a proper settled village-farming community, architecturally well expressed from its deepest levels onward. Something of greater complexity than the overall assemblage indicated by Karim Shahir, M'lefaat, and

---

[1]At the V. internationaler Kongress für Vor- und Frügeschichte, Hamburg, August 24-30, 1958, Dr. K. O. Münnich of the Heidelberg counter described an effect of the screening of natural radioactivity by various possible contaminated atmospheric conditions, calling this "the Autobahn effect." This results in determinations older than the true date of the sample. The more usual types of "geobiochemical" contamination of samples result in determinations younger than the true date of the sample.

Zawi Chemi Shanidar must have preceded the Jarmo phase. It is suggested that the still untested site of Kharaba Qara Chiwar (p. 50) may fill at least part of this postulated gap.

We do not, however, mean to give the impression that this gap was necessarily of very long duration—long enough, for example, for the basic flint-working tradition to have been greatly altered. Such was not the case. The generalized development of the Zarzian-Karim Shahir-Jarmo progression in blade-tool typology and morphology, with its microlithic complement, appears to have been the product of a single evolving tradition. The marble bracelets and perhaps even the simple figurines of Karim Shahir had much more varied counterparts at Jarmo. But we cannot conceive of the whole Jarmo assemblage arising immediately out of that of Karim Shahir. Neither can we—with the two sites less than 2 miles apart on the same wadi—conceive of regional variation as an explanation for the differences.

There can be no question that the Hassunan phase of the era of the primary village-farming community follows that of Jarmo, as the radioactive-carbon determinations indicate and as the Tell Shimshara stratigraphic sequence proves (see below). But it is not clear at what moment in relation to the Jarmo phase the Hassunan began. We have vacillated as to whether a modest gap in the sequence should be suggested between the end of Jarmo and the basal levels of Hassunah and Matarrah. Adams, Caldwell, and Matson are convinced of general ceramic continuity through this range, and the pottery of Gird Ali Agha (pp. 37-38) fits into the picture. The Ali Agha pottery represents an approximate mid-point in the apparent progression from Jarmo to Hassunan types of coarse wares. And there is no appreciable suggestion of discontinuity between the Jarmo and the Hassunan phase in architectural development, if the traces of pits and hearths in the basal levels at Matarrah and Hassunah are assumed to be the remains of very temporary builders' floors, utilized only until the first tauf houses were completed. Perhaps the few architectural traces exposed by our restricted soundings at Ali Agha fit this latter picture, but not enough is known of Ali Agha to place it architecturally. In fact, for all we can say at the moment, if Ali Agha looks like anything else architecturally, it is closest to M'lefaat and Zawi Chemi Shanidar.

There are arguments for a gap between the Jarmo and Hassunan phases, however. It is in the flint and ground stone categories of their respective assemblages that Jarmo and the basal levels of Hassunah and Matarrah show the greatest differences. With the exception of the peculiar and undoubtedly important persistence (in Matarrah, at least) of the transverse microlithic "side blow blade-flake" in obsidian, the older blade-tool tradition is not represented in the Hassunan phase in the piedmont. At the known Hassunan sites of this region, there was, rather, a characterless industry of flake-blades and flakes, with a few projectile points at Hassunah which seem to have been derived from Syro-Cilicia (R. J. and L. Braidwood, 1953, p. 304). Nor is the exquisite Jarmo tradition of marble-working, in bowls, bracelets and rings, and various enigmatic small artifacts such as "pestles," represented at Hassunah and Matarrah. Certainly, also, the bulk and variety of figurines seen in Jarmo were not available from Hassunah and Matarrah.[2]

The radioactive-carbon evidence also complicates the idea of simple continuity. We have assumed (see above) that 6750 B.C. is the "probable true general date" for Jarmo. The single radioactive-carbon determination for basal Matarrah at 5610±250 B.C. (W-623: 7,570±250 years B.P.), taken with that for the roughly comparable materials of basal Mersin at 5990±250 B.C. (W-617: 7,950±250 years B.P.), and the single determination for the well developed materials of the Hassunan phase in Hassunah V at 5080±200 B.C. (W-660: 7,040±200 years B.P.) lead us to suggest that the Hassunan phase was under way by about 5750 B.C. This date, however, leaves 1,000 years between the "probable true general dates" for Jarmo and the Hassunan. So long a span does not seem realistic to us, but this is an example wherein the radioactive-carbon determinations may trick us if we take the

[2]It thus follows that we consider the surface collections made by Harris at Tell Urwell and Tell Raseien, southwest of Tauq (see p. 49), as contemporaneous with the Jarmo phase or its immediate antecedents.

expressed "dates" at face value and ignore the implications of the single standard deviation tolerance.

Thus, for the moment, we do not see much of a gap between the Jarmo and Hassunan phases, nor do we see much basis for complete elucidation now. Pottery and architecture seem to indicate no gap; the chipped and ground stone categories and the figurines appear to suggest one. The circumstances at both Ali Agha and Tell Shimshara need consideration in this connection, but they do not completely solve the problem.

At Tell Shimshara, in the intermontane Dokan-Rania valley a few miles northeast of Jarmo, the Danish expedition (Ingholt, 1957, p. 215) encountered a pertinent stratigraphic sequence in a test pit. Here, Jarmo-like materials in pre-ceramic levels were overlain by Hassunan-Samarran levels. But while the Samarran painted ware was quite "classic" in the piedmont sense, the chipped stone category of the Hassunan-Samarran levels was in our opinion a continuation of a Jarmo-like blade-tool tradition (see p. 49).

Whatever the regional variants of this general range may have been, it seems unlikely that there were long spans of time between the Jarmo and Hassunan horizons. The antecedents of the coarse chipped stone industry of the piedmont remain unknown. The Jarmo phase has not yet been evidenced in excavations on the piedmont, but Harris' surface collections (see p. 161, n. 2) suggest that it may have been represented there.

The two largest exposures of the Hassunan phase were at Matarrah and the type site itself, both located in the piedmont. Both occurrences show the appearance, before the assemblage is superceded by that of the Halafian phase, of the Samarran painted pottery style. The single radiocarbon determination for basal Matarrah (5610±250 B.C.) is from a context that preceded the appearance of Samarran pottery; the single determination for Hassunah—the fifth floor from the bottom (5080±200 B.C.)—is from a context which included Samarran pottery. Our earlier tendency (R. J. and L. Braidwood, 1953) to think of the Samarran painted pottery style as simply an additive element in a normal Hassunan assemblage (presumably due to some local specialization) is now seriously compromised by the surface materials which we collected at Baghuz (see p. 37). That site, near Abu Kemal on the Euphrates, did not yield elements of the normal Hassunan assemblage, although its Samarran painted pottery style is completely characteristic. Therefore, the Samarran pottery may, after all, be part of a full-bodied "Samarran" assemblage or at least an element in some assemblage other than that of the Hassunan phase. Presumably, it had its beginning sometime before 5000 B.C., but exactly where is not yet clear.

Potsherds of the Halafian painted pottery style began to appear in significant numbers in Hassunah VII; a few dozen were found in level VI, into which the Samarran ware continued (Lloyd and Safar, 1945, Fig. 5). A complete vessel with characteristically Halafian painted decoration and profile, as well as a few sherds, appeared at the type site of Samarra itself (Herzfeld, 1930). It is thus apparent that painted pottery of both the Samarran and Halafian styles coexisted for at least a part of their respective durations. Our radiocarbon samples from Baghuz and from the Halafian levels at both Arpachiyah and Banahilk have not yet been counted, but we now suspect that Mallowan (1956, pp. 11-12) is right in dating the Halafian assemblage back to about 5000 B.C. There is no immediate basis for assessing how long the Halafian phase persisted. The next available determination in Iraq, again from a single sample, is from the base of the Eanna pit at Warka, a context containing an early aspect of the conventional southern Iraqi Ubaid phase (as distinct from the still earlier Haji Muhammad and Eridu phases). This determination is at 4110±160 B.C. (H-138/123: 6070±160 years B.P) and seems quite reasonable from the viewpoint of comparative archeological stratigraphy.

The Iraq-Jarmo Project's latest materials are those of the Gird Banahilk assemblage (pp. 33-35), with its Halafian painted pottery style, and we suggest a date of about 5000 B.C. for the establishment of the Banahilk site. We do not know the original focus of formation of the Halafian assemblage. It may have been a hill-country product, and, if so, Banahilk and even Tilki Tepe near Lake Van in Turkey (Reilly, 1940) may have been earlier than the Halafian sites of the piedmont plain. The presence, in Banahilk at least, of the coarse piedmont type of chipped stone industry complicates the picture.

XI

TOWARD THE RECONSTRUCTION OF THE ENVIRONMENTAL SEQUENCE OF NORTHEASTERN IRAQ

Charles A. Reed and Robert J. Braidwood

INTRODUCTION

In chapter v are listed many of the identifications of flora and fauna which serve as clues to the environments within which the several sites flourished at different times. In chapters vii-ix, Wright, Helbaek, and Reed consider certain portions of the evidence yielded by the physiography and the flora and fauna in terms of a much wider perspective than that for northeastern Iraq alone. Clearly the evidence is still a matter of shreds and swatches, so that the following reconstruction is most tentative. We are very sensitive to the fact that "conclusions," once they become crystallized in print and embedded in the literature, may be quoted and misquoted for years to come. Hence we warn that this reconstruction is woefully incomplete and transient in value. It is to be quoted only at the quoter's peril! What is of value, especially in the foregoing chapters of Wright, Helbaek, and Reed, is the clear indication that the environmental evidence is reclaimable and that much may be made of it when it is given the study it deserves.

Our comprehension of how the way of life of the village-farming community came into being will acquire focus only as the environmental reconstruction becomes detailed and reliable. The present evidence leads Wright (p. 72) to conclude that there is not necessarily a cause-and-effect relationship between climatic change and the transition to food-production. This is an important finding and reasserts the significance of the role of culture in the achievement of the transition. Nevertheless, regardless of climatic change or climatic stability, the cultures which achieved the new way of life could only have done so with respect to permissive environmental factors of habitat and biota. We must comprehend these factors if we are to extend our understanding of the cultures of the great transition.

We begin with the impression, gained from the animal bones, the snails, and certain of the woody floral remains, that there has been remarkably little change in the overall biota of northeastern Iraq during the late glacial and postglacial range of time, in spite of Wright's evidence for mountain glaciation, terrace building, and alluviation. However, this impression may be subject to revision in detail as we acquire information from the more delicate tool of pollen analysis; a study has already begun on samples taken from Shanidar cave.

Wright conceives of a certain degree of altitudinal fluctuation of habitats in response to the appearance, and subsequent disappearance, of glaciers in the high Zagros. He believes, however, that the fluctuations arrived at essentially their present state by 12,000 years ago. Furthermore, in an area which rises from a zone of hot desert-steppe through zones of grassland, woodland, forest, and higher alpine meadows, the degrees of climatic changes required to produce—or to eradicate—alpine-type glaciation would not have seriously affected the biota. There would have been some downward movement of the zones and perhaps some compression with respect to the habitats, but the general biota would not need to have changed. Thus, with increased montane precipitation and/or temperature decrease, the snow line moved down, the upper timber line moved down, the forest moved out onto the piedmont, and the grasslands encroached upon the desert. When the climate took its contrary trend, the biota slowly became adjusted in the reverse direction.[1]

Wright suggests that the cold-wet extreme of the fluctuation may have been during the time of the gap in the occupation of Shanidar cave, between levels C and B. By Zarzian times and certainly by about 12,000 years ago, things seem to have returned to "normal." But what is "normal" for northeastern Iraq? From the point of view of a modern conservationist, the transition to food-production, probably about 9,000 years ago, was not "a good thing." It has meant 9,000 years of deforestation, plowing, and overgrazing, with concomitant soil erosion. The present landscape, with its remnant habitats and biotas, can certainly not be considered "normal."

THE PERIOD OF THE MIDDLE PALEOLITHIC FOOD-GATHERERS

Barda Balka (pp. 61-62) is the only excavated site representing this time range. The geological evidence suggests that Barda Balka may be tentatively dated to the closing portion of the Riss-Würm interglacial phase.

We can say relatively little concerning the environment; on the basis of the geological evidence, Wright thinks that the deposits were buried during a period of increased rainfall. The mammals identified are cattle of about the size of Bos primigenius, Indian elephant,

---

[1]Animal life, each species being associated with certain plant communities and thus with a certain habitat, moves easily (in fact, unconsciously) with slow changes in the botanical zones. Thus, if topography, soils, and local climates are permissive in a land of varied altitudes, the biota may naturally survive quite marked climatic changes on a regional scale. We think that most species did so move during the late Quaternary in northern Iraq, but we need much more evidence to clarify the picture. Some animals are better "indicators" than others. In Iraq, the wild pig (Sus scrofa attila) ranges from sea-level marshes to the upper limits of the mountain forest and is obviously a useless ecologic indicator. The land tortoise (Testudo graeca) is similarly useless for similar reasons (Reed and Marx, 1959). The small mammals are usually better zonal indicators, although there are exceptions such as the ubiquitous wild mouse (Mus musculus), which is found in a variety of habitats and environments. In contrast, the gazelle, although a larger and more mobile mammal, is ecologically quite limited.

We follow Picard (1943) in considering that snails are generally better environmental indicators than the large vertebrates. However, a note of caution is required, for Dr. Alan Solem, Curator of Lower Invertebrates at the Chicago Natural History Museum, tells us that under certain circumstances some species of snails might well survive fairly drastic climatic changes, because of their ability to estivate through unfavorable periods and to maintain populations in moist pockets of extremely limited area (sometimes less than one acre). For instance, a semidesert species of a warm-summer Mediterranean-type climate could survive considerable increase in precipitation and decrease in temperature if only one or two of the summer months furnished the requisite environmental situation that had formerly prevailed throughout much of the year; during the optimum months the snails would store enough food reserves to survive in a condition of torpidity through the remainder of the year. Even so, it has seemed logical to us to consider that the presence of snails in an archeological context indicates a general climate not too radically different from that in which those snails are found living today. But Solem's warning indicates that snails are not the very precise climatic indicators that we had hoped they would be. Furthermore, the ecology of the Near Eastern snails must be known in detail before we can set the possible limits on the environments in which they can occur. To be useful to us, the animal remains must be found in the cultural debris being investigated; the effect we call the "cultural filter" is important. We should be without our hundreds of thousands of Jarmo snail shells had the people of Jarmo been as are the present Moslem Kurdish inhabitants of the area, to whom snails as food are anathema.

rhinoceros (not identifiable as to species), an equid (suggestive of the onager but not actually determinable as such), and sheep or goat. Not one of these species is a good climatic indicator, since all have or have had wide distribution; in the Pleistocene, as is well known, certain species of rhinoceros ranged into much colder regions than those in which they are found today, and elephants might still be found in southwestern Asia, as they were in Syria until the ninth century B.C., if they had not been exterminated by man. However, the presence of four shells of Helix salomonica, a semixerophilous snail found today throughout much of the foothill area of southwestern Asia, indicates that the climate could not have differed too radically from that of the present.

The mammalian fauna from Barda Balka suggests that the site was a gathering place of big-game hunters, and we have no subsequent osteological record in Iraq of a fauna which includes rhinoceros or elephant. Lack of such information, however, does not necessarily indicate disappearance of the large mammals or of the people who hunted them; we simply don't know what happened on the piedmont and in the lower foothills for the better part of 100,000 years.

THE PERIOD OF THE DEVELOPED MOUSTERIAN HORIZON IN CAVES

The deep excavation (44 ft.) at Shanidar cave in the mountains of northern Iraq provides one of the longest series of animal bones in the Near East.[2] It is suggested above that the Mousterian horizon of the caves in the Syrian-Iraqi area generally terminated about 40,000 years ago and extended back indefinitely into an interval of 90,000-100,000 years ago.

The animal bones of the interesting sequence represented in Shanidar cave (the cultural details of which are discussed above) were first identified by Dr. Fraser and Miss King at the British Museum of Natural History and then turned over to Reed for more detailed study. While the final report is not yet written, we can state here that the whole sequence indicates that the Zagros Mountains, from the time of the beginning of the occupation of the cave in the Mousterian horizon (Shanidar D), supported a fauna essentially unchanged from that which would be living in the area today had not many of the species been killed off relatively recently by man. Indeed, so definite is the aspect of faunal contemporaneity at Shanidar—even with regard to the bones from the deepest deposits of layer D—that any osteologist, presented merely with the bones and kept in ignorance of the levels, cultural associations, and radiocarbon determinations, would unhesitatingly state that all are of the same age and all recent. The remarkable lack of mineralization in even the oldest of these bones strengthens the mental picture of a single-age, post-Pleistocene fauna.

The more common of these animals are goat (Capra hircus aegagrus) and sheep (Ovis orientalis?), a small type of wild cattle (Bos sp.), pig (Sus scrofa), and land tortoise Testudo graeca). More rare are deer (Cervus and Capreolus), bear (Ursus arctos), fox (Vulpes vulpes), marten (Martes foina), and gerbil (Meriones sp.). While several species at present native to the area are not represented in the cave remains,[3] it is important to note that this group is a completely modern fauna (Hatt, 1959; Reed and Marx, 1959). Even the occasional birds (griffen vulture and chukar partridge) are species of the same region today.

---

[2]It is most fortunate for the present study that Dr. Solecki thoroughly salvaged the animal bones and that they were consigned to Reed for study; further, Dr. Solecki has generously encouraged us to refer to his material here.

[3]It must constantly be remembered that, except for rare intrusive specimens (such as a small rodent), bones in archeological context result from the "cultural filter," representing what the people killed and ate and are not therefore necessarily typical of the fauna as a whole.

The snails[4] from Shanidar cave strengthen our belief in the essential similarity between the former and present environments. Levantina mahanica, a species collected in the immediate Shanidar area by Solecki, was found in the cultural deposits of the cave to a depth of 34 feet and was increasingly common from a depth of 29 feet to the surface. Helix salomonica, known from many of our archeological sites in northeastern Iraq and typical of much of the semixerophilous environment of southwestern Asia, was found to a depth of 29 feet but was common only in layers B and A, where its increased numbers may indicate that it was being gathered for food. Since neither kind of snail occurs naturally in caves, both must have been carried in by men, in the archeological view becoming artifacts. Thus, while the increased use of snails at this time may merely reflect a larger available population of snails following the afore-mentioned cold period, we think it probably is indicative of a people utilizing the available food resources to a more intensive degree.

Each of these snails is a species of the eastern Mediterranean environment, found in that environment today. Their simultaneous presence in Shanidar cave, beginning possibly 70,000 years ago, indicates (with the added evidence of the vertebrate fauna) that the environment during the periods of the cave's occupancy could not have been greatly different from that of the area today, even though there probably was a period of nonoccupancy of some 15,000 years during a cold interval between layers C and B (see p. 169).

It is most interesting, in view of the findings at Shanidar, to note that the fauna reported by Bate[5] from the Mousterian horizon at the Dark Cave (Hazar Merd) is also completely a modern one. In spite of the contemporaneous aspect of the fauna, one finds expressed such ideas as "The Mousterian culture-stage, as represented in the Hazar Merd Cave of this region, appears to have coincided with a phase of intense cold and perhaps also an extension of ice-fields in the mountains" (Huzayyin, 1941, p. 106). Such extreme statements unfortunately are copied and thus perpetuated by subsequent authors (Butzer, 1958, p. 93) to whom the original report (Garrod, 1930) was not available. Since there is such a wide divergence of opinion concerning the environmental conditions at Hazar Merd at the time of its Mousterian occupation, the evidence needs to be re-examined in detail.

In the summary of her report on this site, Miss Garrod (1930, p. 40) wrote the following key sentences: "I have already described how many of the bones and flints from the Mousterian level showed signs of having been subjected to intense heat; other significant facts are the concentration of implements along the walls, and especially behind projecting masses of rock (suggesting that the inhabitants were taking advantage of every bit of shelter they could find), and the absence of implements and hearths in the entrance of the cave. Taken as a whole, this evidence suggests that the Mousterian occupation of the Dark Cave coincided with a period of cold. We have, of course, to bear in mind that the cave has a N. aspect and that even to-day the winter at Sulaimani is severe, the district being often snow-bound till the end of March, but against this one may urge, in the first place, that it is unlikely that the cave was inhabited only in winter, and that under present conditions the summer is very hot; in the second, that the dryness of the cave (noticeable even after a week of heavy rain) and the shelter afforded by its change of direction away from the mouth, to some extent neutralize its unfavorable aspect. On the whole it seems safe to conclude that the temperature of the region in Mousterian times was lower than it is today, but stronger evidence will have to be found before we can decide that the cave-Mousterian of Kurdistan is contemporaneous with a glacial advance."

---

[4]Identified by Dr. Harald Rehder of the U. S. National Museum. We are indebted to Dr. Solecki for permission to utilize these unpublished identifications.

[5]The bones from both Hazar Merd (Bate, 1930a) and Zarzi (Bate, 1930b) were unfortunately few and fragmentary, and no notes were published as to what bones were present or how many for each species. There is, thus, no possibility of reconstructing a complete faunal picture of either period; we must work strictly with the lists of identified species as published.

Miss Garrod's climatic conclusions, thus, were not only moderate but properly cautious. They were, however, based on the position of the artifacts and hearths in the cave, and we suggest, as did she, that the present winter climate is quite rigorous enough to account for much of this particular distribution. The faunal evidence, which must be assessed independently, indicates an environment similar to that which would be found in the region today if that environment had not been quite thoroughly changed by man. Miss Garrod evidently underestimated the importance of the faunal remains: "Unfortunately the animal remains from Hazar Merd are too fragmentary to be of use as evidence of climatic conditions. . . ." It is, however, this particular aggregation of animals[6] that refutes any concept that conditions at the time of occupancy were much, if any, colder than they are at present.

The Hazar Merd mammals, with two exceptions (Hatt, 1959), are known from the area today. Of these two, the red deer (Cervus elaphus) is "native" but now locally exterminated and the burrowing rodent Ellobius (known from adjacent western Iran) is most probably present but as yet unreported because of our great ignorance of the small mammals of the Zagros Mountains. Each of the eight mammals listed may be found in a somewhat colder environment than that of Hazar Merd today, but not one of them is indicative of cold.

Of the birds reported, all are present in Iraq today (Allouse, 1953; Moore and Boswell, 1956). Three species—the chukar partridge, the mistle thrust, and the Alpine swift—

---

[6]The faunal list for Hazar Merd is given below exactly as Miss Bate (1930a) published it, with the common names added in parentheses. Knowledge of this list is necessary for the present discussion, but additionally the article has seldom been cited and the journal in which it originally appeared is not everywhere available.

MAMMALIA

1. Myotis myotis (large mouse-eared bat)
2. Lepus sp. (hare)
3. Ellobius sp. (mole-vole)
4. Apodemus sp. (field mouse)
5. Spalax cf. ehrenbergi (mole rat)
6. Cervus elaphus cf. maral (red deer)
7. Gazella sp. (gazelle)
8. Capra sp. (goat)

AVES

9. Turdus viscivorus (mistle thrush)
10. Small passerine (small songbird)
11. Cypselus melba (Alpine swift)
12. ? Falco sp. (small accipitrine) (small falcon or hawk)
13. Columba sp. (dove)
14. Alectoris chukor (chukar partridge)

MOLUSCA

15. Helix salomonica Naegeli
16. Levantina cf. naegeli Kob.

We think it important for an understanding of the history of the discussion of the climatic conditions at Hazar Merd during the Mousterian period to note that the original faunal list consisted almost entirely of generic and/or generic and specific Latin names. Since these names undoubtedly had little or no meaning to most archeologists and climatologists, they were totally disregarded, particularly in the light of Miss Garrod's opinion as to conditions of a generally colder climate.

are particularly significant for our environmental study. The chukar partridge is at present a common ground bird of open or brushy hillsides in northeastern Iraq and is definitely limited to the eastern Mediterranean biota. The mistle thrush (Witherby et al., 1938, p. 111) is a bird of woodlands and fields and is particularly fond of regions where junipers abound. It breeds north to northeastern Russia, south to the the mountains of the Mediterranean islands and northwestern Africa, and eastward across Asia Minor, Lebanon, and western Iran to central Asia. The Alpine swift (Apus [=Cypsellus] melba) is not, as its name might indicate, a resident of the frigid mountain tops; it merely happens that the Alps, where it was first well known to Europeans, is near the northernmost limit of its range. Actually this bird is a resident of the uplands of the tropical and subtropical regions around the Mediterranean and south through Africa into Madagascar (Peterson et al., 1954, p. 178; Peters, 1940, p. 244). It is found as well in suitable areas of Asia Minor, Palestine (where it nests in the Great Mosque at Jerusalem!), Syria, and Iran. It also breeds in the highlands of southwestern Arabia (Meinertzhagen, 1954). It is a bird of cliff sides (this ecological niche being available directly above the cave mouth at Hazar Merd) and otherwise lives almost entirely on the wing.

It is most revealing, for the purposes of our environmental study, to realize that at present the ranges of the mistle thrust and the Alpine swift overlap only in the upland areas which have a typical Mediterranean climate. Hazar Merd is today in such an upland area, and we can only assume that the environment was similar during the time of the Mousterian occupancy of the cave. The presence of the chukar partridge, strictly a bird of the eastern Mediterranean region, is additional avian evidence for our climatic conclusions.

We believe, moreover, that the two species of snails reported, taken in conjunction with all the other evidence, definitely confirm our climatic conclusions for Hazar Merd. Both Helix salomonica and Levantina naegeli are snails of regions with a Mediterranean-type climate, living in areas with fairly cold winters but with hot dry summers; these conditions are exactly those of the region of Hazar Merd at present. Neither kind of snail occurs naturally in caves, and thus both must have been carried in. Further, since the snails are not obtainable during the winter, because they are inactive in hiding places below ground, they could have been collected only during warmer weather. Thus the cave must have been occupied for at least some part of the nonwinter season.

In toto, then, we visualize for Hazar Merd at the time of its Mousterian occupancy a climate little, if any, different from that of today; the differences in environment are due to recent deforestation and overgrazing. A country such as we envisage—of woodlands, streamside thickets, and areas of open grassland—would have been ideal for deer, hares, burrowing rodents (both Ellobius and Spalax), mistle thrushes, small hawks, doves, chukar partridges, and the snails mentioned. The swifts may have nested on the cliff above the cave (and perhaps still do!), the large mouse-eared bats probably lived in the cave (and perhaps still do!), and the wild goats were probably hunted on the ridges above the cave. The field mouse Apodemus is an animal of rocky hillsides or brushy thickets, which ecological niches were certainly plentiful then, as they are now over much of the area. The gazelles present more of a problem; perhaps they were hunted on the Sulimaniyah plain. If so, they would have required considerable open grassland there, similar to the present conditions (although we believe that most of the present open country in the Sulimaniyah area may be "artificial" and thus that this was not good gazelle country prior to deforestation).

THE UPPER PALEOLITHIC FOOD-COLLECTING HORIZON

The first subdivision of the food-collecting era in northeastern Iraq is to date manifested only in the cave of Shanidar, where it comprises the Baradostian materials of layer C. However, as indicated above, the fauna of the Shanidar sequence is remarkable for its uniformity. Thus our remarks concerning Shanidar D pertain to layer C also.

The radioactive-carbon determinations suggest a time gap in the Shanidar occupation of some 15,000 years between the industries represented by layers C and B. This gap is tentatively correlated by Wright with a period of major glacial intensity in the Zagros Mountains, accompanied (in Wright's opinion) by a depression of the upper tree line of 4,000 feet or more. In spite of such a major environmental change, during which prolonged period the forests may have extended well out onto the Iraqi plain, the animals which had returned to the region by the time of the Zarzian industry (layer B) were no different (with the single exception of a rare beaver) from those of layer C. Since the Shanidar-type biota during this period had undoubtedly shifted out onto the piedmont, it is suggested that archeologists look there for assemblages which would bridge the gap between the Baradostian and the Zarzian.

THE ZARZIAN OR TERMINAL ASPECT OF THE FOOD-COLLECTING ERA

The animal remains from the Zarzi, Palegawra, and Shanidar rock shelters provide hints as to the environment of the uppermost Pleistocene. Since all these animals are found in the area today or presumably would be if they had not been exterminated by man, we conclude that the climate of about 12,000 years ago could not have been much different from that of today. (The biotic environment today is quite different, of course, because of deforestation, overgrazing, soil erosion, and the extermination of many animal species.)

Few bones were recovered at Zarzi (see p. 166, n. 5); the vertebrates consisted only of fox, gazelle, goat, and the ubiquitous land tortoise (*Testudo*). The wild goats were undoubtedly hunted on the rocky ridges behind and above the shelter, but to find gazelles the hunters of Zarzi probably had to go several miles west, through a stream gap and out onto the plains bordering the Little Zab toward Alten Kupri. The aggregation of snails is more revealing, since the four species reported (*Helix salomonica*, *Levantina* cf. *mardinensis*, *Xerophila rrynickii*, and *Petraeus egregius*) occur together only in open grassy areas which are hot and dry for a considerable part of the year. Unfortunately we have no clue as to the number of snails, either in total or as to individual kinds, so that we cannot guess whether they were gathered to be eaten (as would be indicated by large numbers) or perhaps for the making of ornaments. Not one of these snails occurs naturally in caves, and thus in any case they must have been gathered.

The excavations at Palegawra (pp. 57-59) were more extensive than those at Zarzi and yielded correspondingly more faunal evidence, mostly mammalian: an equid (probably the onager), gazelle, red deer, roe deer, wild cattle, wild goat and probably wild sheep, pig, fox, wolf, a lynx-sized cat, hedgehog, many unidentified small rodents, numerous unidentified birds, the ever-present land tortoise, many toads (probably *Bufo viridis*, which still uses this damp cave as a daytime refuge), claws of a fresh-water crab common in northeastern Iraq, and shells of fresh-water clam. Snails, limited to the species *Helix salomonica*, were relatively more plentiful than they had been throughout the preceding periods in other archeological sites, and we conclude that here this snail was being gathered for food.

Palegawra lies amidst low hills close to a lush, well watered, round-bottomed valley. The annual rainfall at present must be about 25 inches (derived by extrapolation from data in De Vaumas, 1955) and was undoubtedly similar in the late Pleistocene. We can picture the hills as covered with a rather open deciduous forest, with oaks predominating but with occasional evergreens. (The latter were most probably *Juniperus*, on the basis of both Barghoorn's tentative identification and present ecology. Junipers are still found scattered at relatively low altitudes in northern Iraq, on cliff ledges and in other protected spots where they have not been cut.) In such a forest lived a variety of animals, ranging from big wild cattle and red deer to mice and shrews; on the higher and rockier ridges were the wild sheep and goats (still found there today), and in the open valley bottom were the equids. The snail, *Helix salomonica*, indicates hot dry summers and some open grassy areas probably other than those in the more verdant valley bottom. Again, we conclude that the general environment was very similar to that conceivable at present had it not been so changed by man.

Remarkably few gazelle bones were found at Palegawra; the valley in front of the cave is narrow and 12,000 years ago was undoubtedly brushy in part; while perhaps a good environment for an equid, it was undoubtedly unsuitable for gazelles. The plains-loving gazelles most likely lived many hours away, as a hunter walked, over a high ridge and across the Chemchemal valley, so that they were rarely hunted.

The known vertebrate fauna from Shanidar B is not a rich one but fits the environmental conclusion reached on the basis of a study of the faunas from Zarzi and Palegawra. It consists mostly of unidentifiable sheep and/or goat and of sheep (Ovis cf. orientalis), Bos or Bison, pig (Sus scrofa), bear (Ursus arctos), fox (Vulpes vulpes), land tortoise (Testudo), and beaver (Castor fiber). The beaver is new to Shanidar. Its presence, on zoögeographic grounds, is no great surprise, although the animal is otherwise unrecorded from Iraq.

The snails from Shanidar B, as previously noted (p. 166), also indicate a climate similar to that of the present. The increase in numbers of Helix salomonica over Levantina mahanica in layer B, as contrasted with the situation in layers C and D, suggests that (as we think true for Palegawra also) the H. salomonica at least was being gathered for food.

THE ERA OF INCIPIENT CULTIVATION IN OPEN-AIR SITES

Most unfortunately the study of the animal bones from Karim Shahir (pp. 52-54), M'lefaat (pp. 50-52), and Zawi Chemi Shanidar has not been completed. But Barth's tentative list of identifications of the Karim Shahir bones is consistent with the faunal lists of both the Zarzian and the Jarmo assemblages. While the elmlike Zelkova(?) did not appear in the woody charcoal samples from either Palegawra or Jarmo, Dr. Fritz Haas's appraisal of the environment called for by the snails (Helicella langloisiana, Helicella vestalis joppensis, Helix salomonica, and Jaminia septemdentata triticea) hardly suggests extreme woodland conditions. Haas informed Reed that the Karim Shahir snail species are typically those seen on Mediterranean hill slopes with some grassland and scattered small bushes; they thrive in an environment that provides both chilly wet winters and long hot dry summers.

Considering the elimination by man of the woody shrubs and the wild cattle and deer, the evidence suggests conditions for Karim Shahir which were not significantly different from those of the present.

THE ERA OF THE PRIMARY VILLAGE-FARMING COMMUNITY

The Jarmo Phase

There is much evidence that from central Palestine around through Syria and into eastern Iraq, from late prehistoric into historic times, there stretched a nearly continuous mountain and foothill woodland, probably in large part of oak, in part dense and in part open and parklike. Reed has been in a remnant of such native forest in northern Iraq at elevations of 4,000-5,000 feet. At these altitudes the winter precipitation is heavy; the trees are large, thick, and spreading, and the underbrush is a tangled mass. Here certainly is the forest primeval, limited now to a few steep mountain sides far from inhabited villages but typical undoubtedly of most if not all of the higher mountain areas at the beginning of postglacial times. This condition would have existed, however, only in the higher regions with more rain and snow. At lower altitudes we visualize a more open type of deciduous forest, probably predominantly of oak, much as one finds over some of the southern California hill country today—a region of similar climatic pattern and approximately the same latitude (Strahler, 1951, Fig. 25:8). We speak of these lower forests as "woodlands," for this word carries more the flavor of the rather open floral assemblage that we visualize.

There are historical and archeological evidences for the presence and subsequent destruction of the "forests" of Palestine (Isserlin, 1955), and Mallowan (1947, p. 15) has discussed the presence of forests in northeastern Syria and the kinds of trees found near Tell Chagar Bazar and Tell Brak in the third and second millenniums B.C.; this region is now completely treeless except for a little scrub atop the Jabal Sinjar, the only considerable hills in the whole area.

For the Zagros areas of Iraq, Zohary (1950, p. 11) says particularly: "The mountainous parts of Iraq in the North and East constitute a woodland with particular flora and vegetation. The most characteristic feature of this vegetation are the oak forests.—Ecologically these forests are much closer to the Eurosiberian than to the Mediterranean forest types though some of their components reoccur in the East Mediterranean Mountains. . . . They [i.e., the forests] are mainly in altitudes of 650 m. to 1700 m. . . ." It is of interest that Jarmo (pp. 38-50), the center of our study for the primary village-farming community, lies within this zone, although at approximately 800 meters it is near the lower limits of it.

We do not know the minimum annual rainfall required to maintain the deciduous trees now sporadically found, but once commonly found, in the foothills of east central Iraq, where Jarmo lies (see p. 26). Nor do we know what the rainfall would be at Zohary's generally lower tree line of 650 meters, but the general Jarmo area (the Chemchemal valley) still supports oak trees, singly or in small groups, where they are given protection. Such protection is generally beside a saint's tomb or in cemeteries; the trees may even have a wall around them to keep out the flocks, and they are invested with enough sanctity, because of their position, to save them from cutting. Some of these trees grow on the tops of knolls, certainly the driest local environment, and one can easily imagine, without postulating any differences in climate, that under earlier conditions trees doubtlessly covered much of the countryside, perhaps in places densely, but in places undoubtedly more sparsely in semi-open parklands. There is today, on the way to Sulimaniyah from Chemchemal but off the main road, an impressive patch of second- or third-growth oaks, spaced at most 50 feet apart (but usually much closer), which shows how at least some of the countryside might once have been covered.

Thus the evidence indicates that the site of Jarmo now lies within the climatic zone of the oak woodland. When the village was founded the area was undoubtedly covered with well spaced large oaks, which gradually disappeared as the need for firewood continued over the centuries. There is today, in the area close to Jarmo, only one large tree; this happens to be a terebinth (Pistacia mutica) and not an oak, but it indicates that the immediate vicinity can still support large trees.

At this point we again emphasize the very tentative and transient nature of our understandings. Reed, impressed by the indications discussed above, tends to reconstruct the Chemchemal valley landscape in terms of an almost continuous scatter of well spaced large oaks and other deciduous trees, with some denser stands, interspersed with brushy thickets along the streams. Helbaek, in discussions during the 1954/55 field season and with respect to his sense for what the cereals required, tended to think of the Jarmo landscape in terms of a grassland climax but with occasional groves of trees. The latter point of view was reached independently by Barth in 1951. A reconstruction of the Jarmo landscape prepared in color for Life magazine (Barnett, 1956, p. 75) followed Helbaek's ideas. Reed believes this reconstruction leans too heavily on the present man-created treeless and semibadland condition in the area and on rainfall estimates which are probably too low. If present rainfall figures are pertinent—and we believe that they are—Wright's (1952) estimate of 16 inches (40 cm.) annual rainfall for the Chemchemal valley may be increased up to 25 inches (64 cm.) by extrapolation from the data of De Vaumas (1955, p. 136). Even if the latter figure is too high by several inches, it justifies the flourishing of the sanctified trees on the knolltops and indicates greater rainfall than one could believe as he surveys the barren landscape. As the detailed study of the evidence proceeds, especially that concerned with the ecology of the snails, the divergent views of Helbaek and Reed will no doubt be resolved.

The animal bones recovered from the Jarmo excavations (pp. 47-48) indicate a site from which hunters could gather animals from both woodland and grassland. Some of these animals are extinct entirely (wild cattle); others (deer, leopard, bear), dependent on the woodlands, are missing from the area now that the trees are gone. The wild pig, the wolf, the fox, and some lesser creatures survive in the more immediate area today in spite of continuous hunting; the wild sheep and the wild goat still exist on the higher rocky ridges to the east, although they will probably disappear in a few years. At least one grassland and/or open-forest animal (an equid, as yet unidentified but possibly the onager) seemingly became extinct in the Jarmo area while the village was occupied, whereas Gazella subgutterosa, another grassland form hunted at the time, still survives to be hunted today.

Thus the Jarmo mammalian fauna suggests a site from which men hunted on the grasslands, in the surrounding woodlands, and in the denser forests of the high ridges. We do not know, of course, the exact boundary between woodland and grassland, although Zohary's figure of an altitude of 650 meters may be suggested as a rough approximation. It is certain that the grasslands (probably the upper levels of the piedmont and the lowermost foothills; see pp. 169 f.) could not have been far away, for gazelles, always animals of the open plains, are represented by numerous bones in the kitchen debris of Jarmo. It is doubtful that this animal would have been hunted for anything but food, and it certainly would not have been carried more than a few hours from the site of the kill to the village. The local distribution of gazelles today may not be a good clue as to their range several thousands of years ago, for they are now found in the Chemchemal valley, all of which we take to be a deforested area naturally barred to gazelles at the time of Jarmo's occupancy.

A comparison of the snails from the Jarmo excavations with the present snail population of the surrounding area would yield ecological information as to the changing conditions of the last several thousand years, if only we knew more of the micro-climatic requirements of the snails involved. The large Helix salomonica, eaten in uncounted hundreds of thousands by the people of Jarmo, was obviously abundant when the village was occupied, but it is extremely rare in the area today. The large snail common in the region now, found almost exclusively along rocky ledges, is the slightly larger Levantina kurdistana. Shells of this snail were rarely found in the excavations; these snails were either selectively rejected as food or were rare in the area then.

In parts of southwestern Asia, we are told by Haas, these two kinds of snails occur together and may be found feeding side by side at night. During the day, however, each retires into a different microniche, the Helix under rocks on the ground or into crevices in the soil and the Levantina into crevices in the rocks (as we also observed). Given certain conditions, thus, both snails can be abundant in the same area, but presumably each can also flourish under circumstances unfavorable to the other. We do not yet know, unfortunately, these ecological variables in any detail; when we do, we shall probably be able to say more about the environmental changes in the Jarmo area than we can now.

The habitat of Helix salomonica, the snail eaten by the people of Jarmo, is supposedly open but stony fields, plains, or glades, and our observations agree, since the very few living individuals that we found were in wheat fields. However, in spite of the fact that the whole Chemchemal valley is now an open plain, these snails are now too rare there to serve as a source of human food; indeed, one has to hunt assiduously to find a single specimen. Though we do not know the ecological variables which led to this extreme decline in population, it may depend on changes in available microhabitats due to deforestation and overgrazing.

The unfortunate situation with the snails, where we have data in hand but do not know what they mean, underlines again the necessity for adequate studies of the contemporary ecology, as well as of past conditions, if the full story of the changing environment is to unfold.

The Hassunah and Halaf Phases

There is very little useful evidence. In chapter ix, Reed notes evidence for animal domesticaion in the Halaf period, at Gird Banahilk (p. 132) and Arpachiyah (p. 143). The Hassunan and Halafian artifactual assemblages appear to call for subsistence activities which suggest no particular environmental conditions different from those of the present day.

SUBSEQUENT HISTORY

The story of northeastern Iraq is one of ever-increasing human exploitation. There may have been minor climatic fluctuations (Butzer, 1958), but any ecologic responses were small relative to the much greater changes wrought by man. Lacking direct biological evidence, we make no attempt to discuss the natural history of the latest prehistoric and earliest historic periods of this region. However, during these periods man was the pre-eminent environmental influence, and the effects of his handiwork are to be seen throughout the Near East.

In general the role of man, of his agriculture and his flocks, has been destructive, and this without any one man meaning to be destructive. The natural tendency toward population increase, however, has resulted in a continuous effort to increase the size of the flocks and the acreage under cultivation. The result is everywhere apparent, but we say here only a few words about the area around Jarmo, with which we are most familiar. Our reconstruction of the contrast between the present landscape of the Chemchemal valley and the landscape of the same area at approximately the time of Jarmo is, of course, largely theoretical, based on such bits of evidence as we now have. As more evidence comes to hand, we may wish to revise the picture to some extent, but we imagine its broad outlines will remain.

Today, throughout much of the once-wooded plain and foothill area of the Chemchemal valley, hardly a shrub remains. On the crests of the Kani Shaitan Hasan-Sagirma Dagh, to the east, the scrub oak rarely is allowed to reach 6 feet in height before it is hacked away by the charcoal burner. With the trees and the brush cover gone and with the grass eaten down to its roots each spring, the soil has largely gone, too, to silt up the rivers and the new canals of the alluvial plains, as the ancient canals were silted before them (Jacobsen and Adams, 1958). Bare rock ridges protrude where once an undulating woodland landscape covered the harsh outlines of the now exposed tilted Miocene sandstones. Floods Mesopotamia has always had, as does any riverine valley whose waters rise in snow-covered hills, but at Jarmo, when the prehistoric village was founded, certainly the soil and vegetation cover held the rain, the streams flowed clear almost the year around, and the run-off was heavy only after the most torrential spring thundershower.

Today at Jarmo (Pl. 8B) bare rock ridges protrude on every side, only the hardiest of goat-eaten shrubs hug the ground, soil washes away on every slope almost as fast as it can form, and the rains rage off the land in chocolate torrents. When Jarmo was an occupied village, the wadi at the base of the site undoubtedly provided water throughout the year, but now it is dry by mid-May except for rare stagnant pools in which a few small fish manage to survive.

This, then, is the story of a land. The trees are gone, the soil is gone, and the larger wild animals that are not gone remain but briefly.

It is not, could not be, the denuded environment of today that spawned the village-farming base upon which the beginnings of civilization were later to be built. Today's land could not, and that land of yesterday is gone.

XII

OBSERVATIONS, QUESTIONS, AND PROSPECTS

INTRODUCTORY REMARKS

We remarked above (p. 1) that "the goal of understanding that we seek will not come within the lifetime of this expedition's staff." This final chapter re-emphasizes that generalization. Various concluding observations are made, but many questions are posed. It may be fair to say that the health and vigor of any focus of research interest may be judged by the questions it poses for itself. Our questions point in a variety of directions and suggest avenues and prospects for further research.

Natural History and Cultural History

The Iraq-Jarmo Project has certainly made a far greater effort in a cross-disciplinary sense than has ever before been attempted in the field in southwestern Asia. What has this cross-disciplinary effort of culture historians and natural historians accomplished? First, speaking as the two senior culture historians involved, we are convinced that the presence of our natural-science colleagues on the staff has prevented us from committing a considerable number of nonsensical generalizations to print, on subjects in which we are naïve and far from well instructed. It also seems that our natural-science colleagues advise us against any easy or sweeping environmental determinism. Having participated with us, in the field and at home, in thinking about a problem in which the primary emphasis is cultural history, Wright, Helbaek, and Reed seem to tell us—either directly or by implication—to render unto culture that which is culture's. They are very sensitive to the ecological potentialities of the situations with which they have dealt, but none of them is an ecological determinist. Helbaek and Reed treat their domesticates as the artifacts of human manipulation, and Wright (p. 97)—ever a cautious generalizer—suggests that ". . . the gradual evolution of culture, with increasing complexity and perfection of tool technology, may have been a more potent factor in bringing about the economic revolution than was the climatic change at the end of the glacial period." Here, though, we ask whether these are to some extent arguments from ignorance still or whether they involve some measure of postponement of decision (for lack of decisive evidence) on the part of the naturalists. Are we not merely at a way stage in fact-finding and reasoning on a problem which is still wide open? These attitudes of the naturalists may be not necessarily a final viewpoint, or an exclusion of other theoretical lines, but rather a tentative reaction, quite strongly and soundly based, to sweeping ecological determinism. In such questions as these, one needs always to bear in mind the very human tendency on the part of either class of protagonist—natural historian or culture historian—to shift the responsibility for dealing with causal factors, when the evidence is still so incomplete, to the bailiwick of the opposite colleague.

It is certainly clear that the natural historians' task, in relation to the problem of our common interest, is far from done. We begin to have some knowledge of the modern life zones of the Palestinian-Lebanese and Iraqi-Kurdistan quarters of southwestern Asia and an inkling of their ecological regimes in antiquity. But over how great an area of southwestern Asia may we fairly, by extrapolation, extend reconstructions? The conception of the hilly-flanks zone as a nuclear area for domestication is encouraged by the available evidence, but what were the exact boundaries of the zone at the pertinent time? Did "nuclearity" for domestication in fact extend somewhat beyond the hilly flanks themselves?

Were the Dead Sea valley and portions of the plateaus of Iran and Anatolia part of the "nuclear area"? Were there perhaps certain critical variations from district to district within the whole zone? Did the critical manipulations of plants occur independetly from, or in any real demonstrably fixed relationship with, those of animals in either space or time within this zone? Will the answer be simple or a mosaic of factors, and, if a mosaic, will it be a simple or a very complex one? We suspect it will be a mosaic.

General Levels of Cultural Activity

The framework of this presentation, the skeleton outline upon which we have hung our snatches of the flesh of once living cultures, is based on a general theoretical scheme of development. This scheme assumes that, in view of the incompleteness of the archeological record, the traces of subsistence and settlement activities of the past cultures serve best to suggest the subdivisions of cultural development into stages and eras. Several trial formulations of this theoretical scheme have been attempted (Braidwood, 1958a-b, 1959, 1960). The headings of chapters x and xi follow the scheme, as does our outline below.

Concentrating our attention on traces of subsistence and settlement activities, for the time range we probe, demands a realistic assessment of the archeological record. We do not believe that enough significant archeological and natural historical evidence has yet been found to allow an adequate interpretation and a successful reconstruction of the full spectrum of cultural activities in the earlier phases. Only toward the end of the sequence with which we deal does the evidence allow relative success.

Beginning with the era of the primary village-farming community, traces of cultural activity evidenced in bands of the spectrum other than those of the subsistence and settlement factors become available. At Jarmo the clay figurines, the bracelets, and the exquisite workmanship of the stone vessels suggest some of the bands of the full cultural spectrum which have not been visible to us in the earlier ranges of our sequence. As the processing and interpretation of these traces of cultural activity proceed, and as more become available, better vehicles than the simple facts of subsistence and settlement will be in hand for the observation of cultural development and change. In fact, as the era of the primary village-farming community yields to the succeeding eras of towns and urban settlements in classic southern Mesopotamia (which is beyond our concern here), the theoretical scheme based on levels of subsistence and settlement activities increasingly loses its primacy for the understanding of culture history. It should be recalled that the primacy allowed to subsistence and settlement activities in our theoretical scheme is not of our own choosing but is imposed upon us by the incompleteness of the archeological record of the earlier ranges.

Our theoretical scheme with its stages and eras conceived of as ideal types—especially the era of incipient cultivation—contains an element of post-factum judgment. Some of our levels, as ideal types, may correspond with reality only in a general way. For example, our era of incipient cultivation cannot have been based for its subsistence entirely on dietary substances derived from activities concerned with "incipient cultivation" alone; most of the dietary intake must still have depended on rather intense food-collecting. In the same way, our theoretical scheme does not primarily visualize what must actually have been the continuity and blends of activities within any given level, any one of which activities might be ideally assignable to each of several levels. The archeological record of fauna, flora, and artifacts, indeed, has always suggested such a continuity. The new activities at each level were an imbrication upon the old, not a replacement or a reweaving, at least at first. With the advent and adoption of the new activities, old ones for a while, or perhaps always, continued compatibly until perhaps some became submerged or dropped away entirely, depending ultimately on some cultural (or natural?) exigency or some event. Our theoretical scheme is, in fact, no more than a model of major landmarks for our convenience in the discussion and interpretation of progressively changing archeological materials in a general process of accretion and discard. The succession of once living cultures of ancient man in Iraqi Kurdistan, or beyond, certainly was not patterned quite so simply and solely for our archeological convenience!

Cultural Influence, Change, and Population

Our attention is focused on Iraqi Kurdistan. We may seem to be writing as if northeastern Iraq existed in a vacuum, as if its own prehistoric cultural succession made transitions from one essentially indigenous subsistence-settlement level to another. Although this may possibly be true to a significant degree, it is probably not the entire story. We believe that, except perhaps at one time in its overall cultural development, Iraqi Kurdistan was predominantly a region which received the impact of outside cultural influences rather than a region which initiated cultural change. We believe that the exception—the one time when Iraqi Kurdistan lay within the central core of a cultural initiation and then only in so far as it lay within the natural-habitat nuclear area of the hilly-flanks zone—was the moment of an interconnected network of achievements in the era of incipient cultivation and in the first flush of the era of the primary village-farming community which followed. But we do not conceive of Jarmo, or Karim Shahir, or the Chemchemal valley, or even the intermontane-valley zone in Iraqi Kurdistan as the center of this cultural initiation; we simply believe that they lay within the general life zone of the hilly-flanks nuclear area where the cultural initiation was made and that they participated in and probably contributed to its beginnings in a manner still to be properly determined.

The source areas, whether local or alien, from which came the impacts bringing cultural change to Iraqi Kurdistan are not clear for any of the levels of our present study. We speak here of only one instance of reputed impact from outside, and that only because it bears on our position regarding Iraqi Kurdistan's role within the conception of the hilly-flanks nuclear area as the scene of a start in cultural change which ended with the achievement of incipient cultivation. Sauer (1952) and von Wissmann (1957; von Wissmann *et al.*, 1956) propose an aboriginal center for all "agricultural" activities in *southeastern* Asia. But such a center is certainly not demonstrable on the grounds of an established archeological sequence of chronology, nor do we see any conceivable traces of westward progress of any diffusion from such a center nor any impact upon Iraqi Kurdistan.[1]

Questions of more immediate application are posed by our chronological chart (Fig. 8). Does its arrangement of the successive sites imply at all points in time internal (Iraqi-Kurdistan region) as well as external direct diffusion of actual people and materials or only an indirect one of ideas and skills? Will some of the chronological levels be found to comprise a single uniform material assemblage, or will progress be found to develop at different speeds? Will there be little if any regional techno-typological variation within the Mousterian industry as seen at Hazar Merd, Shanidar, Spilik, Babkhal, and elsewhere, and ought this common assemblage to have full implications of cultural unity? Certainly something new entered the area with the Baradostian and again with the Zarzian, the latter displaying considerably internal variation as yet unassessed. But how much and what kind of essential change occurred in anything but tool types? Still another new influence or development is evident; in this case we would guess that the new ideas and skills were broadly interchanged throughout the district. But should we hazard the suggestion that there was any wider complete cultural commonality? Iraqi Kurdistan perhaps shared a Mousterian with a wider province, but its Baradostian, its Zarzian, and its Karim Shahir horizons as at present documented cannot be exactly matched morphologically and typolog-

---

[1] Nor do we see any identifiable traces of diffusionary impact upon the hilly-flanks zone from Coon's (1954) postulated center along the Caspian coastal plain, nor from Murdock's (1957) postulated center in the upper bend of the Niger River in Africa. However commendable the Coon, Murdock, Sauer, and von Wissmann postulates may be as flights of imaginative speculation, they remain artifacts of a so far unavoidable ignorance of exactly the kind of archeological and natural historical reconstruction that our cross-disciplinary efforts have tried to adduce for Iraqi Kurdistan.

ically elsewhere, though there are some thought-provoking analogies and perhaps significant comparisons. Contrasting but vaguely analogous clusters of stone industries, or techno-typological assemblages, occur in Syria and Palestine for this general range of time: the so-called Nebekian, Late Capsian, Falitian, and Lower Natufian at Yabrud and the Kebaran and Lower Natufian in Palestine. The fact that the Kurdish assemblages are not specifically comparable in detail suggests that the Kurdish area may have been a somewhat separate cultural entity for a time.

What, further, does the sequence on the chart suggest of the interchange of ideas or of migrations—within Iraqi Kurdistan, or from there to the outside, or from the outside into Iraqi Kurdistan? What is the significance of the steady trickle of obsidian into the area from at least the Baradostian horizon onwards? Why did sites such as Karim Shahir and Zawi Chemi Shanidar largely lack this commodity but share a number of other material categories with Jarmo? How and by what carriers did the impressive bulk of obsidian reach the Chemchemal valley in Jarmo times?

We would suppose that the increasing number of site names on the chart, as time proceeds, means more than simply a reflection upon the present incompleteness of intensive survey. The increase probably does, in fact, suggest population increase with the passage of time. Braidwood and Reed (1957) have attempted to assess a possible population figure for the Chemchemal valley in Jarmo times. Nevertheless, any generalization concerning population increase must remain tenuous until more evidence, both archeological and environmental, becomes available.

THE MIDDLE PALEOLITHIC FOOD-GATHERERS

Barda Balka

Our earliest available trace of human activity within the general stage of food-gathering in Iraq as seen at Barda Balka (pp. 61-62) reflects an era wherein the standardized production of stone tools was already well advanced. The most comprehensively excavated living sites of this era of well developed Acheulean hand axes, pebble tools, and small flakes are probably such sites as Olorgesailie and Isimila in East Africa. They appear to have been temporary open-air encampments or "slaughter sites" along the margins of now extinct lakes or streams. Barda Balka seems to fit this picture.

F. Clark Howell, who dug Isimila, has speculated (in private conversations with us) that "hunting" is too dignified a word to describe the subsistence activities of the Isimila people; "scrounge" or "scavenge" might be more apt.[2] The African sites of this complexion generally yield the bones of the great now extinct Pleistocene animals. In this connection, it may be noteworthy that in Iraqi Kurdistan none of our sites later than Barda Balka has yielded the bones of such animals as the rhinoceros and the elephant.

The Coarse Mousterian of Open-Air Sites

Since none of our sites in this range is yet excavated or, indeed, seems to have any appropriate deposit which might lend itself to extensive examination, we have little basis upon which to assess them. We may note only techno-typological change in the flint tools available to us, as contrasted with those of Barda Balka and of the caves and later sites. Comparable coarse forms stratigraphically precede more developed forms on the Lebanese coast.

---

[2] He now takes the point of view (Washburn and Howell, 1960) that in Africa and Europe from Middle Pleistocene times onward (which include the Isimila occurrence) there is evidence that men "hunted and killed large herbivorous animals in some quantity." He seems inclined to push the "scavenger" level back into the range of the australopithicines. The exact color of meaning to be given to the verb "hunt" is no doubt the issue here.

The Developed Mousterian Horizon in Caves

In our theoretical scheme, we view the developed Mousterian industry, in whatever regional variation, as the archeological trace of the final cultural manifestation of the older stone-age food-gathering and of an advance or shift from what is evidenced by the early open-air industries. We sense that the developed Mousterian horizon in the caves of Iraqi Kurdistan may have been somewhat backward and regionally isolated. To date it cannot be closely matched save on the Iranian plateau, and it seems to show no internal variation or progression. In Shanidar D, Solecki recovered fossil men of the same general Neanderthal type as is usual in the context of Mousterian industries in the westerly portions of the Old World. Steward (1958) sees the general morphology of the Shanidar Neanderthals as more like those of the Palestinian Tabun-type populations than those of the somewhat more modern Skhul type. This view would appear to strengthen our suggestion that the developed Mousterian horizon of Iraq was somewhat more recessive and isolated than that of the Levant coast.

The developed Mousterian, as a general Old World cultural manifestation embracing the sites of Europe and Africa as well as Asia, brings to mind the probable beginnings of the hafting of weapons and conscious burial of the dead. Was there also perhaps some selectivity in the kinds of animals hunted, as we know to be the case slightly later, so that the word "hunting" is probably now acceptable? But, in contrast to the horizon in the harsher surroundings of western Europe, the caves in the latitude and geographic position of Iraqi Kurdistan yield traces of a fauna which is completely modern for the area. The trickle of obsidian may already have begun. There is a hint that the developed Mousterian horizon lies upon the threshold of something new.

THE UPPER PALEOLITHIC FOOD-COLLECTORS

The Broader Implications of the Trend from Gathering to Collecting

As a theoretical generalization the era of food-collecting may be seen as one in which humans adapted themselves with increasing intensity to more regionally restricted environments, as aptly expressed by Garrod (1953, p. 14): "The speeding-up of change and development which begins to show in the period is reflected . . . not only in the greater number of industries having enough individual character to be classified as distinct cultures, but in their restriction in space, since [cultural] evolution now starts to outstrip diffusion." In the more westerly portions of the Old World at least, the beginning of this general trend seems in some way connected with the appearance of both the blade-tool tradition and anatomically modern man. What these apparent coincidences mean is not yet clear.

Garrod once (Garrod and Bate, 1937, pp. 19, 21) saw the area of origin of the blade-tool tradition ". . . possibly in Iran . . . some as yet unidentified Asiatic centre . . .," but she is no longer so certain (e.g. Garrod, 1953), and certainly neither Coon's explorations in Iran nor the available sequence in Iraqi Kurdistan indicate anything either for or against chronological precedence and show no very remarkable variety in blade tools. In the Levant, however, some backed blades and burins do appear intermittently in limited brief previews significantly early—unless one follows the low extreme of chronological reconstruction suggested by Bordes (1955), but we do not—and so also at Mt. Carmel do the more modern skull types of fossil men. It is still fair to leave open the question: Did southwestern Asia have a role in the formation of the blade-tool tradition or in the appearance of anatomically modern man or in both? But it does not appear at the moment that Iraqi Kurdistan could have had much part in these developments if they did take place in southwestern Asia. Nevertheless, the sequence at this range of time for northeastern Iraq is very incomplete.

The Baradostian Horizon

We must—on grounds of typology, strengthened to the degree that we trust the radioactive-carbon chronology—show an X on our chronological table (Fig. 8) both before and after the Baradostian of Shanidar C. The few available radioactive-carbon determinations must be treated with some reserve, however (see p. 160). Is the Baradostian another example of the intermittent occurrence of blade tools such as is known in the "pre-Aurignacian" of Yabrud and on Mt. Carmel? If so, the X phase or phases following the Baradostian might again contain a Mousterian industry. We doubt that such will prove to be the case, but specific evidence is lacking.

Although the industry of Shanidar C is basically in the blade-tool tradition, its general complexion resembles that of the Hazar Merd Mousterian horizon more than it does that of the Zarzian. We are inclined to expect that at least one more industry will eventually be found to fit within the gap marked by the X above Shanidar C in our table.

If, in the trend from simpler food-gathering to more intensified food-collecting, the developed Mousterian horizon was on the threshold of the new way of life, then the Baradostian must have been well within it. At present, however, there is not much to demonstrate the case conclusively in Iraqi Kurdistan. The obsidian trickle continues; the fauna is of the modern type. We wonder whether Turkaka and especially Kowri Khan (pp. 55-57) will eventually prove to link with the Baradostian or lie within the gap immediately following it. If either proves to be the case, is a new trend toward open-site living already under way?

The Zarzian Horizon

The Zarzian industry has a much fuller and more varied and specialized tool kit than any that precedes it, and there are clear hints of both developmental phases within the industry and regional, or at least site, variation even within Iraqi Kurdistan. Some of the older tool types persist, but there are many new forms in the blade-tool tradition as well as a few oddments in ground stone and even some mortar and pestle fragments. The use of obsidian continues, although still as a minor element.

The Zarzian people were the last real cave-dwellers in Iraqi Kurdistan, but the Turkaka and Kowri Khan surface samplings suggest the possibility of open-air sites with a general Zarzian affinity. The fauna of the caves is of modern type and occurs in some bulk, although its study is not yet complete. For the first time snails appear in enough quantity to suggest that they may have been a regular element in the diet.

We see the Zarzian as the terminal aspect of the "pure" food-collecting way of life (if it is conceived of as an ideal type) in Iraqi Kurdistan. Some Zarzian settlements were probably open-air sites, but whether for all of the year or only seasonally and thus alternating with cave dwellings is not yet clear. Further excavations and an exhaustive study of the animal remains may help solve this question (cf. Clark, 1954) and may bear on the question of intensification of cultural adaptation to life within a given more circumscribed region. In this connection, are the suggestions of regional or site variation that we see already significant differences? And how significantly different were the subsistence and settlement ways of the Zarzians from those of the people who were producing roughly comparable blade-tool industries at about the same general time in the Levant (the Kebaran and the upper levels of caves II and III at Yabrud), along the Caspian coastal plain in Iran (Belt and Hotu), and in Soviet Turkmenistan (Peshtera Dzhebel; Okladnikov, 1956)?

It is probably meaningful that what we sense as directly comparable with or a consistent part of the Zarzian assemblage does not extend beyond Iraqi Kurdistan. Even so, we see the Zarzian flint industry as a part of the far vaster <u>oikoumêne</u> of the blade-tool tradition, but we also see the Zarzian manifestation itself as regional. In marked contrast, our feelings about the Barda Balka industry let us range without embarrassment from Tunesia and Rhodesia to the Indian peninsula for comparative material. By Zarzian times regionalism had certainly set in.

THE TRANSITION TO THE FOOD-PRODUCING STAGE

General Considerations

It is very easy to contrast the ways of life of cultures during the grand stages of food-gathering and food-production when these stages are conceived of as ideal types. It is even quite easy to contrast the ways of life of cultures in the terminal aspect of the food-collecting era with those of the primary era of the village-farming community. In any interpretation, or reconstruction, the implications of the Zarzian assemblage, as against those of the Hassunan assemblage or even of the Jarmo assemblage, suggest very different cultural realities as well as different ideal types. It is transparent that the Jarmo assemblage cannot have sprung, fully armed, from the head of the Zarzian. This statement, however, involves an element of post-factum judgment, and trouble begins on the level both of ideal types and of realities.

When we deal with the "mesolithic" in northwestern Europe the matter is not so complicated. Between the terminal aspect of the upper paleolithic and the first trace of the "neolithic" or food-production—which was obviously not indigenously developed and depended on diffusional stimulus—is the range of materials called "mesolithic." The word has real meaning in Europe, where it was coined, in naming those assemblages which show cultural readaptation to a postglacial environment on a level of increasingly intensified food-collection. For example, the difference between the climate and fauna of the Magdalenian and the Maglemosian suggests radical change. And it is not seriously suggested, ex post facto or otherwise, that the Maglemosian lies at the base of an indigenous development of food-production and in itself gives rise to the level of the primary village-farming community.

In southwestern Asia, however, our colleagues in the natural sciences see no evidence for radical change in climate or fauna between the levels of the Zarzian and those of the Jarmo or Hassunah phases. The assemblages of Natufian and Karim Shahir types must be coped with in some fashion, and we believe that they must be intercalated on a basis of morphological and typological development, as they are by relative stratigraphy, between the terminal paleolithic food-collectors and the era of the primary village-farming community. However much post-factum judgment is involved in this reasoning, we nevertheless believe it has real meaning and is somewhere near the truth.

Our way out of this difficulty is to postulate an era of incipient cultivation as an ideal type. We do this in the face of the impossibility of conceiving of its subsistence activities as other than still largely food-collecting (even as an ideal type) and in the face of our extreme difficulties in adducing and demonstrating artifactual evidence for incipient cultivation.

If—even only for the sake of argument—an era of incipient cultivation is allowed, then some interesting questions arise. Was the era manifested only within the natural-habitat hilly-flanks nuclear area? What were the approximate boundaries of this nuclear area, especially toward the Levantine littoral side? If the relatively lush Mediterranean coastal plain was not part of the natural-habitat zone in the strictest sense, do at least the earlier phases of the Natufian represent the contemporary development of an alternative era? Was that development committed to still further intensification on the food-collecting level, or to some kind of incipient cultivation? The domestication of the dog (even were Reed to accept the Natufian evidence wholeheartedly; see p. 128) need not be restricted to the era of incipient cultivation, and the sheen on Natufian sickles may have come from the cutting of a variety of ripe plants with heavy concentrations of silica. We plead not especially for Iraqi Kurdistan but only for a consideration of the location of the effective boundaries of the natural-habitat nuclear area as a whole. Moreover, our natural-science colleagues, at least, are unimpressed with the evidence for an oasis theory of the origins of cultivation. The heartening increase in attention to open-air Natufian sites may soon provide clarification, and, regardless of the question posed above, we will not be surprised if these sites yield some evidence of incipient cultivation. However, we would be surprised by such evidence in the "mesolithic" or even "early neolithic" levels of Belt or Hotu on the very lush Caspian coastal plain, a very different ecological and geographic province.

Clearly, much more investigation of both the cultural and the natural history of this time range is needed before speculation can be replaced by clear delineation. We are embarrassed by the span of two thousand years which our chronological table (Fig. 8) shows for the era of incipient cultivation. We are uncomfortable because of our lack of either artifactual or nonartifactual evidence pointing directly to an incipient stage, however much "making-do" with older tool forms or procedures there must still have been. In the Iraqi-Kurdistan sequence it is not clear whether Turkaka immediately preceded Karim Shahir, and our table shows two critical X's and the as yet unexcavated Qara Chiwar (p. 50) between Karim Shahir and Jarmo. We anticipate learning much from the Palestinian side as the excavation and processing of the materials from Jericho, Mallaha, and Nahal Oren proceed.

The Era of Incipient Cultivation

As with the Zarzian sites, it is fair to ask whether the observable differences in detail in the assemblages of Karim Shahir (pp. 52-54), M'lefaat (pp. 50-52), and Zawi Chemi Shanidar suggest either regional or site variation or else time difference. We have assumed the former. Possibly an element of specialized activities also may be reflected in these differences. In an overall sense, however, we believe the catalogues of the three sites may be lumped together to suggest one reasonably consistent tradition and general horizon.

This phase of the era appears to manifest itself only at open-air sites. Some kind of simple architectual activity, perhaps the making of shallow semisubterranean hut structures, is manifested at M'lefaat and Zawi Chemi Shanidar. In view of the virtual lack of materials of this phase in the fair number of tested caves in Iraqi Kurdistan, it is possible that these open-air settlements may have been occupied throughout the year, although probably for not very many years consecutively. We have no idea how many huts a site contained.

When the fauna of these sites is adequately studied, will we find a trend toward either of the smaller of the potentially domesticable animals? Snail shells now become plentiful in the debris, but we still have no direct evidence of vegetable foods. The numbers of querns, mullers, mortars, and pestles now increase, however. While the overwhelming bulk of the catalogues remains in the chipped stone category, new artifacts appear; the presence of the ground celt is assured, and of ground stone bracelets, pendants, and beads. These, with the pair of Karim Shahir figurines, hint at bands in the cultural spectrum other than simple subsistence and settlement activities.

The position of the Natufian of Palestine is somewhat enigmatic, but we trust that the new work in this horizon will soon bear fruit. At the moment it is quite proper to ask whether the Natufian assemblage—as an ideal type—should be classified as the trace of (1) a highly developed and intensified level of food-collecting or (2) a level of incipient cultivation or (3) an early phase of the level of the primary village-farming community. Or, most important question of all, was it not some sort of blend of two or all three of these ideal types? Such added elements as the harpoon, the fishhook, and the flint projectile point seem to suggest intensification of food-collection. On the other hand, if the bulk of the flint sickle blades are sickles in fact (for the reaping of cereals), then a tough rachis grain is probably implied and might suggest an element of the level of the village-farming community rather than that of incipient cultivation if comparison with the evidence in Iraqi Kurdistan is allowable. In this connection, as regards the pre-ceramic horizon of Jericho, which follows upon the Natufian of that site, we note with interest Zeuner's (1958b, p. 55) observation that ". . . it is worthwhile to consider the alternative that the pre-pottery Jerichoans did not practice agriculture in the strict sense of the word. . . ." The possibility of alternatives and blends must always be kept in mind so that the conception of the ideal types does not force us into unrealistic strait-jackets.

To return to the sequence in Iraqi Kurdistan, it is curious that Karim Shahir showed literally no obsidian and M'lefaat and Zawi Chemi Shanidar very little of it. Does this indicate even more restriction to a given region? On techno-typological grounds we place Qara Chiwar (p. 50) midway between Karim Shahir and Jarmo. Its rather large surface collection yielded only one piece of obsidian. The X's on our chronological table (Fig. 8) above and below Qara Chiwar haunt us, as does the unexcavated condition of Qara Chiwar.

THE ERA OF THE PRIMARY VILLAGE-FARMING COMMUNITY

The Jarmo Phase

With Jarmo we are on firm ground again, although it presents certain problematical implications for what preceded it. Helbaek (p. 103) sees the stage represented by its cereals as having been "accomplished comparatively quickly," and Reed (p. 124) thinks of "more sedentary life" as a precondition for animal domestication. In the face of these implications, we ask again what Qara Chiwar and the X following it in our table will yield. How much time was really involved? We are uncomfortable with the long span of two thousand years for the era of incipient cultivation which is suggested by the radioactive-carbon determinations.

Jarmo (pp. 38-50) was a permanent village establishment with perhaps twenty or more houses and of rather long duration. Its people possessed at least the domestic goat, two kinds of wheat and a barley, and a variety of artifacts adapted to the cultivation, storage, and processing of vegetable foods. Compared to what preceded it the Jarmo assemblage was elaborate, but it retained elements in its flint-working tradition which were at least as early as the Zarzian in ancestry. In fact, a certain Zarzian neatness in the preparation of some tools, which seems to have bypassed the Karim Shahir phase, recurred in Jarmo.

At Jarmo our opportunity for seeing further bands of the whole cultural spectrum broadens considerably. We could speak of leisure for craft pursuits over and above those pertaining to subsistence and settlement alone and of "productive intensity and creativity" (see p. 49) and we could speculate about the function of the vast number of figurines in the matrix of the cultural life of the Jarmo people.

We have noted a curious thing about the oikoumêne or world horizon of the Jarmo people. The lack of obsidian at Karim Shahir suggests the trend toward more intensive adaptation to a given locality or smaller region. At Jarmo the situation is reversed. There are clear traces of a bulk carrying-trade in obsidian. In the following, Hassunan, phase at Matarrah (pp. 35-37) marine shells are present as beads. What does the relatively abrupt opening-up of horizons mean? Does it bear on the increasing number of pre-ceramic village establishments—in Cyprus, Thessaly, and even Afghanistan (the last no doubt due to a slow spread) as well as at Ras Shamra and Jericho? As Lloyd and his associates report increasingly simpler villages in the Burdur region (Mellaart, 1958), it will not surprise us if pre-ceramic villages are discovered on the Anatolian and Iranian plateaus.

Should these occurrences prove to have domesticated cereal and animals, some diffusion out of the natural-habitat zone would presumably have taken place early in the era of the primary village-farming community. If these outlying occurrences do not yield significant traces of cereal and animal domestication, at least two alternative explanations might account for them: (1) Our conception of the restriction of the era of incipient cultivation to the natural-habitat zone or our sense of the location of the natural-habitat zone along the hilly-flanks is in error. (2) Some intensified developments of food-collectors, such as at the "Early Khartum" site of Shaheinab (cf. Braidwood, 1959), involved the borrowing of certain artifactual traits usually associated with food-production but not food-production itself. The possibility of blends of certain elements from each of two or more ideal types of subsistence must never be ignored.

Various assemblages representing the phase seen in Iraqi Kurdistan at Jarmo, Shimshara, and perhaps in a modified form at Ali Agha are to be expected at different points along the hilly-flanks zone. The earliest known aspect of the so-called "dark-faced burnished ware" assemblage in Syro-Cilicia (e.g. in Amuq A and Mersin "lower neolithic") has in its area no known antecedent comparable with the Jarmo assemblage in general complexity, but such must have existed (see R. J. and L. Braidwood, 1960, pp. 499-501). At least part of the pre-ceramic sequence at Jericho must represent such an antecedent phase for inland Palestine. We would expect an assemblage of another complexion in the Siyalk district of Iran and perhaps still another southeast of Diyarbakir in Turkey. Incidentally, the whereabouts of the antecedent of the wretched flint industry of the Hassunan phase still baffles us. The western slopes of the Zagros in Iranian Luristan may yield still another aspect of the phase, and this we hope to test presently.

The importance of Jarmo, on the threshold of the new way of life which was to unfold in Mesopotamia, is manifest. How Jarmo came to be what it was still eludes us.

The Developing Phases

We now reach the more familiar ground of the general literature on Near Eastern archeology. Childe, 1952, and Perkins, 1949, are not essentially affected by our operations in the post-Jarmo phases. The work of the Danes at Shimshara expands the known distribution of Hassunan and Samarran pottery to the Rania plain and provides a firm stratigraphic "fix" for the Jarmo phase. Harris' surface collections from Urwell and Raseien (p. 49) show that flint-working of Jarmo type trickled out onto the piedmont, but we are ignorant of its effect (if any) on the Hassunan phase which followed at near-by Matarrah (pp. 35-37). The full implications of our Ali Agha materials (pp. 37-38) are somewhat enigmatic. Banahilk (pp. 33-35) gives us a new point in the mountain fastness of Kurdistan for the Halafian assemblage but, because it is so remote, may solve no essential questions about the formation of the Halafian assemblage.

PLATES

A

B

A. Air view of the modern city of Erbil, with its central core atop the ancient mound of Arbela. B. An inconspicuous little mound in the hill country, Karim Shahir (with tent)

Plate 2

A

B

A. Desert-steppe country. The Wadi Tharthar at the Iraq Petroleum Company's pipe-line road. B. Piedmont country. The city of Erbil, with the Aqra Dagh beyond to the north

Plate 3

A

B

A. Foothill and intermontane-valley country. The village of Kani Sard in the Chemchemal plain, looking east toward the Kani Shaitan Hasan ridge. B. Kurdish highland country. A village in the Berserini pass east of Ruwanduz (ca. 5,000-ft. elevation)

Plate 4

Qalat Jarmo from the north, above the Cham-Gawra wadi (cf. Pl. 8B). Level of bench at right is at virgin soil in operation I. Below this level is a natural hill with rocky core.

A

B

A. The Greater Zab River, with village of Bekhme beyond head of figure. B. Securing radioactive-carbon sample from floors exposed by road cut through mound of Grai Resh, near the Jabal Sinjar, west of Mosul

Plate 6

A

B

A. Gird Banahilk, looking north beyond Giyana village to the mountains. B. The Khazir River at the Manguba bridge, looking northwest, with Tell al-Khan above river terrace at left and Tell M'lefaat rising immediately beyond and to right of ruined barracks in center

A

B

A. Tell Matarrah from the east. B. The Greater Zab River at Girdamamik village, with Gird Ali Agha partially under cloud shadow and partially visible as light slope to right of river at upper right

Plate 8

A

B

A. Qalat Jarmo from the east, overlooking long axis of the Chemchemal plain. B. Air view of Jarmo approximately from the north. Courtesy of Iraq Petroleum Company, Ltd.

A

B

A. Karim Shahir, above white bluff in middle ground, looking northeast toward the Kani Shaitan Hasan ridge. B. Natural "monolith" (probably a fossil-spring core) at Barda Balka. Gravel slope in background and to left of view yielded stone tools.

Plate 10

A

B

The Zarzi (A) and Palegawra (B) caves

A

B

A. The cave of Barak, near the town of Aqra. B. Within the cave of Hajiyah, above Bekhme village

Plate 12

Random selection of Halafian painted potsherds from Banahilk. Scale, 1:2

A

B

A. Flat river-washed stones set as a hearth at Gird Ali Agha. B. Stone foundations of house and stone pavement at Jarmo. Tauf walls not traceable at this shallow depth (see p. 40)

Plate 14

A

B

Jarmo architecture. A. House with <u>tauf</u> walls and reed bedding for floors (operation II 5). B. Oven with chimney fragment engaged in <u>tauf</u> wall above fire door

Plate 15

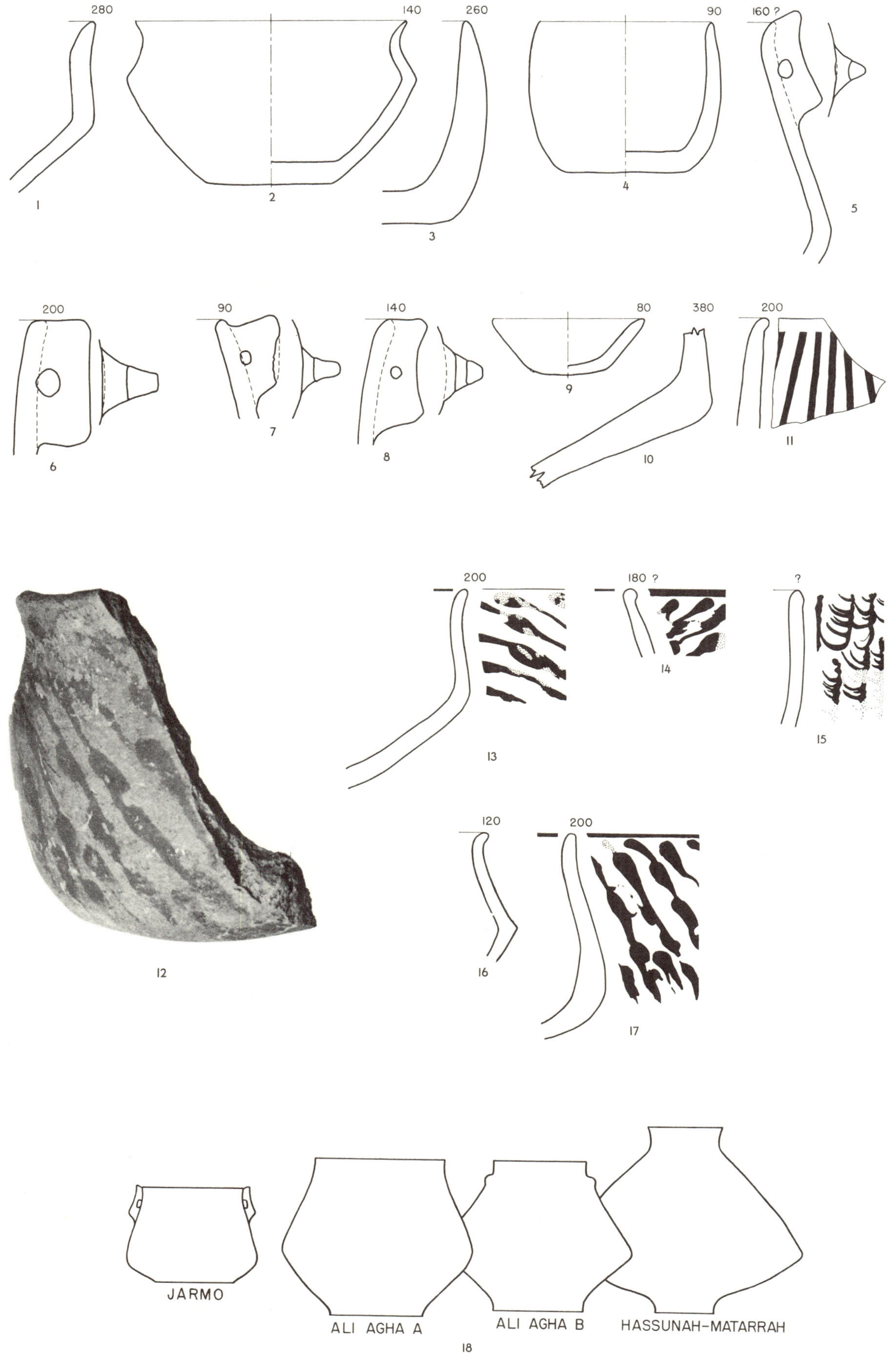

Jarmo pottery. Simple ware (1-11) from the higher floors (operation II 1-3), painted ware (12-17) from the lower floors (II 4-5), and jar profile (18) which persisted from the Jarmo phase into the Hassunan. Scales, 2:3 (12), 1:3 (1-11, 13-17), and 1:10 (18)

Plate 16

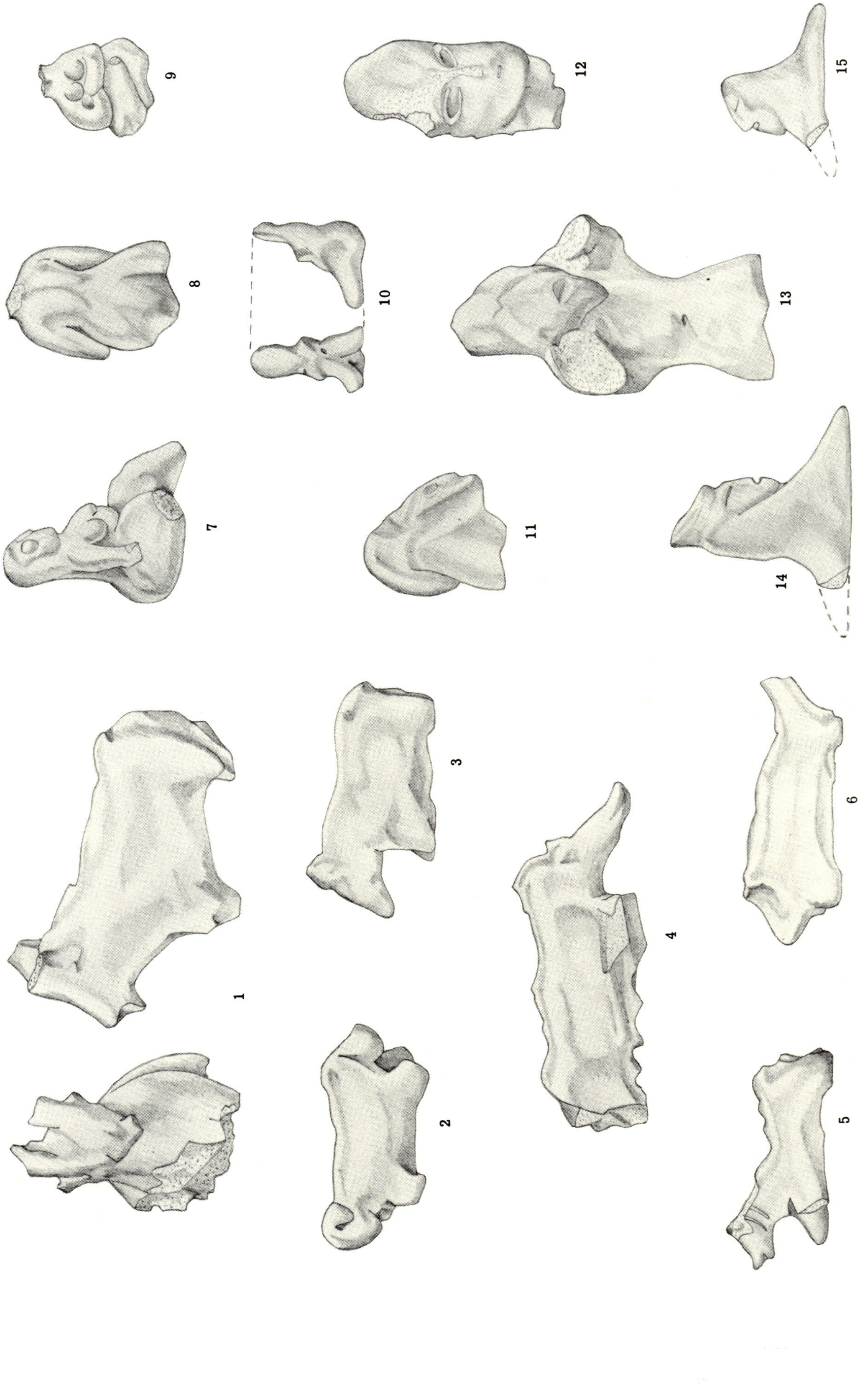

Selected clay figurines of animals (1-6) and human beings (7-15) from Jarmo. Actual size

A

B

Jarmo chipped flint. A. Sickle blades. B. End scrapers and (bottom row) notched blades. Actual size

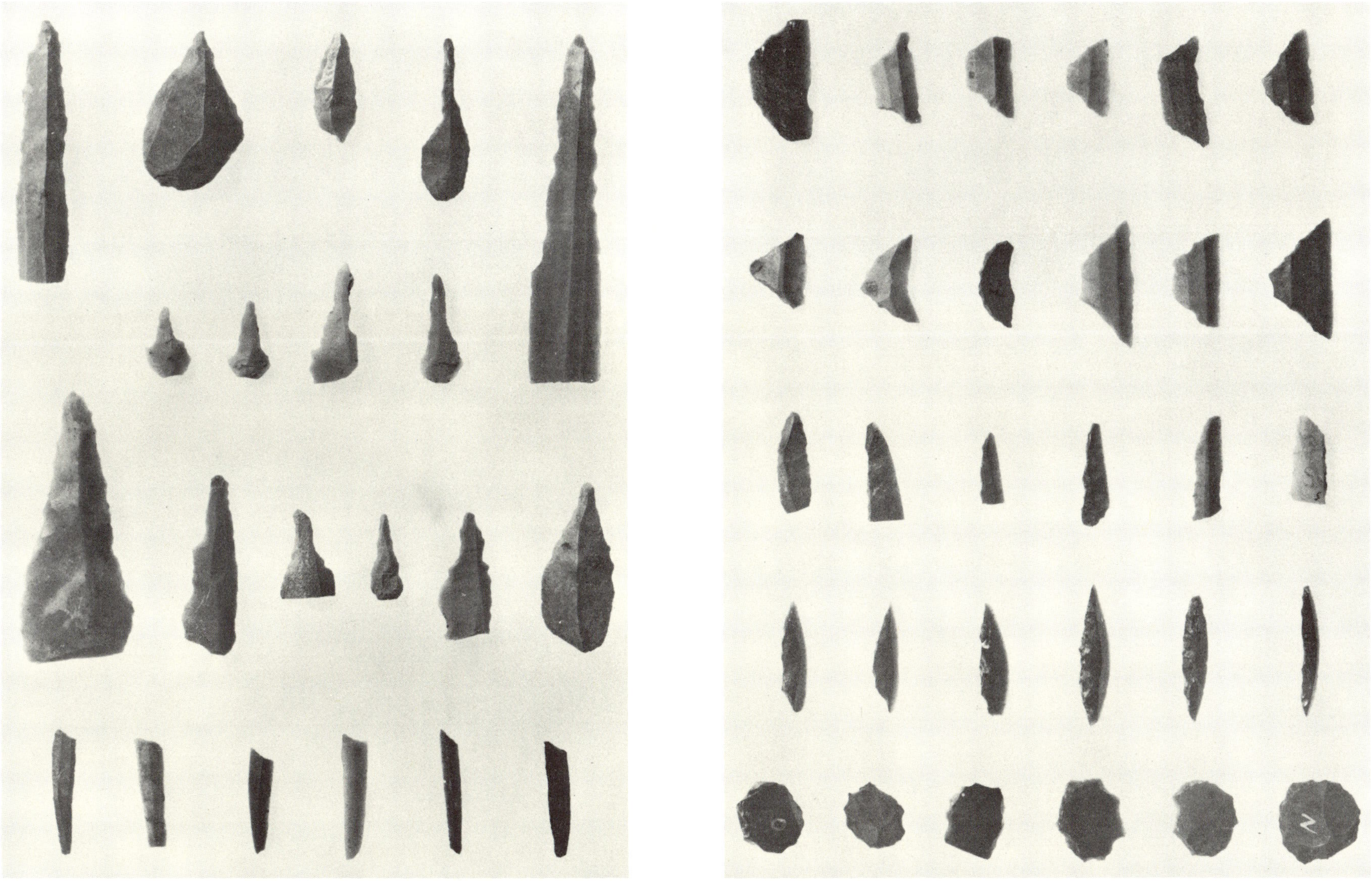

A B

Jarmo chipped flint and obsidian. A. Drills or borers and (bottom row) diagonal-ended bladelets. B. Microlithic trapezoids (top row), triangles, crescent, and trapezoids (2d row), backed bladelets (3d row), "side blow blade-flakes" (4th row), and scrapers (bottom row). Actual size

A

B

Jarmo chipped flint. A. Multinotched side scrapers (top row), side scrapers (middle row), and microlithic blade cores reused as scrapers (bottom row). B. Flake borers (top row) and scrapers. Actual size

Plate 20

Jarmo coarse ground stone. Mortars (1,3), fragmentary pestle (2), upper unit of door pivot (4), and querns (5-6). Scale, 1:4

Plate 21

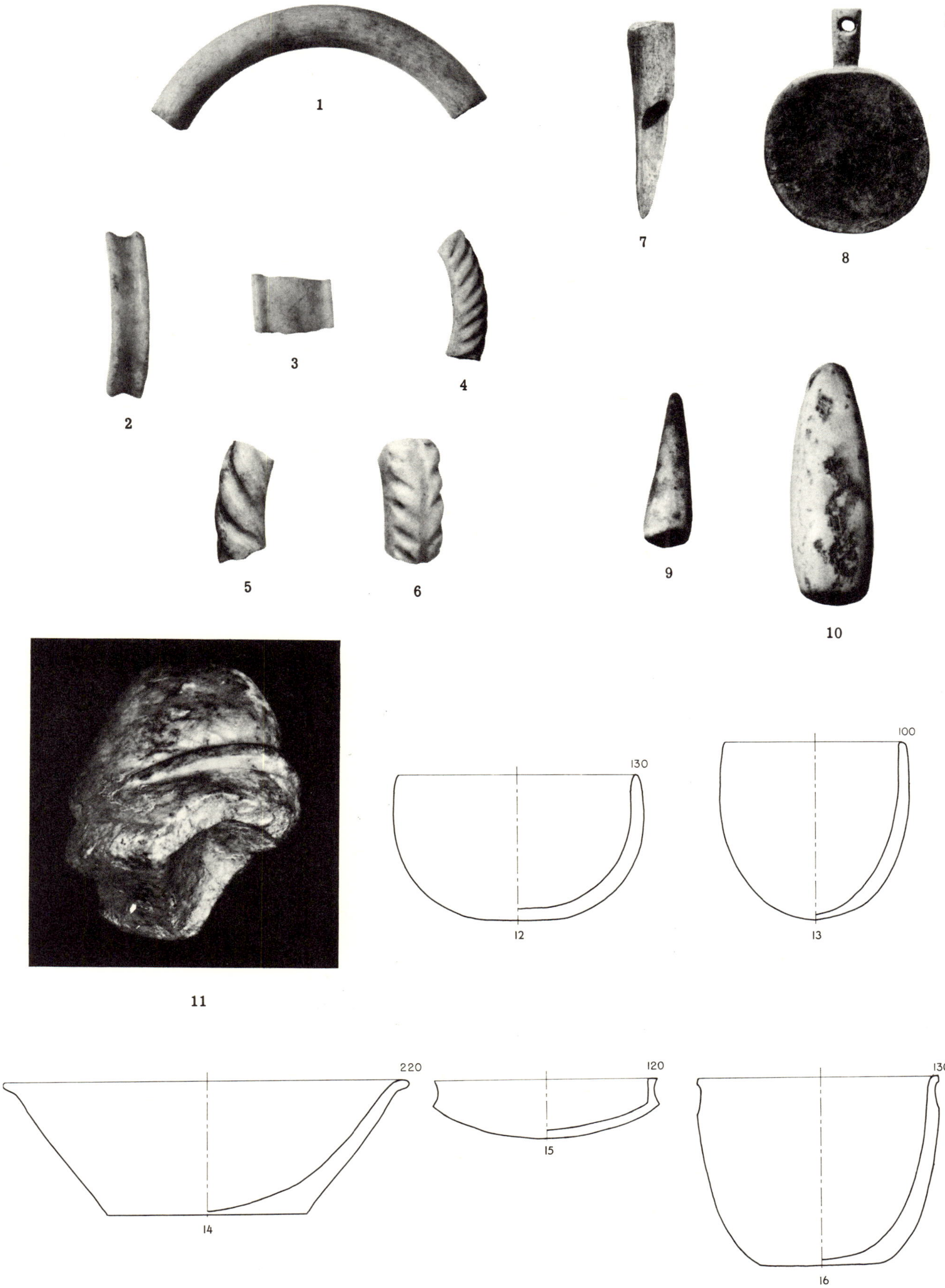

Finely ground marble bracelets (1-6), "pestles" (9-10), "phallus" (11), and selection of bowls (12-16), bone point and spoon (7-8), all from Jarmo. Scales, 4:5 (1-8, 11), 2:3 (9-10), and 1:3 (12-16)

A

B

A. Scatter of cracked limestone pebbles at Karim Shahir. B. Chipped flint celts with polished bits, from Karim Shahir. Scale, 2:3

Plate 23

Coarse ground stone pestles (1-2), muller or grindstone (3), subcuboid hammer (4), grooved rubbing stones (5-6), and fragment of decorated palette or grindstone (7), clay figurine (8), finely ground stone beads and pendants (9-14), marble rings or bracelets (15-16), all from Karim Shahir. Scales, 2:3 (1-7) and 1:1 (8-16)

Plate 24

Palegawra chipped flint. Backed blades, backed bladelets, diagonally truncated and retouched blades, and borers (top row), geometric microliths (2d row), coarse scrapers (3d row), elongated blade core and stubby flake core, both pyramidal with single platform (bottom row). Scale, 3:4

Plate 25

Mousterian chipped flint from Babkhal. Elongated flake-blades (top row, left), broader triangular flakes (top row, right), side scrapers (middle row), spheroid, discoid, and tortoise type cores (bottom row). Scale, 3:4

Plate 26

Hand ax (1), pebble tools (2-3), and flake tools (4-8) from Barda Balka. After Wright and Howe, 1951, Figs. 2-3

Plate 27

A

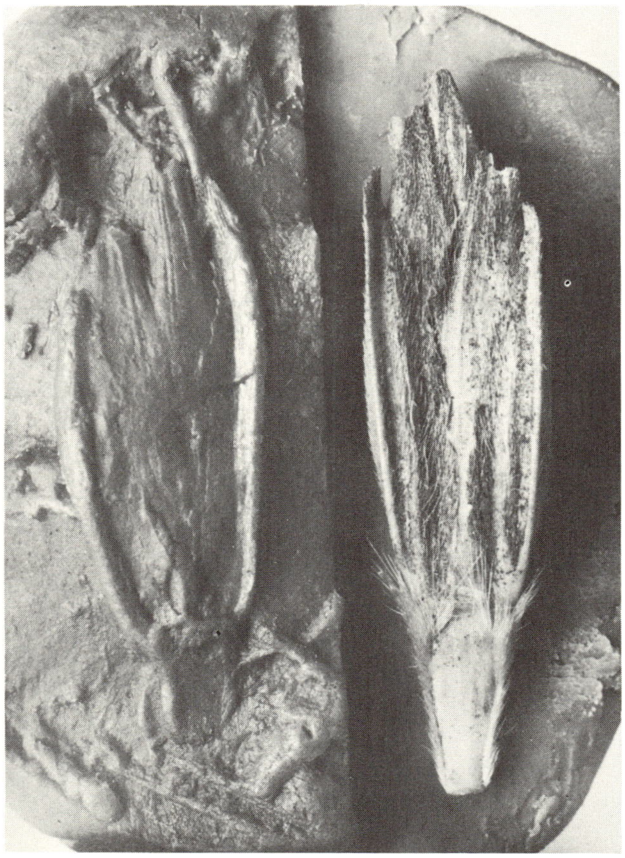

B

C

D

Jarmo wheat. A. Imprint of ventral side of spikelet. B. Cast of imprint shown in A beside fresh spikelet of Triticum dicoccoides. C. Imprint of dorsal side of spikelet. D. Carbonized kernels. Scale, about 4 diam.

Plate 28

A

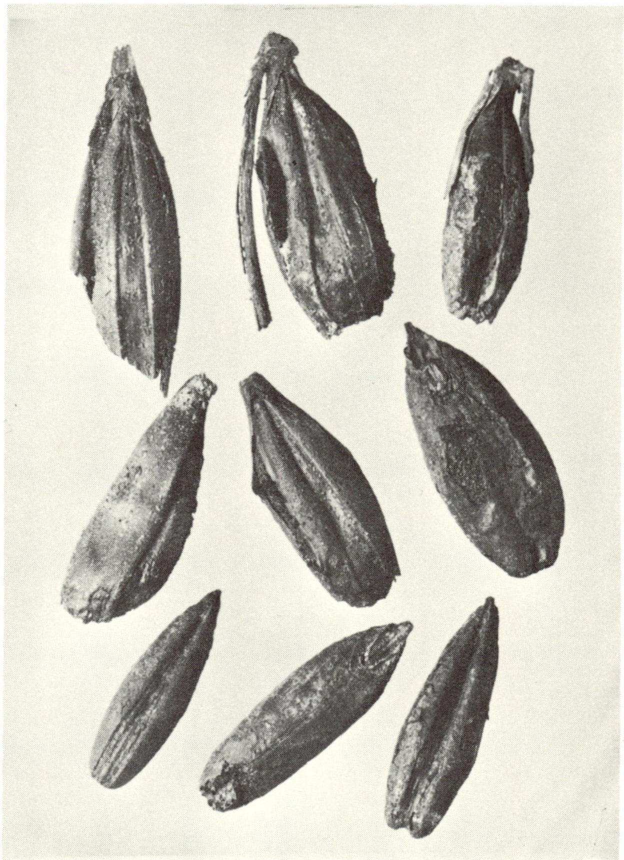

B

C

D

Jarmo plant remains. A. Imprints of two-row barley florets, with kernel partly preserved in lower imprint. B. Carbonized kernels of two-row barley, with internode and one lateral flower partly preserved in top row. C. Carbonized seeds of field peas. D. Carbonized kernels of Pistachia mutica. Scale, about 4 diam.

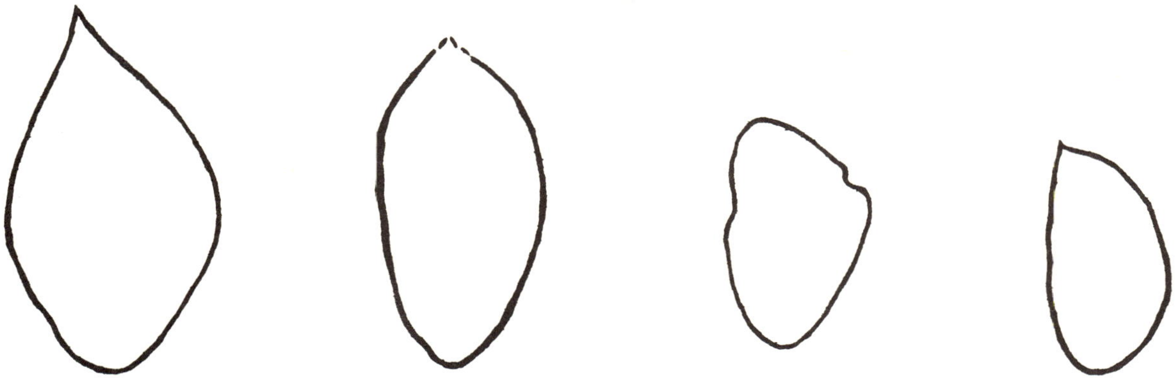

a b c d

A

B

A. Cross sections (taken ca. a third of distance from base toward tip) of right horn cores of male goats, with anterior edge of each at top and median surface to left. Actual size. a. Modern wild goat, *Capra hircus aegagrus* (Chicago Nat. Hist. Mus. No. 84493). b. Presumably domestic goat from Jarmo (No. J 195). c. Domestic goat from Jarmo, *Capra hircus hircus* (No. J 191). d. Modern Kurdish goat, *Capra hircus hircus* (Chicago Nat. Hist. Mus. No. 57253). B. Anterior (left) and lateral (right) views of skull cap and horn cores of modern wild goat